LITIGATING CORPORATE SURVEILLANCE

This book interrogates the legality of corporate surveillance, offering a corrective approach to protecting privacy through litigation—not through legislation.

Explosive revelations, from the Snowden disclosures to the Cambridge Analytica scandal, have shown us that our daily lives are embedded in a network of pervasive, panoptic surveillance designed to manipulate. This corporate surveillance network has grown to encompass and absorb the basic digital substrate of our daily lives. Received wisdom, among commentators, the press, and even legal academia, is that this is all legal: Corporate surveillance has flourished because there are no legal tools to rein in its pervasive and invasive practices. Analyzing recent developments in data privacy law in light of ever-increasing data aggregation and cybersurveillance practices by corporations and governments, this book examines the pervasive, multimodal corporate surveillance practices that now permeate both our digital and offline lives and offers a prescription for fighting back through the courts. Interweaving discussions of the statutory, common law, and constitutional frameworks that are currently being applied in legal challenges to these activities, this book considers current critiques of privacy law as conceptualized by both legal scholars and practitioners. Additionally, it makes suggestions for navigating the future of privacy rights in the face of our increasingly digitized lives.

This book will be of interest to researchers and practitioners in the field of corporate surveillance, digital law, and privacy law.

David Rudolph is Adjunct Professor of Law at University of California College of the Law, San Francisco, where he teaches privacy law, and a partner at Lieff Cabraser Heimann & Bernstein LLP, where he is a member of the firm's Cybersecurity and Data Privacy and Antitrust and Intellectual Property Practice Groups. He has extensive experience litigating privacy class actions. He is a certified information privacy professional (CIPP/US) and regularly presents and lectures on current issues in privacy law. He received his BA in philosophy and JD from the University of California, Berkeley.

LITIGATING CORPORATE SURVEILLANCE

Privacy, Autonomy, Power, and Democracy in the Courtroom

David Rudolph

Routledge
Taylor & Francis Group
LONDON AND NEW YORK

Designed cover image: Getty Images

First published 2026
by Routledge
4 Park Square, Milton Park, Abingdon, Oxon OX14 4RN

and by Routledge
605 Third Avenue, New York, NY 10158

Routledge is an imprint of the Taylor & Francis Group, an informa business

British Library Cataloguing-in-Publication Data
A catalogue record for this book is available from the British Library

ISBN: 978-1-032-53732-0 (hbk)
ISBN: 978-1-032-53733-7 (pbk)
ISBN: 978-1-003-41334-9 (ebk)

DOI: 10.4324/9781003413349

Typeset in Times New Roman
by Apex CoVantage, LLC

For Miki, Noah, and Lev.

"The right to be let alone is indeed the beginning of all freedom."

—William O. Douglas

CONTENTS

Acknowledgments *ix*

Introduction 1

PART I
Foundations of Commercial Surveillance Litigation **9**

1 Privacy as Power Relation 11

2 The Snowden Revelations and Government Cybersurveillance 31

3 Cambridge Analytica and the Unmasking of the Corporate Panopticon 49

PART II
The Current Privacy Battlefield **69**

4 Geolocation Tracking—An Exhaustive Chronicle of Our Daily Lives 71

5 Biometric Information Collection—Through a Face Scanner Darkly 91

6 Internet Activity Tracking: Business as Usual or Egregious Violation of Social Norms? 112

7 Big Data, Data Brokers, and the Corporate Surveillance Cartel 136

8 Harm and Damages Theories 164

PART III
Critiques, Alternative Fronts, and Future **185**

9 Privacy, Performance, and Power 187

10 International Privacy: The Fight for Digital Sovereignty 211

11 The Rise of Hipster Antitrust: A New Front in the Fight for Privacy 232

12 The Future of Privacy Law 249

Index *262*

ACKNOWLEDGMENTS

This book could not have been written without the support of the following people:

Morris Ratner, Academic Dean of UC Law SF, who provided me the opportunity to teach the seminar that formed the basis for this book; the students in my Data Privacy Rights seminar, who provided lively and thoughtful feedback on the issues addressed in this book; the editors at Routledge, particularly Siobhan Poole and Nicola Sharpe, for agreeing to publish the book and for their assistance with the process; my partners at Lieff Cabraser Heimann & Bernstein, especially Michael Sobol, with whom I have spent countless hours fighting the good fight; and my family, including my parents, my siblings, and Miki, Noah, and Lev, to whom this book is dedicated.

The author and/or Lieff Cabraser Heimann & Bernstein LLP, is or was counsel of record for the plaintiffs for the following cases discussed in this book: *In re: Google Location History Litigation*, Case No. 18-cv-05062-EJD (N.D. Cal.); *Campbell v. Facebook Inc.*, Case No. 13-cv-05996-PJH (N.D. Cal.); *In re: Anthem Inc. Data Breach Litigation*, Case No. 15-MD-02617-LHK (N.D. Cal.); *Katz-Lacabe et al v. Oracle America Inc.*, Case No. 3:22-cv-04792-RS (N.D. Cal.). Lieff Cabraser Heimann & Bernstein LLP acts as funder for the Data Privacy Stichting and the Privacy Protection Stichting in the legal actions discussed in Chapter 10.

INTRODUCTION

As a decade of explosive revelations—from the Snowden disclosures to the Cambridge Analytica scandal—have shown us, our daily lives are embedded in a network of pervasive, panoptic surveillance that is designed to manipulate us and bend us to its ends. This network is not (yet) operated in the sole interest of governmental power and control; instead, it is *corporate*. Concomitant with the rise of the Internet, this corporate surveillance network has grown to encompass and absorb the basic digital substrate of our daily lives. Contrary to the cost-of-progress excuses offered by technology apologists over the last two decades, this surveillance network is neither innocuous nor "business as usual." In fact, many of the harms traditionally attendant to mass surveillance, including chilling effects, distrust of the media, and political manipulation, have come to fruition over the last decade as a result of this digital corporate surveillance.

Received wisdom, among commentators, the press, and even legal academia, is that *this is all legal*: Corporate surveillance has flourished because there are no legal tools to rein in its pervasive and invasive practices, and our only hope is to persuade legislators—or even the tech companies behind these practices—to step in to try to stop it. Privacy law is situated at the center of this apparent Gordian knot. We are obsessed with the law of privacy, which is, at its core, the power to protect our autonomy: We extol its importance, lament its demise, and catastrophize about its future. Scholarship on privacy law offers little hope. It generally proceeds by identifying a problem, duly analyzing it, and then suggesting, usually in wildly aspirational terms, that "legislators should," or "courts should," take certain corrective action, without any practical suggestions as to how that would be accomplished. There is collectively very little interest or faith in litigation, a fundamental leveler of power in many democratic societies, as a lever for change.

DOI: 10.4324/9781003413349-1

Indeed, it is received wisdom that privacy litigation is wholly incapable of addressing the harms of corporate surveillance.

The Thesis

Litigating Corporate Surveillance: Privacy, Autonomy, Power, and Democracy in the Courtroom interrogates this prevailing conception and offers a corrective analysis. In contrast to this received wisdom, the book argues that the best path to protecting our privacy is not through legislation—which rests in the hands of institutionally and industry-captured legislators—but rather through litigation, the lever of power that is and always has been within the hands of the people whose privacy rights are threatened. A central thesis of this book is that *current* privacy law is, contrary to the claims of many commentators and privacy scholars, in fact rising to this challenge. Recent developments in privacy jurisprudence at both the federal appellate and district court levels demonstrate a sea change in jurists' views on the legality of digital activity tracking and the compiling of "dossiers" based on that tracking. This change embodies a pro-privacy legal and sociocultural zeitgeist, which has been catalyzed by recent antitrust actions brought by regulators alleging antitrust harm predicated on privacy invasions. The fruits of the pro-privacy zeitgeist include the availability of legal claims to fight privacy-invasive conduct that had previously been considered inapplicable to "commercial" internet activity, including, for example, federal and state criminal wiretapping statutes among the most formidable tools in the privacy law enforcement toolbox.

Litigating Corporate Surveillance analyzes these recent developments in data privacy law in light of ever-increasing data aggregation and cybersurveillance practices by corporations and governments. It excavates and lays bare the pervasive, multimodal corporate surveillance practices that now permeate both our digital and offline lives and offers a prescription for fighting back through the courts. What follows will weave in discussion of statutory, common law and constitutional frameworks that are currently being applied in legal challenges to these activities and consider current critiques of privacy law as conceptualized by practitioners, as well as suggestions for navigating the future of privacy rights as it relates to our increasingly digitized lives.

This book is not a survey of privacy law; it is the first book-length analysis of privacy law specifically through the lens of contemporary litigation. It focuses on the conceptual underpinnings of privacy rights in light of current privacy litigation, critiques of pervasive privacy law–related practices, and prescriptive questions of what privacy law should be, both now and in the future, particularly in light of the disproportionate effect corporate surveillance practices have on marginalized communities and communities of color. The book synthesizes legal source material, technical and forensic analyses, and contemporary legal scholarship to provide readers with an up-to-date understanding of current privacy rights litigation and offers an alternative to the fatalistic view of the future of privacy law that now permeates scholarship and society at large.

Both a diagnosis of the current pathologies of privacy law and a call to arms, this book offers a proposed corrective to the prevailing view that the future of privacy lies in the hands of legislators and technocratic elites. It argues that the future of privacy instead rests on the shoulders of the very people whose rights are being violated, and that it falls on them to vindicate those rights in court. This book provides on-the-ground analysis and roadmap of the fights taking place in courthouses across the country now for our privacy, our democracy, and our autonomy against a breathtakingly pervasive and harmful web of digital corporate surveillance.

The Book

This book is divided into three parts. **Part I**, consisting of Chapters 1–3, lays out the philosophical and historical foundations of privacy law and sets the stage for the analysis of the current privacy litigation battlefield discussed in Part II. **Part II**, consisting of Chapters 4–8, details the on-the-ground developments in the privacy litigation battlefield, from geolocation tracking by tech giants to the compiling of cradle-to-grave dossiers on a vast swath of the world's population by shadowy data brokers. **Part III**, consisting of Chapters 9–12, develops further theory and praxis for successfully addressing ever-encroaching corporate surveillance, with an emphasis on "outsider" approaches to current privacy law issues.

Part I: Foundations of Commercial Surveillance Litigation

Chapter 1 introduces background on the historical and legal foundations of privacy law, including government intrusion and approaches to protecting individual privacy in commercial contexts. It examines various conceptions of the right to privacy, as well the increasingly visible relationship between privacy and functioning democracy. This chapter posits that privacy is fundamentally a power relation. While much legal scholarship generally identifies the legal right to privacy's birth with the publication of Brandeis and Warren's highly influential article "The Right to Privacy," the chapter examines the deep historical foundations of privacy as a form of power relations, which significantly predates Brandeis and Warren's Victorian-era concerns regarding salacious gossip in the press. This chapter sets the stage for the argument that privacy litigation is ultimately about the allocation of power, and that the realignment of power relations is one of the primary functions of civil litigation.

Chapter 2 provides an overview of litigation related to historical and current uses of internet-era mass electronic surveillance by governments in order to expand and exercise their power, from the Snowden revelations to the use of "social credit scores" in China. This chapter draws on the extensive empirical evidence demonstrating the profound "chilling effect" of government cybersurveillance, argues that this effect has concrete implications for the development of personal autonomy, and explains how this fundamental interest is protected under current privacy law. This chapter sets the stage for situating legal challenges to the corporate practices of internet behemoths within the framework of pervasive, all-encompassing state-sponsored surveillance and interrogates the relationship between mass government surveillance and mass surveillance by private entities, arguing that they are at once synergistic, symbiotic, and convergent.

The public response to the Cambridge Analytica scandal, in which whistleblowers revealed that Facebook was routinely making users' private information available to app developers and other third parties, marked the beginning of the current pro-privacy zeitgeist. Chapter 3 describes the history and practices leading up to the scandal, the subsequent regulatory action by the Federal Trade Commission, and the theories underlying current, ongoing legal challenges. The lawsuits related to this scandal are notable in that they challenge surveillance practices that had widely been considered legal for many years. This chapter introduces the discussion of Article III standing post–*Spokeo v. Robbins* and examines how the massive public outcry, and the resulting attention from legislators, was likely important in shaping the courts' pro-plaintiff standing jurisprudence. This chapter also examines the legal fiction of consent that permeates and forms the foundation of much internet privacy law. Finally, this chapter discusses the role of the Federal Trade Commission in addressing the scandal and focuses on criticism of the FTC's settlement, including arguments that the FTC is institutionally incapable of rising to the challenges presented by corporate surveillance practices.

Part II The Current Privacy Battlefield

Geolocation tracking tools that were historically only available for large federal national security or organized crime investigations are increasingly within reach of advertisers, app developers, or anyone who has the wherewithal to access them. Chapter 4 explores the pervasive deployment of this technology—from its embedding within Google's technological ecosystem to the use of geolocation data from phone carriers by bounty hunters—and examines the legal frameworks for challenging the mass implementation of these technologies. Geolocation data is perhaps the most obviously pressing and salient type of personal data that is imperiled by corporate surveillance systems and is thus the first point of departure for a case study analysis. Disputes about the use of geolocation information also exemplify the prevailing attitude that the severe invasions of privacy facilitated by micro-tracking technology are currently legal, and that individuals are largely powerless to stop them beyond asking the corporate surveillance purveyors to stop. This chapter explains why that attitude is incorrect and traces case law developments supporting that conclusion. The Supreme Court's decision in *Dobbs v. Jackson Women's Health Organization* has provided a new urgency to attempts to rein in related corporate surveillance practices in light of the developing cooperative synergies between corporations and law enforcement discussed in Chapter 2.

Facial recognition was once science fiction but is now ubiquitous, from popular social media apps to brick-and-mortar establishments. Chapter 5 examines both the technology and the legal frameworks underlying the use of commercial facial recognition technology. This chapter systematically lays out (1) how facial recognition technology works, (2) the privacy implications of its use, (3) the legal framework within which it operates, and (4) current legal challenges to the use of this technology. The chapter devotes substantial attention to the use of facial recognition technology by Clearview AI, and Facebook, and focuses on the panoply of legally cognizable harms attendant to this use, particularly on marginalized communities and people of color. This chapter also advances the argument that *current* law—as embodied in the Illinois statute that brought Facebook to its knees on the courthouse steps—provides the tools to rein in corporate surveillance practices. This chapter also discusses further developments in Article III standing that counter the received narrative that standing challenges constitute a substantial roadblock to effective privacy litigation. Specifically, despite widespread catastrophizing about the implications of *TransUnion LLC v. Ramirez* for privacy litigation, this chapter demonstrates—based on empirical analyses of recent case outcomes—that privacy litigation continues to flourish, and in fact, *TransUnion* presents no obstacle to the wider utility of privacy litigation as argued for throughout book. As was the case with post–*Spokeo v. Robbins* doomsaying over a half-decade ago, rumors of privacy litigation's demise due to Article III standing are *still* greatly exaggerated.

Chapter 6 covers recent case law developments regarding the legality of tracking users' internet browsing history, which is perhaps the most revealing and intimate personal data available. It traces the evolution of the law over the last 20 years and argues for the viability of current legal challenges to such tracking. The chapter traces the sea change in jurisprudence related to the legality of internet activity tracking and profiling that has developed in the 20 years since the seminal *In re Doubleclick* case held, in essence, that tracking users' internet activity and creating profiles based on that activity was legal. In particular, the Ninth Circuit's 2020 decision in *In re Facebook Inc. Internet Tracking Litigation* substantially and concretely shifted the legal environment in which internet tracking analytics technology operate. In holding that Facebook was potentially liable under federal and state wiretapping laws for tracking users' off-Facebook browsing activity, the court recognized that the extent and the pervasiveness of internet activity surveillance and profiling now constitute significant threats to individual privacy and autonomy, particularly in light of the revelations of voter manipulation at issue in the Cambridge Analytica scandal. Chapter 6 focuses on ongoing litigation against Google for use of its basic analytics technology and highlights the extent to which courts are now rejecting these defendants' arguments that internet activity tracking for ostensible purposes of targeted advertising is "business as usual."

Chapter 7 examines the activities of and legal issues associated with data brokers that collect vast amounts of both online and offline data about individuals and then create digital "dossiers" that are made available for purchase by third parties. This chapter examines how these digital data and database-driven technologies developed, how this has led to the normalization of surveillance, and how these technologies developed by corporations for commercial purposes also offer technological prototypes for panoptic governmental surveillance. Chapter 7 argues that this activity—which, until recently, had largely gone unchallenged in court but has garnered recent interest by regulators—violates various statutory, tort, and constitutional privacy rights. Building on the discussion of the preceding chapters, this chapter argues that data broker conduct is—contrary to incessant pronouncements by the press, legislators, and even legal scholars—clearly illegal under current law. This chapter, which is at the heart of the book's arguments that *current* law, if properly deployed, is up to the task of defending our privacy from corporate surveillance, is the first systematic and comprehensive analysis of the potential legal liability of data brokers under current tort and statutory law. Finally, this chapter will trace the development and progress of a first-of-its kind privacy case against a major data broker filed by the author and his firm on behalf of well-known privacy advocates, *Katz-Lacabe et al. v. Oracle America Inc.*, which embodies the litigation praxis argued for throughout the book.

Chapter 8, as the final chapter in Part II, provides a detailed taxonomy of both the privacy harms inherent in the corporate surveillance practices discussed in detail in the preceding chapters, as well as a discussion of damages theories, that is, the legal mechanisms for obtaining financial redress for privacy harms. Damages theories in privacy litigation embody some of the most vexing questions facing litigants and courts, and the case law on damages is still largely in flux and developing in real time. This chapter examines, as case studies, the ongoing cases related to the use of Google Analytics as legal laboratories in which questions of harm and financial redress are being analyzed by courts and litigants.

Part III Critiques, Alternative Fronts, and Future

Chapter 9 critically engages with Ari Waldman's argument that privacy law as practiced in the field is performative: It has socially constructed what we think privacy law is and should be. Waldman argues that this practice leads to a fundamentally flawed conception of privacy, in which focus on individual rights comes at the expense of population-level harms, and under which the conception of "privacy law as compliance," in fact, reinforces privacy-invasive practices. Chapter 9 also interrogates the notion, promulgated by Waldman and other notable privacy scholars, that privacy class actions are, at best, ineffectual and, at worst, actively normalize the privacy-invasive practices they purport to be fighting against. This chapter concludes by examining the essence of class action litigation and its application to privacy harms. Class action litigation is a central method of vindicating fundamental civil rights and realigning social power relations. Given the aggregate and relational harms inherent in privacy-invasive conduct, class litigation is an ideal vehicle for vindicating these fundamental rights and effecting lasting institutional change. This chapter fully develops the argument that *litigation*, rather than *legislation*, is the best vehicle to address and remedy the structural issues that have allowed both government and corporate digital surveillance to flourish.

Chapter 10 examines current developments in international data transfer law as it relates to US government surveillance practices—namely, the *Schrems II* decision. This chapter first addresses the foundations of EU privacy law and its recognition of privacy as a human right in response to the atrocities of World War II and subsequent, all-encompassing state surveillance in East Germany. The *Schrems II* case is of special significance because it provides a powerful case study of one individual—Max Schrems—refusing to accept the "business as usual" arguments of Meta (as well as much of both the US and EU business communities) to the effect that EU citizens have no right to conduct their daily affairs free from US government surveillance. While the Schrems saga is ongoing, many commentators, and even Meta, have suggested that if Schrems prevails, the fallout will spell the end of modern commerce as we know it. The *Schrems II* decision illustrates the European pushback to Meta's (and Google's) ultimate goals of becoming, in essence, sovereign entities that are not subject to the international rule of law. This chapter concludes by arguing for the rise of European privacy class actions as a powerful mechanism for change.

Current regulatory action by antitrust enforcers has provided a significant impetus for the current pro-privacy zeitgeist that has taken hold in US courts. Chapter 11 examines the "Hipster Antitrust" movement and its relationship to privacy. It provides a detour into the historical foundations of antitrust law as a tool for combating the concentration of corporate power, its turn to focus on economic harm, and its renewed use as a tool to combat privacy violations. The chapter describes the legal theories and progress of current privacy-related antitrust cases. Antitrust law historically developed as a tool to counterbalance growing economic and political power by private entities. However, as has been well-documented in antitrust scholarship, antitrust law has been largely co-opted over the last 50 years by the Chicago School's focus on economic harm as the sole measure of antitrust harm. This chapter examines recent seminal scholarship that has shaken antitrust law to its core and loosened the Chicago School's grip on it. This story illustrates the extent to which unknown aspiring scholars endeavored to get "under the hood" of antitrust law to provide a blueprint for groundbreaking litigation by regulators and private litigants and suggests privacy law is ripe for similar developments. This chapter concludes with an analysis of the ongoing privacy-centered antitrust actions by private plaintiffs.

This final chapter divines the possible trajectories of privacy law and the potential implications of various alternatives in the fight for our privacy and, by extension, our digital souls. It reviews Shoshana's Zuboff's bleak assessment of the mechanisms of "surveillance capitalism" and institutional power, as well as critiques of that heuristic by Julie E. Cohen and others. It illustrates the stakes at issue by sketching a possible dystopian future in which the fight in the courthouse is irremediably lost and much of humanity becomes permanently embedded in a network of digital surveillance and manipulation. Chapter 12 examines current and proposed privacy legislation and analyzes arguments that they are insufficient to address the challenges they face. Chapter 12 concludes by examining the relationship, developed throughout the book, between privacy and functioning democracies and argues that our best hope for protecting both our power and democratic institutions is through the courts, using laws and jurisprudence developed over the past 150 years precisely to protect us from the menace corporate surveillance presents, both at the federal and the state levels. Recent developments in both constitutional law and the American political landscape have shown us that, if nothing else, we can no longer complacently sit by the sidelines as our privacy, autonomy, power, and democracy are eroded from all sides.

The Audience

The material for this book was initially organized and developed for my privacy law seminar at the University of California College of the Law, San Francisco. Accordingly, it is presented as an accessible but comprehensive introduction to the field of privacy litigation. As such, the book would be suitable both as a primary text (with appropriate supplementation) or course accompaniment for privacy law courses. Given its original contributions to the literature as well as its somewhat contrarian take on the utility of privacy litigation, it may be of interest to scholars interested in developments, progress, and theory underlying privacy litigation. The book will also likely be of significant interest to practitioner-litigators on both sides of privacy cases (plaintiffs and defendants) as well as in-house counsel and other privacy law professionals seeking to advise their clients on how to navigate the evolving privacy litigation landscape.

The book also has been calibrated to be of interest to general readers interested in understanding how their privacy rights are currently being fought for in the courts. In particular, the book's systematic exploration and exposé of the practices underlying corporate surveillance, and their relation to privacy rights, will be of interest to readers concerned with understanding how their privacy is being jeopardized.

Finally, due to the rapidly evolving nature of privacy litigation, the author will maintain and update a website, *surveillance.law*, with current resources and case law related to the book; the website will serve as a supplement to and an evolving update of the book.

PART I

Foundations of Commercial Surveillance Litigation

Part I, consisting of Chapters 1–3, *lays out the philosophical and historical foundations of privacy law and sets the stage for the analysis of the current privacy litigation battlefield discussed in Part 2.*

DOI: 10.4324/9781003413349-2

1

PRIVACY AS POWER RELATION

A debate is currently raging among privacy scholars about whether a unified definition of *privacy* is, in principle, possible. At the heart of this controversy is a fundamental clash between "essentialism" and "taxonomic pluralism." Essentialists, as represented by María P. Angel and Ryan Calo, argue that privacy must have clear boundaries and a definitive conceptual core, criticizing the prevailing taxonomic approach for its lack of precision and its tendency to absorb broader concerns, such as algorithmic bias and misinformation.[1] In contrast, preeminent privacy scholar Daniel J. Solove defends a pluralistic, flexible framework, arguing that privacy is best understood as a broad category of related harms rather than a singular concept.[2] In his seminal works *Conceptualizing Privacy* and *A Taxonomy of Privacy*, he asserts that past attempts to define privacy narrowly have either been too restrictive—excluding crucial harms like surveillance and data exploitation—or too vague to provide meaningful guidance.[3] The stakes for privacy law and policy are high: Too narrow a definition risks excluding real harms, while too broad an approach could dilute privacy's legal and normative significance.

This book will navigate these definitional straits through both compromise and fiat, adopting the essentialist thesis that *privacy is fundamentally a power relation* while applying a taxonomic approach to *privacy harms*. Privacy will be examined as a mechanism through which power is distributed, exercised, and contested

1 Maria P. Angel & Ryan Calo, *Distinguishing Privacy Law: A Critique of Privacy as Social Taxonomy*, 124 Colum. L. Rev. 507 (2024).

2 Daniel J. Solove, *Against Privacy Essentialism* (May 13, 2024). GWU Legal Studies Research Paper (forthcoming), available at SSRN: https://ssrn.com/abstract=4826385/

3 Daniel J. Solove, *Conceptualizing Privacy*, 90 Cal. L. Rev. 1087 (2002); Daniel J. Solove, *A Taxonomy of Privacy*, 154 U. Pa. L. Rev. 477 (2006).

DOI: 10.4324/9781003413349-3

in society: Privacy determines who has control over information, who can be observed or hidden, and who can exert agency in digital and physical spaces. The litigation discussed in the following chapters will highlight how privacy is wielded as a tool of power, who benefits from its protection or erosion, and how existing legal frameworks and rights can be wielded to balance these competing interests in an era of pervasive digital surveillance and manipulation.

The Central Concept: Privacy as Power

Etymologies frequently uncover forgotten meanings that illuminate the fundamental nature of concepts. The term "private" emerged in late 14th-century English, meaning "pertaining or belonging to oneself, not shared, peculiar to an individual only." It described things "not open to the public, for the use of privileged persons," or "not shared by Christians generally." These meanings derived from the Latin "privatus"—"set apart from what is public, belonging to oneself (not to the state), peculiar, personal"—used in contrast to "publicus" and "communis."[4]

This etymological insight reveals privacy's deep connection to power relations. The magisterial five-volume *History of Private Life* describes how, in late antiquity, those who maintained "zones of negative privacy" were seen as dangerous precisely because they resisted total submission to religious authority: "The double-hearted [those who would not give the whole of the self in the service of religious law] cut themselves off from God and their neighbors by retiring into those treacherous zones of negative privacy that screened them from such demands."[5] As Mitchell Dean observes, religious authorities sought to eliminate these "zones of negative privacy" that contained "dangerous opacities to both God and community."[6] This framework reveals privacy in its most fundamental form: as the power to resist external demands for transparency and submission to control. Nietzsche recognized this dynamic in his analysis of early Christianity as a "slave revolt" that demanded mobilization of the whole self in service of religious law.[7] On this telling, privacy functions as a counterrevolutionary technique: the creation of protected spaces where individual consciousness could resist the thought-control mechanisms of religious and social authorities.

This tension between private consciousness and religious authority in contemporary American spiritual life is vividly and literally illustrated in T. M. Luhrmann's *When God Talks Back*. Her ethnographic research reveals how modern born-again Christians deliberately train themselves to literally *hear* divine communication in their minds, a process requiring the deliberate surrender of mental privacy. As

4 Oxford English Dictionary (2nd ed., Oxford: Oxford University Press, 1989), s.v. "private."
5 Philippe Ariès & Georges Duby, A History of Private Life, Vol. 1 (Belknap Press, 1987).
6 Mitchell Dean, Governmentality: Power and Rule in Modern Society (SAGE Publications, 2010).
7 Friedrich Nietzsche, On the Genealogy of Morals (Oxford University Press, 1998/1887).

Luhrmann notes, "faith asks that people believe that their minds are not always private"—that true communion with God demands believers accept that their thoughts are not solely their own but rather instruments of divine command.[8] This cognitive retraining represents a voluntary dissolution of those "zones of negative privacy" that early religious authorities sought to eliminate, reframed as the path to spiritual salvation rather than submission to external control.

Much contemporary privacy scholarship treats Warren and Brandeis's 1890 article "The Right to Privacy" as a kind of legal and conceptual Big Bang, relegating earlier concepts of privacy to an inchoate primordial mist. This narrative suggests modern privacy law emerged primarily from Victorian concerns about sexual privacy and media intrusion. While the article's influence on the contemporary notion of privacy is undeniable, this origin story obscures privacy's deeper history as a form of power relations. The developments of the past decade as they relate to digital surveillance are better understood as a re-emergence of this fundamental dynamic. Religious law has been replaced by the profit-generating thought-control mechanisms of surveillance capitalism, discussed in later chapters, but the privacy being fought for remains a crucial bulwark of autonomous thought—a "negative zone" against systems of control and surveillance.

The Panopticon: Surveillance as Power

The notion of privacy as a power relation can be understood through Michel Foucault's analysis of Jeremy Bentham's panopticon prison design. While the panopticon has become a well-worn trope in privacy scholarship, that is for good reason: It is singularly helpful in illustrating what is ultimately at stake in the litigation that will be discussed in later chapters. Bentham's 1798 proposal described a circular prison with cells arranged around a central watchtower. The key innovation was that prisoners could not tell when they were being watched, leading them to regulate their own behavior under the assumption of constant surveillance. Foucault recognized this architectural design as a metaphor for modern power relations, writing that "our society is not one of spectacle but of surveillance. . . . We are neither in the amphitheatre, nor on the stage, but in the panoptic machine."[9] The genius of the panopticon was not just its efficiency in monitoring prisoners but its ability to make subjects internalize the constraints of power. As Foucault wrote, "[h]e who is subjected to a field of visibility, and who knows it, assumes responsibility for the constraints of power; he makes them play spontaneously upon himself."[10] This

8 T.M. Luhrmann, When God Talks Back: Understanding the American Evangelical Relationship with God xii (Vintage Books, 2012).

9 Michel Foucault, Discipline and Punish: The Birth of the Prison (Vintage Books, 1975).

10 Id.

fundamental insight is that surveillance forces the surveilled to internalize their surveiller's power over them.

Foucault's analysis has proved remarkably useful for understanding modern digital surveillance. Today's consumers exist in a state of perpetual visibility through their digital devices and online activities yet can never be certain when and how their data is being collected and analyzed. Like Bentham's prisoners, their autonomy thus is threatened by the corporate panoptic gaze. The power of surveillance technology lies not just in the information gathered, but in how it shapes human behavior and autonomy through the mere intervention of observation.

Privacy as Power: Contemporary Legal Perspectives

Scholarship on privacy law increasingly frames privacy as a mechanism of power. Rather than being conceived of as solely an individual right "to be let alone," privacy is identified as functioning as a crucial tool for maintaining personal and collective autonomy, resisting corporate and governmental overreach, and ensuring democratic participation.[11] Scholars argue that privacy enables individuals to think freely, make independent decisions, and engage in political and social discourse without fear of coercion.[12] As technological advancements continue to expand the capacity for surveillance, the legal and philosophical dimensions of privacy become more urgent and complex. Legal scholars have emphasized that privacy is not simply about secrecy but about control—over personal data, identity, and the ability to exist beyond the reach of ubiquitous data collection. As Julie Cohen puts it, "[p]rivacy is shorthand for breathing room to engage in the processes of boundary management that enable and constitute self-development," rather than merely an individual right to restrict access to personal information.[13]

Contemporary privacy scholars have built upon Foucault's framework to analyze modern surveillance practices. Julie Cohen, in *Between Truth and Power*, argues that privacy should be understood not as an individual right but as a structural feature of social organization that operates at the interface between self and power.[14] According to Cohen, privacy functions as a structural condition produced by the interplay of technological affordances and social and legal practices. For Cohen, "informational capitalism" (discussed in more detail in Chapter 12) has fundamentally reshaped power by embedding data collection within everyday life, making privacy not about secrecy but about negotiating power in an

11 Julie Cohen, *What Privacy Is For*, 126 Harv. Law Rev. 1904 (2013).

12 Id.; Neil M. Richards, Intellectual Privacy: Rethinking Civil Liberties in the Digital Age (Oxford University Press, 2015).

13 Julie Cohen, *What Privacy Is For*, 126 Harv. Law Rev. 1904, 1906 (2013).

14 Julie E. Cohen, Between Truth and Power: The Legal Constructions of Informational Capitalism (Oxford University Press, 2019).

information-driven society.[15] This is echoed by Neil Richards's assertion in *Why Privacy Matters* that privacy is "about the rules governing the extent to which human information is detected, collected, used, shared, and stored and how those activities can be used to affect our lives."[16] Richards identifies four key ways that privacy rules check power: by limiting surveillance, protecting communications, securing intellectual freedom, and ensuring confidentiality. He contends that these protections are essential not just for individual liberty but for the functioning of democratic society. This power-based understanding of privacy explains why corporate surveillance is as insidiously problematic as government surveillance—both represent forms of social control through information flows. As Richards notes, "[w]e live in a society in which information is power, and 'privacy' is the word we use to talk about the struggles over personal information, personal power, and personal control."[17]

Daniel Solove has explored privacy and power in his books *The Digital Person: Technology and Privacy in the Information Age* and *Understanding Privacy*. In *The Digital Person*, he critiques the rise of what he terms "digital dossiers," vast repositories of personal data maintained by both government and corporate entities. He argues that these dossiers fundamentally shift the balance of power by allowing institutions to make consequential decisions about individuals without their knowledge or participation. Solove writes that "the protection of privacy depends upon an architecture that structures power, a regulatory framework that governs how information is disseminated, collected, and networked. We need to focus on controlling power."[18] Unlike Orwell's *Big Brother*, which suggests a centralized system of overt oppression, Solove draws on Kafka's *The Trial* to describe a world in which individuals are subjected to opaque and arbitrary decision-making processes fueled by personal data. In this system, power is exercised not through direct coercion but through bureaucratic structures that people cannot access or challenge. "Under this view, the problem with databases and the practices currently associated with them is that they disempower people. They make people vulnerable by stripping them of control over their personal information."[19]

In *Understanding Privacy*, Solove further dismantles the notion that privacy is simply about secrecy or individual control over information. Instead, he argues for a more nuanced and systemic view, contending that privacy is best understood through a "family resemblance" approach rather than a single universal definition. "Privacy is a sweeping concept," he writes, encompassing a range of concerns,

15 Id.
16 Neil Richards, Why Privacy Matters (Oxford University Press, 2021) 3.
17 Id. at 2.
18 Daniel Solove, The Digital Person: Technology and Privacy in the Information Age (New York University Press, 2004) 101.
19 Id. at 41.

from "freedom of thought" to "freedom from surveillance."[20] He critiques the law's failure to recognize privacy violations that do not result in immediate financial harm, highlighting how privacy's erosion enables broader structural inequalities. Thus, frameworks that focus on individual consent and personal responsibility are inadequate for addressing the realities of data-driven decision-making. Instead, privacy must be understood as a collective and societal issue, one that requires systemic safeguards against unchecked data collection and use. Solove reframes privacy as a struggle over power, not just personal information, critiquing the ways modern surveillance capitalism and state surveillance reinforce existing hierarchies of control.[21] In the digital age, those who control data also control economic opportunities, political expression, and even social mobility. By highlighting the inherent power imbalances created by pervasive data collection, Solove illuminates why privacy is not just about personal choice—it is about protecting individuals and society from the dominance of powerful institutions that operate beyond public accountability.[22]

Carissa Véliz provides a direct theoretical treatment of privacy as power in her aptly named work *Privacy Is Power*.[23] She contends that the modern data economy has fundamentally shifted power dynamics, concentrating control in the hands of corporations and governments that collect and exploit personal data. "Whoever has the most personal data will dominate society," she asserts, warning that surrendering data to companies enables corporate dominance, while handing it over to governments risks authoritarianism.[24] For Véliz, privacy is not merely a right or a protective barrier but an essential mechanism for maintaining individual autonomy and democratic balance. She argues that a society where vast amounts of data are controlled by a few powerful entities erodes democracy and individual agency: "Privacy matters because it gives power to the people."[25] Rather than treating privacy as an individual concern, Véliz advocates for a societal approach to privacy protection, recognizing it as vital infrastructure for democratic governance. She calls for an end to the personal data trade and a reassertion of privacy as a collective good, emphasizing that "the surveillance society has transformed citizens into users and data subjects," and that reclaiming privacy is a necessary step in restoring agency to individuals and democratic institutions.[26]

20 Daniel J. Solove, Understanding Privacy (Harvard University Press, 2008).
21 Id. at 107–112; 180–187.
22 Solove, *Privacy and Power: Computer Databases and Metaphors for Information Privacy*, 53 Stan. L. Rev. 1393, 1401 (2001).
23 Carissa Véliz, Privacy Is Power: Why and How You Should Take Back Control of Your Data (Bantam Press, 2021).
24 Id.
25 Id.
26 Id. at 7.

Ignacio Cofone further refines the concept of privacy as power in *The Privacy Fallacy*, where he critiques existing legal frameworks that rely too heavily on individual consent models. He argues that privacy law fails to account for the collective nature of data harms and the structural power imbalances created by the modern data economy.[27] Cofone argues that "[p]rivacy law's challenge is no longer regulating individual choices, but rather regulating relationships of power."[28] He contends that artificial intelligence and inferential data analytics have created new forms of manipulation and coercion that require legal frameworks focused on corporate accountability rather than mere notice-and-choice mechanisms. In this view, privacy is not just a matter of individual autonomy but a necessary constraint on the power of entities that control and exploit personal data.[29] His work aligns with those of other scholars in arguing that privacy law must evolve to recognize the systemic risks of datafication and the necessity of enforceable protections against its abuses.[30]

Historical Foundations of Privacy

Long before the rise of the digital economy, privacy functioned as a contested site of resistance against institutional authority, shaping societal hierarchies and individual autonomy. To fully understand modern struggles over privacy rights in court, it is helpful to trace its roots in historical conceptions of power. Privacy has been framed as a means of both control and resistance throughout history, from ancient civilizations to early legal doctrines. Examining how privacy was conceptualized and wielded in different sociopolitical contexts helps illuminate the persistent tensions between state authority, corporate power, and individual agency that define privacy law struggles today.

Ancient Conceptions of Privacy as Resistance to Power

The concept of privacy as a form of power relations extends deep into ancient history, taking different forms across cultures but consistently representing a site of contestation between individual autonomy and institutional control. Ancient civilizations developed nuanced understandings of privacy that went far beyond simple

27 Ignacio Cofone, The Privacy Fallacy: Harm and Power in the Information Economy (Cambridge University Press, 2023).

28 Id. at 10.

29 Id.

30 Julie E. Cohen, Between Truth and Power: The Legal Constructions of Informational Capitalism (Oxford University Press, 2019), 107–109; Shoshana Zuboff, The Age of Surveillance Capitalism: The Fight for a Human Future at the New Frontier of Power (PublicAffairs, 2019), 93–97; Daniel J. Solove, Understanding Privacy (Harvard University Press, 2008), 56–59; Paul Ohm, *Broken Promises of Privacy: Responding to the Surprising Failure of Anonymization*, 57 UCLA L. Rev. 1701 (2010).

notions of seclusion or secrecy. In ancient Greece, privacy (expressed through concepts like "idiōtēs" and "oikos") was intimately connected to power relations within the polis. The Greek household ("oikos") represented a zone of privacy protected from political interference—though this protection primarily benefited the male head of household.[31] This asymmetric distribution of privacy rights reflected and reinforced existing power structures, a pattern that would repeat throughout history. Roman law developed more formalized privacy protections through concepts like "ius privatum" (private law) and "dominium" (dominion over private property). The Roman understanding of privacy was fundamentally about power—specifically the power to exclude others and maintain autonomy within one's sphere of control.[32] The famous maxim "domus sua cuique est tutissimum refugium" (a man's house is his safest refuge) expressed this conception of privacy as a shield against external power.[33]

In ancient Jewish tradition, privacy served as a form of resistance against assimilation into dominant cultures. The concept of "tzniut" (modesty/privacy) went beyond simple behavioral rules to encompass the maintenance of cultural and spiritual autonomy.[34] Privacy practices created what James Scott would later term "hidden transcripts"—protected spaces where subordinate groups could maintain their identity and resist dominant power structures.[35] Early Christian communities initially embraced similar privacy practices as protection against persecution. However, as Christianity gained institutional power, religious authorities increasingly viewed private spaces with suspicion. As Peter Brown documents in his work on late antiquity, the "pastoral power" of the church sought to eliminate private spiritual practices in favor of institutionally mediated relationships with the divine.[36] These historical examples demonstrate that privacy has long functioned as a minimal social unit of resistance—the smallest space within which individuals or groups can maintain autonomy from external power.

The Development of Anglo-American Privacy Law

The evolution of Anglo-American privacy law reveals a consistent theme of privacy as resistance to power, though the nature of that power has shifted dramatically over time. This development can be traced through three distinct phases: the

31 Y. Stouraitis (ed.), Identities and Ideologies in the Medieval East Roman World (Edinburgh University Press, 2022).
32 Philippe Ariès & Georges Duby, A History of Private Life, Vol. 1 (Belknap Press, 1987).
33 Coke, Third Institute 160.
34 Jeffrey Rosen, The Unwanted Gaze: The Destruction of Privacy in America (Random House, 2000).
35 James C. Scott, Domination and the Arts of Resistance: Hidden Transcripts (Yale University Press, 1990).
36 P. Brown, The Rise of Western Christendom: Triumph and Diversity, AD 200–1000 (Wiley-Blackwell, 2012).

castle doctrine era, the constitutional period, and the modern digital age. *Semayne's Case* (1603) stands as the foundational articulation of privacy as a form of power in English common law, providing the source for the famous dictum that "the house of every one is to him as his castle and fortress."[37] In 1603, castles were not mere metaphors for domestic tranquility—they were the most visible and explicit embodiments of political power in English society; the revolutionary aspect of *Semayne's Case* was its democratic extension of this form of power to common households. This understanding of privacy as power reached its rhetorical apex in William Pitt's 1763 speech opposing the Cider Bill, which would have granted tax collectors warrantless entry into private homes. Pitt declared:

> The poorest man may in his cottage bid defiance to all the force of the crown. It may be frail—its roof may shake—the wind may blow through it—the storm may enter, the rain may enter—but the King of England cannot enter—all his force dares not cross the threshold of the ruined tenement.[38]

The American Revolution transformed these common-law principles into constitutional rights, particularly through the Third and Fourth Amendments. Legal historian William Cuddihy argues that the Fourth Amendment's prohibition on unreasonable searches and seizures represented a fundamental shift in the relationship between individual and state power.[39] The amendment's warrant requirement institutionalized privacy as a check on government authority. The Supreme Court's early privacy jurisprudence consistently emphasized this power-limiting function. *Boyd v. United States* (1886) described the Fourth Amendment as protecting against "the invasion of [the] indefeasible right of personal security, personal liberty and private property."[40] This framing of privacy as a bulwark against state power would influence Warren and Brandeis's later conceptualization of privacy rights.

Today, the "castle doctrine" must be reconceptualized for an age where the primary threats to privacy come not from kings' soldiers but from corporate algorithms. The threshold of our "ruined tenements" is crossed not by physical intrusion but by digital surveillance, data collection, and algorithmic manipulation. The stakes in this new privacy battlefield thus extend beyond traditional concerns about government overreach or personal embarrassment. As corporate entities develop increasingly sophisticated artificial intelligence systems fed by vast quantities of personal data, privacy becomes essential to maintaining human autonomy and the integrity

37 Semayne's Case (1604) 5 Co Rep 91.

38 15 Hansard, Parliamentary History of England 1307 (1753–65).

39 William John Cuddihy, The Fourth Amendment: Origins and Original Meaning (OUP, 2009), 602–1791.

40 Boyd v. United States, 116 U.S. 616, 630 (1886).

of consciousness itself.[41] The "negative zones" of privacy that historically protected individuals from state and religious authority must now be defended against surveillance capitalism—a system that seeks to predict and control human behavior through the colonization of private experience.[42] This historical trajectory supports that privacy law has always been fundamentally about power relations, though the nature of both privacy and power has evolved. The challenge for modern privacy law is to adapt centuries-old principles of privacy-as-power to address novel threats from corporate surveillance and artificial intelligence systems that seek not merely to observe but to reshape human consciousness itself.

Warren and Brandeis's "The Right to Privacy"

While "The Right to Privacy" is often celebrated for establishing a common-law right to privacy, its most lasting significance lies in its dynamic response to surveillance technologies. Warren and Brandeis were responding specifically to how new technologies had created unprecedented threats to personal autonomy and power relations. Their paper represents the first systematic attempt to address how technological advancement necessitates new legal frameworks for protecting privacy.

The article begins by explicitly linking privacy rights to technological change: "Recent inventions and business methods call attention to the next step which must be taken for the protection of the person, and for securing to the individual what Judge Cooley calls the right 'to be let alone.'"[43] The specific technologies that concerned Warren and Brandeis—instantaneous photographs and newspaper enterprise—may seem quaint today, but they represented a fundamental shift in surveillance capabilities. The invention of the snap camera by Eastman Kodak in 1884 had created, for the first time in history, the ability to photograph people without their knowledge or consent. This technological development, combined with the rise of mass-circulation newspapers and gossip columns, meant that private moments could be captured and disseminated to thousands of readers without any participation by the subject.

Warren and Brandeis's fundamental insight lay in recognizing that existing legal frameworks were insufficient to address these new technological threats. As they noted:

> The narrower doctrine may have satisfied the demands of society at a time when the abuse to be guarded against could rarely have arisen without violating a contract or a special confidence; but now that modern devices afford abundant opportunities for the perpetration of such wrongs without any participation

41 Brett M. Frischmann & Evan Selinger, Re-Engineering Humanity (Cambridge University Press, 2018), 4–5.

42 Shoshana Zuboff, The Age of Surveillance Capitalism: The Fight for a Human Future at the New Frontier of Power (PublicAffairs, 2019).

43 Samuel D. Warren & Louis D. Brandeis, *The Right to Privacy*, 4 Harv. L. Rev. 193 (1890).

> by the injured party, the protection granted by the law must be placed upon a broader foundation.[44]

Their solution was to articulate privacy not as a property right or contractual obligation but as a fundamental right to "inviolate personality." This concept represented an evolving understanding of how surveillance technology threatens not just specific interests but human autonomy itself. As Neil Richards argues, Warren and Brandeis understood that the power to surveil is ultimately the power to shape and control human behavior.[45]

Long after co-authoring "The Right to Privacy," Brandeis continued developing his ideas about the relationship between technology and privacy rights. His most significant contribution to this jurisprudence came in his dissenting opinion in *Olmstead v. United States* (1928), where he confronted the implications of then cutting-edge wiretapping technology. The case provided Brandeis an opportunity to expand on the themes he and Warren had identified nearly four decades earlier about how technological advancement necessitates evolution in privacy protections. Writing in dissent, Brandeis emphasized that "time works changes, brings into existence new conditions and purposes," requiring corresponding evolution in how we understand and protect privacy rights.[46] He recognized that wiretapping represented a fundamentally new kind of privacy threat, arguing that

> subtler and more far-reaching means of invading privacy have become available to the government. Discovery and invention have made it possible for the government, by means far more effective than stretching upon the rack, to obtain disclosure in court of what is whispered in the closet.[47]

Brandeis accurately predicted future technological threats to privacy that, in 1928, must have seemed like science fiction:

> Ways may some day be developed by which the government, without removing papers from secret drawers, can reproduce them in court, and by which it will be enabled to expose to a jury the most intimate occurrences of the home. Advances in the psychic and related sciences may bring means of exploring unexpressed beliefs, thoughts and emotions.[48]

44 Id.
45 N. Richards, Intellectual Privacy: Rethinking Civil Liberties in the Digital Age (Oxford University Press, 2015).
46 277 U.S. 438, 466 (1928).
47 Id.
48 Id.

This prescient warning about both digital surveillance capabilities and potential mind-reading technologies, such as those being currently developed by billionaire Elon Musk,[49] demonstrates how thoroughly Brandeis understood the relationship between technological advancement and privacy threats. The *Olmstead* dissent illustrates the constancy of Brandeis's core insight: Privacy protections must evolve alongside technological capabilities for invading privacy. His dissent provides a conceptual bridge between the Victorian-era concerns that sparked "The Right to Privacy" and contemporary debates about digital surveillance, data mining, and algorithmic manipulation.

The article's origin in Warren's personal frustration with newspaper coverage of his family's social events has led some scholars to dismiss it as merely protecting elite social privileges.[50] However, this reading misses the broader argument about power relations. Warren and Brandeis were concerned with how new technologies had shifted power dynamics between individuals and institutions capable of mass surveillance and information dissemination. Their emphasis on "inviolate personality" as distinct from property rights was a novel development for its time. As Amy Gajda demonstrates, they were arguing that privacy protection should not depend on wealth or social status but should be available to all as a fundamental right.[51] This democratization of privacy rights represented a significant challenge to existing power structures. Moreover, it seems this sentiment was in the air in 1891—as discussed in Chapter 11, the Sherman Act, a seminal tool against the accumulation of power by wealthy monopolists, was also conceived that same year.

The article's framework has proven remarkably adaptable to modern privacy challenges. The core insight—that technological advancement requires reconceptualizing privacy rights—directly informs current debates about facial recognition, data mining, and artificial intelligence. As Daniel Solove notes, Warren and Brandeis's understanding of privacy as protection against unwanted exposure and influence anticipates modern concerns about algorithmic manipulation and behavioral prediction.[52] Their warning that "numerous mechanical devices threaten to make good the prediction that 'what is whispered in the closet shall be proclaimed from the house-tops'" has proven prophetic in an age of ubiquitous digital surveillance.[53]

The development of brain–computer interfaces (BCIs) represents a radical new frontier in privacy law, one that echoes concerns raised nearly a century ago in

49 Jenny Kleeman and James Tapper, *Elon Musk Put a Chip in This Paralysed Man's Brain: Now He Can Move Things with His Mind: Should We Be Amazed—Or Terrified?*, The Guardian (Feb. 8, 2025). www.theguardian.com/science/2025/feb/08/elon-musk-chip-paralysed-man-noland-arbaugh-chip-brain-neuralink.

50 S. Barbas, *Saving Privacy from History*, DePaul Law Rev. 61 (2011).

51 Amy Gajda, *Sunlight and Shadows: Louis D. Brandeis on Privacy, Publicity, and Free Expression in American Democracy*, Touro Law Rev. 33 (2017).

52 Daniel J. Solove, The Digital Person: Technology and Privacy in the Information Age (NYU Press, 2004), 56–57.

53 Samuel D. Warren & Louis D. Brandeis, *The Right to Privacy*, 4 Harv. L. Rev. 193 (1890).

Justice Louis Brandeis's dissent in *Olmstead*. BCIs, which can access, interpret, and potentially modify human thought, mark the realization of Brandeis's worst fears. Unlike traditional surveillance methods that track external actions, BCIs threaten to penetrate the last sanctuary of privacy—the human mind itself.[54] If external actors, whether corporate or governmental, gain the ability to monitor, predict, or manipulate cognition, the very notion of personal agency and intellectual freedom is at risk. The commercialization of BCIs by corporations such as Neuralink and Meta signals an urgent need for these historical privacy rights to be applied proactively in response to technological harms.[55] In this way, the historical foundations of privacy law offer the best defense against the unprecedented dangers of neurological surveillance, reaffirming the right to be let alone in the most literal and urgent sense.

Privacy and Social Power Relations

The distribution of privacy rights has never been equal across society. As Khiara M. Bridges demonstrates in *The Poverty of Privacy Rights*, privacy is not simply an individual entitlement but a mechanism of social power that is differentially allocated based on class, race, and gender.[56] Her analysis reveals that privacy law, despite its universalist aspirations, functions to reinforce existing social hierarchies by systematically denying privacy rights to the poor. Bridges argues that this is not merely a matter of privacy being disproportionately infringed upon in low-income communities; rather, it is fundamentally denied to them. Bridges meticulously documents how state programs targeting the poor demand deeply personal details as a precondition for receiving essential services, such as Medicaid.[57] In the prenatal care context, for example, poor pregnant women are subjected to exhaustive inquiries about their housing, substance use, employment status, and intimate relationships—questions that privately insured women are never required to answer. As Bridges notes, "[t]o be poor is to be subject to invasions of privacy that we might understand as demonstrations of the danger of government power without limits."[58] The invasiveness of these interrogations is not merely a bureaucratic necessity but a means of social control, marking poverty itself as a justification for surveillance. The parallel to Foucault's analysis of power relations is clear: Surveillance is not merely about data collection; it is an instrument of discipline and normalization. This mode of governance positions poor individuals—particularly

54 Yuste, Rafael, et al., *Four Ethical Priorities for Neurotechnologies and AI*, Nature. 551 (2017).

55 Meta, *Using AI to Decode Language from the Brain and Advance Our Understanding of Human Communication*. Feb. 7, 2025. https://ai.meta.com/blog/brain-ai-research-human-communication/.

56 Khiara Bridges, The Poverty of Privacy Rights (Stanford University Press, 2017).

57 Id. at 5.

58 Id.

poor mothers—as objects of state scrutiny, reinforcing the presumption that they are incapable of managing their own lives without intervention.

The disproportionate targeting of marginalized groups is further exacerbated by technological advancements in surveillance and policing. Barry Friedman's *Lawless Surveillance* highlights how unchecked surveillance practices disproportionately impact communities of color, transforming entire neighborhoods into sites of suspicion.[59] Similarly, Chaz Arnett, in *Black Lives Monitored*, documents the excessive surveillance of Black Lives Matter protests, where law enforcement deployed cutting-edge tracking technologies to monitor and suppress political dissent.[60] This echoes Simone Browne's analysis in *Dark Matters: On the Surveillance of Blackness*, where she traces how surveillance has historically been used as a tool of racialized social control—from slave passes to modern-day facial recognition technologies.[61]

Predictive policing technologies, often framed as neutral tools of crime prevention, further entrench racial disparities. As Rashida Richardson, Jason Schultz, and Kate Crawford demonstrate in *Dirty Data, Bad Predictions*, police data is often tainted by historical biases, leading to algorithmic systems that disproportionately target Black and Brown communities.[62] Sandra Mayson, in *Bias In, Bias Out*, builds on this argument by showing how algorithmic decision-making perpetuates racial discrimination under the guise of objectivity.[63] Laura M. Moy expands this critique, categorizing how various forms of police technology—from biometric tracking to social media surveillance—exacerbate racial inequities rather than mitigate them.[64] The problem is not just biased inputs but the very structure of law enforcement technologies that normalize discriminatory practices.

Corporate data extraction compounds these disparities by monetizing personal information in ways that disproportionately impact marginalized groups. As Anita L. Allen warns in *Dismantling the Black Opticon*, surveillance capitalism is particularly insidious for Black communities, as their data is extracted, commodified, and weaponized without their consent: "the Black Opticon searches out and targets vulnerable African Americans online and offline for con-job inclusion. Predatory surveillance is the flip side of the exclusionary-surveillance coin."[65] Mary Anne Franks, in *Democratic Surveillance*, argues that existing surveillance models serve

59 Barry Friedman, *Lawless Surveillance*, 97 N.Y.U.L. Rev. 1143, 1157–1158 (2022).

60 Chaz Arnett, *Black Lives Monitored*, 69 UCLA Law Rev. 1384 (2023).

61 Simone Browne, Dark Matters: On the Surveillance of Blackness (Duke University Press, 2015).

62 Rashida Richardson, Jason M. Schultz & Kate Crawford, *Dirty Data, Bad Predictions: How Civil Rights Violations Impact Police Data, Predictive Policing Systems, and Justice*, 94 N.Y.U.L. Rev. Online 15, 18 (2019).

63 Sandra G. Mayson, *Bias In, Bias Out*, 128 Yale L.J. 2218 (2019).

64 Laura M. Moy, *A Taxonomy of Police Technology's Racial Inequity Problems*, 2021 U. Ill. L. Rev. 139, 144 (2021).

65 Anita L. Allen, *Dismantling the "Black Opticon": Privacy, Race, Equity, and Online Data-Protection Reform*, Yale L.J. Forum 907 (Feb. 20, 2022).

to consolidate power rather than distribute it equitably, reinforcing hierarchies of race and class.[66] The economic incentives of surveillance ensure that privacy remains a privilege rather than a right, with marginalized communities bearing the greatest burden of exposure.

Recognizing privacy as a form of social power highlights the urgent need for legal and policy interventions that address these disparities. As Alvaro Bedoya argues, privacy must be understood as a civil right, essential for resisting oppression and fostering democratic participation.[67] The failure of privacy law to protect marginalized communities is not merely an oversight; it is a deliberate feature of a system designed to control and manage social hierarchies.

Modern Frameworks for Understanding Privacy

With the essentialist notion of privacy as power relation in hand, the remainder of this chapter presents a *taxonomic* overview of privacy rights, violations, harms, and legal sources.

Solove's Taxonomy: Mapping Privacy's Power Relations

As the forgoing makes clear, "privacy" is a site where power is exercised in multiple ways. Daniel Solove's taxonomy of privacy violations offers a comprehensive framework for understanding how privacy operates within power relations, moving beyond a singular definition to capture the varied mechanisms through which privacy harms can occur. His work reveals how privacy violations are not merely individual infractions but manifestations of structural power imbalances embedded within legal, technological, and social institutions. By mapping privacy violations into distinct categories, Solove provides a means to analyze the dynamics of control and vulnerability in the digital age.

One of the central insights of Solove's taxonomy is that privacy violations occur across multiple dimensions, each corresponding to a different mode of power. Solove identifies "four basic groups of harmful activities: (1) information collection, (2) information processing, (3) information dissemination, and (4) invasion."[68] *Information collection* entails direct surveillance and interrogation, where the act of watching or probing influences behavior and reinforces hierarchies of control. Surveillance, Solove argues, functions as a mechanism of social discipline, as individuals modify their actions under the mere possibility of observation, as in Foucault's panoptic model of power.[69] Similarly, interrogation can extend beyond law enforcement, such as manifesting in corporate data collection and mandatory

66 Mary Anne Franks, *Democratic Surveillance*, 30 Harv. J. & Tech. 425 (2017).
67 Alvaro Bedoya, *Privacy as Civil Right*, 50 N.M.L. Rev. 301, 306 (2020).
68 Daniel J. Solove, *A Taxonomy of Privacy*, 154 U. Pa. L. Rev. 477 (2006).
69 Id. at 495.

disclosures that extract information under the guise of consent. Once information is gathered, *information processing* shapes corporate power through data aggregation, identification, and exclusion. *Aggregation* builds detailed digital dossiers that enable new forms of predictive control, while *identification* and *exclusion* determine who is visible, who is monitored, and who is denied agency over their own data.[70] This process is further complicated by *secondary uses* of data, where information originally provided for one purpose is repurposed without consent, expanding surveillance beyond its initial scope.[71]

Privacy violations also arise through *information dissemination*, which governs power by controlling how personal data is shared, accessed, or manipulated.[72] Breach of confidentiality, disclosure, and exposure function as tools that can be wielded to diminish an individual's control over their social identity, shaping public perception in ways that can be coercive or even punitive. Increased accessibility, blackmail, and distortion exacerbate these effects, demonstrating how digital technologies amplify the ability to exploit, misrepresent, or pressure individuals through informational means. Finally, *invasion* captures direct violations of personal space and autonomy, where intrusion disrupts solitude and decisional interference undermines self-governance, revealing how privacy extends beyond data to encompass broader rights to bodily and cognitive freedom.[73]

Solove's taxonomy highlights that privacy law should focus not merely on remedying individual harms but on addressing systemic power asymmetries. By conceptualizing privacy as a function of social control rather than simply as a right to secrecy, his framework provides a lens for examining how privacy protections—or their absence—reinforce broader structures of authority and subordination.

Privacy Harms: The Materialization of Power Relations

In *Privacy Harms*, Danielle Keats Citron and Daniel Solove provide a foundational framework for understanding how privacy violations translate into tangible harms, challenging legal standards that often fail to recognize them.[74] Their taxonomy of privacy harms systematically categorizes the ways privacy violations materialize as exercises of power, demonstrating that privacy breaches extend beyond mere data misuse to shape personal security, economic stability, reputation, mental well-being, autonomy, and social relationships. Under Solove and Citron's "typology of harms," privacy harms can be categorized into physical harms, economic harms, reputational harms, psychological harms (including emotional distress and disturbance), autonomy harms (such as coercion, manipulation, failure to inform,

70 Id.

71 Id.

72 Id. at 488.

73 Id. at 548.

74 Danielle Keats Citron & Daniel J. Solove, *Privacy Harms*, 102 B.U.L. Rev. 793 (2022).

thwarted expectations, lack of control, and chilling effects), discrimination harms, and relationship harms, each reflecting the diverse ways in which privacy violations impact individuals and society. While the harms attendant to the conduct discussed in later chapters of this book will be spelled out in more explicit detail, the following provides a helpful overview of the taxonomic approach to analyzing privacy harms.

Physical Harms: Privacy and Bodily Safety

Physical harm resulting from privacy violations is one of the most severe yet overlooked consequences of data breaches. As Citron and Solove illustrate, the improper disclosure of personal information can facilitate physical violence, particularly against vulnerable individuals. A prominent example is the murder of actress Rebecca Schaeffer, whose home address was obtained through motor vehicle records and used by a stalker to locate and kill her.[75] The legal system has begun to recognize this link, as seen in *Remsburg v. Docusearch Inc.*, where the court held that data brokers have a duty to exercise reasonable care in releasing personal information due to foreseeable risks of criminal misconduct.[76] Despite these precedents, courts often struggle to acknowledge future risks of physical harm as cognizable injuries, a problem that is particularly relevant in cases of doxing, where personal information is maliciously published to enable harassment and violence.

Economic Harms: The Financial Consequences of Privacy Violations

Data breaches frequently result in economic harm, from direct financial losses due to identity theft to more complex and indirect financial burdens. Courts have readily recognized financial injuries in cases of identity theft, as victims suffer fraudulent charges and damaged credit records. However, more nuanced economic harms—such as costs incurred for credit monitoring or loss of employment opportunities due to incorrect data—pose greater legal challenge. Courts remain divided on whether expenses incurred to mitigate potential identity theft constitute compensable harm, reflecting broader struggles in quantifying financial risk associated with data breaches.[77]

Reputational Harms: The Lasting Impact of Data Exposure

Reputational harm arises when privacy violations tarnish an individual's standing in the community, even when the disclosed information is true. Unlike defamation,

75 Id. at 832.
76 Id. at 836.
77 Id.

which involves false statements, reputational harm from privacy invasions often stems from the exposure of sensitive yet accurate information. Citron and Solove highlight the role of digital permanence in amplifying reputational damage, as personal data can spread uncontrollably online, creating what scholars term "digital scarlet letters."[78] Cases such as *Perkins v. LinkedIn* demonstrate how automated data practices can lead to misleading communications that harm professional reputations.[79] The Supreme Court's decision in *TransUnion v. Ramirez*, which denied standing to plaintiffs mislabeled as terrorists unless their credit reports were actually disseminated, illustrates the difficulty in addressing reputational harm that has not yet materialized but poses a significant risk.

Psychological Harms: Emotional and Cognitive Impacts of Privacy Violations

Privacy violations frequently inflict emotional distress, ranging from anxiety and fear to humiliation and mental anguish. Courts have long acknowledged emotional harm as independently actionable, dating back to Warren and Brandeis's argument that privacy violations primarily involve "injury to the feelings."[80] Modern examples include victims of doxing and cyber harassment who experience severe psychological trauma and require professional counseling.[81] A distinct category of psychological harm involves disturbances to peace of mind. Courts have increasingly recognized this harm in cases involving violations of the Telephone Consumer Protection Act (TCPA), acknowledging that unwanted communications can constitute an actionable invasion of privacy.[82] This legal recognition highlights the broader role of privacy in preserving psychological well-being.

Autonomy Harms: Privacy as Self-Determination

Autonomy harms occur when privacy violations impede an individual's ability to make informed decisions and exercise self-governance. These harms manifest in several ways, including coercion, manipulation, and the erosion of informed choice.[83] The Cambridge Analytica scandal (discussed in Chapter 3) is a striking example of how personal data can be weaponized to manipulate voting behavior, demonstrating a profound interference with democratic autonomy. The Federal Trade Commission has recognized that practices preventing consumers from

78 Danielle Keats Citron, *Cyber Civil Rights*, 89 B.U.L. Rev. 61 (2009).
79 Danielle Keats Citron & Daniel J. Solove, *Privacy Harms*, 102 B.U.L. Rev. 793, 838 (2022).
80 Id. at 842.
81 Id. at 841.
82 Id. at 827.
83 Id. at 845.

"effectively making their own decisions" constitute substantial injury.[84] Legal frameworks often attempt to protect autonomy through consent requirements, but failures in notice-and-choice mechanisms undermine their effectiveness.[85] Courts have been inconsistent in recognizing autonomy harms—some, such as the Seventh Circuit in *Robertson v. Allied Solutions*, have found harm in denying individuals information about their rights under privacy laws, while others have dismissed similar claims as speculative.[86]

Discrimination Harms: Privacy and Social Inequality

As discussed earlier, privacy violations disproportionately harm marginalized communities by enabling discrimination through data collection and algorithmic profiling. Information about race, gender, sexual orientation, or disability status can be exploited to deny individuals access to employment, housing, credit, and other essential services. Even seemingly neutral data points can serve as proxies for protected characteristics, facilitating covert discrimination while maintaining plausible deniability. The challenge in addressing discrimination harms lies in detection and proof, as algorithmic decision-making often obscures discriminatory impacts. Courts have been slow to recognize the systemic nature of these harms, limiting legal recourse for those affected.[87]

Relationship Harms: Privacy and Social Bonds

Privacy plays a fundamental role in shaping human relationships, and its violation can damage both personal and professional connections. Trust and intimacy rely on the ability to selectively share information and maintain boundaries; when privacy is breached, it erodes the confidence necessary for meaningful relationships. Courts have long recognized certain relationship-based privacy protections through evidentiary privileges and confidentiality duties, reflecting an understanding that privacy is crucial for interpersonal trust.[88] In professional settings, privacy violations can have significant consequences, undermining workplace relationships and career prospects. The unauthorized disclosure of professional data can damage reputations and erode client confidence in service providers. Courts have been more receptive to recognizing relationship harms in professional contexts, particularly through breach of confidentiality actions.[89]

84 Id. at 848.
85 See Chapters 3, 5, and 9.
86 Id.; see also 902 F.3d 690 (7th Cir. 2018).
87 Id. at 855–859.
88 Id. at 860.
89 Id.

Citron and Solove's typology of privacy harms challenges legal standards that sometimes dismiss privacy violations as inchoate or ephemeral. Their framework demonstrates that privacy invasions materialize as physical, economic, reputational, psychological, autonomy-based, discriminatory, and relational harms. By categorizing these harms, they highlight the structural power imbalances perpetuated by inadequate privacy protections. Solve and Citron argue that the legal system must evolve to recognize privacy harms more comprehensively, ensuring that courts do not dismiss claims simply because they do not fit outdated conceptions of harm.[90]

Conclusion

Understanding privacy as a power relation provides essential context for the litigation strategies discussed in subsequent chapters. Recognizing that privacy has historically functioned as a mechanism through which power is distributed, exercised, and contested contextualizes why modern privacy litigation serves as a crucial tool for rebalancing power in an era of corporate surveillance and algorithmic manipulation. The taxonomic approach to privacy harms, combined with the essentialist understanding of privacy as power, offers a framework for evaluating both the adequacy of existing legal remedies and the need for new ones. As the following chapters will demonstrate, privacy litigation has emerged as a vital counterweight to the power of corporate surveillance, with cases against tech giants like Meta, Google, and Oracle representing not just attempts to enforce atomistic rights but broader efforts to check corporate power and preserve human autonomy. The success of these litigation strategies suggests that while privacy law remains fragmented, even in its current form, it nonetheless provides tools for addressing the fundamental power imbalances that define corporate data-extractive surveillance practices.

90 Id.

2

THE SNOWDEN REVELATIONS AND GOVERNMENT CYBERSURVEILLANCE

In 1999, Google co-founder Sergey Brin shared an ambitious vision for the company's search engine: "The perfect search engine would be like the mind of God."[1] A few years earlier, Google had received its first government research grant from the National Science Foundation, followed shortly by funding from DARPA, the Pentagon's advanced research agency.[2] During this period, Google's early search engine technology was refined with the help of military and intelligence-linked funding, particularly through In-Q-Tel, the CIA's venture capital arm, which sought to leverage Silicon Valley's innovations for national security purposes.[3] Additionally, Google's early infrastructure was developed in close proximity to projects like the Massive Digital Data Systems (MDDS) initiative, a multi-agency program designed to improve large-scale data mining capabilities, sponsored by the NSA, CIA, and other intelligence bodies. By the early 2000s, Google was well-positioned to become a key player in the rapidly expanding surveillance ecosystem, offering not just web search but also tools for mapping, email, and data analytics—each generating vast quantities of user information.

This early confluence between Google's aspirations for omniscient knowledge and government intelligence interests presaged what would become one of the defining features of modern surveillance: the deep interconnection between corporate data collection and state power. The relationship proved fruitful for both

1 John Battelle, The Search: How Google and Its Rivals Rewrote the Rules of Business and Transformed Our Culture (New York: Penguin, Portfolio, 2005).

2 Jeff Nesbit, *Google's True Origin Partly Lies in CIA and NSA Research Grants for Mass Surveillance*, Quartz. Dec. 8, 2017. https://qz.com/1145669/googles-true-origin-partly-lies-in-cia-and-nsa-research-grants-for-mass-surveillance.

3 Yasha Levine, Surveillance Valley: The Secret Military History of the Internet (Public Affairs, 2018).

DOI: 10.4324/9781003413349-4

Google and the government. By 2012, Google had hired DARPA's director as a vice president,[4] while the company's growing repository of search data attracted interest from intelligence agencies. When details emerged in 2013 that Google was a key participant in the NSA's PRISM surveillance program, it highlighted how thoroughly commercial and government surveillance capabilities had become intertwined.[5] What began as an academic search engine project, partially funded by defense research grants, had evolved into a crucial node in the global surveillance infrastructure.

The relationship between privacy and power has become increasingly complex in the internet era as governments expand their capacity for mass electronic surveillance by leveraging corporate infrastructure. This chapter examines how modern surveillance capabilities have transformed traditional privacy doctrine, starting with the seminal *Katz v. United States* and continuing through the Snowden revelations and the emergence of China's social credit system. This chapter explores how government cybersurveillance creates profound chilling effects and analyzes the convergence between state surveillance and corporate data collection practices.

Katz v. United States: Establishing Modern Privacy Doctrine

The Supreme Court's 1967 decision in *Katz v. United States* marked a fundamental shift in Fourth Amendment jurisprudence regarding government surveillance, moving away from property-based concepts of privacy toward a more flexible "reasonable expectation of privacy" test.[6] The case illustrates how privacy jurisprudence has developed to track advancements in surveillance technologies. In *Katz*, FBI agents had placed an electronic listening device on the outside of a public telephone booth to record the defendant's conversations about illegal gambling. Although there was no physical trespass into a constitutionally protected area, the Court held that "the Fourth Amendment protects people, not places."[7] This ruling explicitly rejected the Court's earlier approach in *Olmstead v. United States*, which had held that wiretapping telephone lines did not constitute a search because there was no physical intrusion into a constitutionally protected area.[8] Justice Harlan's concurrence in *Katz* established the now-familiar two-prong test for determining whether government conduct constitutes a search: first, that a person have exhibited an actual, subjective expectation of privacy and, second, that the expectation be one that society is

4 Alexis C. Madrigal, *DARPA's Director Will Soon Be a Google Executive*, The Atlantic (Mar. 12, 2012).

5 Glenn Greenwald & Ewen MacAskill, *NSA Prism Program Taps in to User Data of Apple, Google and Others*, The Guardian (Jun. 7, 2013).

6 *Katz v. United States*, 389 U.S. 347 (1967).

7 Id. at 351.

8 *Olmstead v. United States*, 277 U.S. 438 (1928).

prepared to recognize as reasonable.[9] The *Katz* decision recognized that technological advancement would require privacy protections that transcend physical boundaries. As Daniel Solove notes, *Katz* brought the Fourth Amendment into the 20th century and established a baseline understanding of the legality of government electronic surveillance.[10] As will be seen in subsequent chapters, this doctrine has played a crucial role in the development of privacy law as it relates to commercial surveillance.

The "Nothing to Hide" Argument

The pervasiveness of government surveillance is often defended with what Solove terms the "nothing to hide" argument: If you're not doing anything wrong, you have nothing to fear from surveillance.[11] This argument has proven exceedingly durable, persisting even after revelations of widespread and indiscriminate government surveillance programs. The "nothing to hide" argument reflects and reinforces a particular conception of privacy that fundamentally misunderstands both the nature of privacy rights and the risks of pervasive surveillance. The argument typically manifests in two related forms. The first is direct: Law-abiding citizens need not fear government surveillance because only those engaged in wrongdoing have reason to hide their activities. As Solove documents, this argument gained particular force in the post-9/11 era, with government officials frequently suggesting that only terrorists or criminals would oppose expanded surveillance powers.[12] The second form is more subtle: It suggests that the minimal privacy intrusions experienced by ordinary citizens are a reasonable price for enhanced security. This version emphasizes the limited nature of information collection and the important government interests served by surveillance.[13] Both versions of the argument share a common premise: Privacy is primarily about concealing bad acts or information. As Solove observes, this narrow understanding of privacy "myopically views privacy as a form of concealment or secrecy," rather than recognizing its broader social and political functions.[14] The argument's rhetorical power has made it a powerful tool for advocating limited privacy protections. When the NSA's surveillance programs face criticism, defenders often emphasize that the programs collect "only metadata" or target only foreign communications.[15] Such defenses implicitly rely on the "nothing to hide" logic: If you are not communicating with terrorists or foreign agents, why worry about NSA surveillance?

9 *Katz*, 389 U.S. at 361 (Harlan, J., concurring).
10 Daniel J. Solove, Understanding Privacy (Harvard University Press, 2008), 23.
11 Daniel J Solove, *I've Got Nothing to Hide and Other Misunderstandings of Privacy*, 44 San Diego L. Rev. 745 (2007).
12 Id.
13 Id.
14 Id. at 764.
15 Id. at 766.

Solove presents several powerful counterarguments to this reductive view of privacy. First, he challenges the fundamental premise that privacy is about hiding bad things. Privacy serves many functions beyond concealment, including maintaining autonomy, fostering personal development, and enabling democratic deliberation.[16] Even entirely lawful activities may deserve privacy protection to preserve human dignity and freedom of thought. Second, Solove emphasizes that privacy harms often result from the aggregation of minor intrusions rather than single egregious acts. He draws a compelling analogy to environmental harm: "Privacy problems resemble certain environmental harms which occur over time through a series of small acts by different actors."[17] Just as no single instance of pollution might be catastrophic but the cumulative effect is devastating, the amalgamation of seemingly minor privacy intrusions can fundamentally reshape social behavior and individual liberty. Third, Solove argues that the "nothing to hide" argument fails to account for the power imbalance between citizens and the surveillance state. Even if one has "nothing to hide," the mere awareness of surveillance can chill legitimate speech and association. This creates the potential for surveillance to become a form of social control, regardless of how the information is actually used.[18]

Solove offers a framework for balancing security and privacy interests. He rejects the common framing that pits privacy against security in a zero-sum game. Instead, he argues that

> the security interest should not get weighed in its totality against the privacy interest. Rather, what should get weighed is the marginal limitation on the effectiveness of a government information gathering or data mining program by imposing judicial oversight and minimization procedures.[19]

This nuanced approach recognizes that privacy protections need not fundamentally undermine security programs. Instead, Solove advocates for procedural safeguards, oversight mechanisms, and data minimization requirements that can protect privacy while preserving essential security functions. Only when such procedures would completely impair a security program should the full weight of the security interest be balanced against privacy concerns.[20] Solove's framework moves beyond the false dichotomy often presented by the "nothing to hide" argument. It suggests that the important framing issue is ultimately how society can preserve both security and essential privacy rights. This understanding is particularly relevant in examining the evolution of government surveillance programs, their intersection with commercial surveillance, and their impact on individual liberty.

16 Id. at 761.
17 Id. at 769.
18 Id. at 767.
19 Id. at 771.
20 Id.

Clapper v. Amnesty International: Standing Doctrine as Cloak and Shield

The evolution of the Foreign Intelligence Surveillance Act (FISA) reflects the broader expansion of government surveillance in the digital age.[21] Originally enacted to regulate foreign intelligence collection within US borders, FISA has been repeatedly amended, particularly after 9/11, to expand surveillance authorities and facilitate intelligence sharing between agencies.[22] The FISA Amendments Act (FAA) codified aspects of the NSA's previously secret mass surveillance programs, notably through Section 702, which authorized warrantless collection of foreign communications.[23] These changes significantly eroded traditional judicial oversight, creating a framework for programmatic surveillance that blurred the lines between intelligence gathering and law enforcement.

The Supreme Court's 2013 decision in *Clapper v. Amnesty International* represents a critical moment in digital surveillance jurisprudence, highlighting the significant barriers to challenging government surveillance programs while raising fundamental questions about access to justice in an era of secret surveillance. The case challenged Section 702 of FISA, as amended by the FAA, which dramatically expanded the government's surveillance authority. The FAA marked a significant departure from traditional FISA requirements. Under Section 702, the government no longer needed to demonstrate probable cause that the target of surveillance was a foreign power or an agent of a foreign power. Additionally, the government was not required to specify the nature and location of surveillance facilities or directed surveillance activities. These changes essentially created a framework for programmatic surveillance, moving away from the individualized suspicion model that had characterized previous FISA operations. The plaintiffs—a coalition of attorneys, human rights researchers, journalists, and civil rights organizations—argued that their work required them to communicate with individuals who were likely targets of FAA surveillance.[24] These included foreign activists and dissidents, detained terrorism suspects, government officials in regions of conflict, and sources with knowledge of human rights violations. They contended that the reasonable likelihood of surveillance forced them to take costly protective measures, including traveling abroad for in-person meetings rather than using electronic communications.

In the majority opinion, Justice Alito, joined by four other justices, found that the plaintiffs lacked Article III standing to challenge FISA surveillance. While the concept of standing will be discussed in more detail in Chapter 3, in short, Article

21 Foreign Intelligence Surveillance Act of 1978, Pub. L. No. 95–511, § 105(e), 92 Stat. 1783, 1791–1792.

22 Id.

23 FISA Amendments Act of 2008, Pub. L. No. 110–261, § 702, 122 Stat. 2436, 2438.

24 *Clapper v. Amnesty Int'l USA*, 568 U.S. 398 (2013).

III of the US Constitution limits the jurisdiction of federal courts to "cases" and "controversies," a restriction that forms the basis for the doctrine of "standing"—the requirement that a plaintiff must have a sufficient stake in a dispute to bring a lawsuit in federal court. Standing serves as a gatekeeping function, ensuring that courts adjudicate only concrete disputes rather than hypothetical or abstract disagreements.

To establish Article III standing, a plaintiff must satisfy three essential elements[25]:

1. *Injury in fact.* The plaintiff must have suffered or be imminently threatened with a "concrete and particularized" injury. This injury cannot be hypothetical or conjectural; it must be real and specific to the plaintiff.
2. *Causation.* There must be a direct causal link between the defendant's conduct and the plaintiff's injury. The harm must be traceable to the challenged action rather than resulting from an independent third-party decision.
3. *Redressability.* A favorable court decision must be capable of remedying the plaintiff's injury. If a ruling in the plaintiff's favor would not meaningfully change the situation, standing does not exist.

In cases involving government surveillance and secrecy, meeting these criteria proved to be particularly challenging. Plaintiffs have struggled to demonstrate that they have been directly harmed by a surveillance program when the details of such programs are classified. This creates a paradox: Without proof of monitoring, plaintiffs cannot establish standing, yet such proof is difficult or impossible to obtain without government disclosure or leaks.

In *Clapper*, the Supreme Court applied an especially stringent version of the injury-in-fact requirement. The Court's analysis focused on three central issues. First, the Court held that the plaintiffs could not demonstrate that the threat that their communications were to be monitored was *certainly impending*, dismissing their fears as based on a "highly attenuated chain of possibilities."[26] This reasoning relied on speculation about whether the government would target their foreign contacts, whether the Foreign Intelligence Surveillance Court would authorize such surveillance, and whether the government would ultimately succeed in acquiring the communications. Second, the Court rejected the argument that costs incurred to avoid surveillance could establish standing, characterizing these as "self-inflicted injuries" resulting from fears of hypothetical future harm. Justice Alito wrote that plaintiffs "cannot manufacture standing merely by inflicting harm on themselves based on their fears of hypothetical future harm that is not certainly impending."[27] Finally, the majority opinion reflected concerns about judicial intervention in

25 *Lujan v. Defenders of Wildlife*, 504 U.S. 555, 560–561 (1992).
26 *Clapper*, 568 U.S. at 410.
27 Id. at 416.

matters of national security and foreign intelligence, repeatedly emphasizing the need for deference to executive branch decisions in these areas.[28]

Justice Breyer's dissent, joined by three other justices, offered a sharp critique of the majority's approach. First, he contended that the majority's "certainly impending" standard was inconsistent with previous standing decisions, noting that the Court had frequently found standing based on reasonable probabilities rather than certainties. In a particularly striking passage, he wrote with respect to the anticipated surveillance of the plaintiffs:

> Indeed it is as likely to take place as are most future events that commonsense inference and ordinary knowledge of human nature tell us will happen. This Court has often found the occurrence of similar future events sufficiently certain to support standing.[29]

Second, Breyer emphasized that courts should be permitted to draw reasonable inferences about government conduct. Given the government's stated counterterrorism objectives and the broad authority granted by the FAA, he argued that it was reasonable to conclude that the plaintiffs' communications would be intercepted. He colorfully noted:

> Perhaps, despite pouring rain, the streets will remain dry (due to the presence of a special chemical). But ordinarily a party that seeks to defeat a strong natural inference must bear the burden of showing that some such special circumstance exists.[30]

Finally, Breyer pointed to the concrete costs incurred by plaintiffs—such as travel expenses and secure communication systems—as sufficient to establish injury in fact. He argued that these were not "self-inflicted" but rather reasonable professional responses to the realistic threat of surveillance.[31]

The timing of *Clapper* proved particularly ironic. Just months after the decision, Edward Snowden's revelations confirmed many of the surveillance practices the plaintiffs had alleged. This sequence of events highlighted the catch-22 of standing in surveillance cases: Plaintiffs cannot challenge surveillance programs without evidence of monitoring, but such evidence typically remains secret unless leaked. The decision's impact extended beyond surveillance cases: In 2017, Professor Margot Kaminski observed that *Clapper* had become a potential barrier to privacy litigation more broadly, with courts applying its stringent standing requirements

28 Id. at 422–423.
29 Id. at 432 (Breyer, J., dissenting).
30 Id. at 436.
31 Id. at 438.

to dismiss challenges to corporate data practices and government–private surveillance partnerships.[32] However, as subsequent chapters discuss, the Snowden and Cambridge Analytica revelations eventually affected a shift in judicial perspectives on standing in privacy cases.

The Snowden Revelations

The Snowden disclosures in 2013 provided a rare glimpse into the hidden architecture of the global surveillance apparatus, demonstrating the scale and depth of government surveillance with direct corporate cooperation. These revelations stemmed from tens of thousands of classified NSA documents leaked to journalists, exposing secret programs that had operated in the shadows for years. The disclosures upended previous assumptions about the limits of intelligence collection, confirming the extent to which digital communications—once thought to be private—were systematically intercepted, stored, and analyzed.

Edward Snowden, a former NSA contractor, initially sought to expose what he saw as a radical expansion of government surveillance powers that had outpaced both public awareness and democratic oversight. In his own words, he acted out of a sense of duty to inform the public about how their data was being collected en masse, often without meaningful legal constraints.[33] Snowden had worked as a systems administrator for intelligence contractors Booz Allen Hamilton and Dell, with access to highly classified systems, including NSA's XKEYSCORE database. His concerns intensified after witnessing the extent of warrantless mass data collection, which he believed violated constitutional and international privacy rights. Snowden's decision to leak documents was a calculated effort to inform the public while minimizing harm to national security. He first reached out to journalist Glenn Greenwald and documentary filmmaker Laura Poitras, eventually meeting them in Hong Kong to hand over the documents.[34] The first revelations, published in *The Guardian* and *The Washington Post*, focused on the NSA's mass collection of Verizon phone records and the PRISM program, which gave the NSA direct access to user data from major technology firms.[35] Subsequent reporting expanded on these programs, unveiling a comprehensive surveillance ecosystem spanning multiple agencies and allied governments. Snowden's 2013 disclosures provided unprecedented insight into the scale of government surveillance programs—deeply aided by commercial entities themselves engaged in commercial internet surveillance—revealing a surveillance apparatus of staggering scope and sophistication. The revelations exposed what Professor

32 Margot E. Kaminski, *Standing after Snowden: Lessons from National Security Litigation*, 66 DePaul L. Rev. 413, 419 (2017).

33 Edward Snowden, Permanent Record (New York: Metropolitan Books, 2019).

34 Id.

35 G. Greenwald, *NSA Collecting Phone Records of Millions of Verizon Customers Daily*, The Guardian (Jun. 6, 2013).

Margaret Hu termed a "cybersurveillance state," characterized by multiple overlapping programs designed to achieve total information awareness.[36]

The surveillance infrastructure revealed by Snowden centered on several key collection programs[37]:

1. *PRISM*. The PRISM program represented perhaps the most direct intrusion into everyday digital life, providing the NSA with direct access to user data from nine major technology companies, including Facebook, Google, Apple, and Microsoft.[38] Through PRISM, the government could target the communications of non-US persons outside the United States by sending "selectors" (such as email addresses) to these service providers, who were then compelled to share all communications associated with those selectors.[39]
2. *Upstream collection*. While PRISM gathered data from tech companies, "Upstream" collection involved direct interception of communications from the internet backbone—the fiber-optic cables carrying global internet traffic.[40] This collection directly from the servers of US service providers allowed for massive-scale surveillance of both metadata and content.[41]
3. *Bulk telephony metadata*. Under Section 215 of the PATRIOT Act, the NSA operated a program collecting bulk telephone metadata from major telecommunications providers. While not capturing call content, this program allowed the agency to map comprehensive social networks through call patterns and connections.[42] The program's scope was vast: By 2013, it was collecting metadata on billions of calls daily.

The Snowden documents revealed what Glenn Greenwald described as the "literal, explicitly stated aim of the surveillance state: to collect, store, monitor, and analyze all electronic communication by all people around the globe."[43] This was not hyperbole—internal NSA documents outlined a "New Collection Posture" organized around five key imperatives[44]:

1. "Collect It All": Comprehensive data collection programs.
2. "Process It All": Systems for analyzing collected data.

36 Margaret Hu, *Orwell's 1984 and a Fourth Amendment Cybersurveillance Nonintrusion Test*, 92 Wash. L. Rev. 1819 (2017).

37 Margaret Hu, *Taxonomy of the Snowden Disclosures*, 72 Wash. & Lee L. Rev. 1679 (2015).

38 Id. at 1694.

39 Id.

40 Id.

41 Id.

42 Id. at 1693.

43 Glenn Greenwald, No Place to Hide: Edward Snowden, the NSA, and the U.S. Surveillance State (2014).

44 Margaret Hu, *Taxonomy of the Snowden Disclosures*, 72 Wash. & Lee L. Rev. 1679, 1689–1700 (2015).

3. "Exploit It All": Programs to leverage information for intelligence purposes.
4. "Sniff It All": Technologies for identifying and isolating valuable data.
5. "Know It All": Databases and systems for storing and accessing intelligence.

This framework demonstrated the NSA's ambition to achieve total information awareness through technological means. As Professor Hu notes, these programs collectively represented a sea change in the government's approach to intelligence gathering, moving from targeted surveillance toward "big data cybersurveillance."[45] The revelations highlighted serious questions about the legal framework governing these programs. While conducted under the authority of FISA and the PATRIOT Act, many programs operated in legal gray areas or relied on novel interpretations of statutory authority.[46] The FISA Court's role in overseeing these programs was also questioned, as documents showed the court repeatedly rubber-stamping broad surveillance authorizations with minimal scrutiny.[47]

The Snowden revelations illuminated a crucial aspect of modern surveillance: the deep interconnection between government and corporate surveillance systems. This relationship manifests in three overlapping ways: synergistic, symbiotic, and convergent surveillance practices.

Synergistic surveillance. Government and private surveillance systems amplify each other's capabilities in ways that transcend their individual capacities. Corporate data collection creates vast repositories of personal information that government agencies can access through legal processes or informal cooperation. Meanwhile, government requirements and preferences shape corporate data practices, creating what Professor Alan Rozenshtein terms "surveillance intermediaries."[48] For example, the PRISM program's effectiveness relied entirely on the vast data collection already undertaken by major technology companies for commercial purposes.

Symbiotic interdependence. Beyond mere synergy, government surveillance and private surveillance have developed a symbiotic relationship where each sector depends on the other's surveillance infrastructure. Private companies rely on government security apparatus to protect their networks and data, while government agencies increasingly depend on private sector technology and data analysis capabilities. As Professor Julie Cohen notes, this creates a "surveillance-innovation complex," where the boundaries between public and private surveillance continuously blur.[49]

45 Margaret Hu, *Small Data Surveillance v. Big Data Cybersurveillance*, 42 Pepp. L. Rev. 773 (2015).
46 Glenn Greenwald, *No Place to Hide* (Penguin Books, 2015 edition).
47 Id.
48 Alan Z. Rozenshtein, *Surveillance Intermediaries*, 70 Stan. L. Rev. 99, 99 (2018).
49 Julie E. Cohen, *The Surveillance-Innovation Complex: The Irony of the Participatory Turn*. The Participatory Condition in the Digital Age 207. Eds. Darin Barney et al. (Univ. of Minn. Press, 2015).

Surveillance convergence. Perhaps most significantly, we are witnessing what scholars describe as surveillance "convergence"—the gradual merger of government and private surveillance systems into a unified surveillance infrastructure.[50]

This convergence manifests in several interconnected mechanisms. Government and private databases increasingly form interconnected networks rather than isolated silos. The Department of Homeland Security's Automated Targeting System, for instance, combines government watchlists with commercial data from airlines, financial institutions, and social media companies.[51] This integration is facilitated by both formal mechanisms (like PRISM) and informal channels, such as the growing market for commercial data brokers who aggregate and sell personal information to government agencies.[52] Surveillance technologies and techniques regularly migrate between government and private sectors. Facial recognition systems developed for military applications now power commercial security systems and social media photo tagging.[53] Similarly, corporate innovations in big data analytics are quickly adopted by intelligence agencies. The Snowden documents revealed numerous examples of this cross-pollination, including the NSA's adoption of commercial data mining techniques and private companies implementing government-developed encryption standards.[54] A revolving door between government surveillance agencies and private sector surveillance companies ensures the continuous transfer of expertise, practices, and institutional culture. Former NSA and CIA officials frequently take leadership positions at technology companies and defense contractors, while private sector technologists move into government roles.[55] Perhaps most importantly, this public–private partnership has normalized pervasive surveillance as a standard feature of modern life. Government agencies cite private sector data collection to justify their own surveillance programs, while companies point to national security requirements to defend expansive data gathering.[56]

The implications of this public–private surveillance partnership are profound. Traditional legal frameworks focused solely on government surveillance fail to account for the corporate surveillance complex. Constitutional protections against

50 Benjamin J. Hayes, *The Surveillance-Industrial Complex.* Routledge Handbook of Surveillance Studies 200. Eds. Kirstie Ball et al. (Routledge, 2012).

51 Rachel Levinson-Waldman & Jose Gutierrez, Overdue Scrutiny for Watch Listing and Risk Prediction, Brennan Center for Justice at 4–5 (Brennan Center for Justice, Oct. 19, 2023).

52 Id., n. 84.

53 Kelly A. Gates, Our Biometric Future: Facial Recognition Technology and the Culture of Surveillance (NYU Press, 2011).

54 Glenn Greenwald, No Place to Hide: Edward Snowden, the NSA, and the U.S. Surveillance State (Metropolitan Books, 2014).

55 See Shane Harris, @War: The Rise of the Military-Internet Complex (Eamon Dolan/Houghton Mifflin Harcourt, 2015).

56 See David Lyon, Surveillance after Snowden (Polity Press, 2015).

government searches offer little protection when private companies willingly share data with government agencies or when government agencies can simply purchase data from commercial data brokers, as described in Chapter 7. Moreover, this convergence creates a hybrid system where government surveillance and corporate surveillance reinforce each other while evading traditional accountability mechanisms. The Snowden disclosures thus revealed not just the scope of government surveillance programs but the emergence of a new surveillance paradigm that transcends traditional public–private distinctions.

Chilling Effects and the New American Surveillance State

Since the Snowden revelations, the relationship between government surveillance and private sector technology companies has only evolved and deepened. As journalist Byron Tau documents in "Means of Control: How the Hidden Alliance of Tech and Government Is Creating a New American Surveillance State," what was once an uneasy partnership has transformed into a comprehensive surveillance apparatus that combines corporate data collection with government power.[57] The post-Snowden era has seen a further shift from direct government surveillance to surveillance by proxy, where government agencies increasingly rely on commercial data brokers and tech companies to gather information they cannot legally collect themselves.[58] This arrangement allows agencies to circumvent constitutional restrictions while maintaining plausible deniability about the scope of their surveillance activities. A key development in this new surveillance landscape is the rise of specialized data brokers who serve as intermediaries between tech companies and government agencies. These firms aggregate vast amounts of personal data from commercial sources and package it for government consumption. The scale of this data trade is staggering—as described in more detail in Chapter 7, a single broker may have detailed profiles on hundreds of millions or even billions of individuals.[59]

The surveillance capabilities revealed by Snowden have been significantly amplified by advances in artificial intelligence and machine learning. Modern surveillance systems can now analyze patterns of life across multiple data sources, allowing intelligence agencies to predict behavior and identify anomalies. These systems also enable the creation of highly detailed social network maps, tracking individuals across both physical and digital spaces. Additionally, real-time risk assessments can be generated, enhancing the ability to monitor and respond to perceived threats. According to Tau, these advancements create unprecedented opportunities for social control

57 Byron Tau, Means of Control: How the Hidden Alliance of Tech and Government Is Creating a New American Surveillance State (Crown, 2024).

58 Id.

59 See Chapter 7.

and manipulation.[60] The emergence of this new surveillance state raises fundamental questions about democratic governance and individual liberty. The combination of corporate data collection and government power creates a system of soft totalitarianism, where control is exercised through prediction and prevention rather than overt coercion. This system threatens to fundamentally alter the relationship between citizens and state, creating what Ryan Calo and Danielle Citron term an "automated administrative state," where decisions about individuals are increasingly made by algorithms operating on surveillance data.[61]

Recent empirical research has demonstrated concrete "chilling effects" from awareness of government surveillance. Professor Jonathon Penney's 2022 study *Understanding Chilling Effects*[62] is a comprehensive analysis of how government surveillance impacts public behavior, particularly in the realm of online activity and political expression. His work builds upon prior empirical studies, including his research on Wikipedia traffic patterns, but expands the scope to explore the broader social, legal, and psychological dimensions of chilling effects.[63] His findings indicate that state surveillance does not merely inhibit illegal or illicit activities but significantly deters lawful, socially valuable forms of expression, inquiry, and participation in democratic discourse. One of the key innovations in Penney's study is his critique of conventional deterrence-based theories of chilling effects, which have historically been rooted in First Amendment jurisprudence. Conventional legal theories, such as those advanced by Frederick Schauer, assume that individuals engage in rational decision-making, weighing the risks of legal sanction before altering their behavior.[64] However, Penney argues that this model is overly simplistic and empirically weak. Drawing from behavioral psychology, he highlights that individuals often do not engage in rational cost–benefit analyses regarding surveillance; rather, their behavior is shaped by implicit social pressures and a general sense of being watched. This means that chilling effects occur not only when individuals consciously censor themselves but also when they subconsciously conform to perceived social norms.[65]

Penney introduces the *Social Conformity Theory of Chilling Effects,* which shifts the focus from individual self-censorship to broader societal dynamics.[66] He explores various dimensions of chilling effects that extend beyond traditional legal models, beginning with legal and regulatory chilling effects. These occur

60 Byron Tau, Means of Control: How the Hidden Alliance of Tech and Government Is Creating a New American Surveillance State (Crown, 2024).

61 Ryan Calo & Danielle K. Citron, *The Automated Administrative State: A Crisis of Legitimacy*, 70 Emory L.J. 797 (2021).

62 Jonathon W. Penney, *Understanding Chilling Effects*, 106 Minn. L. Rev. 1451, 1455 (2022).

63 Id.

64 Id. at 1456.

65 Id.

66 Id. at 1488.

when vague or overly broad laws discourage individuals from engaging in lawful activities due to fear of legal repercussions. While this type of chilling effect has been extensively examined in legal scholarship, it does not fully account for the wider behavioral changes induced by surveillance and data collection. Beyond legal deterrence, Penney examines the impact of surveillance and data collection on individual behavior. His empirical work, including studies on Wikipedia traffic following the Snowden revelations, demonstrates that mere awareness of state surveillance can lead to significant behavioral modifications.[67] Even in the absence of direct legal threats, individuals may avoid certain topics or limit their online activity out of concern that their actions could be scrutinized.

Penney introduces the concept of the *Chilling Effects Curve*, which provides a predictive framework for understanding how different forms of surveillance and regulation impact behavior.[68] His model suggests that chilling effects do not operate in a linear fashion but rather fluctuate based on the visibility of enforcement, the level of uncertainty about surveillance practices, and the perceived severity of consequences. This model helps explain why chilling effects may be more pronounced in certain contexts, such as marginalized communities or politically sensitive discussions.

Penney's research has important implications for constitutional law, privacy law, and digital governance. He argues that mitigating chilling effects demands not only legal reforms but also broader structural interventions in the digital ecosystem—interventions that, as Kevin Werbach explores in his analysis of social credit systems, reveal how surveillance increasingly functions as a mechanism of behavioral regulation.

Social Credit Systems: Surveillance as Explicit Social Control

Kevin Werbach's *Orwell That Ends Well: Social Credit as Regulation for the Algorithmic Age*[69] critically engages with the complexity of panoptic surveillance systems beyond the typical dystopian narrative. Werbach argues that while China's social credit system (SCS) is widely perceived in the West as a tool of authoritarian oppression, it is, in fact, the most advanced prototype of algorithmic regulation, presenting both opportunities and risks for governance in the digital age. The Snowden revelations exposed the extent of government cybersurveillance in liberal democracies, but Werbach argues, China's social credit system represent a fundamentally different model of surveillance. Rather than being focused solely on intelligence gathering for national security, it seeks to engineer compliance through algorithmic governance. Werbach's analysis suggests that

67 Id.

68 Id. at 1523.

69 Kevin Werbach, *Orwell That Ends Well? Social Credit as Regulation for the Algorithmic Age*, 2022 U. Ill. L. Rev. 1417 (2022).

SCS is not simply a mechanism of social control but also an effort to modernize regulatory enforcement through data-driven governance. The West's critique of China's SCS often serves to obscure the ways in which surveillance capitalism has already created similar, albeit decentralized, forms of behavioral regulation in democratic societies.

Werbach frames social credit as a regulatory system that operates through three key mechanisms: data as infrastructure, feedback loops to shape behavior, and an oversight regime meant to provide legal constraints.[70] This framing moves beyond the notion that SCS is merely a repressive tool and instead positions it within broader debates about digital governance. He argues that SCS is an evolution of systems that already exist in the West, such as credit scoring, reputation-based incentives, and algorithmic decision-making in criminal justice and employment.[71] However, what sets China's model apart is its integration into a state-driven, systematic approach to governing social and economic behavior. One of the core arguments Werbach makes is that social credit in China is not a monolithic, centralized system but rather a collection of overlapping initiatives at various levels of government and private industry.[72] While some implementations are more punitive, others resemble traditional regulatory measures designed to encourage financial responsibility and legal compliance. Werbach argues this nuance is often lost in Western discourse, which tends to portray SCS as a totalizing system of control reminiscent of Orwell's *1984*. In reality, Werbach argues, SCS is an experiment in algorithmic governance that reflects broader global trends, including the increasing use of machine learning and data analytics to manage societal behavior.[73] The oversight mechanisms in China's SCS attempt to balance the system's benefits with potential abuses. Werbach notes that the Chinese government has introduced "safeguards," such as transparency measures and legal constraints on the application of blacklists.[74]

However, these safeguards remain limited by China's lack of judicial independence and political pluralism. As a result, the system can still be weaponized for political repression, particularly against marginalized groups, such as the Uighurs, and political dissidents. The potential for arbitrary enforcement remains a critical concern for Werbach; he highlights that while China's system is state-led, Western forms of algorithmic governance are largely driven by corporate actors, such as Google, Meta, and credit agencies. These entities use similar data-driven techniques to shape user behavior, whether through personalized advertising, content moderation, or predictive analytics in law enforcement. The difference is that in China, these mechanisms are formalized into a coherent regulatory framework,

70 Id.
71 Id.
72 Id. at 1431.
73 Id. at 1422.
74 Id.

whereas in the West, they operate through a fragmented and opaque set of private sector practices.[75]

Werbach also challenges the assumption that social credit necessarily leads to dystopian outcomes. He suggests that in a different political context, a system based on social credit principles could be designed to enhance fairness and accountability rather than suppress individual freedoms. For instance, algorithmic regulation could be used to enforce corporate compliance with environmental laws, reduce corruption, or ensure more equitable access to financial services.[76] However, the risks of overreach and discrimination remain significant, particularly in the absence of strong legal protections and democratic oversight. In the context of the Snowden revelations, Werbach's analysis provides a counterpoint to the view that surveillance in liberal democracies is categorically different from China's approach. While the legal and institutional frameworks differ, the fundamental logic of using data analytics for governance is increasingly universal. The key question Werbach presents is not whether societies *should* employ algorithmic regulation but how to do so in a way that preserves individual rights and prevents abuse.

While Werbach presents a compelling argument that China's social credit system is an advanced prototype of algorithmic regulation rather than purely an authoritarian tool, his perspective underestimates the systemic harms embedded in the Chinese model and its broader implications for liberal democracies. The SCS is not simply an evolution of financial credit scoring or regulatory enforcement; rather, it represents a fundamental shift toward a comprehensive panoptic surveillance infrastructure that integrates all aspects of social life into a centralized system of control. This level of surveillance and behavioral regulation, once normalized, is likely to be replicated—albeit through different legal and corporate structures—in Western nations, particularly the United States.

A primary concern Werbach downplays is the inherent coerciveness of the SCS. Scholars such as Rogier Creemers emphasize that, regardless of its stated regulatory objectives, the SCS serves as a mechanism for state control, reinforcing government ideology and suppressing dissent under the guise of maintaining social harmony.[77] Creemers argues that SCS is structured to create a self-policing society where individuals internalize state-approved norms, not just through legal enforcement, but through the social and economic consequences of deviating from them.[78] Unlike traditional legal sanctions which operate through formal legal procedures, the SCS leverages pervasive data analytics to create an omnipresent, inescapable framework of digital discipline. This effectively diminishes individual agency by embedding social control into everyday transactions and interactions. Another

75 Id. at 1464.

76 Id.

77 R. Creemers, *China's Social Credit System: An Evolving Practice of Control*. 2018. Available at SSRN: www.ssrn.com/abstract=3175792.

78 Id.

significant omission in Werbach's analysis is the role of corporate complicity in social credit–style governance. While he rightly observes that algorithmic governance is already widespread in Western digital economies, he does not fully engage with the ways in which corporate surveillance has evolved to mirror—and potentially even surpass—the intrusiveness of state surveillance in China. Legal scholars such as Shoshana Zuboff and Frank Pasquale argue that the expansion of surveillance capitalism has created an environment where private corporations, not governments, exert primary control over digital life through data monopolies, predictive analytics, and algorithmic nudging.[79] In China, the corporate–state synergy is explicit, with companies like Alibaba and Tencent partnering with government agencies to develop SCS infrastructure.[80] In the United States and Europe, the partnership is less overt, but no less consequential—companies like Google, Meta, and Amazon act as de facto regulatory bodies, making determinations about access to platforms, services, and even financial opportunities based on opaque algorithmic assessments. Werbach's account of SCS minimizes the structural risks posed by comprehensive data-driven governance. If anything, China's social credit experiment should be viewed not as a potential model for democratic societies but as a warning of the direction in which Western digital surveillance is headed. The difference between China's state-led approach and the West's market-driven surveillance capitalism is one of degree, not kind.

In the end, whether surveillance is justified on regulatory grounds (as Werbach suggests) or framed as a service optimization tool (as corporate actors claim), the underlying effect is the same: a new form of digital subordination in which individuals are perpetually assessed, ranked, and disciplined by opaque, unaccountable systems. The West's response to China's SCS should therefore not be one of relief that democratic societies do not (yet) have a similar system, but of urgency in recognizing that a parallel, corporate-driven version is already emerging. Chapter 3 discusses the nationwide awakening to this concern through the revelations of the Cambridge Analytica scandal, which unearthed the broad power digital surveillance has to manipulate populations at scale, with potentially world-altering outcomes.

Conclusion

The evolution of digital surveillance illustrates an undeniable convergence between government and private sector, fundamentally altering traditional understandings of power and control in democratic societies. Historically, the most pervasive and

79 S. Zuboff, The Age of Surveillance Capitalism: The Fight for a Human Future at the New Frontier of Power (PublicAffairs, 2019); F. Pasquale, The Black Box Society: The Secret Algorithms That Control Money and Information (Harvard University Press, 2015).

80 See, for example, Daithí Mac Síthigh & Mathias Siems, *The Chinese Social Credit System: A Model for Other Countries?*, 82 Mod. L. Rev. 1034–1071, 18 (2019).

coercive forms of surveillance were wielded by states, justified under the imperatives of national security, law enforcement, and governance. Today, however, private corporations have amassed surveillance capacities that rival, and in some cases exceed, those of governments. This transformation signals a shift in power once reserved for sovereign states into the hands of for-profit enterprises that operate with far less transparency, accountability, or democratic oversight.

Government surveillance, as revealed by the Snowden disclosures, has long relied on comprehensive data collection and predictive analytics to monitor and influence populations. The architecture of modern corporate surveillance—built on consumer data tracking, behavioral targeting, and algorithmic filtering—necessarily mirrors these techniques. Corporations like Google and Meta systematically monitor user interactions, collecting vast amounts of personal data to refine predictive models and influence behavior at scale. The following chapters discuss efforts by private citizens to combat that digital coercion by exercising their rights to privacy in court.

3

CAMBRIDGE ANALYTICA AND THE UNMASKING OF THE CORPORATE PANOPTICON

While the Snowden revelations brought the extent of panoptic government digital surveillance to light, the Cambridge Analytica scandal marked an important moment in privacy law and public consciousness regarding the extent of corporate digital surveillance. While privacy advocates had long warned about the dangers of unchecked data collection and algorithmic manipulation, it took the dramatic revelations about Facebook's role in enabling political manipulation during the 2016 presidential election to catalyze widespread demands for reform. This chapter examines how the scandal helped shape privacy law doctrine, particularly regarding Article III standing requirements, consent theory, and regulatory enforcement.

The Scandal and Its Implications

Background

The Cambridge Analytica scandal emerged through a complex web of academic research, political consulting, and social media data exploitation that exemplified the dangers of corporate surveillance. At its center was Aleksandr Kogan, a Cambridge University researcher who created a personality quiz app called "thisisyourdigitallife" in 2013.[1] The app's seemingly innocuous nature masked a sophisticated data harvesting operation that would ultimately compromise the privacy of millions.[2]

1 Carole Cadwalladr & Emma Graham-Harrison, *Revealed: 50 Million Facebook Profiles Harvested for Cambridge Analytica in Major Data Breach*, The Guardian (Mar. 17, 2018).
2 Matthew Rosenberg et al., *How Trump Consultants Exploited the Facebook Data of Millions*, N.Y. Times (Mar. 17, 2018).

DOI: 10.4324/9781003413349-5

Kogan's app utilized Facebook's "Graph API v1.0," which allowed third-party developers to collect not only information about users who installed their apps but also detailed data about those users' Facebook friends.[3] This "friends permission" feature meant that each user who installed the app created a gateway to potentially hundreds of additional profiles. While only about 270,000 users actually installed Kogan's app, it ultimately harvested data from approximately 87 million Facebook users through this multiplier effect.[4] The scope of data collection was staggering: Through the Graph API, Kogan's app accessed users' and their friends' Facebook likes, timeline posts and photos, religious and political affiliations, relationship status and sexual orientation, employment and education history, private messages, and location data.[5] This data was then transferred to Cambridge Analytica, a political consulting firm founded by Robert Mercer and Steve Bannon.[6] The firm combined this Facebook data with other commercial and political datasets to create detailed psychological profiles of voters. Using what it termed "psychographic targeting," Cambridge Analytica claimed it could predict and influence voting behavior through highly targeted advertising.[7]

The timeline of Facebook's knowledge of and responsibility for this conduct became a crucial point of contention. Facebook purportedly learned of Cambridge Analytica's data collection in 2015 through media reports.[8] While the company claims it then demanded that Cambridge Analytica delete the data, internal documents revealed that Facebook took minimal steps to verify compliance or notify affected users.[9] Moreover, Facebook continued allowing similar data access to other developers through secret "whitelisting" agreements even after publicly announcing it would end such practices.[10] The scandal broke into public consciousness in early 2018 through the revelations of Christopher Wylie, a former Cambridge Analytica employee-turned-whistleblower.[11] Wylie's disclosures to *The Guardian* and *The New York Times* detailed how the firm had weaponized Facebook data for political manipulation.[12] The revelations about the firm's work for Donald Trump's

3 First Amended Consolidated Complaint at ¶¶ 148–156, In re Facebook, Inc. Consumer Privacy User Profile Litigation, No. MD 18–02843 (N.D. Cal. Feb. 22, 2019).

4 In re Facebook, Inc. Consumer Privacy User Profile Litigation, 402 F. Supp. 3d 767, 779 (N.D. Cal. 2019).

5 First Amended Consolidated Complaint, supra note 3, at ¶¶ 157–165.

6 Nicholas Confessore & Matthew Rosenberg, *Spy Contractor's Idea Helped Cambridge Analytica Harvest Facebook Data*, N.Y. Times (Mar. 27, 2018).

7 Brittany Kaiser, Targeted: The Cambridge Analytica Whistleblower's Inside Story of How Big Data, Trump, and Facebook Broke Democracy and How It Can Happen again (Harper, 2019).

8 Harry Davies, *Ted Cruz Using Firm That Harvested Data on Millions of Unwitting Facebook Users*, The Guardian (Dec. 11, 2015).

9 Elizabeth Dwoskin & Tony Romm, *Facebook's Zuckerberg Just Survived 10 Hours of Questioning by Congress*, Wash. Post (Apr. 11, 2018).

10 Kashmir Hill, *Facebook Has Been Sharing User Data with Phone Makers for Years*, Gizmodo (June 3, 2018).

11 Christopher Wylie, Mindf*ck: Cambridge Analytica and the Plot to Break America (Random House, 2019).

12 Carole Cadwalladr, *The Cambridge Analytica Files: 'I Made Steve Bannon's Psychological Warfare Tool'*, The Guardian (Mar. 18, 2018).

2016 presidential campaign immediately raised questions about the role of data exploitation in democratic processes.[13]

The technical architecture that enabled this massive privacy invasion was not inadvertent; as internal Facebook documents later revealed, the company had deliberately designed its platform to maximize data collection while obscuring these practices from users.[14] The Graph API's friend permission feature, for instance, was known internally as a "magic door" that would encourage developer adoption by offering access to massive amounts of user data.[15] Cambridge Analytica itself operated within a broader ecosystem of political firms and consultancies skilled in data-driven political manipulation. The company was an offshoot of SCL Group, a British political consulting firm with ties to military psychological operations.[16] Its methodologies built on earlier "microtargeting" techniques developed by firms like Aristotle International and Catalist, but with unprecedented access to intimate psychological data through Facebook's platform.[17]

The scandal's revelations triggered multiple parallel investigations. Beyond the FTC's investigation into Facebook's compliance with its 2012 consent decree, the company faced scrutiny from the Securities and Exchange Commission regarding disclosures to investors, state attorneys general investigating consumer protection violations, the Department of Justice examining potential criminal violations, and parliamentary investigations in the UK and EU. These overlapping investigations revealed a pattern of corporate behavior that prioritized growth and data collection over user privacy. As one internal Facebook email obtained by investigators revealed, the company's modus operandi was to maximize the amount of sharing with third parties while simultaneously giving users the impression of control over their data.[18]

Democratic Implications

The Cambridge Analytica scandal vividly demonstrated to the general public how privacy violations could have profound implications for democratic processes. Unlike previous privacy controversies that focused primarily on commercial exploitation or individual harms, the scandal illustrated how corporate surveillance

13 David E. Sanger, *How Russian Trolls Helped Keep the Women's March Out of Lock Step*, N.Y. Times (Jan. 20, 2019).

14 United Kingdom House of Commons, *Digital, Culture, Media and Sport Committee*, Disinformation and 'Fake News': Final Report (Feb. 18, 2019).

15 Carole Cadwalladr & Emma Graham-Harrison, *Revealed: 50 Million Facebook Profiles Harvested for Cambridge Analytica in Major Data Breach*, The Guardian (Mar. 17, 2018).

16 Adam Satariano & Nicholas Confessore, *Cambridge Analytica's Parent Company Helped Shape Saudi Arabia's Reform Movement*, N.Y. Times (May 31, 2019).

17 Daniel Kreiss, Prototype Politics: Technology-Intensive Campaigning and the Data of Democracy (Oxford University Press, 2016).

18 United Kingdom House of Commons, Digital, Culture, Media and Sport Committee, Disinformation and 'Fake News': Final Report (Feb. 18, 2019).

could be weaponized to manipulate and effectuate world-historic election outcomes.[19] The firm repeatedly claimed it could use this data to identify voters' personalities and influence their behavior through microtargeted advertising; while the specific role of Facebook in affecting the election results remains disputed, it is undeniable that the platform's vast troves of personal data, combined with opaque algorithmic curation and psychological profiling, created a powerful avenue for political influence.[20]

The gravity of these implications was reflected in the unprecedented congressional hearings that followed the scandal. In April 2018, Mark Zuckerberg testified before joint sessions of the Senate Judiciary and Commerce Committees and the House Energy and Commerce Committee. These hearings were a pivotal moment in tech regulation, marking the first time a major platform CEO was compelled to publicly answer for his company's privacy practices.[21] The hearings revealed both the depth of congressional concern and the challenges of effective oversight. Senators expressed particular alarm about Facebook's role in enabling foreign interference in elections. As Senator Dianne Feinstein stated, "We have seen how foreign actors are abusing social media platforms like Facebook to interfere in elections and take millions of Americans' personal information without their knowledge in order to manipulate public opinion and target individual voters."[22] This framing of privacy as a democratic rather than merely individual concern marked an important shift in regulatory discourse. However, the hearings also exposed significant knowledge gaps between lawmakers and tech platforms. Many observers noted that basic questions about Facebook's business model and technical operations consumed much of the questioning time.[23]

The hearings produced several notable exchanges that would shape subsequent privacy debates. When pressed about Facebook's data collection practices, Zuckerberg repeatedly emphasized user control and consent mechanisms. Yet as Senator Richard Durbin demonstrated through questions about Zuckerberg's own privacy preferences, this focus on individual choice obscured the systemic nature of surveillance practices.[24] Perhaps most significantly, the hearings highlighted the limitations of existing regulatory frameworks; Facebook had already been subject to a 2012 FTC consent decree meant to prevent precisely these types of privacy

19 Nicholas Confessore & Matthew Rosenberg, *Spy Contractor's Idea Helped Cambridge Analytica Harvest Facebook Data*, N.Y. Times (Mar. 27, 2018).

20 Brittany Kaiser, Targeted: The Cambridge Analytica Whistleblower's Inside Story of How Big Data, Trump, and Facebook Broke Democracy and How It Can Happen again (Harper, 2019).

21 Elizabeth Dwoskin & Tony Romm, *Facebook's Zuckerberg Just Survived 10 Hours of Questioning by Congress*, Wash. Post (Apr. 11, 2018).

22 www.govinfo.gov/content/pkg/CHRG-115shrg37801/pdf/CHRG-115shrg37801.pdf.

23 Cecilia Kang et al., *Knowledge Gap Hinders Ability of Congress to Regulate Silicon Valley*, N.Y. Times (Apr. 12, 2018).

24 U.S. Sen. Dick Durbin, *Durbin Questions Facebook CEO Mark Zuckerberg*. Apr. 10, 2018. www.durbin.senate.gov/newsroom/press-releases/durbin-questions-facebook-ceo-mark-zuckerberg.

violations.[25] The company's ability to continue aggressive data collection while purportedly technically complying with that order demonstrated the need for more robust enforcement.

This revelation sparked widespread public outrage and regulatory scrutiny not just because of the scale of the privacy violation but because it exposed how surveillance practices previously justified as necessary for targeted advertising could be repurposed for political manipulation. The scandal thus highlighted the inadequacy of corporate privacy discourse premised on individual consent and "mere" commercial use.

Legal Aftermath and Doctrinal Evolution

The Consolidated Class Action Complaint

The scandal led to the almost immediate filing of dozens of related privacy class actions in federal and state courts across the country. The consolidated complaint in *In re Facebook Inc. Consumer Privacy User Profile Litigation* reflected both the broad scope of Facebook's alleged privacy violations and the challenges of translating those violations into cognizable legal claims. Lead plaintiffs' counsel, representing approximately three dozen Facebook users, filed a sprawling complaint that sought to represent a class of all Facebook users in both the United States and the United Kingdom whose personal information had been compromised between 2007 and 2018.[26] The complaint's breadth reflected the systemic nature of the privacy violations at issue. Rather than focusing narrowly on Cambridge Analytica's acquisition of data, the plaintiffs challenged Facebook's entire approach to user privacy. As Judge Chhabria—the federal district court judge in the Northern District of California who ultimately oversaw the litigation—characterized it, the complaint seemed to identify "anything Facebook has ever been reported to have done wrong and then made sure to sprinkle in at least a few allegations about it."[27]

The plaintiffs' core allegations centered on Facebook's practice of making users' personal information available to third parties without meaningful consent. This included intimate details, such as private messages, photographs, videos, location data, and political and religious preferences.[28] The complaint alleged that Facebook had architected its platform to facilitate widespread data harvesting while deliberately obscuring these practices from users. Particularly significant was the

25 Fed. Trade Comm'n, *Facebook Settles FTC Charges That It Deceived Consumers by Failing to Keep Privacy Promises*. Nov. 29, 2011. www.ftc.gov/news-events/news/press-releases/2011/11/facebook-settles-ftc-charges-it-deceived-consumers-failing-keep-privacy-promises.

26 In re Facebook, Inc. Consumer Privacy User Profile Litigation, 402 F. Supp. 3d 767, 776 (N.D. Cal. 2019).

27 Id. at 777.

28 Id.

allegation that Facebook's privacy violations persisted even after the company entered into a consent decree with the FTC in 2012. The complaint detailed how Facebook continued allowing preferred developers access to friend data through secret "whitelisting" agreements, even after publicly announcing it would end such practices.[29] This alleged pattern of public promises followed by private circumvention became central to the plaintiffs' claims.

The complaint advanced multiple theories of harm. Beyond traditional privacy injuries, plaintiffs alleged economic damages from the loss of their data's value and increased risk of identity theft. They also emphasized broader societal harms, including the use of harvested data for voter manipulation and political propaganda.[30] The complaint asserted an array of specific legal claims, including invasion of privacy under federal and state law, violations of the Stored Communications Act, violations of the Video Privacy Protection Act, breach of contract and implied covenant of good faith, negligence and gross negligence, deceit by concealment, violations of state consumer protection statutes, and unjust enrichment.[31] Notably, the plaintiffs sought both monetary damages and injunctive relief, requiring Facebook to reform its privacy practices. The breadth of remedies sought reflected the complaint's dual aims of compensating individual users while addressing systemic privacy issues.

The Litigation Process and Allegations

The procedural history of the Cambridge Analytica litigation illustrates both the complexities of modern privacy litigation and the challenges courts face in managing cases involving widespread privacy violations. After numerous similar lawsuits were filed across the country, the Judicial Panel on multidistrict litigation (MDL) consolidated the cases before Judge Vince Chhabria in the Northern District of California.[32] The MDL process, designed to promote efficient adjudication of similar cases and avoid conflicting rulings, proved particularly significant in the Facebook litigation. As Judge Chhabria explained, while the process contemplates eventually returning cases to their original jurisdictions for trial, the practical effect was to create "one large proposed class action" that could potentially resolve all private claims against Facebook arising from its data-sharing practices.[33] The consolidated complaint reflected both the strengths and the weaknesses of the MDL process. The lead counsel attempted to manage the complexity by dividing claims into "prioritized" and "non-prioritized" categories.[34] However, the court found this strategy "interfere[d] significantly with the clarity and effectiveness of the

29 Id. at 778.
30 Id.
31 Id. at 779–780.
32 Id.
33 Id. at 778.
34 Id.

plaintiffs' presentation."[35] In the court's view, the complaint's scope had expanded well beyond Cambridge Analytica to challenge Facebook's entire business model. Nevertheless, the court was able to distill four core categories of alleged wrongdoing, each representing a distinct aspect of Facebook's data-sharing practices.[36]

First, Facebook's practice of giving app developers broad access to user data went far beyond what users might reasonably expect. When users accessed apps on the Facebook platform between 2009 and 2015, developers could obtain not just information about the users who directly interacted with their apps but also extensive data about those users' friends. Even if users had adjusted their privacy settings to restrict access to "friends only," app developers could still obtain this information through their friends' use of apps. The court noted that tens of thousands of developers had this level of access during this period.[37] Second, Facebook's conduct regarding "whitelisted" apps revealed a significant discrepancy between public promises and private practices. In 2014, responding to growing criticism, Facebook publicly announced it would restrict app developers' access to friend data. However, the company continued to allow a preferred list of developers to access such information through private agreements. This list included major companies like Airbnb, Netflix, and Lyft, demonstrating how Facebook's public privacy commitments were undermined by private business arrangements.[38] Third, Facebook maintained a separate information-sharing program with "business partners," including device manufacturers like Samsung and Blackberry, as well as companies like Amazon and Microsoft.[39] This program, which Facebook characterized as involving "integration partnerships," represented another layer of data sharing that occurred largely without users' knowledge or meaningful consent. Particularly concerning was the inclusion of entities like Yandex, a Russian search engine, among these privileged partners.[40] Fourth, Facebook's failure to prevent misuse of shared information by third parties represented a systemic breakdown in privacy protections. While Facebook claimed to have policies restricting how app developers could use obtained information, the complaint alleged that Facebook "did nothing to enforce this policy."[41] This created a facade of privacy protection while countless developers could use acquired data for purposes far beyond their stated intentions. The court found this pattern particularly troubling as it suggested Facebook was "intent solely on generating revenue from the access it was providing."[42]

35 Id. at 779.
36 Id.
37 Id. at 780.
38 Id.
39 Id. at 781.
40 Id.
41 Id.
42 Id.

This consolidation and refinement of claims allowed the court to systematically address novel questions about standing, consent, and remedies in the context of modern corporate surveillance practices.

*Facebook's Challenge: Article III Standing Post-*Spokeo

Facebook moved to dismiss the lawsuit, arguing that the plaintiffs lacked Article III standing because they failed to demonstrate concrete harm. The motion served as an important test of privacy standing doctrine in the post-*Spokeo* era, reflecting broader judicial debates about the nature of intangible injuries. Facebook contended that the mere exposure of personal data, without tangible economic loss or identity theft, was insufficient to establish standing. The court's analysis ultimately underscored the evolving recognition of data privacy violations as legally cognizable harms. As discussed throughout this book, motions to dismiss, which generally take place at the outset of a lawsuit, are critical for defining the contours of the rights at issue, and in this case, the court's ruling helped shape the boundaries of privacy rights in the context of pervasive corporate surveillance.

Article III standing is a central concept in privacy litigation jurisprudence. While it will be discussed further in Chapter 5, in brief (and as noted in the previous chapter), Article III standing addresses whether a plaintiff has the legal right to bring a case in federal court, by demonstrating a concrete and particularized injury. Rooted in the US Constitution's "case or controversy" requirement, the doctrine requires plaintiffs to establish three key elements: (1) an *injury in fact* that is concrete, particularized, and actual or imminent; (2) a *causal connection* between the injury and the defendant's conduct; and (3) *redressability*, meaning that a favorable court decision would likely remedy the harm.[43] These requirements have been the subject of significant judicial interpretation in privacy cases, where harms often involve intangible injuries, data misuse, or heightened risk of future harm.

The development of Article III standing doctrine in privacy cases cannot be understood without recognizing the broader critiques of standing as a constitutional barrier to important litigation. Article III's "case or controversy" requirement has evolved through Supreme Court jurisprudence into a demanding three-part test requiring plaintiffs to show injury in fact, causation, and redressability.[44] However, as scholars have noted, this test represents a relatively recent and controversial innovation in constitutional law. Cass Sunstein has argued that modern standing doctrine is fundamentally ahistorical, noting that English and early American courts regularly heard cases brought by private citizens challenging unlawful

43 *Lujan v. Defenders of Wildlife*, 504 U.S. 555 (1992).
44 Id.

conduct without requiring any showing of personal injury.[45] The current framework, he contends, emerged primarily as a mechanism for courts to avoid hearing certain types of cases, particularly those involving government misconduct or systematic corporate wrongdoing.[46] Similarly, Heather Elliott has demonstrated how the Supreme Court's increasingly strict standing requirements have functioned to keep important public law cases out of federal courts.[47] She argues that the injury-in-fact requirement, in particular, has become a shield against judicial review rather than a meaningful test of whether cases belong in federal court.[48] This critique has particular resonance in privacy cases, where harms are often diffuse or difficult to quantify. As Seth Kreimer argues, standing doctrine's demand for "concrete" and "particularized" injury sometimes sits uneasily with privacy rights that are inherently about maintaining social conditions necessary for individual autonomy.[49]

The Supreme Court's 2016 decision in *Spokeo Inc. v. Robins* brought these tensions to the fore.[50] *Spokeo* involved a lawsuit under the Fair Credit Reporting Act (FCRA), where the plaintiff, Thomas Robins, sued Spokeo, a data aggregation company, for publishing inaccurate information about him online. Robins argued that Spokeo's dissemination of false personal data—such as misstating his education level and financial status—violated his statutory rights under the FCRA. The Court, in a 6–2 decision, held that while Congress could identify intangible harms as legally cognizable injuries, a plaintiff must still demonstrate that the harm is both "concrete" and "particularized" to satisfy Article III standing.[51] The ruling introduced a historical framework for evaluating intangible injuries, requiring a close analogy to harms recognized in the common law. This decision initially created some uncertainty for plaintiffs, as courts were left to determine whether data privacy violations, in the absence of demonstrable financial or reputational damage, constituted a sufficiently concrete injury for standing. While the Court recognized that "intangible" injuries could satisfy Article III, it demanded that such injuries bear a "close relationship to a harm that has traditionally been regarded as providing a basis for a lawsuit in English or American courts."[52] This historical test posed potential challenges for privacy plaintiffs seeking to challenge novel forms of corporate surveillance.

Against this backdrop, the Cambridge Analytica litigation represented an important early test of whether standing doctrine would effectively immunize Facebook's

45 C.R. Sunstein, *Standing and the Privatization of Public Law*, 88 Colum. L. Rev. 7, 1432–1481 (1988).

46 Id.

47 H. Elliott, *The Functions of Standing*, 61 Stan. L. Rev. 3, 459–522 (2010).

48 Id.

49 Seth F. Kreimer, *'Spooky Action at a Distance': Intangible Injury in Fact in the Information Age*, 18 U. Pa. J. Const. L. 745 (Feb. 2016).

50 578 U.S. 330 (2016).

51 Id.

52 Id.

privacy practices from judicial review. The plaintiffs alleged three distinct types of injury to establish standing. First, they claimed a direct privacy injury from Facebook's widespread disclosure of sensitive information, including photographs, videos, religious preferences, and private messages. Second, they argued the data sharing increased their risk of identity theft. Third, they contended they were deprived of the economic value of their personal information.[53] Facebook contended that "mere" privacy violations, without additional concrete harm, could not satisfy Article III.[54] Facebook argued aggressively that users lacked standing because they could not show concrete harm from the sharing of their data.

The court's analysis of these alleged harms was an important moment in privacy standing doctrine. At the time, it was far from clear how the court would rule on the standing issue; *Spokeo* was still a relatively new decision, and in early hearings, the court expressed skepticism about whether the alleged manipulation of the plaintiffs through political propaganda was any more harmful than run-of-the-mill commercial "propaganda" in the form of personalized clothing advertisements.[55] In the end, Judge Chhabria rejected the second and third theories as insufficient. The identity theft risk was deemed "too speculative to confer standing," while the economic loss theory failed because plaintiffs could not "plausibly allege that they intended to sell their non-disclosed personal information" or that "someone else would have bought it as a stand-alone product."[56] However, the court held that the first alleged injury—the privacy violation itself—was sufficient for Article III standing. Judge Chhabria roundly rejected Facebook's argument that a "bare" privacy violation, without "credible risk of real-world harm" like identity theft or economic consequences, could not constitute an Article III injury.[57] The court grounded this holding in both precedent and principle. First, it noted that *Spokeo* explicitly recognized that intangible injuries could be concrete for standing purposes.[58] Second, it emphasized the historical recognition of privacy violations as actionable harms, citing statutes like the Electronic Communications Privacy Act. Most fundamentally, the court reasoned that "to say that a 'mere' privacy invasion is not capable of inflicting an 'actual injury' serious

53 *In re Facebook, Inc., Consumer Privacy User Profile Litig.*, 402 F. Supp. 3d 767, 786 (N.D. Cal. 2019).

54 Id.

55 Transcript of July 18, 2018, hearing in Case No. 18-md-02843-VC at 38 ("**THE COURT:** I mean, it sort of brings me back to the question, the initial question I asked, about standing, right? I mean, let me give you a real world—it's not a hypothetical because it's something that actually happens to me sometimes, right? Like I'm on ESPN and I'm reading about the 49ers. And all of a sudden they figure out that I keep going to the 49ers and so these ads pop up for Jimmy Garoppolo jerseys, right? for me to buy. So they've collected information about me, about my preferences, and they have subjected me to propaganda about Jimmy Garoppolo jerseys. How have I been injured by that? And if I haven't been injured by that, how is the—how is this case different from that?").

56 *In re Facebook, Inc., Consumer Privacy User Profile Litig.*, 402 F. Supp. 3d 767, 784 (N.D. Cal. 2019).

57 Id.

58 Id.

enough to warrant the attention of the federal courts is to disregard the importance of privacy in our society."[59] The specific nature of the privacy violations alleged also influenced the standing analysis. The plaintiffs claimed Facebook had exposed (1) sensitive communications, including photographs, videos, and private messages, (2) that they had intended to share only with specific people or groups, (3) in ways that enabled third parties to develop detailed dossiers, including information about locations, religious and political preferences, and video-watching habits.[60] The concrete and particularized nature of these allegations helped distinguish the case from more abstract privacy claims.

Judge Chhabria's ruling on Article III standing in the *Cambridge Analytica* litigation was significant not only for its doctrinal implications but also because it reflected the broader political and social context in which the case unfolded. The massive public outcry over Facebook's data-sharing practices—exacerbated by widespread media coverage, congressional hearings, and bipartisan condemnation—likely played a role in shaping the court's approach to standing. As illustrated by the *Clapper* case discussed in Chapter 2, federal courts had, in some instances, been hesitant to recognize standing in privacy cases, often requiring plaintiffs to show tangible economic harm rather than dignitary or informational injuries. However, in this case, the overwhelming public response to Facebook's actions may have helped shift judicial perceptions of privacy harm, reinforcing the idea that violations of personal data rights are not merely abstract concerns but important injuries that warrant federal adjudication. The political landscape surrounding the *Cambridge Analytica* scandal undoubtedly influenced how the court viewed the plaintiffs' allegations; in the wake of the revelations, lawmakers on both sides of the aisle criticized Facebook's handling of user data, leading to multiple hearings in which CEO Mark Zuckerberg was forced to answer for the company's practices. The scandal also prompted legislative proposals aimed at strengthening consumer data protections, such as the California Consumer Privacy Act (CCPA) and various federal privacy bills. This heightened political scrutiny likely underscored for courts that the alleged privacy violations were not just isolated grievances but part of a larger crisis in digital governance. Judge Chhabria's ruling, which recognized that the unauthorized disclosure of sensitive personal data itself constituted a concrete injury for standing purposes, aligned with this broader movement toward acknowledging the significance of data privacy harms. Judge Chhabria's ruling thus highlights the interplay between public opinion, legislative action, and judicial decision-making in shaping privacy law. By recognizing the sufficiency of privacy violations as an Article III injury, the court signaled growing judicial receptiveness to arguments that personal data misuse can cause concrete harm, even in the absence of direct economic loss.

59 Id.
60 Id.

The Fiction of Consent

The Cambridge Analytica litigation also highlighted fundamental problems with consent-based privacy frameworks in the internet era. Facebook's primary defense rested on the argument that users had consented to the sharing of their data through acceptance of the platform's terms of service.[61] The court's treatment of this argument exposed not just the limitations of consent in this particular case but the broader failings of notice-and-consent as a privacy protection framework. The court began by articulating three principles that govern consent in the digital context. First, the question of consent was fundamentally one of contract interpretation under California law. Second, and most strikingly, the court stated it must "pretend that users actually read Facebook's contractual language before clicking their acceptance, even though we all know virtually none of them did," noting the court was "[c]onstrained by this fiction."[62] Third, if contract language is reasonably susceptible to multiple interpretations, with one suggesting consent and another belying it, the issue cannot be resolved at the motion to dismiss stage.[63]

The court's explicit recognition of consent as legal *fiction* rather than empirical reality echoes a growing body of scholarly criticism. As Daniel Solove has argued, the notice-and-consent model of privacy regulation has become a "privacy self-management" regime that overwhelms individuals with decisions while providing little meaningful protection.[64] Solove's analysis of "murky consent" provides a particularly useful framework for understanding the failures of consent in the Cambridge Analytica context.[65] Solove identifies several fundamental problems that make consent in modern privacy law inherently problematic. First, he argues that consent is "murky" in its scope—people cannot meaningfully understand or anticipate all the ways their data might be used when consenting.[66] This was precisely the issue with Facebook's friend-sharing feature, where users who "consented" to sharing with app developers could not foresee how that data would be aggregated into psychological profiles for political manipulation. Second, Solove explains that consent is often "murky" in its actual expression—it is unclear whether and to what extent people are actually agreeing to specific practices.[67] The court's acknowledgment that it must "pretend" users read terms of service exemplifies this murkiness. As Solove notes, this fiction of consent serves

61 Id. at 789.
62 Id.
63 Id.
64 Daniel J. Solove, *Privacy Self-Management and the Consent Dilemma*, 126 Harv. L. Rev. 1879, 1880 (2013).
65 Daniel J. Solove, *Murky Consent: An Approach to the Fictions of Consent in Privacy Law*, 104 B.U.L. Rev. 593 (2024).
66 Id.
67 Id.

to legitimize data practices while providing no meaningful protection.[68] Third, and perhaps most importantly, Solove argues that consent is "murky" in its legitimacy—even when clearly expressed, consent may not be legitimating if it occurs under problematic circumstances or involves problematic choices. This speaks directly to Facebook's attempts to justify its data-sharing practices through formal compliance with notice-and-choice frameworks, even while designing its platform to maximize data collection in ways users could not meaningfully understand or resist. These multiple layers of murkiness, Solove argues, mean that consent often fails to fulfill its essential normative function of legitimating privacy-invasive practices.[69] Solove warns that privacy law creates a regulatory environment where fictional consent is fabricated to legitimize data practices that compromise autonomy through a person merely visiting a website or app—a dynamic Paul Schwartz has referred to as a "consent trap."[70]

Woodrow Hartzog and Neil Richards have advanced critiques of notice-and-consent frameworks, demonstrating how they function less as mechanisms for exercising autonomy and more as tools for legitimizing corporate power.[71] They argue that digital consent has become a manufactured or coerced process, failing to protect individuals while enabling unchecked data collection. Rather than ensuring informed decision-making, consent mechanisms overwhelm users with dense, unreadable policies, leading to what they describe as "consent fatigue," where individuals become desensitized to privacy choices and simply click "agree" out of habit rather than genuine understanding.[72] The constant barrage of consent requests, they note, creates a burden that inhibits meaningful choice, as digital consumers are asked to accept data collection practices across nearly every website, app, and service they use daily. This problem is exacerbated by what Hartzog and Richards describe as an illusion of control, where companies claim to offer user autonomy while structuring consent processes in ways that manipulate or nudge individuals into compliance.[73] They emphasize that users lack the cognitive bandwidth to process the sheer scale of privacy-related decisions required to navigate modern digital ecosystems, making the current consent regime an inadequate safeguard against exploitation.[74] This aligns with Judge Chhabria's recognition that courts must participate in a collective "fiction" that users actually read and understand terms of service, reinforcing a legal framework that privileges corporate surveillance over individual rights.

68 Id.
69 Id.
70 Paul M. Schwartz, *Privacy and Democracy in Cyberspace*, 52 Vand. L. Rev. 1609, 662 (1999).
71 Neil Richards & Woodrow Hartzog, *The Pathologies of Digital Consent*, 96 Wash. U.L. Rev. 1461 (2019).
72 Id.
73 Id.
74 Id.

Ari Waldman expands on this critique by describing notice-and-consent as a system of extractive legitimation—a mechanism that allows companies to extract as much data as possible while maintaining the appearance of legitimacy through formal compliance.[75] Waldman argues that notice-and-consent is not merely ineffective but actively harmful because it provides a legal shield for predatory data practices. By engaging in just enough superficial "disclosure" of their practices buried in never-read legalese, firms can claim compliance while still designing their systems to maximize data collection, often in ways users cannot anticipate or meaningfully resist.[76] In *Privacy, Practice, and Performance*, Waldman argues that companies like Facebook have "weaponized" consent, using it as both a shield against accountability and a tool for mass data extraction. Rather than serving as a genuine mechanism for expressing autonomy, the consent doctrine has been strategically leveraged to justify extensive surveillance while absolving corporations of responsibility for privacy violations.[77] As Waldman explains, "[o]n the misleading premise that individuals are capable of making their own informed choices about what they share and with whom they share it, industry weaponizes consent in ways that make other individual rights of control mostly meaningless."[78] This manipulation ensures that users "agree" to surveillance under circumstances that favor corporate interests—whether through dark patterns, default settings, or legalistic, incomprehensible privacy policies.

Waldman identifies the invocation of consent as a legal defense against privacy claims in litigation as one of its most insidious deployments. Facebook, Waldman notes, has repeatedly invoked user consent to argue that it bears no responsibility for data breaches or exploitative data practices. In court, the company has repeatedly claimed that users "consented" to surveillance simply by using its services, regardless of whether they understood the implications. Waldman notes that during the motion to dismiss proceedings in the Cambridge Analytica case, Facebook's lawyer argued:

> There is no privacy interest in any information Facebook has. . . . [Users] consented to the terms of service and engaged in an affirmative social act to publish, which under centuries of common law . . . negated any reasonable expectation of privacy.[79]

As such, consent is exploited as a means of waiving user rights, rather than protecting them.

Waldman further argues that "consent" is often coercive—users have no real alternative but to accept invasive data collection practices. Facebook, for instance,

75 A. Waldman, *Privacy, Practice, and Performance*. 110 Cal. L. Rev. 4, 989–1025 (2022).
76 Id.
77 Id.
78 Id.
79 Id.

has designed its services so that refusal to consent results in loss of functionality or exclusion from the platform entirely. Waldman explains that this dynamic creates a false sense of voluntariness, where users appear to agree but are actually left with no meaningful alternatives. In these cases, users are not making an active choice but are merely complying with an imposed framework. Waldman warns that the weaponization of consent undermines all other privacy rights, making protections like data deletion or opt-out mechanisms effectively meaningless: "[W]herever consent is operable in the information economy, it is both a weapon of data extraction and a shield against accountability."[80]

The Facebook litigation exemplifies these critiques in practice. While the company pointed to disclosures and settings as evidence of user consent, internal documents revealed a systematic effort to collect as much data as possible while maintaining legal cover. This underscores the reality that notice-and-consent frameworks are not about user empowerment but about regulatory compliance strategies that permit maximal data extraction under the guise of voluntary agreement. The court's ultimate resolution of the consent issue reflected these tensions. While finding that some users had consented to certain data-sharing practices through Facebook's disclosures, it held that the complaint plausibly alleged lack of consent for three of the four categories of challenged conduct.[81] This split decision highlighted both the continued doctrinal centrality of consent and its effective bankruptcy as a viable privacy protection framework.

The Progress of the Litigation and Settlement

The path to resolution in the Facebook MDL was marked by contentious discovery disputes that themselves illustrated the challenges of holding tech platforms accountable. By 2022, the litigation had devolved into accusations of systematic discovery misconduct by Facebook, leading to an extraordinary sanctions hearing that highlighted the power imbalances inherent in privacy litigation. During the sanctions hearing, Judge Chhabria expressed profound frustration with what he characterized as Facebook's pattern of obstruction:

> Any little ambiguity in something that a judge says, or special master says, or plaintiff says, Facebook and [its lawyers] Gibson Dunn would pounce on that and use it as part of their effort to obstruct, and delay and resist the production of obviously responsive materials.[82]

80 Id. at 1257.
81 *In re Facebook, Inc., Consumer Privacy User Profile Litig.*, 402 F. Supp. 3d 767, 798 (N.D. Cal. 2019).
82 Amanda Brostad, *'Gibson Dunn Would Pounce': Judge Grills Facebook's Lawyers at Sanctions Hearing*, Law.com. Sept. 15, 2022. www.law.com/therecorder/2022/09/15/gibson-dunn-would-pounce-judge-grills-facebooks-lawyers-at-sanctions-hearing.

This judicial rebuke reflected broader concerns about tech behemoths' ability to use their resources and complexity to evade meaningful oversight. The sanctions motion focused on Facebook's handling of discovery related to "whitelisted" apps—those that received continued access to friend data after Facebook claimed to have ended such access. Internal documents suggested Facebook had maintained a program of privileged data access for preferred developers far longer than previously acknowledged. Judge Chhabria rejected Facebook's attempt to moot the sanctions motion through settlement, noting that "it can't be that a company can engage in serious dilatory litigation misconduct, and then receive a motion for sanctions, and then settle the case and avoid the consequences."[83] This sentiment reflected a growing judicial willingness to impose consequences for blatant discovery abuses in data privacy cases and a growing weariness at the systematic gamesmanship and mendacity of the defense counsel.

The litigation ultimately resulted in a $725 million settlement in 2022, which the plaintiffs' counsel characterized as "the largest recovery ever achieved in a data privacy class action."[84] Beyond the monetary relief, Facebook argued that it had already implemented several structural changes to its data-sharing practices that provided the plaintiffs with the same relief they would have been able to obtain at trial, including deprecation of capabilities and APIs that enabled third parties to obtain non-public friend data, enhanced monitoring and restrictions on how third parties acquire and use Facebook user information, and development of more robust tools for users to understand what information Facebook collects and shares.[85] The settlement was particularly notable, given Facebook's early arguments that users suffered no concrete harm from its data-sharing practices. Significantly, Facebook confirmed in sworn declarations that it had "no plans to revise or restore any methods that would permit third parties to access private friend data without the explicit authorization of each user."[86] This commitment represented a retreat from the "friend permission" feature that had enabled Cambridge Analytica's data harvesting. The settlement also highlighted evolving estimations of privacy damages; while early data privacy cases had struggled to establish concrete harm, the Facebook settlement reflected growing recognition that "mere" privacy violations themselves warrant substantial compensation. The per-user recovery, while modest, established an important precedent for valuing privacy rights.

However, Facebook's discovery misconduct in the Cambridge Analytica MDL leading up to the settlement warrants close examination. It was not merely an attempt to resist disclosure; it reflected the company's broader posture that it is not fully subject to the rule of law. The platform's ability to manipulate legal

83 Id.

84 Plaintiffs' Notice of Motion and Motion for Attorneys' Fees, Expenses, and Service Awards, Case No. 18-md-02843-VC.

85 Id.

86 Id.

proceedings, delay compliance, and then use settlement as an escape hatch demonstrated its view that the law is just another obstacle to be navigated, rather than a genuine limitation on its conduct. In this sense, Facebook's conduct aligned with a larger pattern of corporate defiance, where massive technology firms leverage their financial and legal power to test the limits of governmental authority, effectively operating in a space that exists between occasional regulation and impunity.[87]

The *Cambridge Analytica* litigation exemplified this strategy in several ways. First, Facebook's obstructionist approach to discovery was not incidental but structural—it used its vast resources to exhaust plaintiffs and regulators, engaging in gamesmanship to delay resolution of the case for as long as possible. Judge Chhabria's comments about the company "pouncing" on ambiguities underscored a deliberate pattern: Facebook and its legal team, led by the massive, worldwide law firm Gibson Dunn, systematically identified every loophole, delay tactic, and legal gray area available to them and attempted to exploit them. This behavior mirrored the company's well-documented history of pushing regulatory boundaries until external forces compelled it to stop.[88] Facebook's entanglements with contempt proceedings and potential sanctions further illustrate how the company actively probed the boundaries of state power. The platform did not merely resist discovery for strategic advantage; it used the legal system itself as a proving ground for how far it could go in defying judicial orders before facing real consequences.

Facebook's response to the sanctions motion demonstrated a corporate strategy that treated judicial oversight as a game of endurance. When the plaintiffs sought discovery on whitelisted apps, the company selectively disclosed information, revealing only as much as necessary to keep the litigation moving forward while concealing crucial evidence. Judge Chhabria's frustration reflected an understanding that Facebook's goal was not to comply in good faith but to see how much resistance it could sustain before penalties became unavoidable. In effect, the company was not just fighting a lawsuit—it was testing the willingness of the judiciary itself to rein in its conduct. Facebook's willingness to test the power of the courts in the *Cambridge Analytica* case was not an isolated incident but part of a broader pattern of legal defiance that has surfaced in multiple jurisdictions. In previous cases, the company has ignored governmental directives, delayed compliance with regulatory orders, and engaged in aggressive lobbying to weaken enforcement mechanisms. For example, in its battles with the FTC, Facebook has repeatedly negotiated massive fines—such as the record $5 billion penalty in 2019—without admitting wrongdoing or fundamentally changing its data practices. Similarly, in Europe, Facebook has challenged the authority of regulators seeking to enforce

87 See, for example, Mike Scarcella, *Google Hit with $971K Sanction for Litigation Misconduct in Privacy Suit*, Reuter. Jul. 18, 2022. www.reuters.com/legal/transactional/google-hit-with-971k-sanction-litigation-misconduct-privacy-suit-2022-07-15/.

88 See, for example, Facebook's conduct in the *Schrems* litigation discussed in Chapter 10.

the General Data Protection Regulation (GDPR), often citing technical obstacles or jurisdictional disputes to justify its delays—conduct discussed in more detail in Chapter 10. This persistent resistance to legal oversight reflects a deep corporate philosophy: Facebook does not see itself as bound by the rule of law. Instead, it operates as a quasi-sovereign entity, wielding more power than many nation-states and treating government regulation as just another variable to be managed and, eventually, eliminated. The *Cambridge Analytica* litigation, and Facebook's attempt to escape accountability through strategic settlement, fits squarely within this model of corporate governance.

Regulatory Response and Institutional Constraints

The Federal Trade Commission's $5 billion settlement with Facebook was the largest privacy fine in history. However, the settlement faced significant criticism, particularly from FTC Commissioner Rohit Chopra, who argued that it failed to meaningfully address the underlying business model that incentivized privacy violations.[89] Rather than forcing structural changes to Facebook's data-driven revenue model, the settlement primarily imposed governance reforms, such as the establishment of an "independent privacy committee," which critics described as largely symbolic, lacking real authority to challenge Facebook's core operations.[90]

The *Cambridge Analytica* aftermath exposed potential limitations in the FTC's ability to regulate privacy practices effectively. The agency's primary enforcement authority under Section 5 of the FTC Act is limited to prohibiting "unfair or deceptive practices," a framework that focuses on broken promises rather than imposing substantive privacy protections.[91] As a result, some scholars have argued, the FTC's ability to address systemic surveillance practices remains weak, allowing companies to exploit data with little oversight. Scholars such as Ari Waldman have argued that this enforcement model is structurally incapable of protecting users.[92] Instead of restricting data extraction, the FTC has relied on self-regulatory mechanisms, effectively allowing companies to define their own compliance standards. Waldman has criticized this approach as creating an illusion of accountability, where companies appear to follow privacy rules while continuing exploitative data practices.[93] This is exacerbated by the FTC's overwhelming reliance on settlements and consent decrees, rather than litigation, to resolve privacy violations. These settlements often do not require admissions of wrongdoing and frequently impose

89 Dissenting Statement of Commission Rohit Chopra, In re Facebook, Inc., File No. 1823109 (Jul. 24, 2019).

90 Id.

91 Section 5(a) of the FTC Act provides that "unfair or deceptive acts or practices in or affecting commerce . . . are . . . declared unlawful." 15 U.S.C. Sec. 45(a)(1).

92 Ari Ezra Waldman, *Privacy Law's False Promise*, 97 Wash. U.L. Rev. 773 (2020).

93 Id.

compliance measures that are easy for companies to meet without changing their fundamental business practices.[94]

Another limitation of the FTC's enforcement model is its reliance on financial penalties that may ultimately be too small to serve as effective deterrents. While the Facebook fine was historic, critics, including Commissioner Chopra, pointed out that it was insignificant compared to Facebook's annual revenue—meaning, it had little impact on the company's financial incentives.[95] Waldman has argued that these fines amount to little more than the cost of doing business, allowing companies to continue privacy-invasive practices knowing that any penalties will be minor compared to their profits.[96] Without the ability to impose fines that significantly alter corporate behavior, the FTC remains a weak regulatory force.

Further compounding the issue is the FTC's close relationship with the industries it regulates. Rather than acting as a strict enforcer, the agency often positions itself as a partner to big tech, regularly consulting with industry representatives to "monitor the marketplace." This reliance on industry cooperation has led to a form of regulatory capture where major technology firms exert significant influence over the very rules meant to regulate them. Waldman has described this as "privacy law's false promise," a system where government oversight is shaped by corporate interests rather than public protections.[97] The FTC has frequently included industry perspectives in its reports and guidance, allowing companies to dictate the terms of their own regulation. This dynamic has normalized a regulatory approach that prioritizes voluntary compliance and corporate self-policing over meaningful government enforcement.

The FTC's historic approach has been fundamentally reactive rather than proactive. It intervenes only after a violation has occurred, rather than setting forward-looking rules that could prevent privacy abuses in the first place. The limitations of this model were evident in the Facebook settlement, which did little to prevent future data exploitation. Even after the $5 billion fine, Facebook continued to engage in controversial data-sharing practices, demonstrating that existing penalties are insufficient to alter corporate behavior. The agency's reliance on industry self-regulation, coupled with financial penalties that do not meaningfully impact major tech companies, has (at least until recently) allowed surveillance capitalism to continue largely unchecked.

Scholars have argued that for the FTC to become an effective privacy regulator, structural reforms are necessary. Scholars argue that the agency needs expanded rulemaking authority, allowing it to create substantive privacy regulations rather

94 Id.
95 Dissenting Statement of Commission Rohit Chopra, In re Facebook, Inc., File No. 1823109 (Jul. 24, 2019).
96 A. Waldman, *Privacy, Practice, and Performance*, 110 Cal. L. Rev. 4, 989–1025 (2022).
97 Ari Ezra Waldman, *Privacy Law's False Promise*, 97 Wash. U.L. Rev. 0773 (2020).

than relying on case-by-case enforcement actions.[98] Additionally, scholars suggest financial penalties should be scaled to company revenue to ensure that violations come with meaningful economic consequences.[99] Finally, reducing industry influence over the FTC's regulatory process is critical to ensuring that privacy enforcement serves societal rather than corporate interests. Until these reforms are implemented, scholars such as Waldman and Hartzog have argued, the FTC's privacy enforcement will remain performative rather than substantive (a concept discussed in more detail in Chapter 9), reinforcing a system where tech companies can violate user trust with minimal consequences. However, as we will see in the next chapter, this criticism has been tempered by the FTC's recent aggressive turn in suing data brokers under Lina Khan's leadership, implementing many of the changes these scholars called for. These recent developments suggest that the will of highly motivated enforcers can suffice to break through the numerous structural impediments scholars have identified.

Conclusion

The Cambridge Analytica scandal marked a turning point in both privacy law and public consciousness of corporate surveillance and was the catalyst for the pro-privacy zeitgeist that the successful privacy litigations discussed in subsequent chapters exemplify. While the immediate legal aftermath produced doctrinal evolution, particularly regarding standing, the fundamental challenges of regulating surveillance capitalism continue to be addressed through ongoing litigation, as discussed in Part II of this book.

98 Id.
99 Id.

PART II

The Current Privacy Battlefield

Part II, consisting of Chapters 4–8, *details the on-the-ground developments in the privacy litigation battlefield, from geolocation tracking to the compiling of cradle-to-grave dossiers on a vast swath of the world's population by shadowy data brokers.*

DOI: 10.4324/9781003413349-6

4

GEOLOCATION TRACKING—AN EXHAUSTIVE CHRONICLE OF OUR DAILY LIVES

Chapters 1–3 established the theoretical framework of privacy as power and examined both government and corporate surveillance systems. This chapter now turns to one of the most intimate and pervasive forms of modern surveillance: geolocation tracking. While the Cambridge Analytica scandal revealed how social media data could be weaponized to influence democratic processes, the tracking of physical movements through geolocation technology represents an equally fundamental intrusion into personal autonomy. This surveillance capability, once the exclusive domain of sophisticated government agencies, has now proliferated throughout the corporate world, creating detailed chronicles of individuals' daily movements that raise profound questions about the power dynamics established in Chapter 1 and the government–corporate surveillance symbiosis explored in Chapter 2. The legal challenges to geolocation tracking thus serve as a case study in how courts are grappling with novel privacy intrusions in an era of ubiquitous digital surveillance. As this chapter will demonstrate, emerging jurisprudence and regulatory actions suggest that neither constitutional protections nor consumer privacy laws are impotent in the face of these practices, as has sometimes been assumed.

The Constitutional Framework: *Carpenter* and Comprehensive Location Surveillance

The Supreme Court's landmark decision in *Carpenter v. United States* significantly reshaped privacy law jurisprudence as applied to modern location tracking technologies.[1] The case arose from the FBI's warrantless acquisition of Timothy

1 *Carpenter v. United States*, 138 S. Ct. 2206 (2018).

DOI: 10.4324/9781003413349-7

Carpenter's cell site location information (CSLI) from wireless carriers, which placed his phone near four robbery locations. At issue was whether this procurement of historical location records constituted a "search" under the Fourth Amendment, requiring a warrant. The government's primary argument relied on the third-party doctrine established in *Smith v. Maryland* and *United States v. Miller*, contending that Carpenter had no reasonable expectation of privacy in records voluntarily conveyed to his wireless carriers.[2] This position reflected decades of precedent holding that individuals forfeit Fourth Amendment protection for information shared with third parties.

However, writing for the majority, Chief Justice Roberts recognized that CSLI presented a qualitatively different privacy concern. The Court opened the opinion by reiterating the bedrock principle that "[a] person does not surrender all Fourth Amendment protection by venturing into the public sphere."[3] The Court emphasized that cell phones generate a "detailed chronicle of a person's physical presence compiled every day, every moment, over several years," and that "[t]here is a world of difference between the limited types of personal information addressed in *Smith* and *Miller* and the exhaustive chronicle of location information casually collected by wireless carriers today."[4] This comprehensive tracking capability created what the Court termed a "distinct category of information" deserving of Fourth Amendment protection despite its third-party transmission. The Court's analysis broke new ground in its treatment of the "voluntary exposure" rationale underlying the third-party doctrine. Rather than accepting that cell phone users voluntarily assume the risk of location tracking, the majority emphasized the "indispensable" role of cell phones in modern life, describing them as "almost a 'feature of human anatomy.'"[5] This recognition that individuals effectively cannot opt out of location tracking without foregoing essential technology marked a crucial evolution in Fourth Amendment analysis. The Court placed particular emphasis on the comprehensive nature of CSLI tracking. Unlike traditional surveillance methods or discrete business records, CSLI creates an "all-encompassing record" of an individual's movements, revealing not only particular locations but also patterns of behavior that can expose "familial, political, professional, religious, and sexual associations."[6] This ability to reconstruct an individual's movements retrospectively over extended periods presented privacy concerns far beyond those contemplated in earlier cases.

While declining to overturn the third-party doctrine entirely, the Court established what scholars have recognized as a key jurisprudential development in privacy

2 Id.
3 Id.
4 Id. at 2220.
5 Id. at 2218.
6 Id.

protections against comprehensive digital tracking.[7] The opinion underscored several critical distinctions between CSLI and traditional third-party records. First, it highlighted the automatic and pervasive nature of CSLI collection, emphasizing that location data is continuously generated without any affirmative action by the user.[8] Additionally, the Court noted that individuals have no meaningful voluntary choice in whether to share this data, as carrying a cell phone—a necessity in modern life—inevitably results in location tracking.[9] The retrospective quality of CSLI surveillance further heightened its privacy implications, allowing law enforcement to reconstruct a person's movements over extended periods with precision far beyond what was possible with conventional investigative techniques.[10] Beyond its temporal scope, CSLI also reveals highly intimate details about an individual's life, including associations and routines that can expose sensitive personal, political, religious, and professional information.[11] Finally, the Court recognized the accessibility and affordability of CSLI data, stressing that the low cost of obtaining and analyzing such records makes widespread surveillance by the government far more feasible than traditional investigative methods.[12] These factors collectively distinguished CSLI from other types of third-party records and underscored the need for stronger Fourth Amendment protections against warrantless location tracking.[13]

Although *Carpenter* directly addressed only government acquisition of CSLI, its reasoning has important implications for commercial location tracking. The Court's recognition that comprehensive location data deserves special privacy protection has influenced both statutory interpretation and common-law privacy analysis in cases involving private sector surveillance. As discussed in what follows, courts have increasingly drawn on *Carpenter*'s privacy framework when analyzing reasonable expectations of privacy in commercial location tracking contexts.

Commercial Location Data Tracking Practices

Scale and Scope of Data Collection

The full extent of commercial location tracking remained largely obscured from public awareness until a series of investigative reports in 2019 and 2020 exposed its immense scale. A *New York Times* analysis of a single dataset containing over 50 billion location pings from 12 million phones revealed not only the sheer volume

7 Matthew Tokson, *The Next Wave of Fourth Amendment Challenges after Carpenter*, 59 Washburn L.J. 1 (2020).
8 Carpenter v. United States, 138 S. Ct. 2206, 2210 (2018).
9 Id. at 2218.
10 Id. at 2219.
11 Id. at 2217.
12 Id. at 2216.
13 Id. at 2223.

of data collection but also the profound level of detail it captured.[14] This dataset, just a fragment of the broader location data marketplace, enabled journalists to track individuals to highly sensitive locations, including medical facilities, places of worship, private residences, and political gatherings.

The precision of modern location tracking surpasses what most consumers believed their devices were capable of recording. The *New York Times* investigation demonstrated that location data typically includes latitude and longitude coordinates accurate to within a few meters, timestamps recorded to the second, device identifiers that persist across multiple applications, movement speed and direction, and even altitude data capable of distinguishing specific floors within buildings.[15] This level of detail allows for a pattern-of-life analysis, in which an individual's daily routines, social connections, and personal habits can be reconstructed with striking accuracy. The investigation illustrated this capability by tracking individuals to politically sensitive locations, including high-profile estates, protests and political rallies, known residences and workplaces, and specialized medical treatment facilities. Notably, the authors opined that "it's perfectly legal to collect and sell all this information," expressing a common but fatalistic viewpoint which the litigation discussed in this chapter demonstrates is incorrect.[16]

Modern smartphones generate location data at an almost-continuous rate. Research cited in the *Google Location History* litigation discussed later found that a typical Android phone communicates its location to Google 340 times within a 24-hour period, even when not in active use.[17] Moreover, approximately 90% of applications hosted by Google transmit location data regardless of whether location services are necessary for their function. Compounding the privacy risks, location history data is often retained indefinitely, unless users specifically request deletion. The persistence of this data collection has led Professor Paul Ohm to observe that modern surveillance does not merely capture isolated moments but instead enables "the power to gather information that is the 'modern-day equivalent' of activity that has been held to be a Fourth Amendment search."[18] He describes how databases containing vast amounts of personal information, collected continuously and often imperceptibly, allow for retrospective tracking and analysis of an individual's movements over extended periods.[19] This phenomenon illustrates how the storage and retrieval capabilities of modern technology effectively create a "time machine"

14 Stuart A. Thompson & Charlie Warzel, *Twelve Million Phones, One Dataset, Zero Privacy*, N.Y. Times (Dec. 19, 2019). www.nytimes.com/interactive/2019/12/19/opinion/location-tracking-cell-phone.html.

15 Id.

16 Id.

17 *In re Google Location History Litig.*, 514 F. Supp. 3d 1147, 1155 (N.D. Cal. 2021).

18 Paul Ohm, *The Many Revolutions of Carpenter*, 32 Harv. J.L. & Tech. 357, 394 (2019).

19 Id. at 372–375.

for law enforcement, allowing them to reconstruct a person's historical presence across time and space.[20]

The location data market has become a multi-billion-dollar industry within the larger data broker ecosystem, discussed in Chapter 7. The overall data broker industry generated over $250 billion in revenue in 2023, with location data representing a significant and growing segment.[21] A 2021 investigation by *The Markup* identified 47 companies engaged in the collection, aggregation, and sale of location data in the United States, highlighting the scale of the industry.[22] These brokers collect data from hundreds of millions of mobile devices, with individual devices potentially generating dozens of location data points daily. The immense economic value of location data has driven increasingly aggressive collection practices. Data brokers actively market their ability to track individuals across multiple devices and applications, correlate location data with demographic and behavioral profiles, provide real-time location monitoring, and generate detailed movement patterns and predictive analyses.[23]

Beyond its commercial applications, location data has become an invaluable tool for various institutional functions. It is widely utilized in law enforcement investigations, immigration enforcement, financial services risk assessments, insurance underwriting, political campaign targeting, and public health monitoring.[24] This extensive institutional adoption has contributed to the "surveillance-industrial complex," in which commercial data collection seamlessly integrates with government and institutional surveillance mechanisms.[25] This fusion enables data initially gathered for commercial purposes to be repurposed for law enforcement, intelligence operations, and other governmental functions, often circumventing traditional constitutional safeguards designed to protect individual privacy.

Law Enforcement Use of Commercial Data

Law enforcement agencies have increasingly turned to commercial location data, particularly through Google's *Sensorvault* system, a vast repository containing

20 Id. at 366.

21 SNS Insider, *Data Brokers Market to USD 441.4 Billion by 2032*, Owing to Increasing Demand for Targeted Marketing and Consumer Insights. Feb. 18, 2025. https://finance.yahoo.com/news/data-brokers-market-usd-441-150000955.html; *The Location Data Market, Data Brokers, and Threats to Americans' Freedoms, Privacy, and Safety: Hearing on Pending Legislation Before the J. Comm. on Consumer Prot. & Pro. Licensure*, 2023 Leg., 193rd Sess. 7–8 (Mass. 2023) (written testimony of Justin Sherman, Duke Univ. Sanford Sch. of Pub. Pol'y).

22 J. Angwin & T. Parris, *There's a Multibillion-Dollar Market for Your Phone's Location Data*. The Markup (Sept. 30, 2021).

23 Id.

24 J. Sherman, Data Brokers and Sensitive Data on US Individuals (Duke University Sanford Cyber Policy Program, 2021).

25 Julie Cohen, Between Truth and Power (Oxford University Press, 2019), 93.

years of geolocation records for millions of devices.[26] Unlike traditional investigative methods, geofence warrants allow law enforcement to request anonymized data for all devices in a specified location during a given time period, later narrowing the list to identify suspects. While this technique has been instrumental in solving crimes, it has also led to wrongful arrests, as in the case of Jorge Molina, who was jailed for nearly a week before authorities realized his phone had been used by someone else at the time of a murder.[27]

The Molina case illustrates the dangers of relying on location data as definitive evidence. Even highly precise geolocation records cannot account for shared devices, GPS inaccuracies, or the nuances of human movement. The broad scope of geofence warrants raises serious Fourth Amendment concerns, as they resemble the Colonial-era "general warrants"—that "specif[y] only an offense," leaving "to the discretion of executing officials the decision as to which persons should be arrested and which places should be searched"[28]—that the Constitution was designed to prohibit.[29] Unlike traditional warrants, which require specific probable cause, geofence warrants sweep up data from everyone in a given area, often including innocent bystanders. Critics argue that such indiscriminate surveillance violates constitutional protections against unreasonable searches and seizures.[30] Privacy advocates warn that the use of geofence warrants can turn unsuspecting individuals into investigative targets simply because they were near a crime scene. This risk is exacerbated for communities of color and low-income neighborhoods, which experience a higher degree of police scrutiny.[31] Some courts have begun to push back against geofence warrants, with a federal judge in Virginia ruling that they fail to meet the particularity requirement of the Fourth Amendment.[32]

The Location Data Marketplace

In the 1982 Ridley Scott film *Blade Runner*, despite the film's depiction of a futuristic world filled with advanced surveillance and biometric tracking technologies, the notion of near-omniscient geolocation tracking seemed so utterly far-fetched

26 Jennifer Valentino-DeVries, *Tracking Phones, Google Is a Dragnet for the Police*, N.Y. Times (Apr. 13, 2019). www.nytimes.com/interactive/2019/04/13/us/google-location-tracking-police.html.

27 Id.

28 *Steagald v. United States*, 451 U.S. 204, 220 (1981).

29 Orin Kerr, *Geofence Warrants and the Fourth Amendment*, 135 Harv. L. Rev. 1023, 1042–1045 (2022).

30 Id.; *see also Riley v. California*, 573 U.S. 373, 386 (2014) (holding that digital data requires heightened Fourth Amendment protection).

31 *See* Abby Dennis, *How Google's Surveillance Technology Endangers Communities of Color*, Medium. May 20, 2020. https://medium.com/breaking-down-the-system/how-googles-surveillance-technology-endangers-communities-of-color.

32 *United States v. Chatrie*, 590 F. Supp. 3d 901, 905 (E.D. Va. 2022) ("[T]he Court concludes that this particular geofence warrant plainly violates the rights enshrined in that Amendment.").

as to not factor into bounty hunter Rick Deckard's toolkit at all. Yet today, as investigations into the location data marketplace reveal, real-time tracking of individuals—by bounty hunters and others—has become not just possible but a routine and profitable industry, operating with minimal oversight and often circumventing traditional legal protections. The commercialization of location data has given rise to a vast and largely unregulated marketplace in which data brokers collect, analyze, and resell geolocation information harvested from mobile devices. Companies across industries, including advertising, law enforcement, and intelligence services, purchase this data to track consumer behavior, enforce legal actions, and even directly surveil specific individuals. The lack of clear regulatory oversight has enabled a thriving industry where location data is repurposed and sold to the highest bidder, without the knowledge or consent of the individuals being tracked.

An investigation by *Motherboard* in 2019 (incidentally, the same year in which *Blade Runner* was set) exposed how this system operates in practice. For as little as $300, bounty hunters could gain access to real-time location data from major US telecom providers, including AT&T, T-Mobile, and Sprint. This access was facilitated through a convoluted chain of data brokers that acquired and resold location data under the pretense of supporting legitimate services, such as roadside assistance and emergency response systems.[33] In theory, these data flows were subject to strict contractual and regulatory limitations. However, in practice, they were rife with vulnerabilities, as the intermediaries lacked meaningful oversight mechanisms. Telecom providers often entrusted third-party companies with access to subscriber location data, assuming they would comply with usage restrictions. These third-party companies, in turn, passed the data to other intermediaries, eventually leading to unauthorized access by individuals who had no legitimate reason to obtain it.[34] The investigation revealed that, rather than being tightly controlled, the sale of location data had become a lucrative side business for many data brokers. These brokers marketed their services to bail bond agents, private investigators, and bounty hunters, who used the information to locate people without the need for subpoenas, warrants, or judicial oversight.[35] The resale of location data in this manner not only circumvented traditional due process protections but also demonstrated how easily sensitive geolocation information could be exploited for profit.

The use and abuse of this location data marketplace extend far beyond bounty hunters and law enforcement. Advertisers, insurance companies, and financial institutions also participate in this ecosystem, leveraging location data to assess

33 Joseph Cox, *I Gave a Bounty Hunter $300: Then He Located Our Phone*, Motherboard. Jan. 8, 2019. www.vice.com/en/article/nepxbz/i-gave-a-bounty-hunter-300-dollars-located-phone-microbilt-zumigo-tmobile.

34 Id.

35 Id.

creditworthiness, determine insurance rates, and personalize marketing campaigns.[36] Individuals unknowingly contribute to this marketplace every time they use certain mobile applications that request location access, as many app developers collect this information through ubiquitous software development kits (SDKs) that routinely collect such information, regardless of whether the app directly uses location information, and then sell this data to brokers who aggregate and analyze it for resale.[37] Studies have shown that even anonymized location data can be de-anonymized with relative ease, allowing data brokers to reconstruct detailed movement patterns and infer personal habits, including visits to medical clinics, religious institutions, and political gatherings.[38]

The exposure of these practices led to increased scrutiny, with telecommunications companies pledging to curb the sale of location data to third parties. In response to public outrage and congressional inquiries, AT&T, T-Mobile, and Verizon announced plans to terminate agreements with location data aggregators.[39] However, enforcement of these pledges has been inconsistent, and reports suggest that some location data brokers continue to find ways to access and distribute sensitive geolocation information through alternative means.[40] The FCC ultimately fined these carriers $200 million in 2024 for illegally sharing location information.[41]

Reproductive Health-Care Surveillance

The increasing commercialization of location data has raised particularly grave concerns in the realm of reproductive health care. Investigations have revealed that data brokers have been selling sensitive geolocation data that can reveal visits to abortion clinics, fertility centers, and other reproductive health-care facilities.[42]

36 *See* Wolfie Christl, *Corporate Surveillance in Everyday Life*, Cracked Labs. Jun. 2017. https://crackedlabs.org/en/corporate-surveillance/.

37 *The Location Data Market, Data Brokers, and Threats to Americans' Freedoms, Privacy, and Safety: Hearing on Pending Legislation before the J. Comm. on Consumer Prot. & Pro. Licensure*, 2023 Leg., 193rd Sess. 7–8 (Mass. 2023) (written testimony of Justin Sherman, Duke Univ. Sanford Sch. of Pub. Pol'y).

38 Yves-Alexandre de Montjoye, César A. Hidalgo, Michel Verleysen & Vincent D. Blondel, *Unique in the Crowd: The Privacy Bounds of Human Mobility*, Sci. Rep. 3, 1376 (2013). www.nature.com/articles/srep01376.

39 Brian Krebs, *Verizon to Stop Sharing Customer Location Data with Third Parties*, Krebs on Security. Jun. 19, 2018. https://krebsonsecurity.com/2018/06/verizon-to-stop-sharing-customer-location-data-with-third-parties/.

40 Federal Communications Commission (FCC), *FCC Fines Largest Wireless Carriers for Sharing Location Data*, FCC.gov. Apr. 2024. www.fcc.gov/document/fcc-fines-largest-wireless-carriers-sharing-location-data.

41 Id.

42 *The Location Data Market, Data Brokers, and Threats to Americans' Freedoms, Privacy, and Safety: Hearing on Pending Legislation Before the J. Comm. on Consumer Prot. & Pro. Licensure*, 2023 Leg., 193rd Sess. 7–8 (Mass. 2023) (written testimony of Justin Sherman, Duke Univ. Sanford Sch. of Pub. Pol'y).

Such data, once aggregated and analyzed, enables third parties to infer highly intimate details about individuals, including whether they may be seeking an abortion, undergoing fertility treatments, or obtaining contraception counseling.

Among the most egregious examples of reproductive health-care surveillance is the use of geofencing technology to target individuals in abortion clinic waiting rooms. Copley Advertising, a marketing firm, used geofencing to create digital perimeters around abortion clinics, allowing anti-abortion organizations to send targeted advertisements directly to the mobile devices of individuals who entered these locations.[43] These ads, often containing misleading or manipulative messages, attempted to dissuade individuals from obtaining abortions by directing them to crisis pregnancy centers, which are facilities that present themselves as health-care providers while often lacking licensed medical professionals and promoting anti-abortion messaging.[44] The ability to send such ads in real time to vulnerable individuals sitting in waiting rooms or consulting with medical providers raised serious ethical and legal concerns about coercion and digital harassment. Massachusetts regulators took action against Copley Advertising, arguing that its practices violated consumer protection laws, but the case exposed broader systemic issues about the nature of location-based advertising and its potential for abuse in the health-care sector.[45]

Beyond targeted advertising, reproductive health-care data has been harvested, repackaged, and sold by data brokers to third parties, including law enforcement agencies, advocacy organizations, and private actors with unknown intentions. Investigations by journalists and privacy advocates have found that data brokers offer packages of anonymized but easily de-anonymized location datasets that track visits to Planned Parenthood clinics and other reproductive health providers.[46] Some of these datasets, available for purchase online, included information on thousands of individuals who visited such facilities, with details about the duration of their visit, frequency of visits, and travel patterns before and after leaving the clinic. While these brokers claim that the data is anonymized, research has repeatedly shown that with just a few data points, it is possible to re-identify individuals with alarming accuracy.[47]

The Supreme Court's 2022 decision in *Dobbs v. Jackson Women's Health Organization*[48] has brought the potential harms associated with the trafficking of location

43 Id.

44 Id.

45 *AG Reaches Settlement with Advertising Company Prohibiting 'Geofencing' Around Massachusetts Healthcare Facilities*, Mass.Gov. Apr. 4, 2017. www.mass.gov/news/ag-reaches-settlement-with-advertising-company-prohibiting-geofencing-around-massachusetts-healthcare-facilities.

46 Joseph Cox, *Data Broker Is Selling Location Data of People Who Visit Abortion Clinics*, Vice (May 3, 2022). www.vice.com/en/article/m7vzjb/location-data-abortion-clinics-safegraph-planned-parenthood.

47 Id.

48 142 S. Ct. 2228 (2022).

data into acute focus. The Supreme Court's decision overturned *Roe v. Wade*, eliminating the federal constitutional right to abortion and allowing states to regulate or ban the procedure as they see fit.[49] The decision has highlighted how commercial surveillance systems can become tools for law enforcement in ways that threaten constitutional liberties and individual autonomy. Recent investigations have documented how location data brokers continue to collect and sell information about visits to reproductive health-care facilities, despite the clear risks such practices pose in a post-*Dobbs* environment.[50] Private sector data collection thus effectively circumvents constitutional protections against government surveillance, allowing law enforcement in abortion-restricting states to surveil their populace and hunt down women seeking abortions.[51] While *Carpenter* requires law enforcement to obtain a warrant for cell site location information from carriers, no such requirement exists when the same information is purchased from commercial data brokers.

The risks are not merely theoretical. In Nebraska, prosecutors used Facebook messages obtained through a search warrant to bring charges related to an alleged self-managed abortion.[52] Similar cases in Mississippi and Indiana have seen prosecutors attempt to use internet search histories and text messages as evidence in pregnancy-related prosecutions.[53] These cases demonstrate how commercial surveillance infrastructure can be repurposed for law enforcement objectives that may chill constitutionally protected activities. Danielle Keats Citron has highlighted the dangers posed by the modern surveillance economy in the wake of *Dobbs*, emphasizing how location tracking, data brokering, and law enforcement surveillance jeopardize intimate privacy.[54] Citron argues that the commodification of intimate data—including information on reproductive health, location tracking of clinic visits, and online searches for abortion-related services—creates significant risks for individuals seeking reproductive health care, their providers, and those assisting them.[55]

The collection and sale of reproductive health-care-related location data became so alarming that, in 2023, Senator Elizabeth Warren, along with a coalition of lawmakers, launched an investigation into data collection practices at crisis pregnancy centers. These facilities, often affiliated with religious organizations, have

49 Id.

50 Justin Sherman, *The Data Broker Caught Running Anti-Abortion Ads—to People Sitting in Clinics*, Lawfare. Sept. 19, 2022. www.lawfareblog.com/data-broker-caught-running-anti-abortion-ads-people-sitting-clinics.

51 Id.

52 Jason Koebler & Anna Merlan, *This Is the Data Facebook Gave Police to Prosecute a Teenager for Abortion*, Vice. Aug. 9, 2022, 2:44 PM. www.vice.com/en/article/n7zevd/this-is-the-data-facebook-gave-police-to-prosecute-a-teenager-for-abortion.

53 Kylie Cheung, *Abortion in the Surveillance State*, JEZEBEL. Nov. 22, 2021. https://jezebel.com/abortion-in-the-surveillance-state-1848076906.

54 Danielle Keats Citron, *Intimate Privacy in a Post-Roe World*, 75 Fla. L. Rev. 1033 (2023).

55 Id.

been accused of misleading individuals into believing they provide comprehensive reproductive health care while actually collecting personal information that can later be used for anti-abortion advocacy or even legal action. Lawmakers expressed concerns that this data, if obtained by hostile actors or state governments in jurisdictions where abortion is now criminalized, could be weaponized against individuals seeking care, as well as against providers offering reproductive health services.[56] Despite these concerns, legislative enforcement mechanisms remain weak, and many privacy advocates argue that self-regulation by data brokers is insufficient. Some states, such as California, have introduced privacy laws aimed at restricting the sale of sensitive health-related location data, but these protections remain fragmented.[57] Legislative proposals have emerged to address these concerns, including the My Body, My Data Act and the Health and Location Data Protection Act.[58] However, these efforts face significant political headwinds and have stalled in Congress. The post-*Dobbs* environment thus presents a crucial test case for current privacy law's ability to address the weaponization of commercial location surveillance.

Legal Challenges to Commercial Location Tracking

The Google Location History Litigation

While legislative attempts to directly rein in these practices have gained little traction, over the past half-decade, aggressive enforcement of *existing* rights through litigation has shown promise in curtailing commercial geolocation surveillance. In *In re Google Location History Litigation*, filed in 2018, Google app users challenged the company's practice of collecting and storing location data even after they had explicitly disabled the "Location History" setting.[59] The case's progression through multiple rounds of motions to dismiss illustrates the evolving judicial understanding of privacy expectations in the digital age. The plaintiffs' initial complaint focused on the deceptive nature of Google's Location History toggle, arguing that users reasonably believed disabling this setting would prevent all location tracking. After Google moved to dismiss the complaint, the court, however, found these allegations insufficient to establish a reasonable expectation of privacy. It

56 Abigail Abrams, *Elizabeth Warren and Senate Democrats Press Crisis Pregnancy Centers on Abortion Data Gathering*, Time. Sept. 20, 2022. https://time.com/6214503/elizabeth-warren-crisis-pregnancy-centers-abortion-data.

57 California Consumer Privacy Act of 2018, Cal. Civ. Code § 1798.100 et seq.

58 *My Body, My Data Act of 2023*, S.1656, 118th Cong. (2023). www.congress.gov/bill/118thcongress/senate-bill/1656/text.

59 In re Google Location History Litig., 5:18-cv-05062-EJD (N.D. Cal.).

emphasized that users voluntarily used Google's services and had not alleged specific sensitive information being tracked, making the initial claims inadequate.[60]

In response to the court's ruling, the amended complaint presented detailed technical evidence demonstrating the pervasive nature of Google's tracking practices. Plaintiffs highlighted how Google's mobile apps gather location data almost incessantly, even when users are not actively interacting with them. The amended complaint further alleged that approximately 90% of Google-hosted applications send personal data to Google regardless of user engagement. It also revealed that a dormant Android phone communicates location information to Google approximately 340 times over a 24-hour period, or roughly every 4 minutes. Additionally, location tracking was shown to occur even through applications that have no obvious connection to location services, such as music streaming and payment processing apps.[61]

The court's analysis of the amended complaint reflected a more nuanced understanding of how continuous, comprehensive tracking differs from discrete data collection. Several factors proved important in establishing the reasonable expectation of privacy. The court emphasized that, unlike previous cases involving specific, limited instances of tracking, Google's practices created an exhaustive chronicle of users' movements.[62] It also found particularly significant that data collection continued even when users were not actively engaging with Google services, undermining the argument that users voluntarily disclosed this information.[63] The court also recognized how Google's ability to integrate location data across multiple apps and services created surveillance capabilities far beyond what users could reasonably expect or understand.[64] The court ultimately found plaintiffs adequately pled that Google's alleged conduct gave rise to claims for intrusion upon seclusion under the common law, violation of the California Constitution's right to privacy, and unjust enrichment.[65]

The ruling illustrated several important principles. The court determined that the "reasonable expectation of privacy" analysis for the common law intrusion upon seclusion claim[66] must consider the totality of data collection practices rather than just individual instances of tracking. It also held that companies cannot rely on generalized service usage to negate privacy expectations when tracking extends beyond the scope of active user engagement. The court further concluded that

60 514 F. Supp. 3d 1147 (N.D. Cal. 2021).

61 Id.

62 Id.

63 Id.

64 Id.

65 Id.

66 Under California common law, for an intrusion upon seclusion claim, courts ask (1) whether there exists a reasonable expectation of privacy, and (2) whether the intrusion was highly offensive. *In re Facebook, Inc. Internet Tracking Litigation*, 956 F.3d at 601 (citing *Hernandez v. Hillsides, Inc.*, 47 Cal. 4th 272, 286 (2009)).

"[w]hether Google's collection and storage of location data when Location History was set to off was highly offensive to a reasonable person is a question of fact," for the jury to decide, and that "allegations of continuous tracking or storage of comprehensive location data" and that Google "tracked the plaintiffs after the plaintiffs stopped using the defendant's services" could support a finding that the conduct was "highly offensive."[67] The court explicitly connected commercial location tracking to the Supreme Court's Fourth Amendment analysis in *Carpenter v. United States*, recognizing that comprehensive private surveillance can implicate privacy interests previously considered primarily in the law enforcement context.[68] This framework represented a departure from previous judicial approaches that largely deferred to corporate practices justified by generalized user consent. By shifting the focus to the totality of data collection and integrating principles from constitutional privacy law, the ruling set important precedent for evaluating privacy violations in the location data context.

The *Google Location History* class action also served as a catalyst for broader enforcement efforts, demonstrating how private litigation can spark governmental action and ultimately lead to comprehensive remediation. Following the court's denial of Google's motion to dismiss the private action, state attorneys general began launching their own investigations and lawsuits targeting similar practices. In January 2022, state attorneys general from Indiana, Texas, Washington, and the District of Columbia filed parallel lawsuits against Google, building directly on the factual allegations developed in the private litigation.[69] These complaints expanded on the original case by emphasizing how Google's practices violated various state consumer protection laws. By November 2022, the coalition had grown to include 40 state attorneys general, representing the largest coordinated state privacy enforcement action to date. The state investigations revealed additional details about Google's location tracking practices; for instance, the Arizona attorney general's investigation uncovered internal emails showing that even Google's own engineers had difficulty determining when location tracking was enabled or disabled, with Google engineers stating, "Speaking as a user, WTF? More specifically I **thought** I had location tracking turned off on my phone," and "So our messaging around this is enough to confuse a privacy focused [Google software engineer]. That's not good."[70] This evidence strengthened both the public and private cases by undermining Google's arguments about user consent and control.

67 Id. at 1158.

68 Id.

69 *AG Racine Leads Bipartisan Coalition Suing Google for Deceiving Consumers and Invading Their Privacy*, Office of the Attorney General for the District of Columbia. Jan. 24, 2022. https://oag.dc.gov/release/ag-racine-leads-bipartisan-coalition-suing-google.

70 Jerod Macdonald-Evoy, *Unsealed Google Lawsuit Docs Show Its Own Engineers Were Confused by Privacy Settings*, Arizona Mirror. Aug. 24, 2020. https://azmirror.com/2020/08/24/unsealed-google-lawsuit-docs-show-its-own-engineers-were-confused-by-privacy-settings/.

The convergence of private and public enforcement actions ultimately led to a comprehensive settlement announced in late 2022. As part of the agreement, Google committed to paying $391.5 million to state attorneys general offices to resolve allegations related to its location tracking practices. In addition to the financial penalty, the settlement imposed several requirements aimed at enhancing user privacy and transparency. Google agreed to provide clearer disclosures about its location tracking policies, ensuring that users have a more accurate understanding of how their data is collected and used. To further safeguard user data, Google committed to automatically deleting location information after specified periods, reducing the risk of long-term retention and potential misuse.[71]

The parallel private class action settled shortly thereafter for an additional $62.5 million and similar injunctive relief.[72] These settlements represent the largest geolocation privacy lawsuit resolution in history and establish an important precedent for future privacy enforcement. The settlement's requirements went beyond retrospective monetary compensation, mandating specific technical changes to Google's products. The company was required to provide users with detailed information about the location data collected by different Google services, create new controls for managing location settings, and modify its data retention policies to offer users greater control over their information, requiring that any location information be automatically deleted by default within 18 months.[73]

The success of these coordinated enforcement actions challenges prevailing narratives about the ineffectiveness of privacy litigation. The combination of private class actions and state enforcement proved particularly powerful, with each type of action leveraging different legal theories and remedial powers to achieve comprehensive reform. This model of complementary enforcement has since been replicated in other privacy contexts, suggesting a potential framework for future privacy regulation.

FTC Enforcement Actions

The Federal Trade Commission's enforcement action against location data broker Kochava marked a pivotal shift in the FTC's role in regulatory oversight of the location data marketplace, testing the agency's authority to regulate data brokers under Section 5 of the FTC Act. In August 2022, anticipating FTC enforcement action, Kochava took the unusual step of filing a preemptive lawsuit against the

71 *Attorney General Josh Shapiro Announces $391 Million Settlement with Google Over Location Tracking Practices, Pennsylvania Office of Attorney General* (Nov. 14, 2022). www.attorneygeneral.gov/taking-action/attorney-general-josh-shapiro-announces-391-million-settlement-with-google-over-location-tracking-practices/.

72 *Google Location History Settlement Website*, GoogleLocationHistorySettlement.com. www.googlelocationhistorysettlement.com/.

73 Id.

FTC in the US District Court for the District of Idaho. The company sought declaratory judgment that its data practices did not violate Section 5, arguing that its location data was anonymized and that the FTC lacked authority to regulate location data sales absent specific statutory authorization.[74] This defensive maneuver came just days before the FTC filed its own enforcement action, creating parallel proceedings that highlighted the complex jurisdictional and substantive issues surrounding location data privacy.

The FTC's initial complaint focused primarily on the sensitive nature of locations tracked by Kochava, including health-care facilities and places of worship, arguing that the mere sale of such data constituted an unfair practice. However, the court found these allegations insufficient, requiring more than just theoretical privacy concerns. Specifically, the court sought concrete examples of actual consumer harm and clearer explanations of how Kochava's data could identify individuals.[75]

The FTC responded with an amended complaint that reconceptualized the nature of the privacy harms at issue. Rather than focusing solely on the sensitivity of tracked locations, the FTC provided a detailed technical analysis of Kochava's data collection and sales practices. The complaint alleged that Kochava provides its customers with vast amounts of essentially non-anonymized information about millions of mobile device users, including their past physical locations, personal characteristics (such as age, ethnicity, and gender), religious and political affiliations, marital and parental statuses, economic statuses, and more.[76] Far from merely selling isolated "bits and pieces" of data available through other lawful means, the FTC alleged that Kochava offers comprehensive, aggregated collections of both raw and synthesized data, designed to give its customers a "360-degree perspective" on the unique traits of millions of individual device users.[77] Significantly, the amended complaint directly addressed the de-anonymization question that had troubled the court in its initial ruling. The FTC explained how mobile advertising IDs (MAIDs) function as persistent identifiers that, when combined with location patterns, can effectively identify individuals. This technical analysis was supplemented with documentation of services that explicitly match MAIDs to personal information, demonstrating how Kochava's supposedly anonymous data could be used to identify and track specific individuals.[78] The complaint also meticulously documented how Kochava's "Collective" and "Raw Feed" products capture precise latitude and longitude coordinates, tracking approximately 94 billion geo-transactions monthly, with an average of 90 daily transactions per device.[79] This level of granularity underscored the vast surveillance capacity of Kochava's data products,

74 *Kochava, Inc. v. Fed. Trade Comm'n*, 2:22-cv-00349-BLW, 3 (D. Idaho May 3, 2023).

75 Complaint, FTC v. Kochava Inc., No. 2:22-cv-00377 (D. Idaho 2022).

76 Amended Complaint, FTC v. Kochava Inc., No. 2:22-cv-00377 (D. Idaho 2023).

77 Id.

78 Id.

79 Id.

reinforcing the FTC's argument that the company's practices pose substantial risks to consumer privacy. As will be seen in Chapter 7, this approach mirrors (and was perhaps inspired by) the comprehensive allegations against data broker Oracle by the private plaintiffs in the *Katz-Lacabe et al. v. Oracle* litigation, demonstrating the further synergies between public and private enforcement of privacy rights.

The FTC also substantially strengthened its allegations regarding concrete privacy risks. Rather than relying on abstract concerns about sensitive location tracking, the amended complaint documented specific scenarios where location data could enable stalking and domestic abuse. It provided examples of how the data could facilitate discrimination in health care, employment, and housing contexts. Crucially, the FTC included evidence of actual cases where similar types of location data had been misused, helping establish that the potential harms were neither speculative nor hypothetical.[80]

The court's analysis of the amended complaint reflected an evolving understanding of these modern data surveillance practices. In denying Kochava's second motion to dismiss, the court accepted the FTC's theory that the sale of comprehensive location data could constitute substantial injury. The court recognized that Kochava's conduct plausibly "causes or is likely to cause" substantial injury to consumers by selling "massive amounts of private and encyclopedic information" that puts consumers at a significant risk of suffering secondary harms.[81] Recognizing privacy as a long-established legal interest at the state, local, and federal levels, the court emphasized that an invasion of privacy can, on its own, constitute substantial consumer injury under Section 5(a) of the FTC Act. In assessing the severity of this intrusion, the court drew upon Supreme Court and Ninth Circuit precedent, including *Carpenter v. United States*, *Patel v. Facebook* (discussed in Chapter 5), and *In re Facebook Internet Tracking Litig*ation (discussed in Chapter 6), which acknowledged the unique threats posed by modern technology in enabling pervasive surveillance. The court noted that Kochava's sale of non-anonymized geolocation data—linked to mobile advertising IDs and other identifiers—created a comprehensive record of individuals' movements, allowing its customers to track visits to sensitive locations, such as abortion clinics, religious institutions, and medical facilities. In doing so, Kochava did not merely sell isolated data points but rather provided a "360-degree perspective" on individual consumers, a practice the court likened to the kind of highly intrusive profiling that had previously been deemed a "highly offensive" invasion of privacy in *In re Facebook Internet Tracking Litigation*. Rejecting Kochava's argument that its data only inferentially revealed personal information, the court found that Kochava's datasets, combined with its ability to make inferences about users' behaviors and attributes, strengthened the plausibility of substantial injury. Because the FTC sufficiently alleged

80 Id.
81 Order Denying Motion to Dismiss Amended Complaint, FTC v. Kochava Inc. (D. Idaho 2023).

that Kochava's practices exposed consumers to significant privacy harms beyond standard data collection, the court concluded that the claims met the standard of substantial injury under Section 5(a), justifying denial of the motion to dismiss.[82]

The Kochava litigation illustrates several important principles for privacy enforcement litigation. It confirms that the FTC can challenge data practices based on risk of harm rather than requiring evidence of specific, completed injury. The case also emphasizes the importance of technical details about data collection and potential de-anonymization in establishing unfairness. Perhaps most significantly, it suggests that location data brokers cannot rely solely on technical pseudonymization when dealing with sensitive location data, particularly given the comprehensive nature of modern tracking systems.

Following this success in the *Kochava* case, the FTC intensified its scrutiny of the location data marketplace, initiating enforcement actions against several prominent data brokers. In December 2024, the FTC filed a complaint against Mobilewalla, alleging that the company collected and sold sensitive location data without obtaining consumers' informed consent.[83] The complaint highlighted Mobilewalla's creation of detailed consumer profiles, including analyses of participants in Black Lives Matter protests, where the company attempted to infer protesters' racial identities by tracking their mobile devices to locations such as Black churches and Hindu temples. The proposed settlement of the case (filed simultaneously with the complaint, as is common in FTC actions) prohibits Mobilewalla from selling sensitive location data and mandates the deletion of previously collected data associated with sensitive locations.[84] Additionally, Mobilewalla is required to implement a comprehensive privacy program to ensure compliance with the order.[85]

In a parallel action, the FTC targeted Gravy Analytics and its subsidiary, Venntel, for unlawfully selling sensitive consumer location data.[86] The complaint alleged that these companies collected precise geolocation information from mobile devices and sold data that could be used to track individuals to sensitive locations, such as health-care facilities, places of worship, and political events. The FTC asserted that Gravy Analytics and Venntel failed to obtain consumers' consent and continued to use location data even after learning that consumers had not provided informed consent. The proposed settlement of this case prohibits these companies from selling, licensing, or sharing sensitive location data, except in

82 Id.

83 *FTC Takes Action against Mobilewalla for Collecting and Selling Sensitive Location Data*, Federal Trade Commission. Dec. 2024. www.ftc.gov/news-events/news/press-releases/2024/12/ftc-takes-action-against-mobilewalla-collecting-selling-sensitive-location-data.

84 Id.

85 Id.

86 *FTC Takes Action against Gravy Analytics and Venntel for Unlawfully Selling Location Data and Tracking Consumers*, Federal Trade Commission. Dec. 2024. www.ftc.gov/news-events/news/press-releases/2024/12/ftc-takes-action-against-gravy-analytics-venntel-unlawfully-selling-location-data-tracking-consumers.

limited circumstances involving national security or law enforcement.[87] They are also required to establish a sensitive data location program designed to prevent the misuse of consumers' visits to sensitive locations. These enforcement actions underscore the FTC's renewed commitment to curtailing the collection and sale of sensitive location data.

These enforcement actions reflect an aggressive interpretation of the FTC's existing authority to address modern privacy challenges. During the 2010s, scholars engaged in vigorous debate about the FTC's authority to regulate data practices under Section 5 of the FTC Act. Some scholars saw the FTC developing a promising "common law of privacy" through enforcement actions, arguing that the agency was effectively establishing privacy norms by leveraging its authority against companies engaged in deceptive or unfair practices.[88] Others have expressed deep skepticism about the agency's ability to effectively regulate commercial surveillance practices without new legislation, contending that the FTC's case-by-case approach lacked consistency and failed to address the structural problems in the data economy.[89] Scholars also pointed to limitations in the FTC's statutory authority, questioning whether Section 5's unfairness standard could meaningfully constrain sophisticated data collection practices.[90] The success of recent enforcement actions suggests that the agency's authority may have been more robust than skeptics assumed, though perhaps requiring more aggressive interpretation and application than previous leadership pursued. Khan's enforcement strategy demonstrates that the FTC's perceived limitations may have been more about institutional will than statutory authority. The FTC under Khan has interpreted "substantial injury" to encompass privacy risks even absent concrete financial harm,[91] treated the sale of sensitive location data as inherently unfair regardless of disclosure,[92] held data brokers accountable for downstream misuse of their data,[93] and required complete deletion of illegally collected location data.[94] The FTC's aggressive enforcement stance has already begun reshaping industry practices. Following the commencement

87 Id.

88 Daniel J. Solove & Woodrow Hartzog, *The FTC and the New Common Law of Privacy*, 114 Colum. L. Rev. 583, 599 (2014).

89 Ari Ezra Waldman, *Privacy Law's False Promise*, 97 Wash. U.L. Rev. 773, 776 (2020).

90 Woodrow Hartzog & Daniel J. Solove, *The Scope and Potential of FTC Data Protection*, 83 Geo. Wash. L. Rev. 2230 (2015).

91 Complaint in *FTC v. Kochava, Inc.*, No. 2:22-cv-00377 (D. Idaho, filed Aug. 29, 2022).

92 Press release, *FTC Order Prohibits Data Broker X-Mode Social and Outlogic from Selling Sensitive Location Data*. Jan. 9, 2024. www.ftc.gov/news-events/news/press-releases/2024/01/ftc-order-prohibits-data-broker-x-mode-social-outlogic-selling-sensitive-location-data.

93 Press release, *FTC Order Will Ban Avast from Selling Browsing Data for Advertising Purposes*, Require It to Pay $16.5 Million Over Charges the Firm Sold Browsing Data after Claiming Its Products Would Block Online Tracking. Feb. 22, 2024. www.ftc.gov/news-events/news/press-releases/2024/02/ftc-order-will-ban-avast-selling-browsing-data-advertising-purposes-require-it-pay-165-million-over.

94 Id.

of enforcement actions, major data brokers announced they would stop collecting or selling precise location data,[95] demonstrating how vigorous enforcement of existing laws can drive market-wide changes. The success of Khan's enforcement strategy has prompted scholars to reassess earlier critiques of the FTC's privacy authority.[96] While previous scholarship emphasized the need for comprehensive federal privacy legislation, recent developments on the ground suggest that aggressive interpretation of Section 5's unfairness authority may well provide a workable framework for FTC enforcement. This evolving understanding highlights how institutional leadership and enforcement priorities can be as important as formal legal authority in shaping privacy doctrine.

Conclusion

The successful litigation discussed in this chapter directly challenges the common narrative that individuals are powerless against corporate surveillance practices. This perspective, perhaps understandable given the pervasive nature of location tracking, fails to account for these significant developments in both private litigation and regulatory enforcement that demonstrate the legal system's evolving capacity to address invasive surveillance practices.

The *Google Location History* class action litigation provides perhaps the clearest refutation of this perceived powerlessness. The court's recognition that the plaintiffs maintain a reasonable expectation of privacy in their comprehensive location data, even when using commercial digital services, establishes that privacy rights persist in the modern age, where individuals essentially have no choice but to constantly use such services. More significantly, the case demonstrates that the current privacy doctrine can address systemic privacy violations in the absence of comprehensive—but largely elusive—legislative fixes. The FTC's successes against Kochava, Mobilewalla, and Gravy Analytics further undermine the notion that invasive location tracking practices are beyond legal remedy. The FTC's ability to challenge location data sales as "unfair" under Section 5, even in the absence of specific examples of consummated harms, provides a powerful tool for addressing privacy invasions before they cause irreparable damage. The court's acceptance of this theory suggests that the legal system is adapting to recognize how modern surveillance practices can constitute actionable wrongs consistent with traditional notions of privacy harms.

The sophistication of recent court decisions in both private and government enforcement litigation also reveals an evolving judicial understanding of privacy

95 J. Cox, *SafeGraph to Close Digital Shop That Sold Abortion Clinic Location Data*, Vice. Sept. 30, 2022. www.vice.com/en/article/g5vw3b/safegraph-to-close-shop-abortion-clinic-location-data.

96 Alicia Solow-Niederman, *The Overton Window and Privacy Enforcement*, 34 Harv. J.L. & Tech. 1007 (2024).

in the digital age. Courts are increasingly recognizing that corporatized concepts of consent and disclosure are insufficient to justify comprehensive tracking practices, particularly when data collection extends beyond the scope of user expectations or understanding. This evolution in legal doctrine provides new avenues for challenging surveillance practices that might previously have been considered legally permissible; rather than demonstrating powerlessness, the litigation discussed in this chapter reveals an emerging framework for forceful privacy advocacy.

5

BIOMETRIC INFORMATION COLLECTION—THROUGH A FACE SCANNER DARKLY

In Philip K. Dick's dystopian novel *A Scanner Darkly*, technology blurs the line between reality and digital surveillance, capturing the lives of individuals under the gaze of invasive "holoscanners." These devices document and distort reality, tracking individuals' every move with an almost-forensic level of detail; by stripping individuals of their privacy and identity, the holoscanners reinforce the novel's central anxiety: the erosion of personal autonomy under all-seeing, intrusive surveillance. The novel also features the "scramble suit," a high-tech disguise that anonymizes its wearer by constantly shifting their appearance. The protagonist, an undercover narcotics agent, struggles with identity loss as he observes, and is observed, gradually fracturing under the pressures of panoptic surveillance and drug addiction. Written decades before modern facial recognition technology, Dick's narrative offers a prescient glimpse into the themes explored in this chapter.[1] Just as Dick's holoscanners scrutinized and scrambled human lives with invasive precision, modern facial recognition technology raises profound questions about autonomy, privacy, and the societal impact of unrelenting observation.

What was once confined to the realm of science fiction has now become an unsettling reality, as demonstrated by Madison Square Garden Entertainment's recent controversial deployment of facial recognition technology. The venue's owner began using this technology not to enhance security or prevent crime but to identify and deny entry to attorneys involved in litigation against his business

1 See Jennifer Rhee, *Surveillance and Counter-Surveillance in Philip K. Dick's A Scanner Darkly*. 50 Mosaic: An Interdisciplinary Critical Journal 2 (June 2017), 133. *Gale Literature Resource Center*. link.gale.com/apps/doc/A497271460/LitRC?u=anon~c9060ba3&sid=googleScholar&xid=b415131b. Accessed 7 Feb. 2025.

DOI: 10.4324/9781003413349-8

interests or affiliated venues.[2] This system scanned the faces of thousands of paying customers as they entered the arena, checking them against a database of lawyers from firms engaged in legal disputes with the company.[3] The practice resulted in multiple incidents where legitimate ticket-holders were turned away from concerts and sporting events simply because they worked for law firms representing clients in cases against Madison Square Garden's owner.[4] As Adam Schwartz of the Electronic Frontier Foundation recognized, this "punitive as opposed to protective" use of facial recognition technology was a "major jump forward that needs to be treated as radical"; would companies now start using facial recognition to exclude individuals who had picketed the business, or even those who had simply given them negative reviews?[4] This real-world application of facial recognition technology as a tool for corporate retaliation illustrates how biometric surveillance systems are now being weaponized to serve cynical private interests.[5]

Facial recognition technology (FRT) is now a pervasive reality. From unlocking smartphones to surveilling public spaces, FRT has become deeply embedded in daily life. However, this technology's rapid adoption presents significant challenges to privacy and civil liberties. This chapter delves into the multifaceted world of commercial FRT, examining its technological underpinnings, privacy implications, governing legal regimes, and the pivotal litigation shaping the contours of its acceptable uses.

Facial Recognition Technology

FRT generally operates through a sophisticated multi-step process that transforms human facial features into mathematical representations, called "faceprints," or "face templates."[5] Understanding these technical processes is important for appreciating both the technology's capabilities and its limitations. The transformation of a human face into actionable data occurs through distinct stages, each building upon the previous to create an increasingly sophisticated representation of facial characteristics. The process begins with face detection, where specialized algorithms scan images or video feeds to locate regions containing human faces. This foundational step employs advanced computer vision techniques to distinguish facial patterns from complex backgrounds.[6] Once a face is detected,

2 Kasmir Hill and Corey Kilgannon, *Madison Square Garden Uses Facial Recognition to Ban Its Owner's Enemies*, N.Y. Times (Dec. 22, 2022). www.nytimes.com/2022/12/22/nyregion/madison-square-garden-facial-recognition.html.

3 Id.

4 Id.

5 Electronic Frontier Foundation, *Face Recognition Technology: Commonly Used Terms* (Oct. 2021). www.eff.org/deeplinks/2021/10/face-recognition-technology-commonly-used-terms.

6 Patrick Grother et al., *Face Recognition Vendor Test (FRVT) Part 3: Demographic Effects*, Nat'l inst. of Standards & Tech. (Dec. 2019). https://doi.org/10.6028/NIST.IR.8280.

the system proceeds to face analysis and feature extraction, the most technically intricate stage of the process. During this phase, the system maps between 68 and 78 key facial landmarks, creating a detailed topographical representation of the face.[7] The software measures precise geometric relationships between facial features, including interocular distance, nasal dimensions, jaw configuration, and cheekbone positioning.[8] The next stage, template creation, transforms these raw measurements into a standardized mathematical representation suitable for efficient storage and comparison. The final stage involves template comparison and matching, where the system evaluates the similarity between different facial templates.

Despite their sophistication, these systems must contend with numerous technical challenges. Variations in pose and orientation can significantly impact recognition accuracy, as can changes in illumination conditions. Systems must also account for natural variations in facial expression and the effects of aging on facial features. Individual facial features and their distinctiveness can significantly impact recognition accuracy, with some faces proving easier to recognize than others. Perhaps most critically, demographic factors have been shown to significantly affect recognition accuracy, raising important questions about algorithmic bias and fairness.[9] Research has consistently demonstrated lower accuracy rates for certain demographic groups, particularly affecting women and people of color. These disparities often stem from imbalances in training data, where certain populations may be underrepresented or poorly represented. The technology frequently struggles with diverse facial characteristics, and existing biases can become amplified through the machine learning process.[10]

Face recognition technology encompasses several interconnected capabilities, each serving distinct functions but often working in tandem.[11] At its core, *face detection* identifies whether an image contains a human face, a relatively benign application often used to obscure identifiable faces in publicly released footage. Once a face is detected, it can be analyzed in several ways. *Face identification* involves comparing a given faceprint to a database of known individuals in an attempt to determine identity. This process may yield multiple results, often accompanied by a confidence score that indicates the likelihood of a correct match. In contrast, *face verification* focuses on confirming whether two faceprints belong

7 ResearchGate, *68 Facial Landmarks in Face Recognition.* www.researchgate.net/figure/facial-landmarks_fig1_338048224.

8 Id.

9 P. Grother et al., *Face Recognition Vendor Test (FRVT) Part 3: Demographic Effects*, NIST Internal Report 8280.

10 J. Buolamwini & T. Gebru, *Gender Shades: Intersectional Accuracy Disparities in Commercial Gender Classification*, Conference on Fairness, Accountability and Transparency (2018).

11 Electronic Frontier Foundation, *Face Recognition Isn't Just Face Identification and Verification.* Oct. 2021. www.eff.org/deeplinks/2021/10/face-recognition-isnt-just-face-identification-and-verification.

to the same person. This method is commonly employed in security applications, such as unlocking smartphones or authorizing financial transactions. Beyond simple identification, face recognition technology is also used for *face tracking,* which follows an individual's movements through physical spaces using surveillance cameras. Similarly, *face analysis,* also known as inference, attempts to extract information about an individual's demographics, emotional state, or other characteristics based on their facial features. While sometimes marketed as a tool for understanding consumer behavior or detecting deception, these analyses are often criticized for their inaccuracy and potential for bias.[12] Another related capability is *face clustering,* which groups together images of similar-looking faces without necessarily identifying the individuals. This function is commonly used in organizing large datasets, such as sorting photos in digital libraries or social media platforms. Underpinning all these processes is *faceprinting,* a technique that translates facial characteristics into a unique mathematical representation. The collection and storage of these faceprints pose significant privacy risks, as they can be used for surveillance or exploited in data breaches.[13]

Each of these capabilities plays a significant role in the broader application of face recognition technology, with varying implications for privacy and security. The legal status of face recognition technology varies, with some capabilities facing significant restrictions due to privacy and ethical concerns. Face identification and face tracking are among the most legally curtailed, with bans on government use in cities like San Francisco and Portland and strict regulations under laws like the EU's GDPR and Illinois's BIPA. Face analysis, particularly emotional recognition, faces increasing scrutiny, with the EU considering bans in workplaces and schools.[14] Meanwhile, face verification is widely accepted due to its ubiquitous commercial applications, and face clustering and face detection generally encounter fewer restrictions unless tied to biometric data collection. Faceprinting, while fundamental to recognition systems, is regulated under laws like BIPA, requiring consent for data storage. As concerns over bias, surveillance, and privacy grow, governments continue to propose stricter regulations on high-risk applications of facial recognition.

12 Id.

13 Id.

14 *See,* for example, 5 Years After San Francisco Banned Face Recognition, Voters Ask for More Surveillance, *Wired* (May 2024). www.wired.com/story/san-francisco-banned-face-recognition-voters-ask-for-more-surveillance/; *Prohibit the Use of Face Recognition Technologies by Private Entities in Public Spaces, City of Portland Code 34.10.* www.portland.gov/code/34/10; Status of State Laws on Facial Recognition Surveillance, *Tech Policy Press* (2024). www.techpolicy.press/status-of-state-laws-on-facial-recognition-surveillance-continued-progress-and-smart-innovations/; Top 5 Things Employers Need to Know about the EU's Latest AI Guidelines, *JD Supra* (Feb. 6, 2025). www.jdsupra.com/legalnews/top-5-things-employers-need-to-know-6620552/.

Privacy Implications and Harms

The collection and processing of biometric data raise substantial privacy concerns that extend beyond traditional data protection frameworks. Unlike passwords or identification numbers, biometric identifiers are immutable—they cannot be changed if compromised. This permanence amplifies the consequences of privacy invasions, making individuals more vulnerable to identity theft, wrongful surveillance, and unauthorized tracking. The mass collection of biometric data also increases the risk of government and corporate misuse, particularly when such data is shared across agencies or with third-party vendors. Laws like the GDPR in the European Union and the Illinois Biometric Information Privacy Act attempt to curb these risks by requiring explicit consent and imposing strict storage and security requirements. However, enforcement remains inconsistent, and many jurisdictions lack comprehensive biometric data protection laws.

As noted earlier, facial recognition systems have been shown to exhibit significant accuracy disparities across demographic groups, disproportionately affecting communities of color. Studies, including those conducted by the National Institute of Standards and Technology (NIST), have found that Black and Asian individuals are up to 100 times more likely to be misidentified than White individuals.[15] These inaccuracies can lead to false arrests, wrongful detentions, and discriminatory outcomes in hiring, banking, and housing decisions.[16] The biases in these systems stem from the lack of diversity in training datasets, as well as systemic issues in how the technology is developed and deployed. When used in law enforcement, facial recognition technology amplifies existing racial disparities in policing, disproportionately targeting communities of color, who already face heightened scrutiny in the criminal justice system.[17] Calls for stricter regulations and outright bans on police use of the technology continue to gain traction, as civil rights groups push for policies that limit its deployment in high-risk scenarios.[18] Anita Allen's scholarship highlights the ethical dimensions of these disparities, framing the issue as a fundamental violation of privacy and dignity. Allen contends that the unchecked deployment of FRT exacerbates a surveillance culture that disproportionately burdens marginalized groups, eroding their autonomy and perpetuating cycles of

15 Patrick Grother et al., *Face Recognition Vendor Test (FRVT) Part 3: Demographic Effects*, Nat'l Inst. of Standards & Tech. (Dec. 2019). https://doi.org/10.6028/NIST.IR.8280.

16 American Civil Liberties Union (ACLU), *Biased Technology: The Automated Discrimination of Facial Recognition*, ACLU of Minnesota (Feb. 29, 2024). www.aclu-mn.org/en/news/biased-technology-automated-discrimination-facial-recognition.

17 Kate Crawford & Trevor Paglen, *Excavating AI: The Politics of Training Sets for Machine Learning*. https://excavating.ai.

18 Electronic Frontier Foundation (EFF), *Police Use of Face Recognition Continues to Wrack Up Real-World Harms*. www.eff.org/deeplinks/2025/01/police-use-face-recognition-continues-wrack-real-world-harms.

mistrust and alienation.[19] By normalizing the extraction and misuse of biometric data, FRT undermines the ability of individuals in these communities to navigate public life without fear of undue scrutiny. The concept of the "Black Opticon," as detailed in Allen's article "Dismantling the 'Black Opticon,'" further illustrates the structural and cultural dimensions of FRT's impact on Black communities.[20] The *Black Opticon* refers to the pervasive visibility and hypersurveillance of Black individuals, in which they are treated as inherently suspicious and subject to disproportionate monitoring and manipulation. FRT intensifies this phenomenon by automating and institutionalizing discriminatory practices, embedding racial bias into ostensibly neutral technologies.

The pervasive use of facial recognition technology has a chilling effect on constitutionally protected activities, including free speech, political expression, and the right to assembly.[21] The fear of being monitored and recorded, particularly at protests, discourages individuals from participating in demonstrations or engaging in activism.[22] This is especially concerning in societies with a history of surveillance-based repression, where marginalized communities are already disproportionately targeted.[23] The deployment of facial recognition at public gatherings, combined with real-time tracking and data-sharing among law enforcement agencies, creates an environment where individuals may self-censor to avoid potential government scrutiny or retaliation. The use of this technology in private spaces, such as retail stores or workplaces, further erodes personal privacy, as individuals may feel compelled to modify their behavior due to continuous monitoring.[24]

Legal Frameworks

The Illinois Biometric Information Privacy Act (BIPA) is paradigmatic biometric privacy legislation, establishing what remains the most comprehensive and stringent regulatory framework for biometric data collection in the United States.[25] Enacted in 2008, BIPA responded to growing concerns about the commercial collection of biometric data following the bankruptcy of Pay by Touch, a

19 Anita L. Allen, *Dismantling the "Black Opticon": Privacy, Race Equity, and Online Data-Protection Reform*, 131 Yale L.J.F. 2021 (2021).

20 Id.

21 J. Lynch, *Face Off. Law Enforcement Use of Face Recognition Technology*, Electronic Frontier Foundation. www.eff.org/files/2020/04/20/face-off-report-2020_1.pdf.

22 S. Kaplan, *To Be a Face in the Crowd: Surveillance, Facial Recognition, and a Right to Obscurity*. Everyday Life in the Culture of Surveillance. Eds. L. Samuelsson, C. Cocq, S. Gelfgren & J. Enbom (Nordicom: University of Gothenburg, 2023), 45–66.

23 Anita L. Allen, *Dismantling the "Black Opticon": Privacy, Race Equity, and Online Data-Protection Reform*, 131 Yale L.J.F. 2021 (2021).

24 Lindsey Barrett, *Ban Facial Recognition Technologies for Children—and for Everyone Else*, 26 B.U.J. Sci. & Tech. L. 223 (2020).

25 740 ILCS 14/1 et seq. (2008).

fingerprint-based payment system that left customers uncertain about the fate of their stored biometric information.[26] BIPA's approach centers on consumer choice and corporate accountability. The statute requires organizations to obtain written consent before collecting or processing biometric data, moving beyond the passive "notice and choice" model common in other privacy contexts.[27] This affirmative consent requirement reflects legislative recognition that biometric identifiers, unlike passwords or social security numbers, cannot simply be changed if compromised.[28] The law mandates that companies provide clear information about their data retention practices and intended uses of biometric information, enabling consumers to make informed decisions about sharing their biometric data.[29]

The statute also imposes substantive limitations on how companies may handle biometric data. Organizations must develop and publicly disclose detailed schedules for both storing and, ultimately, destroying biometric information.[30] These requirements reflect legislative understanding that the risks of biometric data collection extend beyond initial collection to encompass long-term storage and potential future misuse. BIPA further prohibits companies from selling or otherwise profiting from stored biometric information, addressing concerns about the commercialization of personal biological characteristics.[31] Perhaps most significantly, BIPA provides a private right of action with substantial statutory damages—$1,000 for each negligent violation, and $5,000 for each intentional or reckless violation.[32] This enforcement mechanism has proven crucial to the law's effectiveness, as demonstrated by major settlements with companies like Facebook and TikTok.[33] The availability of statutory damages recognizes the legislature's determination that while privacy harms may be difficult to quantify in monetary terms, they nonetheless deserve meaningful redress.[34]

Other states have adopted varying approaches to biometric privacy protection, though none match BIPA's comprehensive scope. Texas and Washington have enacted biometric privacy laws that share some of BIPA's core requirements but

26 H.R. Debate Transcript, 95th Gen. Assemb. No. 276, at 249 (Ill. 2008) (statement of Rep. Kathy Ryg).
27 Daniel J. Solove & Woodrow Hartzog, *The FTC and the New Common Law of Privacy*, 114 Columbia Law Review 583, 592–596 (2014).
28 H.R. Debate Transcript, 95th Gen. Assemb. No. 276, at 249 (Ill. 2008) (statement of Rep. Kathy Ryg).
29 740 ILCS 14/15(b) (detailing written notice and consent requirements).
30 740 ILCS 14/15(a) (establishing requirements for written policy development and schedule disclosure).
31 740 ILCS 14/15(c) (prohibiting profit from biometric data).
32 740 ILCS 14/20 (establishing private right of action and statutory damages).
33 In re Facebook Biometric Info. Privacy Litig., No. 15-cv-03747-JD, 2021 WL 757025 (N.D. Cal. Feb. 26, 2021) ($650 million settlement); TikTok, Inc. Consumer Privacy Litig., No. 20-cv-04699 (N.D. Ill. Oct. 1, 2021) ($92 million settlement).
34 Danielle Keats Citron & Daniel J. Solove, *Privacy Harms*, 102 Boston University Law Review 793, 831–835 (2022).

lack its private right of action, leaving enforcement to state attorneys general.[35] This limitation has resulted in significantly less litigation and, some argue, less-effective enforcement. California addresses biometric information through its broader California Consumer Privacy Act (CCPA) and California Privacy Rights Act (CPRA), treating biometric data as a subset of personal information subject to general privacy protections.[36] Recent years have seen increased legislative activity around biometric privacy. States, including Maryland, Mississippi, and New York, have considered BIPA-style legislation, though technology industry opposition has often impeded passage.[37] Some jurisdictions have adopted more targeted approaches—Portland, Oregon, banned private sector use of facial recognition technology entirely, while Virginia's Consumer Data Protection Act includes specific provisions for biometric data processing.[38] The varying state approaches highlight ongoing debates about how best to regulate biometric information. BIPA's emphasis on informed consent and private enforcement has proven influential, but scholars have questioned whether consent-based frameworks adequately protect privacy given power imbalances between individuals and data collectors.[39]

Such laws highlight the problems with legislation which seeks to regulate, rather than ban, privacy-invasive conduct. Critics argue that existing biometric privacy laws, including BIPA, continue to rely too heavily on notice-and-consent frameworks that fail to address the fundamental problems posed by biometric surveillance. These scholars contend that the focus on disclosure and consent mechanisms misses the broader social and ethical implications of normalized biometric data collection, and argue that certain forms of biometric surveillance are inherently problematic regardless of whether individuals nominally consent to them. Drawing on legal scholar Nancy Kim's consentability framework[40] and their own research on obscurity and privacy, Evan Selinger and Woodrow Hartzog argue that facial surveillance has a "fatal consent problem" that makes traditional notice-and-choice frameworks inappropriate and insufficient as regulatory mechanisms.[41] Selinger and Hartzog argue that facial recognition enables an unprecedented form of surveillance that is "categorically different" from previous technologies. Unlike traditional surveillance tools, facial recognition allows for real-time tracking and behavior policing of entire populations at scale. The technology can create a pervasive "chill" that deters constitutionally protected activities, erode due process by

35 Tex. Bus. & Com. Code § 503.001; Wash. Rev. Code § 19.375.020.

36 Cal. Civ. Code § 1798.100 et seq.

37 Matthew B. Kugler, *From Identification to Identity Theft: Public Perceptions of Biometric Privacy Harms*, 10 UC Irvine Law Review 107, 130–131 (2019).

38 Portland, Or., Code § 34.10.030 (2020); Va. Code Ann. § 59.1–578 (2021).

39 Neil Richards & Woodrow Hartzog, *The Pathologies of Digital Consent*, 96 Wash. U.L. Rev. 1461, 1463, 1487 (2019).

40 Nancy Kim, Consentability: Consent and Its Limits (2019).

41 Evan Selinger & Woodrow Hartzog, *The Inconsentability of Facial Surveillance*, 66 Loyola Law Rev. 101 (2019).

recasting citizens as risk profiles, and enable systematic abuse of power through automated enforcement.[42] Central to their analysis is the concept of "obscurity"—the practical difficulties in finding and correctly interpreting information about people.[43] Historically, obscurity has been protected by structural constraints like technological limitations and human cognitive capacity. Facial recognition threatens to eliminate these natural protections by making identification, tracking, and analysis of individuals trivially easy. Selinger and Hartzog argue that obscurity serves vital individual and collective interests, enabling everything from intimate relationships to intellectual development to democratic participation.

Selinger and Hartzog identify fundamental and insurmountable flaws in consent-based approaches to facial surveillance regulation. At the individual level, they argue that the risks of facial surveillance are "impossibly opaque," preventing people from meaningfully understanding or evaluating how the technology could impact their autonomy and privacy.[44] This opacity problem is compounded by the collective nature of surveillance harms, which cannot be effectively addressed through individual choice mechanisms. Even when some individuals withhold consent, the participation of others helps build and legitimize surveillance infrastructure that affects everyone in society.[45] The gradual expansion of surveillance technologies presents another critical challenge, as the incremental nature of the threat masks its severity. No single decision to allow facial surveillance appears significant enough to motivate resistance, leading to what the authors characterize as "death by a thousand cuts."[46] This dynamic is further complicated by issues of privilege and power—marginalized groups often bear disproportionate surveillance harms, yet their interests may be ignored when privileged groups make individual choices about adopting and accepting the technology.

Most fundamentally, the authors argue, facial surveillance is "inconsentable" because it inevitably corrodes collective autonomy interests that should take precedence over individual choices.[47] They contend that even highly regulated, consensual uses will normalize invasive technology, entrench organizational practices, and fuel investment in surveillance capabilities that ultimately undermine democratic values. Rather than trying to regulate facial surveillance through procedural protections like warrant requirements or consent frameworks, the authors advocate for outright bans, particularly on government use. They argue this is the only approach that can prevent the gradual erosion of obscurity and preserve collective autonomy interests. Selinger and Hartzog argue that allowing facial surveillance to become entrenched through either government or private sector use will

42 Id.
43 Id.
44 Id.
45 Id.
46 Id. at 116.
47 Id. at 104.

inevitably lead to unacceptable harms to obscurity and collective autonomy: Even if advocates got everything on their "wish list" of consent requirements and procedural protections, society would still suffer from "a barrage of I agree buttons and search warrants powered by government and industry's unquenchable thirst for more access to our lives."[48] Given these dynamics, the authors argue, the only defensible policy response is to ban facial surveillance entirely.

The lawsuits discussed in what follows, while working within the available statutory frameworks, have functioned to highlight both the pernicious harms of facial recognition technology as well as the ability of strategic private litigation to curb these biometric surveillance practices.

Legal Challenges

Clearview AI Litigation

The Clearview AI litigation raised central questions at the intersection of privacy rights and First Amendment protections. The company's business model, which involved scraping billions of photographs from social media platforms without consent to create a facial recognition database, sparked widespread public outcry and multiple legal challenges. The *ACLU v. Clearview AI* case emerged in 2020, when the American Civil Liberties Union, along with several other advocacy organizations and individuals, filed suit against Clearview AI in Illinois state court under the Illinois Biometric Information Privacy Act (BIPA).[49] The case centered on Clearview AI's practices of scraping over 20 billion photographs from social media platforms and other websites without obtaining consent from the photographed individuals.[50] The company used these images to create a vast facial recognition database, which it then marketed and sold to private companies, law enforcement agencies, and other entities.[51]

The plaintiffs alleged that Clearview AI's practices violated BIPA in several ways: by collecting and storing biometric identifiers without written consent, by failing to maintain a publicly available data retention policy, and by profiting from individuals' biometric information. The suit sought injunctive relief to stop these practices and statutory damages, which under BIPA can range from $1,000 to $5,000 per violation. Following the initial filing, the case underwent several procedural developments. The litigation proceeded through extensive discovery, during which the scale and scope of Clearview's data collection practices became

48 Id. at 122.

49 ACLU v. Clearview AI, No. 2020-CH-04353 (Ill. Cir. Ct. filed May 28, 2020).

50 *See* Kashmir Hill, *The Secretive Company That Might End Privacy as We Know It*, N.Y. Times (Jan. 18, 2020).

51 Ryan Mac et al., *Clearview's Facial Recognition App Has Been Used By the Justice Department, ICE, Macy's, Walmart, and the NBA*, BuzzFeed News (Feb. 27, 2020).

more fully understood. The ensuing litigation established an important precedent for regulating commercial surveillance technologies in the context of biometric privacy protection.

At the heart of the legal dispute lay Clearview's novel First Amendment defense. The company argued that its collection and analysis of publicly available photographs constituted protected speech, comparing its activities to those of search engines and news organizations. The company contended that BIPA's restrictions on collecting and using biometric information amounted to an unconstitutional restriction on protected speech. This argument required the court to balance competing constitutional interests: the right to collect and disseminate publicly available information against individual privacy rights in biometric data. The court's rejection of Clearview's First Amendment defense was an important, if not wholly unexpected, development in privacy jurisprudence. While acknowledging that faceprinting involves expression entitled to some First Amendment protection, the court determined that Clearview's activities warranted only intermediate scrutiny rather than strict scrutiny. This determination rested on the court's finding that Clearview's faceprints did not address matters of public concern and served purely commercial purposes. Under intermediate scrutiny, the court found that Illinois had demonstrated important governmental interests in protecting privacy and security, particularly given the "difficulty in providing meaningful recourse once a person's biometrics have been compromised."[52] The court emphasized that BIPA's opt-in consent requirement was "no greater than necessary" to advance the state's privacy interests, as it "returns control over citizens' biometrics to the individual whose identities could be compromised."[53] This ruling effectively rejected Clearview's argument that the public nature of source photographs negated privacy interests in biometric data derived from them. As the court noted, "[t]he fact that something has been made public does not mean that anyone can do with it as they please."[54]

After Clearview's primary defense was rejected, the litigation eventually culminated in a notable settlement that restructured Clearview's business practices nationwide.[55] The company agreed to a permanent nationwide ban on providing private entities access to its facial recognition database, with narrow exceptions specified in BIPA. This restriction effectively ended Clearview's commercial ambitions in the private sector, limiting its operations primarily to government and law enforcement clients.[56] Within Illinois specifically, the settlement imposed more stringent restrictions. Clearview agreed to cease providing database access to any state or local government entity in Illinois for five years, including law enforcement

52 *ACLU v. v. Clearview AI, Inc.*, No. 20 CH 4353, slip op. (Ill. Cir. Ct. Cook Cnty. Aug. 27, 2021).
53 Id.
54 Id.
55 *ACLU v. Clearview AI, Inc.*, No. 20 CH 04353, Consent Order of Permanent and Time-Limited Injunctions, slip op. (Ill. Cir. Ct. Cook Cnty. May 11, 2022).
56 Id.

agencies. This provision prevented Clearview from utilizing BIPA's government contractor exception. The company also committed to blocking access by private entities in Illinois for the same period, regardless of potential statutory exceptions.[57] The settlement also established novel mechanisms for individual privacy protection. Clearview agreed to maintain an opt-out system allowing Illinois residents to upload photos to ensure their faceprints would be blocked from search results, even in searches conducted by law enforcement users. To ensure meaningful implementation of this provision, the company committed substantial resources to publicizing the opt-out mechanism, and the settlement prohibited Clearview from using opt-out photos for any purpose other than implementing the blocking system.[58] The settlement also extended to Clearview's data collection practices: The company agreed to maintain filters designed to prevent the collection of photographs taken in or uploaded from Illinois, demonstrating the potential for geographic restrictions on biometric data collection. Finally, the settlement also ended Clearview's practice of offering free trial accounts to individual police officers without departmental oversight, addressing concerns about uncontrolled proliferation of surveillance capabilities.[59]

The *Clearview* litigation and settlement helped solidify the durability of privacy rights under biometric surveillance statutes. The rejection of First Amendment challenges to biometric privacy regulations provided clear precedent for future privacy legislation, and the settlement's nationwide scope demonstrates the potential for state-level privacy laws to influence corporate practices across jurisdictions. Moreover, the case illustrates how private rights of action, coupled with strong statutory protections, can effectively curb—if not outright eliminate—commercial surveillance practices.

Standing: Rosenbach v. Six Flags Entertainment Corp.

In *Rosenbach v. Six Flags Entertainment Corp.*,[60] the Illinois Supreme Court addressed a different but equally foundational legal question regarding the application and enforcement of BIPA: whether a plaintiff qualifies as an "aggrieved" person under BIPA without demonstrating additional "actual injury or adverse effect" beyond a statutory violation—the Illinois state analogue of Article III standing. The case arose after Six Flags required a minor to provide a fingerprint for a season pass without providing the required disclosures or obtaining written consent. The plaintiff, through her mother, argued that these actions violated BIPA and sought damages under the statute. The defendants asserted that the plaintiff "had suffered

57 Id.
58 Id.
59 Id.
60 2019 IL 123186.

no actual or threatened injury" beyond the statutory violation "and therefore lacked standing to sue" because the plaintiff was not "aggrieved" by the "mere" statutory violation.[61] The Illinois Supreme Court held that a person is "aggrieved" under BIPA whenever their statutory rights are violated, regardless of whether additional harm is alleged. Drawing on long-standing Illinois jurisprudence, the Court explained that being aggrieved means having a "substantial grievance; a denial of some personal or property right."[62] The Court further elaborated that an individual need not suffer pecuniary harm to have standing; rather, the violation of statutory rights itself constitutes sufficient injury.[63] This interpretation aligns with the legislature's intent to protect biometric privacy by enforcing procedural safeguards before harm occurs. The Court rejected the appellate court's characterization of statutory violations as mere "technicalit[ies]," emphasizing that the unauthorized collection of biometric data represents a significant intrusion into personal privacy.[64] It concluded that allowing claims for statutory violations without requiring additional harm was essential to achieving BIPA's preventative and deterrent purposes.

The Illinois Supreme Court's decision in *Rosenbach v. Six Flags Entertainment Corp.* had significant implications for Article III standing in BIPA litigation in federal courts. The ruling established that a plaintiff is "aggrieved" under BIPA when their statutory rights are violated, even in the absence of additional harm. This decision clarified that violations of procedural safeguards can constitute concrete injuries, ensuring that plaintiffs can seek enforcement without proving additional damage. By recognizing the loss of statutory privacy rights as a sufficient injury, *Rosenbach* influenced federal standing doctrine; courts interpreting Article III standing under *TransUnion* and *Spokeo*—including *Patel v. Facebook*—have looked to *Rosenbach* as evidence that privacy laws inherently protect concrete interests. This decision provided a counterpoint to restrictive interpretations of standing and also underscored the importance of state-level privacy laws in shaping federal jurisprudence, as BIPA's private right of action continues to be a model for other jurisdictions seeking to enforce biometric data protections.

Patel v. Facebook: *A Durable Framework for Standing*

The Ninth Circuit's decision in *Patel v. Facebook*, drawing on *Rosenbach*, illustrates the employment of an effective framework for Article III standing analysis. The dispute centered on Facebook's "Tag Suggestions" feature, which deployed facial recognition technology to analyze users' photographs and create facial

61 *Rosenbach v. Six Flags Ent. Corp.*, 2019 IL 123186.
62 Id.
63 Id.
64 Id.

templates without obtaining the notice and consent required by BIPA. The litigation began in 2015 with multiple class action complaints filed in Illinois state courts alleging that Facebook's facial recognition technology violated BIPA's notice-and-consent requirements. Facebook removed these cases to federal court, leading to their consolidation in the Northern District of California through the multi-district litigation process.

Facebook's initial defense strategy focused heavily on challenging the application of BIPA to its conduct. The company argued that a California choice-of-law provision in its user agreement precluded the application of Illinois law. The district court rejected this argument in February 2018, finding that Illinois had a materially greater interest in protecting its residents' biometric privacy than California had in applying its law to the dispute.[65] Following this ruling, Facebook mounted a vigorous challenge to the plaintiffs' Article III standing. The company argued that its facial recognition practices caused no concrete harm to users (alleged lack of concrete harm is an argument that Facebook/Meta appears to have made in virtually every privacy lawsuit that has ever been brought against it, despite that argument's near-universal failure rate),[66] characterizing any BIPA violations as mere procedural infractions; this argument reflected a broader strategy by tech companies to leverage the Supreme Court's decision in *Spokeo v. Robins* to defeat privacy claims at the motion to dismiss stage. The district court denied Facebook's motion to dismiss on standing grounds, leading to an interlocutory appeal to the Ninth Circuit. The appeal attracted significant attention from privacy advocates, tech companies, and legal scholars. Numerous amicus briefs addressed both the standing question and broader implications for privacy litigation. Privacy advocates emphasized the unique sensitivity of biometric data and the importance of statutory enforcement mechanisms, while tech industry groups warned about the potential for excessive liability and impediments to innovation.[67]

The Ninth Circuit's standing analysis demonstrated a nuanced application of *Spokeo*'s framework, discussed in Chapter 3, articulating the Ninth Circuit's two-step approach to the Article III standing analysis. The first step examines whether the statutory provisions at issue protect concrete interests rather than purely

65 In re Facebook Biometric Info. Privacy Litig., 185 F. Supp. 3d 1155 (N.D. Cal. 2016).

66 See, for example, *In re Facebook, Inc. Consumer Privacy User Profile Litig.*, 402 F. Supp. 3d 767, 787 (N.D. Cal. 2019) (denying Facebook's motion to dismiss and finding unauthorized data-sharing sufficient for Article III standing); *Campbell v. Facebook, Inc.*, 951 F.3d 1106, 1117 (9th Cir. 2020) (finding standing where Facebook intercepted private messages for advertising purposes); *In re Meta Pixel Healthcare Litig.*, No. 22-cv-03580 (N.D. Cal. 2023) (rejecting Meta's argument that unauthorized health data collection did not result in concrete harm); *In re Facebook Internet Tracking Litig.*, 956 F.3d 589, 601 (9th Cir. 2020) (holding that Facebook's unauthorized tracking of user browsing outside its platform constituted a concrete injury).

67 *See,* for example, Brief for Electronic Privacy Information Center as Amicus Curiae Supporting Plaintiffs-Appellees, *Patel v. Facebook, Inc.*, No. 18-15982 (9th Cir. Dec. 17, 2018).

procedural rights.[68] This analysis draws on both historical practice and legislative judgment to determine whether the privacy right at issue has substantive weight. In *Patel*, the court traced BIPA's protections to their roots in the common-law right to privacy, beginning with Warren and Brandeis's seminal article and extending through modern Supreme Court jurisprudence. This historical analysis concluded that "an invasion of an individual's biometric privacy rights 'has a close relationship to a harm that has traditionally been regarded as providing a basis for a lawsuit in English or American courts.'"[69] The second step considers whether the specific violations alleged actually harm or present a material risk of harm to those interests. Here, the Court recognized that Facebook's collection and storage of biometric data creates immediate, concrete injury by violating "the right not to be subject to the collection and use of such biometric data."[70] This finding rejected Facebook's argument that plaintiffs needed to show additional consequential harm beyond the statutory violation itself.

This analysis was important in several ways. First, it explicitly recognized that technological advances can create new privacy threats, requiring new protections. Drawing on Supreme Court precedents like *United States v. Jones* (regarding GPS monitoring) and *Carpenter v. United States* (addressing cell site location information), the Court acknowledged that privacy law must evolve to address emerging technological capabilities. The Court particularly emphasized the unique sensitivity of biometric data, noting that its collection can be "detailed, encyclopedic, and effortlessly compiled," leading to the special harms that can arise from its unauthorized collection.[71] *Patel v. Facebook*'s influence has extend beyond BIPA litigation, providing a model for establishing standing in various privacy cases. The decision demonstrated the connection of modern privacy violations to historical protections and recognized that unauthorized data collection itself creates concrete injury.

Standing in biometric privacy cases was far from a forgone conclusion at the time the case was decided, and it was an important moment that reinforced standing in statutory privacy cases post-*Spokeo*. In part due to this ruling (but also after the case went through multiple rounds of appeals, including to the Supreme Court, and was on the eve of trial), the case culminated in a blockbuster $650 million settlement, one of the largest ever in a privacy-related lawsuit.[72] The settlement not only provided financial compensation to affected users but also included injunctive relief, requiring Facebook to overhaul its biometric data practices, enhancing transparency and user control over facial recognition technology. This outcome underscored the broader impact of *Patel*, demonstrating the potential for privacy

68 *Patel v. Facebook, Inc.*, 932 F.3d 1264, 1270 (9th Cir. 2019).
69 Id.
70 Id.
71 Id.
72 In re Facebook Biometric Info. Privacy Litig., 522 F. Supp. 3d 617, 624 (N.D. Cal. 2021).

litigation to drive meaningful corporate accountability and commercial surveillance business practice changes.

This Article III framework has proven particularly resilient in the face of subsequent developments in standing doctrine. While the Supreme Court's decision in *TransUnion LLC v. Ramirez* emphasized the need for concrete harm beyond bare statutory violations, *Patel*'s careful analysis of how privacy violations create concrete injury provided a roadmap for satisfying *TransUnion*'s requirements while maintaining robust privacy protections. This adaptability helps explain why courts across jurisdictions continue to adopt *Patel*'s reasoning in biometric privacy cases and other privacy contexts.

The Resilience of Privacy Litigation Post-*TransUnion*

Two pivotal Supreme Court decisions—*Spokeo Inc. v. Robins* and, more recently, *TransUnion LLC v. Ramirez*—were both initially predicted to create significant obstacles for plaintiffs bringing privacy-related claims in federal court, which many feared would effectively close the courthouse doors to privacy claims. Privacy scholars and advocates have roundly criticized these decisions, arguing that they unnecessarily restrict access to justice and undermine legislative efforts to empower individuals to enforce privacy laws.[73] Yet the actual impact of these decisions tells a more nuanced story. While *TransUnion* has guided Article III standing analysis, it has not created the insurmountable barrier that many initially feared. As discussed later, recent empirical studies of post-*TransUnion* cases reveal that privacy plaintiffs continue to successfully establish standing, with federal courts increasingly recognizing that intangible harms can satisfy the concrete injury requirement.[74]

TransUnion centered on TransUnion's practice of adding alerts to consumers' credit reports that inaccurately identified them as potential matches to names on a Treasury Department list of terrorists, drug traffickers, and other serious criminals.[75] While 8,185 class members had such alerts placed in their credit files, only 1,853 had their misleading credit reports actually disseminated to third parties, in violation of the provisions of the Fair Credit Reporting Act.[76] In a 5–4 decision, the Court held that only the class members whose misleading credit reports were actually disseminated to third-party businesses during the relevant period had demonstrated concrete harm sufficient for Article III standing. Writing for the majority,

73 Daniel J. Solove & Danielle Keats Citron, *Standing and Privacy Harms: A Critique of TransUnion v. Ramirez*, 37 Berkeley Tech. L.J. 1 (2022).

74 *See* Noelle Wilson & Amanda Reid, *Intangible Harms, Tangible Consequences: Analyzing the Impact of TransUnion on Standing to Sue for Data Breach, forthcoming* Missouri Law Rev. (2025). https://ssrn.com/abstract=5019503.

75 *TransUnion LLC v. Ramirez*, 141 S. Ct. 2190 (2021).

76 Id. at 2202.

Justice Kavanaugh emphasized that for the other 6,332 class members, "the mere presence of an inaccuracy in an internal credit file, if it is not disclosed to a third party, causes no concrete harm."[77] The Court also rejected the plaintiffs' argument based on the risk of future disclosure to third parties, explaining that in a suit for damages, plaintiffs must demonstrate that "the risk of future harm materialized."[78] The Court concluded that these class members did not demonstrate that the risk materialized—that is, "that their credit reports were ever provided to third parties or caused a denial of credit"—and thus they suffered no concrete harm and therefore lacked standing: "No concrete harm, no standing."[79] The Court's reiteration of *Spokeo*'s emphasis on concrete harm "traditionally recognized by American courts" reinforced a framework that appeared to some scholars to present a challenge for privacy claims involving intangible harms or risks of future injury.[80]

The (Un)Catastrophic Impact of TransUnion *on Privacy Litigation*

TransUnion has been described by legal scholars Danielle Citron and Daniel Solove as a significant impediment for privacy litigation in their articles "Standing and Privacy Harms: A Critique of *TransUnion v. Ramirez*" and the generative "Privacy Harms" discussed in the first chapter. In their comprehensive critique, they argue that the decision represents a substantial narrowing of standing doctrine, one that undermines the ability of individuals to seek redress for privacy harms and effectively enforces the legislative intent of privacy laws. They emphasize that the decision reflects a fundamental misunderstanding of privacy harms and jeopardizes the enforcement mechanisms necessary to protect privacy in the modern digital age.[81] A central concern raised by Citron and Solove is that *TransUnion* imposes an unnecessarily restrictive view of harm by requiring plaintiffs to demonstrate injuries that are closely related to harms traditionally recognized by common law: According to the authors, this framework is ill-suited for modern privacy harms, which often involve intangible injuries, such as the loss of control over personal information, reputational harm, or the risk of future misuse. They argue that the Court's insistence on tying privacy harms to historical common-law analogues problematically "ossifies" privacy law and fails to account for the distinctive and evolving nature of privacy violations.[82]

Citron and Solove argue that *TransUnion* also represents a significant judicial encroachment on legislative prerogatives. Privacy statutes such as the FCRA were

77 Id. at 2208–2209.

78 Id.

79 Id. at 2214.

80 Daniel J. Solove & Danielle Keats Citron, *Privacy Harms*, 102 B.U.L. Rev. 793, 815–816 (2022).

81 Id.

82 Id.

designed by Congress to empower individuals to enforce legal protections and hold entities accountable for privacy violations. These statutes often include private rights of action and statutory damages to address the difficulty of proving concrete harms. However, by requiring plaintiffs to demonstrate additional harm beyond statutory violations, *TransUnion*, Solove and Citron argue, effectively nullifies the enforcement mechanisms embedded in privacy laws.[83] By erecting additional hurdles to standing, the Court "significantly undermined the effectiveness of many privacy laws" and "enables courts to rewrite privacy laws to alter how they are enforced."[84]

Citron and Solove predicted that the *TransUnion* decision would have a chilling effect on privacy litigation, discouraging individuals from pursuing claims and emboldening corporations to engage in privacy-invasive conduct. They argue that *TransUnion* sends a clear message to companies: As long as privacy violations do not immediately result in tangible harm, they can operate with near impunity.[85] To mitigate the "malignant" effects of *TransUnion*, Citron and Solove called for a doctrinal shift that better aligns with the realities of modern privacy harms. They propose that courts embrace a broader understanding of harm, one that reflects the full scope of injuries caused by privacy violations, including risks, anxieties, and loss of control.[86]

Other legal scholars have extensively criticized *TransUnion* for its anticipated impact on privacy litigation. Many have argued, along with Solove and Citron, that the decision significantly limits the ability of plaintiffs to bring statutory privacy claims, thereby reinforcing corporate impunity. Bernard Chao contends that *TransUnion* represents a major setback for privacy enforcement by effectively dismantling private rights of action under privacy statutes.[87] He argues that the Supreme Court's insistence on plaintiffs demonstrating a concrete, historical common-law injury severely limits the ability of individuals to hold companies accountable for privacy violations. Paul Schwartz has criticized the ruling for narrowing the scope of standing in privacy cases, arguing that it favors corporate wrongdoers over consumers: "The Supreme Court's case law regarding privacy standing demonstrates how it manipulates doctrine to select the litigants that it wishes to favor."[88] This manipulation, he argues, risks undermining decades of legislative efforts to protect consumer data. Schwartz also highlights the broader risk posed by *TransUnion* to privacy law, noting that the ruling places undue emphasis on historical

83 Id.

84 Daniel J. Solove & Danielle Keats Citron, *Standing and Privacy Harms: A Critique of TransUnion v. Ramirez*, 101 B.U.L. Rev. Online 62 (2021).

85 Privacy Harms, at 796.

86 Id. at 829.

87 Bernard Chao, *Unjust Enrichment: Standing up for Privacy Rights*, 108 Iowa L. Rev. Online 49 (2023).

88 Paul M. Schwartz, *Privacy Standing*, 104 B.U.L. Rev. 1795 (2024).

common-law analogs while disregarding the realities of modern privacy harms.[89] Peter Ormerod argues that the *TransUnion* ruling creates an "enormous problem" and nearly insurmountable barrier for plaintiffs in privacy cases, and that "the Court's restrictive interpretation of Article III suggests that abusive informational practices are incapable of individual enforcement."[90] Neil Richards and Woodrow Hartzog also argue that *TransUnion* weakens the role of privacy law in protecting individuals from corporate exploitation.[91] They contend that "privacy law fails to stop companies from engaging in self-serving, opportunistic behavior at the expense of those who trust them with their data," and *TransUnion* exacerbates this problem by making legal recourse even more difficult.[92] Ignacio Cofone further explores how *TransUnion* has impacted class action certification, arguing that the Court's myopic view of concrete harm undermines the effectiveness of collective privacy litigation.[93] As one commentator, summarizing this view, put it, after *TransUnion*, "a huge number of Americans harmed by a flagrant violation of the law will be locked out of the federal judiciary altogether"[94]

*Evidence From Post-*TransUnion *Litigation*

These scholars paint a bleak picture of the future of privacy litigation brought by private litigants. However, empirical analysis of post-*TransUnion* developments in court reveal that dire predictions about *TransUnion*'s impact were overly pessimistic. A comprehensive study by Amanda Reid and Noelle Wilson examining post-*TransUnion* privacy cases found that 60% of plaintiffs in data breach cases successfully demonstrated injury in fact based on intangible harms.[95] These findings illustrate courts' growing sophistication in recognizing concrete privacy injuries, even when those injuries cannot be reduced to "easily measurable economic or reputational harms like identity theft and fraud."[96] The authors note that while some circuits have shown greater receptivity to claims involving intangible harms, others have adopted more restrictive approaches. Despite these regional differences, the overall success rate of plaintiffs in establishing standing suggests that federal courts have found ways to accommodate privacy claims within *TransUnion*'s

89 Id.

90 Peter Ormerod, *Making Privacy Injuries Concrete*, 79 Wash. & Lee L. Rev. 101, 107 (2022).

91 Neil M. Richards & Woodrow Hartzog, *A Duty of Loyalty for Privacy Law*, 99 Wash. Univ. Law Rev. 961 (2021).

92 Id.

93 Ignacio Cofone, *Certifying Privacy Class Actions*, 37 Harv. J.L. & Tech. 225 (2023).

94 Mark Joseph Stern, *The Supreme Court's Conservatives Issued a Decision Too Extreme for Clarence Thomas*, Slate (Jun. 25, 2021). https://slate.com/news-and-politics/2021/06/transunion-kavanaugh-thomas.html.

95 Reid & Wilson, supra note 74.

96 Id.

framework.[97] Reid and Wilson's study of 96 federal data breach cases decided post-*TransUnion* provides an empirical counterpoint to Solove and Citron's warnings of systemic collapse. As they note, despite fears that *TransUnion* would effectively "nullify the private right of action" for privacy violations, their results indicate that a significant number of plaintiffs successfully establish standing based on intangible harms.[98] If anything, further empirical data suggest the chance of privacy cases surviving standing challenges has gotten *better* post-*TransUnion*. While using different methods and criteria, another empirical study found that close to 60% of data privacy cases heard in federal courts from 2000 to 2020 (i.e., prior to *TransUnion*) were *dismissed* for a failure to Article III standing requirements.[99] This suggests that far from having an apocalyptic impact on privacy litigation, *TransUnion* has reinforced privacy standing in many contexts.

In addition to this data, much of the litigation discussed throughout this book—most of which takes place within the Ninth Circuit Court of Appeals—survived standing challenges post-*TransUnion*. The Ninth Circuit has emerged as a particularly important venue for testing *TransUnion*'s impact on privacy litigation, given the commercial surveillance ecosystem's central presence in Silicon Valley, with several landmark decisions demonstrating how courts can reconcile modern privacy harms with traditional legal frameworks. These cases reveal nuanced judicial approaches that recognize the concreteness of privacy injuries while staying within *TransUnion*'s doctrinal boundaries. This trend is evident in *Brown v. Google*,[100] *Rodriguez v. Google LLC*,[101] *In re Google RTB Consumer Privacy Litigation*,[102] and *Katz-Lacabe v. Oracle America Inc.*,[103] each of which survived standing challenges despite defendants' reliance on *TransUnion*. While these cases will be discussed in more detail in Chapters 6 and 7, they are illustrative of the way courts have ruled with respect to standing in particularly important recent privacy class actions. In these cases, the courts largely rejected arguments that privacy violations without additional consequences failed to establish concrete harm, affirming that violations of the privacy rights analogous to those at issue in modern corporate surveillance cases "have long been actionable at common law,"[104] and that an "invasion of privacy can be a harm in and of itself."[105] The courts found that the unauthorized collection of private browsing data (even if anonymized), continued tracking despite

97 Id.

98 Id.

99 Christopher Muhawe & Masooda Bashir, *Privacy as Pretense: Empirically Mapping the Gap Between Legislative & Judicial Protections of Privacy*, 2023 U. Ill. J.L. Tech. & Pol'y 257.

100 685 F. Supp. 3d 924 (N.D. Cal. 2023).

101 *Rodriguez v. Google LLC*, No. 20-cv-04688-RS, at 12 (N.D. Cal. Jan. 7, 2025).

102 *In re Google RTB Consumer Privacy Litigation*, 606 F. Supp. 3d 935, 945 (N.D. Cal. 2022).

103 *Katz-Lacabe v. Oracle America, Inc.*, 668 F. Supp. 3d 928, 939 (N.D. Cal. 2023).

104 Id. at 940.

105 *Rodriguez v. Google LLC* at 12 (quoting Facebook Tracking, 956 F.3d at 598, and Campbell v. Facebook, Inc., 951 F.3d 1106, 1117 (9th Cir. 2020)).

privacy-protective settings, auctioning of user data without consent, and creation of comprehensive user profiles for sale all constituted concrete privacy injuries sufficient for standing. These decisions consistently relied on the Ninth Circuit precedent in *Campbell v. Facebook* and *In re Facebook Internet Tracking Litigation* (both discussed in Chapter 6), reaffirming that the intrusion itself makes defendants subject to liability regardless of downstream consequences.

These successful adaptations echo the legal system's response to *Spokeo,* showing once again that predictions about privacy litigation's demise due to Article III standing issues were premature. For example, Peter Ormerod warned in 2020 that *Spokeo* would "gut putative privacy law reform" and "shut [privacy plaintiffs] out of federal courts."[106] Similarly, the *Harvard Law Review* cautioned in 2018 that *Spokeo* would "jeopardize[e] the breadth of many laws" by making it harder for plaintiffs to sue, even when statutory violations clearly injured a class of plaintiffs.[107] But as illustrated earlier, courts post-*Spokeo* demonstrated considerable flexibility in recognizing evolving forms of privacy harm as supporting Article III standing. This resilience strengthened the role of private enforcement in addressing emerging technological challenges, particularly in contexts like biometric surveillance, where the potential for harm is both significant and difficult to quantify. To be sure, numerous privacy cases across the country have been dismissed on standing grounds post-*TransUnion*; however, the weight of authority and prevailing trends demonstrate that *TransUnion* has not proven to be a significant impediment to meaningful privacy litigation. This resilience is particularly salient in the context of biometric privacy, where the permanent and uniquely personal nature of the data at issue makes effective enforcement mechanisms especially important.

Conclusion

Current legal frameworks provide powerful tools for addressing commercial surveillance practices. While challenges remain in ensuring equitable protection across communities, recent litigation successes—including surviving standing challenges under *Spokeo* and *TransUnion*—demonstrate the continued vitality of privacy litigation in confronting and remediating technological intrusions into historically bound privacy rights.

106 Peter C. Ormerod, *Privacy Injuries and Article III Concreteness*, 48 Fla. St. U.L. Rev. 133 (2020).
107 Recent Cases, *Standing—Class Actions—Ninth Circuit Allows Fair Credit Reporting Act Class Action to Proceed Past Standing Challenge.—Robins v. Spokeo, Inc., 867 F.3d 1109 (9th Cir. 2017)*, 131 Harv. L. Rev. 894 (2018).

6

INTERNET ACTIVITY TRACKING

Business as Usual or Egregious Violation of Social Norms?

The past two decades have witnessed a transformation in judicial approaches to privacy litigation challenging internet activity tracking and related profiling. What was once viewed as an acceptable or even necessary component of the economic engine that is the internet has increasingly come to be recognized as a potentially serious invasion of privacy that warrants legal intervention. This evolution in jurisprudence reflects both a growing awareness of the intimate nature of browsing data and mounting concerns about how such data can be weaponized to manipulate individual autonomy and the democratic process. This chapter traces the arc of this legal transformation through an analysis of key cases that have shaped the landscape of internet tracking litigation. This chapter examines the seminal 2001 decision in *In re DoubleClick*, which effectively blessed widespread commercial internet tracking practices.[1] This chapter then discusses how the 2020 *Facebook Internet Tracking* decision marked a decisive shift in judicial attitudes post–Cambridge Analytica.[2] Finally, the chapter explores recent cases involving Google's analytics technology that continue to push the boundaries of legal challenges to commercial surveillance practices.

The Application of Wiretapping Statutes to Commercial Internet Surveillance

Before examining the evolution of internet tracking jurisprudence, it is important to establish why modern corporate surveillance practices unquestionably fall within the intended scope of current wiretap statutes. A common argument by defendants in internet surveillance litigation is that the wiretapping statutes frequently at

1 *In re DoubleClick Inc. Privacy Litigation*, 154 F. Supp. 2d 497 (S.D.N.Y. 2001).
2 *In re Facebook, Inc. Internet Tracking Litigation*, 956 F.3d 589 (9th Cir. 2020).

DOI: 10.4324/9781003413349-9

issue in those cases simply were not intended by their framers to apply to modern internet technology.[3] This is incorrect; examination of the legislative histories of the Electronic Communications Privacy Act (ECPA) and the California Invasion of Privacy Act (CIPA) reveals that their framers were remarkably prescient in anticipating and intending to address the precise types of harms posed by comprehensive commercial surveillance and electronic dossier-building.[4]

The statutory histories of CIPA and the ECPA demonstrate that their framers were acutely aware of, and intended to protect against, the harms posed by computerized surveillance, including the creation of what Daniel Solove has termed "digital dossiers."[5] Despite being enacted before the full development of the modern internet and digital ecosystems, the legislative records and surrounding legal discourse show that policymakers understood the broader implications of emerging technologies for privacy. This historical intent underscores their relevance in addressing today's concerns about corporate surveillance and data aggregation. CIPA, enacted in 1967—the same year the US Supreme Court determined that individuals have a right to privacy in their telephone conversations in *Katz v. United States*—was passed during a period of significant societal concern about technological invasions of privacy. California lawmakers were responding to the rise of advanced surveillance tools, such as wiretaps and recording devices, that allowed for pervasive monitoring of private communications. However, the framers of CIPA went beyond physical or audio eavesdropping and explicitly designed the statute to anticipate future technological advancements that could facilitate broader invasions of privacy. Early legislative debates reveal an awareness of the growing role of electronic devices in creating permanent records of personal behavior.[6] The

3 See, for example, U.S. Chamber of Commerce & Retail Litigation Center, Inc., Amicus Brief in Support of Defendant-Appellee and Affirmance, *Gutierrez v. Converse, Inc.*, No. 24-4797 (9th Cir. Jan. 22, 2025) (CIPA "by its terms, is directed at the unauthorized and intentional tapping of 'any telegraph or telephone wire, line, cable, or instrument.' . . . The legislature could have used or later added text that is expansive enough to capture internet communications. But it did not—and courts may not adopt a broad reading of statutory text that conflicts with its plain language.").

4 *See* Alan Westin, *Privacy and Freedom* (1967); H.R. Rep. No. 99-647 (1986) (ECPA legislative history documenting intent to address computerized surveillance).

5 Daniel J. Solove, *The Digital Person: Technology and Privacy in the Information Age 8* (N.Y.U. Press, 2004).

6 *See* Assembly Speaker Jesse M. Unruh, *Statement for the Floor on Assembly Bill 860*, Relating to Invasions of Privacy (May 2, 1967) ("The bill is a result of my increasingly strong conviction that as our society develops more sophisticated technology, together with the ever-increasing stakes which successful industrial espionage and eavesdropping present to the unscrupulous operator, the right of the California citizen to be reasonably secure in his private communications and conversations is seriously threatened. The continual development and use of highly sophisticated devices for eavesdropping—and their ready availability on the market in my opinion creates a serious threat to our right of privacy and the free exercise of personal liberty."); *see also* CIPA Legislative History, Assembly Speaker Unruh Press Release (Mar. 1, 1967) ("Recent advances in technology and science . . . have made the description of the American society as 'the open society' much more than a cliché . . . As it becomes more and more apparent that we must live in 'glass houses', it becomes all the more urgent that government protect the right of the individual to reasonable privacy in his personal affairs.").

concern over the aggregation of personal information into centralized systems is apparent in the discussions leading to the law's passage.[7] Similarly, the legislative history of the 1968 Wiretap Act (the precursor to the ECPA) underscores deep concerns about the rise of computerized surveillance and mass data aggregation, warning that intelligence-gathering bureaus in nearly every major police department were compiling vast amounts of information on individuals without specific investigative purposes.[8] Lawmakers feared that advances in electronic eavesdropping and computerized intelligence systems would allow for the creation of computerized dossiers on nearly every American, with much of this data obtained through unconstitutional surveillance. The legislative record cautioned that the unchecked expansion of such technology could lead to a "Big Brother" state, where electronic surveillance is pervasive and beyond public oversight.[9]

By the time Congress enacted the ECPA in 1986, concerns about computerized surveillance and data aggregation had become even more pronounced. The ECPA was introduced in response to the widespread adoption of computers, early networking technologies, and database systems capable of aggregating personal information into detailed electronic profiles.[10] The legislative history of the ECPA highlights the framers' understanding of these dangers. Congress explicitly acknowledged the risks posed by both government and private entities using computers to capture, store, and analyze electronic communications.[11] While the ECPA was motivated in part by public outrage over government surveillance abuses revealed by the Church Committee in 1976, its framers were equally concerned about the potential for private sector misuse of digital surveillance technologies. The inclusion of private actors under the statute's purview demonstrates this intent to protect against a broader set of harms. Legal scholarship at that time further underscores the framers' awareness of the harms posed by computerized surveillance. Alan Westin's seminal book *Privacy and Freedom* (1967), which influenced privacy debates in the lead-up to both CIPA and the Wiretap Act, warned of a "surveillance society" enabled by emerging computer systems. Westin identified the danger of such systems collecting and compiling vast amounts of personal information.[12] Similarly, scholars such as Arthur R. Miller critiqued the rise of "data banks" that aggregated disparate pieces of information into comprehensive profiles.[13] These concerns informed legislative efforts to protect individual privacy, with legislators

7 Id.; *People v. Superior Court (Smith)* 70 Cal. 2d 123, 75 Cal. Rptr. 1, 449 P.2d 230 (1969)).

8 S. REP. 90-1097, S. Rep. No. 1097, 90TH Cong., 2ND Sess. 1968 (noting that "data transmission and computer systems have become a pervasive part of the business and home environments.").

9 Id.

10 Daniel J. Solove, *Reconstructing Electronic Surveillance Law*, 72 Geo. Wash. L. Rev. (2003); H.R. Rep. No. 99-541, at 2–3, 5 (1986); H.R. Rep. No. 99–647, at 16–19 (1986).

11 (House Report No. 99-647, 99th Cong., 2d Sess. 19 (1986)).

12 Alan Westin, *Privacy and Freedom* (1967) (directly informing CIPA debates); H.R. Rep. No. 99-647 (1986).

13 Arthur Miller, *The Assault on Privacy* (1971).

noting how the increasing encroachment of digital technology meant that a "computerized consolidation" of "information [that] has been obtained through illegal, unconstitutional, and unconscionable electronic eavesdropping" could "certainly make available some sort of information on almost 9 out of every 10 citizens in the country."[14] The ECPA's extension of privacy protections to stored communications was groundbreaking at that time, addressing concerns that emails, files, and other forms of digital communication could be intercepted, retained, and analyzed as part of larger data aggregation efforts. These statutory provisions show that both laws were designed to safeguard individuals against long-term retention and analysis of their communications, even as the underlying technology evolved.[15]

The legislative histories of these statutes also reveal an early understanding of the harms of commercial surveillance. Although government surveillance dominated much of the public discourse, lawmakers recognized the increasing role of private corporations in collecting and monetizing personal data. ECPA's applicability to private actors reflects an intent to prevent the commercial exploitation of intercepted communications.[16] Legislative records further indicate awareness of how electronic surveillance could serve as a tool for financial gain, a concern that has proven well-founded in the era of surveillance capitalism, where personal data is a primary commodity.[17] These concerns are particularly relevant to internet privacy challenges, such as electronic dossier-building by companies like Google and Facebook.[18] These practices, which involve real-time interception of communications and long-term data aggregation, parallel the harms the framers sought to address. The statutes' emphasis on consent and control over personal information remains critical in this context. Contemporary practices, such as hidden tracking scripts and opaque terms of service, discussed later, directly contravene these principles, highlighting the need to enforce the protections envisioned by these statutes. The evolution in judicial interpretation of these statutes—from *DoubleClick* to recent cases like *In re Facebook Internet Tracking Ligation* and *Brown v. Google*—thus reflects not just changing social norms but growing recognition of their framers' broader privacy-protective purposes. As subsequent sections demonstrate, courts have increasingly acknowledged that commercial surveillance practices, however widespread, can trigger precisely the statutory protections that legislators envisioned decades ago. Modern practices of real-time interception, coupled with long-term data retention and analysis to compile detailed profiles,

14 *See* S. Rep. 90-1097, S. Rep. No. 1097, 90TH Cong., 2ND Sess. 1968. (Individual Views of Mr. Long of Missouri and Mr. Hart in Opposition to Title Ill).

15 (See *S. Rep. No. 99-541, 99th Cong., 2d Sess.* (1986)).

16 See *House Judiciary Committee Report on ECPA*, H.R. Rep. No. 99-647 (1986) (noting the intent of the Act was to prevent unauthorized access to electronic data for the purposes of "financial advantage" or "private commercial gain").

17 Id.

18 Solove, Digital Person.

represent exactly the type of comprehensive surveillance that the framers sought to regulate through broad, adaptable statutory language emphasizing principles of consent and control.[19]

Statutory Frameworks for ECPA, SCA, and CIPA

The statutory frameworks governing electronic privacy in the United States have evolved to address the complex challenges posed by digital surveillance and data collection. The ECPA, the Stored Communications Act (SCA), and CIPA each plays a critical role in regulating various aspects of electronic surveillance, data interception, and consumer privacy.

The ECPA was enacted in 1986 as an extension of the 1968 Wiretap Act to regulate the interception of computerized communications. At its core, the ECPA prohibits the unauthorized interception, access, and disclosure of electronic communications, including emails and other forms of digital messaging. However, the statute includes exceptions, such as the consent of one party to the communication and service provider exemptions, which have been widely utilized by technology companies to justify data collection practices.[20] Courts have wrestled with the applicability of ECPA to modern internet tracking technologies, with some rulings narrowing its scope by construing consent broadly or interpreting some types of internet tracking as falling outside the definition of "interception" under the statute.[21]

The SCA, a subset of ECPA, was designed to protect the privacy of electronic communications that are stored by third-party service providers. The SCA limits government and private entity access to stored electronic communications without user consent or appropriate legal authorization, such as a warrant. However, the Act's distinction between "electronic storage" and "post-transmission storage" has resulted in interpretative challenges, particularly in the context of cloud computing and behavioral tracking.[22]

CIPA, passed in 1967, imposes strict requirements on the recording and interception of communications. Unlike the federal ECPA, which permits one-party consent, CIPA requires the consent of *all* parties to a communication before it can be recorded or intercepted. This broader protection has made CIPA a key legal tool in challenging online tracking technologies, particularly those that operate without direct user awareness. Courts have interpreted CIPA's applicability to include website tracking methods that capture user interactions with webpages, such as session

19 See H.R. Rep. No. 99-647, at 17–19 (1986) (emphasizing need for adaptable statutory framework to address evolving surveillance technologies).

20 See, for example, *In re DoubleClick Inc. Privacy Litigation*, 154 F. Supp. 2d 497 (S.D.N.Y. 2001).

21 18 U.S.C. §§ 2510–2523.

22 *Quon v. Arch Wireless Operating Co.*, Case No. 07-55282 (9th Cir. June 18, 2008); 18 U.S.C. §§ 2701–2712.

replay scripts and keystroke logging.[23] As discussed later, recent litigation under CIPA also has targeted the use of tracking pixels and analytics scripts that transmit user behavior to third parties without consent.

The California Computer Data Access and Fraud Act (CDAFA) and the federal Computer Fraud and Abuse Act (CFAA) also provide important legal frameworks for addressing unauthorized access to digital systems and user data. The CDAFA, enacted to combat computer-related crimes in California, prohibits unauthorized access, tampering, and misuse of computer networks and systems.[24] It has been increasingly applied in privacy litigation against companies engaging in surreptitious data collection and invasive tracking practices. The CFAA, a federal statute, was originally designed to criminalize hacking but has since been used in civil litigation against entities accused of unauthorized access to computer systems.[25] Recent Supreme Court interpretations, such as in *Van Buren v. United States*, have narrowed the scope of CFAA liability, emphasizing that mere violations of terms of service do not necessarily constitute unauthorized access.[26] Nonetheless, both statutes remain powerful tools in legal actions challenging invasive digital surveillance practices.

Internet Tracking Technologies

The cases discussed in this chapter involve an array of internet tracking technologies that facilitate the collection, retention, and monetization of user data. These technologies, ranging from cookies to JavaScript injections, form the backbone of digital advertising and analytics but have also become central to privacy litigation and regulatory scrutiny.

Cookies are small text files placed on a user's browser by websites to store information about user preferences, login credentials, and browsing activity. First-party cookies are set by the website a user visits directly, whereas third-party cookies originate from external domains, often serving advertising and tracking purposes. While cookies enable website functionality, they also allow advertisers to build extensive profiles on users by tracking them across multiple websites, leading to concerns about persistent online surveillance. Legislative efforts such as the GDPR mandated stricter consent requirements for cookie-based tracking, influencing global regulatory approaches to privacy.[27]

Tracking pixels, also known as web beacons or pixel tags, are small, invisible image files embedded in websites or emails that send information back to a server

23 Cal. Penal Code §§ 630–638; *see also Javier v. Assurance IQ*, LLC, No. 20-cv-02860 (N.D. Cal. 2023) (applying CIPA to session replay technologies).

24 Cal. Penal Code § 502.

25 18 U.S.C. § 1030; *Facebook, Inc. v. Power Ventures, Inc.*, 844 F.3d 1058 (9th Cir. 2016).

26 *Van Buren v. United States*, 593 US 374 (2021).

27 In re Meta Pixel Healthcare Data Litigation, No. 22-cv-03580 (N.D. Cal. 2022).

when loaded. These pixels allow advertisers and analytics firms to monitor user engagement, determine email open rates, and track conversions. Facebook's Pixel and Google's tracking scripts are among the most widely used, enabling companies to link browsing behavior with user profiles. The legal scrutiny of tracking pixels has intensified in recent years, particularly in cases where plaintiffs argue that pixels operate as unauthorized wiretaps by capturing user data without explicit consent.[28] The origins of tracking pixels can be traced to covert surveillance techniques developed in the late 1990s, when marketers began embedding 1 × 1 transparent GIF images in HTML emails. Initially described as "spy pixels," these tracking mechanisms allowed senders to surreptitiously monitor whether recipients opened messages, when they were viewed, and even the approximate location of the recipient.[29] Despite these nefarious origins, the technique was rapidly commercialized across digital marketing platforms. By 2021, spy pixels were described as "endemic," with a study estimating that approximately 70% of commercial emails included some form of pixel-based tracking technology, and they are now ubiquitous on commercial websites.[30]

JavaScript-based tracking scripts enable more sophisticated data collection by dynamically executing code on a webpage. These scripts can log keystrokes, track mouse movements, and capture form inputs, often relaying this data to third-party servers in real time. Session replay software, a subset of JavaScript-based tracking, records a user's interactions with a webpage, including scrolling behavior and text entry. Some courts have found that such scripts may violate wiretapping laws by intercepting communications between users and websites in real time.[31] These tracking technologies have faced increasing legal challenges, and the application of statutes such as ECPA, SCA, and CIPA to these technologies continues to evolve in the litigation discussed in the following pages, delimiting the legal boundaries of internet tracking in an era of endemic commercial surveillance.

In re DoubleClick: Early Internet Tracking Jurisprudence

The *In re DoubleClick* case of 2001 presented one of the first major judicial examinations of internet tracking technologies.[32] DoubleClick (later acquired by Google) operated an advertising network that collected user data through cookies placed on users' computers when they visited affiliated websites. This data was used to

28 Id.

29 See Leo Kelion, *Spy Pixels in Emails Have Become Endemic*, BBC News (Feb. 17, 2021). www.bbc.com/news/technology-56071437.

30 See Steven Englehardt, Jeffrey Han & Arvind Narayanan, *I Never Signed Up for This! Privacy Implications of Email Tracking*, Procs. on Privacy Enhancing Techs. (2018). https://petsymposium.org/2018/files/papers/issue1/paper42-2018-1-source.pdf.

31 Katz-Lacabe v. Oracle Am., 668 F. Supp. 3d 928, (N.D. Cal. 2023).

32 *In re DoubleClick Inc. Privacy Litigation*, 154 F. Supp. 2d 497, 503 (S.D.N.Y. 2001).

build detailed demographic profiles of users for targeted advertising purposes. The company maintained profiles on over 100 million users, tracking their movements across billions of web page visits.[33] The plaintiffs alleged violations of three federal statutes: the SCA, the Wiretap Act, and the CFAA.[34] The court's analysis of these claims proved influential in shaping the legal framework for internet tracking over the following decades.

The Southern District of New York's approach to DoubleClick's practices reflected the prevailing zeitgeist of the early commercial internet: The court emphasized the importance of allowing innovative business models to flourish and showed significant deference to industry practices. Addressing the Stored Communications Act claims first, the court focused on whether websites could authorize DoubleClick's access to user communications. The plaintiffs argued that DoubleClick's placement of cookies on users' hard drives constituted unauthorized access under the statute. However, the court found an exception applied; the SCA does not prohibit conduct authorized by a user of that service with respect to a communication intended for that user, and the court determined that affiliated websites qualified as "users" under the statute and could therefore authorize DoubleClick's access. The court found it "implausible to infer that the Web sites have not authorized DoubleClick's access" even while acknowledging that "officers of certain Web sites might not understand precisely how DoubleClick collects demographic information through cookies."[35]

The court's analysis of the Wiretap Act claim proved particularly influential in shaping subsequent internet privacy jurisprudence. The key issue was whether DoubleClick's conduct fell within the statute's exception to the consent to the interception exception, where the interception was conducted for "criminal or tortious" purposes (sometimes referred to as the "exception to the exception" for consent).[36] DoubleClick argued its activities fell within this exception because (1) it was a party to the communications through its relationships with affiliated websites, and (2) its commercial purposes precluded finding the requisite criminal or tortious intent. The court agreed on both counts in an analysis that effectively immunized most commercial tracking from Wiretap Act liability. The court's treatment of the crime-tort exception proved especially significant. It held that establishing a "tortious" purpose required showing that the defendant's "primary motivation" or a "determining factor" was to "injure plaintiffs tortiously"—a concept the court did not define.[37] The court further found the plaintiffs have failed to "articulate any facts that could support an inference that DoubleClick accessed plaintiffs' electronic

33 Id. at 505.
34 Id. at 500.
35 Id. at 510–511.
36 Id. at 514.
37 Id. at 515.

communications with the 'insidious' intent to harm plaintiffs or others."[38] This interpretation effectively created a commercial-purpose "safe harbor" from Wiretap Act liability.[39]

The *DoubleClick* court relied on this reasoning to reinforce the principle that commercial activity conducted for profit, even if later deemed invasive, does not inherently establish a tortious purpose under the Wiretap Act. This framework would prove highly influential in subsequent cases, with courts regularly—but illogically—finding that commercial motivations precluded finding the requisite tortious intent, *even where the commercial conduct was unquestionably tortious*. In an oft-cited passage, the court held: "DoubleClick's purpose has plainly not been to perpetuate torts on millions of Internet users, but to make money by providing a valued service to commercial Web sites."[40] Thus, the court—nonsensically—held that where a party commits a wiretap violation in furtherance of a tortious act but does so with the intent to "make money," it is immunized from liability under the Wiretap Act. This makes no sense—blackmailers and trade secret thieves have the goal of "making money" through wiretapping, yet those are paradigmatically "tortious" acts that would be excepted under the *DoubleClick* court's reasoning. However, as discussed later, several courts, including the court in *Brown v. Google*, have more recently rejected this judicially created "commercial intent exception" to the ECPA.

Finally, addressing CFAA claims, the court rejected arguments that users suffered legally cognizable harm from the collection and monetization of their data. The CFAA required showing "damage" of at least $5,000, which plaintiffs argued could be established because companies paid DoubleClick for users' attention and demographic information.[41] The court found this theory "dubious," holding that users had no economic interest in their own browsing histories. The court reasoned that "demographic information is constantly collected on all consumers by marketers, mail-order catalogues and retailers" without being considered damage to consumers.[42]

DoubleClick's permissive approach to commercial tracking shaped the legal landscape for nearly two decades. Its core holdings—that website operators could consent to tracking on users' behalf, that commercial purposes precluded Wiretap liability, and that users suffered no economic harm from tracking—became hooks that courts relied upon to dismiss privacy challenges to tracking technologies. While only a district court case, *DoubleClick*'s reasoning resounded throughout the intervening decades, shaping jurisprudential views on internet tracking across the county. This judicial framework thus facilitated (at least indirectly) the explosive

38 Id. at 518.
39 Id. at 512.
40 *In re DoubleClick Inc. Privacy Litigation*, 154 F. Supp. at 518.
41 Id. at 520.
42 Id. at 525.

growth of the behavioral advertising industry. Companies like Google (which ultimately acquired DoubleClick) and Facebook built massive advertising businesses premised on comprehensive tracking of user activity across the internet.

Campbell v. Facebook

While there was little meaningful litigation addressing corporate surveillance in the decade after *DoubleClick*, one early, pre–Cambridge Analytica legal challenge to Facebook's data collection practices was *Campbell v. Facebook*, a case that examined whether Facebook's scanning of private messages to extract URLs for various purposes violated federal and state wiretapping laws.[43] In 2013, the plaintiffs alleged that Facebook systematically intercepted private messages containing URLs and used that data to increase engagement metrics on its platform, share information with third parties, and refine targeted advertising, arguing that this practice constituted unauthorized wiretapping under the ECPA and CIPA. The case raised important early questions about the scope of privacy protections afforded to digital communications and whether Facebook's actions could be classified as unauthorized interception under existing legal frameworks.

The district court initially denied Facebook's motion to dismiss the ECPA and CIPA claims, in which Facebook contended that its scanning of messages fell within the "ordinary course of business"[44] exception under ECPA and that users had implicitly consented to the practice through its terms of service, allowing the case to proceed through extensive discovery.[45] Notably, the court "reject[ed] the suggestion that any activity that generates revenue for a company should be considered within the 'ordinary course of its business.'"[46]

After years of litigation, including an order in which the court granted class certification for injunctive relief but *not* for damages, the parties reached a settlement. Facebook agreed to discontinue certain data-sharing practices and provide disclosures in its Help Center regarding its message-scanning activities. The settlement did not include monetary compensation for class members but preserved their ability to seek damages in individual litigation.[47]

A key issue on appeal[48] was whether the plaintiffs had demonstrated Article III standing. The Ninth Circuit held that the plaintiffs had sufficiently alleged a concrete injury

43 *Campbell v. Facebook Inc.*, Case No. 13-cv-05996 (N.D. Cal).

44 The Wiretap Act creates an exception for interceptions conducted by an "electronic communications service provider" occurring in "the ordinary course of its business." *See* id.

45 Campbell v. Facebook Inc., 77 F. Supp. 3d 836, 838 (N.D. Cal. 2014).

46 Id.

47 *Campbell v. Facebook Inc.*, Case No. 13-cv-05996-PJH, 2 (N.D. Cal. Aug. 18, 2017).

48 Serial objector Ted Frank represented objectors who appealed the district court's approval of the settlement, arguing that the settlement was impermissible because it did not provide for payment to the class.

under *Spokeo Inc. v. Robins*, emphasizing that unauthorized interception of private messages implicates historically recognized privacy harms. The court held that plaintiffs identified a concrete injury by claiming that Facebook violated ECPA and CIPA when it "intercepted, catalogued, and used without consent URLs that users had shared in private messages."[49] The court noted "the harms protected by these statutes bear a 'close relationship' to ones that have 'traditionally been regarded as providing a basis for a lawsuit,'" and that one of the several privacy torts historically recognized was "unreasonable intrusion upon the seclusion of another," which traditionally extends to, among other things, "tapping . . . telephone wires" as well as "opening . . . private and personal mail."[50] The court observed that the plaintiffs' allegations that Facebook collected the contents of users' individual private messages without consent sufficiently stated a violation of the concrete privacy interests that ECPA and CIPA protect, regardless of how the collected data was later used; as the court emphasized, "[n]o more is needed to support standing under Spokeo."[51] This ruling—which has since been cited repeatedly for the proposition that violations of ECPA and CIPA alone give rise to Article III standing without further allegations of harm—reinforced judicial recognition of privacy harms in the emerging landscape of internet surveillance litigation.

In re Facebook Internet Tracking: A Sea Change

One month after the Ninth Circuit's ruling in *Campbell v. Facebook*, the court issued another significant decision in *In re Facebook Internet Tracking*, further clarifying the scope of privacy protections against commercial surveillance.[52] The years between the district court proceedings in *Campbell* and the appellate ruling saw a dramatic shift in public and legal perspectives on data privacy, largely influenced by the Cambridge Analytica scandal. That scandal revealed the extensive harm Facebook's data practices had inflicted, demonstrating how internet tracking and profiling could be weaponized for mass political manipulation. The decision must also be viewed in the broader context of heightened regulatory scrutiny of technology companies: In the years following *Cambridge Analytica*, Facebook and Google both faced numerous antitrust actions brought by government enforcers, alleging monopolistic practices that stifle competition and harm consumers.[53] At the same time, the COVID-19 pandemic underscored the extent to which modern life depends on digital platforms, further fueling public discourse on privacy rights and corporate responsibility. The convergence of these factors has led to a pro-privacy zeitgeist, with courts and regulators increasingly willing to challenge the

49 *Campbell v. Facebook, Inc.*, 951 F.3d 1106, 1117 (9th Cir. 2020).
50 Id.
51 Id. at 1119.
52 *In re Facebook Internet Tracking Litig.*, 956 F.3d 589, 603 (9th Cir. 2020).
53 See Chapter 11.

surveillance-based business models of major technology firms. Against this backdrop, the *In re Facebook Internet Tracking* decision reflected growing judicial and societal recognition of the dangers posed by widespread corporate surveillance.

Standing and Privacy Harms

The Ninth Circuit held that the plaintiffs had standing to bring their claims, applying the standard articulated in *Spokeo* that requires a plaintiff to demonstrate (1) an injury in fact (2) that is fairly traceable to the challenged conduct of the defendant and (3) that is likely to be redressed by a favorable judicial decision.[54] The court held that Facebook's unauthorized tracking of users after they logged out of the platform constituted an invasion of a legally protected privacy interest which was sufficient to confer standing.[55] The court's analysis focused on the significant privacy harms arising from Facebook's tracking practices. First, Facebook continued to collect users' browsing data even after they had logged out of the platform, contrary to its representations.[56] Second, the court emphasized the indiscriminate nature of Facebook's tracking, noting that it occurred "no matter how sensitive" or personal a user's browsing history was.[57] Third, Facebook continuously compiled and updated its database with users' browsing activities, amassing an extensive repository of personal information.[58] This tracking enabled Facebook to aggregate behavioral data far beyond the confines of its platform, creating a pervasive and intrusive digital profile of users' lives. Finally, by correlating users' browsing history with their personal Facebook profiles, which could include employment history, political affiliations, and religious beliefs, Facebook constructed what the court described as "cradle-to-grave" profiles without user consent—a phrase which echoed the language used by the framers of the California constitutional right to privacy, as explained further in Chapter 7.[59]

In determining that these harms were sufficient to confer standing, the court relied on *Spokeo*'s holding that intangible injuries can constitute concrete harms when they bear a "close relationship to a harm that has traditionally been regarded as providing a basis for a lawsuit in English or American courts."[60] Citing *Campbell v. Facebook,* the court held that statutory privacy protections, including those enshrined in ECPA and CIPA, "codify a substantive right to privacy, the violation of which gives rise to a concrete injury sufficient to confer standing."[61] The Ninth

54 Id. at 597.
55 Id.
56 Id. at 596.
57 Id. at 598.
58 Id. at 602.
59 Id. at 601.
60 Id. at 598, quoting Spokeo, 136 S. Ct. at 1549.
61 Id. at 599.

Circuit also rejected the notion that plaintiffs must demonstrate direct economic loss to establish standing. Facebook had argued that because the plaintiffs had not suffered out-of-pocket financial losses, they lacked standing. The court disagreed, noting that "California law recognizes a right to disgorgement of profits resulting from unjust enrichment, even where an individual has not suffered a corresponding loss."[62] Thus, "[b]ecause California law recognizes a legal interest in unjustly earned profits, Plaintiffs have adequately pleaded an entitlement to Facebook's profits from users' personal data sufficient to confer Article III standing."[63]

Recognizing the broader implications of digital surveillance, the court cited the Third Circuit's ruling in *In re Google Inc. Cookie Placement Consumer Privacy Litigation*,[64] which held that "the assertion that federal courts are powerless to provide a remedy when an internet company surreptitiously collects private data is untenable."[65] This alignment with other federal appellate courts underscored the increasing judicial recognition that unrestricted commercial surveillance poses concrete harms warranting legal redress. Thus, the court held that plaintiffs had adequately alleged an invasion of their privacy sufficient to confer standing under the Wiretap Act, CIPA, and the common-law claims for invasion of privacy and intrusion upon seclusion.

Reasonable Expectation of Privacy and Statutory Claims

The Ninth Circuit's recognition of plaintiffs' reasonable expectation of privacy in their internet activity was grounded in both the nature of the data collected and the manner in which Facebook acquired it. The court emphasized that Facebook's post-logout tracking was "surreptitious and unseen," which made it fundamentally different from tracking that users had knowingly consented to.[66] The court reasoned that "[t]echnological advances provide 'access to a category of information otherwise unknowable' and 'implicate privacy concerns' in a manner different from traditional intrusions as a 'ride on horseback' is different from 'a flight to the moon.'"[67] Facebook's tracking practices, by operating invisibly and without consent, allowed the company to collect an "enormous amount of individualized data" from users, creating a "vast repository of personal data."[68] The court found that this type of mass surveillance was not only invasive but also ran counter to established privacy norms.

62 Id.
63 Id.
64 934 F.3d 316, 325 (3d Cir. 2019).
65 Id.
66 Id. at 603.
67 Id. at 604, quoting *Patel v. Facebook, Inc.*, 932 F.3d 1264, 1273 (9th Cir. 2019).
68 Id.

Moreover, the court stressed that the sensitivity of the collected data further supported plaintiffs' privacy claims. Facebook's tracking extended across 7 million third-party websites incorporating Facebook plug-ins, enabling it to build a comprehensive record of users' online activities. The data collected, "no matter how sensitive the websites visited," could include financial, medical, religious, and political information, as well as details about a user's interests and habits.[69] The court rejected Facebook's argument that plaintiffs needed to identify specific pieces of sensitive information, stating that the legal inquiry should focus on "whether the manner [in which] it was collected—after users had logged out—violates social norms."[70] Ultimately, the Ninth Circuit concluded that Facebook's collection of post-logout browsing data, its misleading disclosures, and the breadth of its surveillance practices established a reasonable expectation of privacy.[71] The ruling underscored a growing recognition of the privacy risks associated with pervasive digital surveillance and willingness to scrutinize companies that mislead users about the extent of their data collection practices.

Finally, the court's treatment of specific statutory claims further demonstrated its willingness to adapt decades-old statutes to modern privacy threats. Unlike *DoubleClick*, the Ninth Circuit rejected arguments that Facebook's status as a "party" to communications through embedded "like" buttons exempted it from liability. The court adopted the First and Seventh Circuits' view that "simultaneous, unknown duplication and communication of GET requests do not exempt a defendant from liability under the party exception."[72] The court reasoned that accepting Facebook's interpretation "would render permissible the most common methods of intrusion, allowing the exception to swallow the rule."[73] This marked a significant departure from *DoubleClick*'s permissive approach to commercial internet tracking.

Settlement

In 2022, after the case had been remanded to the district court for further proceedings, Facebook agreed to pay $90 million to settle the litigation.[74] The settlement demonstrated the growing financial risk to companies engaged in aggressive tracking practices. The decision also reflected broader shifts in judicial thinking about internet privacy following the Cambridge Analytica scandal. Where *DoubleClick* had emphasized allowing innovative business models to develop unfettered, *In re Facebook Internet Tracking* demonstrated growing judicial recognition that

69 Id. at 603.
70 Id. at 604.
71 Id.
72 Id. at 608.
73 Id.
74 In re Facebook Internet Tracking Litig., 5:12-md-02314-EJD (N.D. Cal. Nov. 10, 2022).

unrestricted commercial surveillance posed genuine risks to individual privacy and autonomy. The ruling also reflects California's particularly strong privacy protections. Unlike many other states, California has enshrined privacy as an explicit constitutional right, declaring that all individuals have an inalienable right to "pursuing and obtaining safety, happiness, and privacy."[75]

The Google Analytics Cases: Challenging Business-as-Usual

In re Facebook Internet Tracking's recognition that purportedly "standard" commercial surveillance practices can constitute actionable violations of privacy rights has led to substantial litigation over the last half-decade. A series of recent cases challenging Google's analytics and tracking practices have built upon *Facebook Internet Tracking*'s foundation while pushing into new territory. These cases—*Brown*, *Calhoun*, and *Rodriguez*—reflect courts' increasing willingness to scrutinize even widely used tracking technologies.

Brown v. Google: *Private Browsing Expectations*

The *Brown v. Google* litigation represented a direct challenge to Google's core analytics practices by targeting its collection of browsing data while users were in "Incognito" private browsing mode. The case's progression through multiple procedural stages illustrated courts' increasing willingness to scrutinize even widespread tracking technologies, while also highlighting the ongoing challenges of obtaining monetary relief for privacy violations.

The court's March 2021 denial of Google's motion to dismiss marked an important victory for privacy advocates challenging corporate surveillance practices. Drawing heavily on the Ninth Circuit's analysis in *Facebook Internet Tracking*, the court rejected Google's argument that its privacy disclosures adequately warned users about tracking in private browsing mode. Judge Koh's analysis emphasized how Google's disclosures could mislead reasonable users about the scope of private browsing protections, noting that Google's splash screen for Incognito mode stated that users could "browse privately" and listed specific entities that might still see their activity—"websites you visit, your employer or school, your internet service provider"—conspicuously omitting Google itself from this list.[76]

A pivotal moment in the case came during a February 2021 hearing, when Google's attorney attempted to defend the company's tracking practices by pointing out that the Northern District of California's own court website used Google Analytics to track visitors. This argument appeared to spectacularly backfire: Judge Koh expressed deep concern over the allegation, halting oral arguments to investigate

75 Cal. Const. Art. I, § 1.
76 *Brown v. Google LLC*, 525 F. Supp. 3d 1049, 1065 (N.D. Cal. 2021).

the claim. Judge Koh was "deeply disturbed" by Google's suggestion that the court's website was complicit in the same tracking methods under scrutiny in the lawsuit.[77]

The motion to dismiss order not only reflected the court's legal reasoning but also exemplified Judge Koh's growing skepticism of—and at times outright pique at—Google's arguments. In her written order, Judge Koh repeatedly emphasized the misleading nature of Google's disclosures and the company's failure to adequately address the implications of its tracking practices. She criticized Google's assertion that its privacy policies sufficiently informed users of ongoing surveillance in Incognito mode, noting that such disclosures were ambiguous at best and actively deceptive at worst.[78] The order underscored the fundamental disconnect between what Google told users and what it actually did, finding that reasonable users could—and likely did—believe that Incognito mode provided greater privacy than it actually did. The court also found that Google's privacy disclosures were "misleading partial disclosure[s]," which further obscured the true extent of its data collection and justified the application of the fraudulent concealment doctrine.[79] The language of the order, combined with Koh's visible frustration in hearings, sent a clear message: The court would not permit Google to rely on vague, self-serving policies to justify extensive and undisclosed data collection.

The *Brown* court also diverged from *DoubleClick*'s narrow interpretation of the ECPA's crime-tort exception, rejecting Google's invocation of *DoubleClick*'s reasoning that a commercial motive necessarily negates tortious intent. Instead, the court held that plaintiffs had plausibly alleged that Google's interception of private browsing data was committed for the purpose of associating that data with existing user profiles—a form of electronic dossier-building that itself could constitute tortious conduct.[80] This alignment of the interception with tortious use, regardless of Google's profit-driven motives, was sufficient to preclude application of the consent defense under the Wiretap Act. In doing so, the court acknowledged that commercial surveillance practices can indeed be both profit-seeking and tortious. This marked a notable departure from *DoubleClick*'s implied "safe harbor" for commercial surveillance and underscored the court's recognition that data aggregation for profiling may itself be a legally cognizable harm.

Judge Koh's ruling also marked an important moment in the power dynamics of modern privacy law, serving as a direct rebuke to Google's implicit assertion that its surveillance practices were so ubiquitous and inevitable that even the court itself must ultimately submit to them. By pointing to the Northern District of California's

77 Koh 'Deeply Disturbed' By Google Tracking Court Site Users. law360.com.

78 Id. at 22 ("omitted Google from the entities that could see a user's private browsing activity and presented private browsing as a way that users could maintain their privacy and control what Google collects").

79 Id. at 30.

80 Id.

own use of Google Analytics as emblematic of the normalization of its surveillance, Google was presenting itself as an inescapable force in the digital ecosystem, one that even the judiciary must relent to. Judge Koh's sharp reaction to this argument, halting proceedings to investigate the court's own website and demanding a detailed declaration from Google on its data collection practices, was more than just a procedural response—it was a direct assertion that the courts remain a venue where even the most dominant tech firms can be brought to heel. In an era where digital surveillance is often framed as an unavoidable inevitability, the court's order served as a reminder that courts can act as levelers of power, pushing back against corporate attempts to unilaterally dictate the terms of online privacy.

The class certification proceedings in *Brown v. Google* revealed both the potential and the challenges of privacy class actions. After the case had been transferred to a new district court judge after Judge Koh was elevated to the Ninth Circuit, the court certified a Rule 23(b)(2) class for injunctive relief while denying certification of a damages class under Rule 23(b)(3). The newly assigned judge, Judge Yvonne Gonzalez Rogers, rejected Google's argument that its sheer size rendered class treatment impractical, emphasizing that "the notion that Google is too big to be held accountable does not persuade."[81] However, the court found that individual issues of implied consent would predominate in any damages claim, as class members had differing levels of awareness regarding private browsing limitations. Specifically, the court reasoned that some users may have been misled by Google's representations about Incognito mode, while others—particularly those with greater technical expertise or familiarity with past media coverage—may have understood that private browsing did not prevent all tracking.[82] This variation in user knowledge and expectations led the court to conclude that class-wide adjudication of monetary claims would be inappropriate.

Despite denying class certification for damages, the court certified a Rule 23(b)(2) injunctive relief class, allowing plaintiffs to seek structural reforms to Google's tracking practices.[83] The plaintiffs sought an injunction that would preclude Google from collecting further private browsing data, require the deletion of previously gathered information, and mandate the removal of any services developed using private browsing data. Additionally, they requested the appointment of an independent monitor to oversee compliance and ensure that Google adhered to any court-ordered restrictions. By certifying the class for injunctive relief, the court acknowledged that privacy harms extend beyond financial damages and that widespread digital tracking could warrant structural remedies, and that "[t]hese would be important changes to reflect transparency in the system."[84]

81 *Brown v. Google*, No. 20-CV-03664-YGR, Docket no. 803 at 2 (N.D. Cal. Dec. 12, 2022).
82 Id. at 30–31.
83 Id. at 33.
84 Id. at 34.

The court's summary judgment ruling in *Brown v. Google* proved the viability of such cases to make it to trial.[85] In rejecting Google's again-asserted argument that plaintiffs lacked standing, the court reaffirmed that privacy harms that result from common commercial surveillance practices can constitute concrete injuries. Citing *TransUnion* and *In re Facebook Internet Tracking*, the court held that Google's unauthorized collection and retention of private browsing data amounted to an invasion of a legally protected privacy interest. The court emphasized that the plaintiffs' claims arose under statutes codifying substantive privacy rights, making the injuries sufficiently concrete to confer standing, holding that the "intrusion into privacy itself is what makes a defendant liable" under both statutory and common-law theories.[86]

The court also rejected Google's reliance on the "ordinary course of business" exemption under the Wiretap Act. Google had argued that its data collection was necessary for improving its services, but the court held that there must be some nexus between the need to engage in the alleged interception and the provider's ultimate business, that is, the ability to provide the underlying service or good, and that Google's tracking of Incognito users failed this test.[87] Internal Google documents played a significant role in the court's analysis. The court highlighted emails in which Google employees warned that the company's disclosures regarding private browsing were misleading. Specifically, internal communications indicated that employees themselves recognized that "most users are not aware of session-based tracking" and that Google's explanations regarding private browsing protections were ambiguous.[88]

The *Brown v. Google* court's rejection of all of Google's pre-trial challenges to the plaintiffs' case demonstrated that meaningful privacy class actions can navigate all the supposed hurdles—standing, class certification, and challenges on the merits—that scholars have suggested make privacy class actions inherently ineffectual, as discussed more in Chapter 9. In mid-2024—shortly before the case was scheduled to go to trial—the parties reached a settlement providing injunctive relief for the certified (b)(2) class.[89] The parties had squared off and were days away from a trial that would have been a singular event in privacy law history, given the stakes at issue and the powerhouse law firms on both sides (the plaintiffs were represented by David Boies, of *United States of America v. Microsoft Corporation* fame, and one of the most well-known and feared trial attorneys in the United States). While the settlement required significant changes to Google's tracking practices, the inability to obtain certification of a damages class meant monetary compensation remained elusive in federal court. However, in a unique litigation strategy

85 *Brown v. Google LLC*, 685 F. Supp. 3d 909 (N.D. Cal. 2023).
86 Id.
87 Id. at 934.
88 Id. at 925.
89 Settlement Agreement, Case 4:20-cv-03664-YGR Document 1097–4. filed April 1, 2024.

innovation, tens of thousands of plaintiffs filed parallel state court actions in order to pursue the individual damages claims they were denied at class certification.[90] This bifurcation of injunctive and monetary relief between federal and state courts may provide a model for future privacy litigation seeking both systematic changes and individual compensation where courts deny certification of a damages class. The *Brown* litigation thus illustrates both the progress in judicial recognition of privacy rights and the continuing procedural challenges in obtaining monetary relief for privacy violations. While courts have grown increasingly willing to scrutinize surveillance practices, the path to a class-wide damages verdict at trial remains complex.

Rodriguez v. Google: *Challenging App Analytics Practices*

The *Rodriguez* litigation—brought by the same law firms representing the plaintiffs in *Brown*—mounted a similar challenge to Google's analytics practices by focusing on its web and app activity ("WAA") settings.[91] The plaintiffs alleged that Google misled users regarding the extent to which its WAA settings controlled data collection. Despite representations that turning WAA off would prevent Google from saving certain user activity, the plaintiffs claimed that Google continued to collect data from users' interactions with third-party apps, violating their privacy expectations. The case's progression through multiple procedural stages illustrates courts' increasing sophistication in analyzing complex privacy issues as they relate to online tracking technologies.

At the motion to dismiss stage, the court focused on whether Google's disclosures adequately explained the scope and limitations of its privacy controls. The plaintiffs advanced claims under the California Constitution's right to privacy, common-law intrusion upon seclusion, and the California Computer Data Access and Fraud Act (CDAFA).[92] The court found the plaintiffs had plausibly alleged that Google's WAA disclosures were misleading. While Google argued that the settings only controlled whether data was "saved in [the user's] Google account," the court found a reasonable user could interpret the controls as preventing any collection of their data.[93] The court also expressed skepticism toward Google's reliance on technical ephemera in its disclosures. The court noted that while Google's engineers may have understood the nuanced ways in which data collection continued despite WAA settings, the average user would not have the same level of technical expertise. As Judge Seeborg memorably remarked, "[t]he average internet user is not a

90 Kat Black, *Google at the Center of a 'Perfect Storm' of Privacy Litigation*, The Recorder (May 20, 2024). www.law.com/therecorder/2024/05/20/google-at-the-center-of-a-perfect-storm-of-privacy-litigation/.

91 *Rodriguez v. Google LLC*, Case No. 20-cv-04688-RS, (N.D. Cal.).

92 The plaintiffs originally brought a wiretap claim as well, but that claim was ultimately dismissed.

93 *Rodriguez v. Google LLC*, Case No. 20-cv-04688-RS, 3 (N.D. Cal. May. 21, 2021).

full-stack engineer; he or she should not be treated as one when Google explains which digital data goes into which digital buckets, and where the corresponding spigots might be found."[94]

The class certification proceedings in *Rodriguez* diverged from those in *Brown*, demonstrating the viability of financial remedies for privacy violations on a class-wide basis. The court's certification analysis focused on whether Google's uniform practice of collecting data despite WAA being turned off created common questions that predominated over individual inquiries. Unlike in *Brown*, where user knowledge about private browsing varied significantly and complicated certification of a damages class, the court in *Rodriguez* found that Google's standardized treatment of WAA settings across all users favored class treatment.[95] Google's data collection occurred regardless of individual users' understanding of the WAA controls, making the harm suffered by class members fundamentally similar. Significantly, the court rejected Google's argument that individual issues of consent would defeat certification. Google contended that users had different levels of awareness regarding WAA's functionality and thus may have implicitly consented to data collection. The court disagreed, finding that class members' uniform conduct—explicitly turning WAA off—constituted a consistent withdrawal of consent for Google to save app activity data.[96] The Court ultimately certified both an injunctive relief *and* damages classes, setting the stage for potentially billions of dollars in liability for Google.

The court's January 2025 summary judgment ruling established several key holdings that further clarified the legal frameworks governing privacy disclosures and user expectations. First, the court found Google's WAA disclosures to be ambiguous as a matter of law, concluding that they failed to clearly explain what data collection was actually prevented when users disabled the setting.[97] Second—as in the *Brown* case—internal Google communications played a pivotal role in the court's analysis. The court highlighted emails in which Google employees had warned that WAA disclosures needed modification, with some staff explicitly stating that WAA-off should prevent any data collection.[98] The court also pointed to internal discussions where Google employees acknowledged that the company was being "intentionally vague" about the technical distinctions involved in its privacy settings.[99] Finally, the court rejected Google's argument that its data retention practices were harmless, finding that there were genuine disputes about whether its conduct was "highly offensive" under the common-law claim for invasion of

94 Id.

95 *Rodriguez v. Google LLC*, No. 20-cv-04688-RS, Docket No 352 (N.D. Cal. Jan. 3, 2024).

96 Id. at 24.

97 *Rodriguez v. Google LLC*, 20-cv-04688-RS, 7 (N.D. Cal. Jan. 7, 2025).

98 Id. at 12.

99 Id.

privacy.[100] Employee concerns about misleading disclosures, coupled with Google's ambiguous representations, raised substantial questions about whether reasonable users would find such tracking unacceptable. The *Rodriguez* litigation thus illustrates how courts have moved beyond the early, superficial analyses seen in cases like *DoubleClick*, shifting toward an approach that accounts for both legal formalities and real-world user understanding. As of this writing, the case is continuing to move toward trial.

Calhoun v. Google: *Consent and Privacy Expectations*

The *Calhoun* litigation challenged Google's Chrome browser data collection practices when users chose not to sync their browsers with their Google accounts. The plaintiffs alleged that Google unlawfully collected and stored personal browsing data from users of its Chrome browser, even when those users had chosen not to sync their browsers with their Google accounts. Despite Chrome's privacy notices suggesting that data would not be sent to Google unless users enabled sync, plaintiffs claimed that Google nevertheless collected browsing history, unique identifiers, and other personal data, violating privacy expectations and privacy laws.

At the motion to dismiss stage, the court examined whether the plaintiffs had plausibly alleged that Google's privacy disclosures failed to adequately inform users about Chrome's data collection practices. The court selected ten claims to proceed, including allegations under the Wiretap Act, the Stored Communications Act, various California privacy statutes, common-law privacy torts, and contract-based theories.[101] The court's initial analysis centered on whether Google's various privacy policies and disclosures, when read together, could establish user consent. Google argued that its "general" privacy policy provided sufficient notice of its data collection practices. However, the court found that "Chrome-specific" privacy representations could reasonably be interpreted as limiting data collection in ways that conflicted with Google's broader privacy policy.[102]

The district court's summary judgment ruling—again, like *Brown*, transferred from Judge Koh to Judge Yvonne Gonzalez-Rogers after the motion to dismiss—marked a significant shift in the consent analysis. The court found that Google's general privacy policy and account creation agreements established user consent to data collection as a matter of law.[103] At the core of the court's reasoning was its determination that Google's data collection practices were "browser-agnostic" rather than Chrome-specific. The court reached this conclusion after examining expert testimony analyzing approximately 80 GB of server log files, which

100 Id.
101 *Calhoun v. Google LLC*, 526 F. Supp. 3d 605 (N.D. Cal. 2021).
102 Id.
103 *Calhoun v. Google, LLC*, 645 F. Supp. 3d 916(N.D. Cal. 2022).

demonstrated that Google collected the same categories of data regardless of whether users accessed websites through Chrome, Safari, Edge, or Firefox browsers. This technical finding was then relied upon by the court as grounds to look beyond Chrome-specific privacy representations to Google's broader privacy policies.[104]

Building on this "browser-agnostic" framework, the court held that Google's general privacy policies and terms of service governed the collection of user data. The court reasoned that because the same data collection occurred across all browsers, users' acceptance of Google's general privacy policy when creating accounts established consent for these universal practices.[105] Controversially, the court also determined that Chrome-specific privacy representations could not override or nullify this express consent framework. While acknowledging that the Chrome privacy notice contained certain privacy-protective language, the court held that these statements had to be read in conjunction with Google's broader privacy disclosures rather than in isolation.[106] This consent analysis represented a marked departure from the motion to dismiss stage's more nuanced treatment of potentially conflicting privacy representations. Where Judge Koh had initially found that the confusing interplay between Chrome-specific and general privacy policies created factual questions, the summary judgment ruling effectively established a hierarchy privileging general privacy policies over product-specific privacy promises. The district court concluded that based on the record, Google adequately disclosed, and plaintiffs consented to, the collection of the at-issue data.[107]

But in another doctrinal twist, the Ninth Circuit then reversed this summary judgment ruling in 2024. The appellate court emphasized that consent analysis must center on "whether a reasonable user reading them would think that he or she was consenting to the data collection," making clear that user understanding—not technical policy wording—must be the touchstone of privacy determinations.[108] Additionally, the Ninth Circuit held that Google's Chrome privacy policy could reasonably be read as a binding commitment regarding data collection. The court reasoned that, in the light most favorable to plaintiffs, "Google did make a promise in its Chrome Privacy Policy that it would not collect certain information absent a user's voluntary decision to sync, so Google may be 'bound by [those] promises.'"[109]

The Ninth Circuit also rejected the lower court's reliance on a "browser agnosticism" theory, which had suggested that Google's data collection practices were permissible because they were consistent across different browsers. The Ninth

104 Id. at 929.
105 Id. at 925.
106 Id. at 937.
107 Id.
108 *Calhoun v. Google, LLC*, 113 F.4th 1141, 1148 (9th Cir. 2024).
109 Id.

Circuit criticized this approach, stating that "by focusing on 'browser agnosticism' instead of conducting the reasonable person inquiry, the district court failed to apply the correct standard, despite its recitation of it."[110] The court emphasized that the proper analysis should assess how a reasonable user would interpret Google's disclosures, rather than whether Google's practices were uniform across different browsing environments. Memorably—and echoing the district court's sentiment in *Rodriguez*—the appellate court held:

> Whether a "reasonable" user of Google's computer software at issue in this case consented to a particular data collection practice is not to be determined by attributing to that user the skill of an experienced business lawyer or someone who is able to easily ferret through a labyrinth of legal jargon to understand what he or she is consenting to. Instead, a determination of what a "reasonable" user would have understood must take into account the level of sophistication attributable to the general public, which uses Google's services.[111]

The Ninth Circuit's approach in *Calhoun* thus reflected a growing judicial consensus that defendants cannot escape liability for privacy-invasive corporate surveillance practices by burying them in incomprehensible disclosures.

Conclusion

The evolution from *DoubleClick*, through *Campbell* and *In re Facebook Internet Tracking*, to the current Google Analytics cases illustrates a clear evolution in jurisprudential approaches to the legality of internet activity surveillance practices that had been openly adopted for years. First, courts increasingly recognize internet surveillance–related privacy harms as concrete injuries deserving legal protection. Second, judges now show greater willingness to question whether ubiquitous business practices can nonetheless violate established privacy norms; the mere fact that corporate internet surveillance is commonplace no longer immunizes it from judicial scrutiny. Third, courts place a growing emphasis on user expectations and understanding rather than technical compliance with jargon-filled disclosures.

The transformation in judicial approaches to internet tracking over the past two decades reflects broader societal recognition of privacy's importance in the digital age. Importantly, these cases have the potential to significantly reshape—and even eliminate—numerous pervasive corporate surveillance practices. If any of the Google Analytics cases discussed earlier were to go to trial, it could potentially result in a jury verdict of *tens of billions* of dollars in statutory damages and a court

110 Id.
111 Id. at 1151.

order requiring the cessation of core business practices—a potentially ruinous outcome even for a company as powerful as Google.

As the Cambridge Analytica scandal starkly illustrated, the comprehensive tracking of online activity and attendant manipulation poses severe, potentially world-historic risks beyond mere commercial exploitation. Courts' increasing willingness to scrutinize and restrict internet tracking practices suggests the era of unfettered internet-based commercial surveillance may be drawing to a close—or, at the very least, will no longer be immune from legal challenges in court.

7

BIG DATA, DATA BROKERS, AND THE CORPORATE SURVEILLANCE CARTEL

Data brokers surreptitiously collect, aggregate, and sell vast amounts of personal data, creating comprehensive digital "dossiers" that are sold to third parties, including individuals, advertisers, corporations, and governments. The chapter examines the development of data broker business practices, their role in normalizing surveillance, and their impact on societal power structures. It further explores how these technologies—originally developed for commercial purposes—have become instrumental in governmental surveillance initiatives. This chapter also argues that, despite widespread pronouncements to the contrary, the activities of data brokers are not only ethically questionable but also illegal under existing statutory, tort, and constitutional privacy laws. Drawing from key case studies, this chapter provides a systematic analysis of data broker liability and outlines a strategic roadmap for litigation against these entities.

The data broker conduct discussed in this chapter represents a synthesis of the invasive corporate surveillance practices detailed in Chapters 2, 3, 4, and 6. As Chapter 2 demonstrated, mass government surveillance has laid the groundwork for widespread digital tracking—normalizing the collection, storage, and exploitation of vast quantities of personal data—in symbiosis with the "surveillance–innovation complex." Chapter 3 expanded on this by detailing how corporate surveillance, epitomized by the Cambridge Analytica scandal, leveraged these same techniques for commercial and political manipulation. Chapter 4 highlighted the ways geolocation tracking has been seamlessly integrated into the data ecosystem, ensuring that individuals' physical movements are continuously mapped and monetized, further eroding privacy and autonomy. Chapter 6 explored how internet activity tracking has become pervasive and nearly inescapable, allowing companies to compile detailed behavioral profiles on billions of people. Data brokers represent the culmination of these surveillance practices, acting as the clearinghouses where

DOI: 10.4324/9781003413349-10

disparate streams of personal data—ranging from web browsing habits to geolocation data—are aggregated, repackaged, and sold. As discussed in what follows, this consolidation of surveillance power makes data brokers a particularly urgent target for remedial litigation.

Data Brokers: The Rise of Commercial Mass Surveillance

Data brokers are central nodes in the commercial surveillance ecosystem.[1] A *data broker*, as defined under California law, is a business that "knowingly collects and sells to third parties the personal information of a consumer with whom the business does not have a direct relationship."[2] Unlike companies that gather data from their own users—such as social media platforms or e-commerce sites—data brokers operate in the background, aggregating vast amounts of personal, behavioral, and demographic information from various sources, including public records, online tracking, third-party transactions, and commercial databases. These brokers analyze and categorize individuals based on factors such as browsing habits, purchasing behavior, financial status, and even inferred characteristics, like political affiliation or health interests.[3] The resulting consumer profiles are then sold to advertisers, financial institutions, insurers, and other entities seeking to target, predict, or influence consumer behavior.[4] The emergence of data brokers represents a fundamental transformation in how personal information is collected, analyzed, and monetized in modern society. While much attention has focused on the privacy implications of consumer-facing technology companies such as Meta and Google, data brokers have—up until recently—operated largely outside of public view, constructing vast surveillance networks that create detailed digital dossiers on hundreds of millions of individuals.[5] This surveillance infrastructure has profound implications for privacy, autonomy, and democratic integrity.

1 See Wolfie Christl, *Corporate Surveillance in Everyday Life: How Companies Collect, Combine, Analyze, Trade, and Use Personal Data on Billions* (Cracked Labs, 2017).
2 Cal. Civ. Code § 1798.99.80.
3 Christl, supra n. 1.
4 Id.
5 During the course of the writing of this book, regulators have begun to direct significantly more attention to data brokers than in the past two decades of internet surveillance. See, for example, Federal Trade Commission, *FTC Explores Rulemaking to Crack Down on Commercial Surveillance and Lax Data Security Practices*, FTC Press Release (Aug. 11, 2022). www.ftc.gov/news-events/news/press-releases/2022/08/ftc-explores-rulemaking-crack-down-commercial-surveillance-lax-data-security-practices; U.S. Senate Committee on Commerce, Science, and Transportation, *Protecting Americans' Privacy from Data Brokers*, Hearing (Sept. 21, 2023). www.commerce.senate.gov/hearings/protecting-americans-privacy-from-data-brokers; California Privacy Protection Agency, *Proposed Data Broker Regulations Under CPRA*. https://cppa.ca.gov (last visited Feb. 2025).

Data Broker Surveillance Techniques

The technological architecture that underpins mass commercial surveillance developed gradually over several decades through the convergence of multiple technological and business practices. In the 1970s, early data brokers such as Acxiom began compiling basic marketing lists using public records and survey data.[6] The introduction of credit cards and loyalty programs in the 1980s provided new streams of consumer transaction data, but a significant transformation came with the rise of the commercial internet in the 1990s.[7] This era ushered in unprecedented capabilities for tracking individual behavior, with the development of cookie technology by Netscape in 1994 serving as a pivotal moment. Initially designed to facilitate basic website functions like shopping carts, cookies quickly evolved into sophisticated tracking tools.[8] The emergence of third-party cookies enabled cross-site tracking and established the foundation for today's surveillance infrastructure. Companies such as DoubleClick, now part of Google (as discussed in the previous chapter), played a substantial role in pioneering behavioral advertising techniques, setting many of the technical standards that persist today.

The mobile revolution of the 2000s significantly expanded the scope of surveillance. Smartphones introduced new data streams, including location tracking, app usage patterns, and sensor data. The development of mobile advertising identifiers, such as Apple's IDFA and Google's AAID, allowed for persistent tracking beyond the limitations of traditional cookies.[9] Simultaneously, advances in computing power and storage capacity made it feasible to collect and analyze vast amounts of personal data at an unprecedented scale. More recently, the rise of machine learning and artificial intelligence has transformed how data brokers process and monetize personal information.[10] These advancements have led to increasingly sophisticated methods for identity linking, behavioral prediction, and psychological profiling.

Modern data brokers have developed advanced "identity resolution" technologies that enable them to track individuals across multiple devices, platforms, and contexts.[11] By leveraging probabilistic and deterministic matching techniques, companies like LiveRamp can connect various identifiers and establish a unified profile of an individual.[12] For instance, when a user logs into an email account on both a smartphone and a laptop, data brokers can link these devices to the same

6 Christl, supra n. 1.

7 Id.

8 John Schwartz, *Giving Web a Memory Cost Its Users Privacy*, N.Y. Times (Sept. 4, 2001). www.nytimes.com/2001/09/04/business/giving-web-a-memory-cost-its-users-privacy.html.

9 Jennifer Valentino-DeVries et al., *Your Apps Know Where You Were Last Night, and They're Not Keeping It Secret*, N.Y. Times (Dec. 10, 2018).

10 Shoshana Zuboff, *The Age of Surveillance Capitalism: The Fight for a Human Future at the New Frontier of Power* (New York: Public Affairs, 2019).

11 Christl, supra n. 1.

12 Id.

person; "probabilistic" matching can also be used to guess that the same user is using both devices, even if not logged in to the same account.[13] These connections are further reinforced by incorporating "offline" data, such as credit card transactions and loyalty card usage, allowing brokers to build comprehensive profiles that integrate both digital and physical activities.[14] Even attempts to obscure one's identity—such as clearing browsing data or using private browsing modes—can often be circumvented through techniques like cookie syncing and browser fingerprinting, ensuring that persistent identification remains intact.[15]

In addition to tracking identity, data brokers employ advanced machine learning algorithms to infer highly sensitive personal attributes from seemingly innocuous data points. By analyzing browsing history, app usage, and purchasing behavior, they can predict characteristics such as health conditions, sexual orientation, political beliefs, and financial status with remarkable accuracy.[16] The well-known *Target* case where changes in shopping habits allowed the retailer to infer a customer's pregnancy before she had disclosed it exemplifies the power of these inference engines.[17] As these systems continuously process larger datasets, their predictive capabilities become increasingly refined, allowing them to generate intimate insights without directly collecting sensitive information. Beyond identifying existing traits, data brokers use historical data and behavioral patterns to anticipate future actions. Their predictive models forecast likely purchases, major life events, and even shifts in political views or personal relationships.[18] These predictive capabilities extend beyond advertising, raising concerns about manipulative practices that exploit moments of vulnerability or heightened susceptibility. The development of psychological profiling techniques further enhances the ability of data brokers to analyze and influence individuals. By examining patterns in online activity, social media behavior, and consumer transactions, brokers construct detailed "psychographic" profiles that include personality traits, emotional states, cognitive styles, and decision-making tendencies.[19]

The rise of location data brokers like Kochava and Mobilewalla—discussed in Chapter 4—has expanded commercial surveillance beyond digital tracking to real-world movements. These companies collect and sell precise geolocation data from mobile devices, often sourced from everyday apps.[20] By analyzing GPS signals and Wi-Fi connections, they construct detailed movement patterns, revealing

13 Id.
14 Id.
15 Id.
16 Id.
17 K. Hill, *How Target Figured Out a Teen Girl Was Pregnant before Her Father Did*. Forbes (2012). www.forbes.com/sites/kashmirhill/2012/02/16/how-target-figured-out-a-teen-girl-was-pregnant-before-her-father-did/.
18 Christl, supra n. 1.
19 Id.
20 See Chapter 4.

where people live, work, shop, or seek medical care. Investigations into Kochava, for instance, found its datasets included visits to sensitive locations, like reproductive health clinics and places of worship.[21] Similarly, Mobilewalla tracks location alongside demographic data, enabling targeted profiling based on race, income, and age.[22]

Perhaps the most significant development in the commercialization of personal data is the establishment of the real-time bidding (RTB) infrastructure. Data brokers play a central role in the RTB ecosystem by aggregating, analyzing, and supplying user data to advertisers in real time.[23] When an individual visits a website or opens an app, their data—including browsing history, location, device type, and behavioral profiles—is instantly collected and transmitted to multiple ad exchanges, where advertisers bid on the opportunity to display targeted ads.[24] Data brokers increase the invasiveness of this surveillance process by "enriching" user profiles with external datasets, enabling advertisers to make more precise bidding decisions.[25] Through identity resolution techniques such as cross-device tracking, browser fingerprinting, and probabilistic matching, data brokers ensure that advertisers can reach the same user across different platforms and devices, even when traditional identifiers like cookies are absent.[26] This infrastructure has transformed digital advertising into a high-speed, data-driven auction system where personal information is continuously surveilled, collected, and monetized without individuals' knowledge or consent. The widespread deployment of RTB technology has sparked significant concerns among privacy advocates and regulators; the sheer volume and sensitivity of the data being traded have been described as the "the biggest data breach ever recorded."[27]

The litigation described in this chapter sought to innovatively challenge this conduct, using existing historically bound legal frameworks, to hold data brokers accountable for their role in enabling mass surveillance, privacy violations, and the commodification of personal information.

The Normalization of Surveillance

Data brokers flourish in an environment of increasing "digital resignation." The normalization of commercial surveillance has occurred through a series of interrelated processes that gradually obscure its pervasiveness. Digital tracking functions

21 Id.

22 Id.

23 B. Cyphers & G. Gebhart, *Behind the One-Way Mirror: A Deep Dive Into the Technology of Corporate Surveillance*. Tech. rep., Electronic Frontier Foundation (2019).

24 Id.

25 Id.

26 Id.

27 Irish Council for Civil Liberties, *Real-Time Bidding (RTB)*. www.iccl.ie/rtb/.

seamlessly and often without user awareness, making it difficult for individuals to grasp the extent of data collection or its implications. This technical opacity fosters a sense of complacency, as surveillance becomes an imperceptible but constant presence. At the same time, industry actors have played an active role in shaping public perceptions of surveillance through strategic rhetoric and framing. Data collection is frequently presented in terms of "personalization" and "relevance," masking the reality of comprehensive behavioral tracking.[28] Technical jargon and convoluted privacy policies further obscure the mechanisms of surveillance, making it challenging for consumers to fully understand how their personal information is gathered, stored, and monetized. Research demonstrates that majority of individuals lack the knowledge necessary to provide meaningful consent to commercial surveillance practices. A national survey conducted by the Annenberg School for Communication at the University of Pennsylvania found that Americans overwhelmingly do not understand basic corporate and governmental data collection practices, nor do they believe they have control over how their data is used.[29] The study revealed that 77% of respondents failed a test measuring their understanding of key data practices, with many incorrectly assuming that laws such as HIPAA protect them from data brokers selling their information.[30] Moreover, 91% of Americans express a desire to control how companies collect data about them, but 79% believe they have little or no control over these processes.[31] This lack of understanding and control fosters a state of in which individuals do not consent to the conduct but feel helpless to challenge the inevitability of data extraction.[32] The study's findings challenge the fundamental legitimacy of the notice-and-consent framework, suggesting that genuine informed consent at scale is not possible in the modern corporate surveillance environment.[33]

As a practical matter, integration of surveillance technologies that feed into the data broker ecosystem with essential services has left individuals with little choice but to participate.[34] As digital tracking systems become embedded in critical areas such as communication, finance, and online commerce, avoiding surveillance becomes increasingly impossible. The normalization of surveillance has been further reinforced by deliberate corporate strategies designed to entrench data

28 Joseph Turow et al., *Americans Reject Tailored Advertising and Three Activities That Enable It*, Annenberg Sch. for Commc'n, U. of Pa. 4–8 (2009). https://repository.upenn.edu/asc_papers/137/.

29 Joseph Turow, Yphtach Lelkes, Nora A. Draper & Ari Ezra Waldman, *Americans Can't Consent to Companies' Use of Their Data*, Univ. of Pa. Annenberg Sch. for Commc'n (2023), at 2.

30 Id. at 9–10.

31 Id. at 12.

32 Id. at 15.

33 Id. at 17 ("This study has found that overwhelmingly and to an extent not known before, Americans neither understand commercial surveillance practices and policies nor feel they are capable of doing anything about rampant data extraction.").

34 Julie E. Cohen, *Between Truth and Power: The Legal Constructions of Informational Capitalism* (2019).

collection as the de facto standard.[35] Many platforms default users into tracking by design, with opt-out options intentionally buried in complex settings.[36] Together, these factors contribute to a social and economic environment in which commercial surveillance is pervasive. Scholars have described this gradual expansion of monitoring as "surveillance creep", where surveillance measures that initially seem highly invasive or unacceptable gradually become normalized and permanent. Evan Selinger and Judy Rhee argue that as surveillance tools become more widespread, people grow habituated to their presence, making it increasingly difficult to resist their expansion or question their legitimacy.[37] Their work builds on moral psychology research showing that people tend to accept practices as socially and ethically acceptable simply because they are common—meaning that surveillance expansion can reshape attitudes over time without individuals consciously recognizing the shift.[38] This creeping normalization erodes individual privacy, further entrenching commercial surveillance as a "default" feature of modern digital life.

Data Broker Surveillance as Government Prototype

The data trafficking infrastructure developed by data brokers has increasingly been repurposed for government use, creating what privacy scholars have termed "surveillance intermediaries."[39] Rather than collecting personal data directly, law enforcement and intelligence agencies purchase vast amounts of commercially available information, circumventing constitutional protections against warrantless surveillance.[40] Data brokers regularly sell vast quantities of location data harvested from mobile apps, allowing agencies to track individuals' movements without a warrant. This data originates from apps that collect location information under the guise of services like weather forecasting, navigation, or fitness tracking.[41] Once aggregated and repackaged, the data is sold to government agencies, effectively bypassing Fourth Amendment protections by leveraging the private market.[42] Investigative work by privacy researchers, including Justin Sherman, Johnny Ryan, and Wolfie Christl, has documented how military personnel have

35 See Chapter 11, discussing Facebook's systematic process of pushing surveillance boundaries in order to normalize intrusive conduct.

36 Norwegian Consumer Council, Deceived by Design: How Tech Companies Use Dark Patterns to Discourage Us from Exercising Our Rights to Privacy 14–18 (2018). https://fil.forbrukerradet.no/wp-content/uploads/2018/06/2018-06-27-deceived-by-design-final.pdf.

37 See Evan Selinger & Judy Hyojoo Rhee, *Normalizing Surveillance*, 22 N. Eur. J. of Phil. 49, 56–61 (2021).

38 Id.

39 Alan Rozenshtein, *Surveillance Intermediaries*, 70 Stan. L. Rev. 99 (2018).

40 Byron Tau, Means of Control: How the Hidden Alliance of Tech and Government Is Creating a New American Surveillance State (Crown, 2024).

41 Id.

42 Matthew Tokson, *Government Purchases of Private Data*, 59 Wake Forest L. Rev. 269, 274 (2024).

been targeted through these same commercial channels, with data brokers selling location data linked to sensitive military sites.[43] This practice raises national security concerns, as adversaries or malicious actors could also exploit the same commercial datasets to track US troops.

Social media monitoring further illustrates how government agencies exploit commercial surveillance. Rather than conducting direct surveillance on individuals, agencies contract with third-party data brokers that aggregate, analyze, and cross-reference social media activity.[44] These services combine public posts, geolocation data, and behavioral patterns with other datasets purchased from data brokers, generating detailed profiles of individuals and communities. The result is a sophisticated monitoring system that enables government agencies to track online discourse, identify potential dissenters, and anticipate social unrest—practices that would raise significant constitutional concerns if executed directly by the state.[45] The expansion of predictive policing exemplifies how commercial surveillance feeds algorithmic control. Law enforcement agencies increasingly rely on data broker–driven systems that aggregate commercial datasets, including credit histories, social media activity, and purchasing behavior, to assess individuals' likelihood of engaging in criminal activity.[46] Predictive policing algorithms built on data broker services reinforce existing biases and disproportionately target marginalized communities.[47] Such practices demonstrate how commercial surveillance, originally developed for advertising and market analytics, now directly influences state policing strategies.

By exploiting the vast and unregulated data broker ecosystem, the state has effectively privatized key aspects of digital surveillance, expanding its reach while evading traditional legal constraints. This hidden alliance between corporate data brokers and government agencies is now woven into the very infrastructure of commercial digital services.[48]

43 Johnny Ryan & Wolfie Christl, *America's Hidden Security Crisis*. www.iccl.ie/wp-content/uploads/2023/11/Americas-hidden-security-crisis.pdf; Justin Sherman et al., *Data Brokers and the Sale of Data on U.S. Military Personnel: Risks to Privacy, Safety, and National Security* (Duke Univ. Sanford Sch. of Pub. Pol'y, Nov. 2023). https://techpolicy.sanford.duke.edu/data-brokers-and-the-sale-of-data-on-us-military-personnel/.

44 Id.

45 Id.

46 Sarah Brayne, *Predict and Surveil: Data, Discretion, and the Future of Policing* (Oxford University Press, 2020).

47 Id.

48 Id.

Data Broker Harms: The Erosion of Privacy, Autonomy, and Democracy

The data broker industry operates largely in the shadows, yet its conduct has far-reaching consequences for privacy, security, and societal power dynamics. By aggregating, analyzing, and selling vast amounts of personal information without consent, data brokers contribute to an ecosystem where individuals lose control over their own data. As Daniel Solove recognized over two decades ago in "Privacy and Power: Computer Databases and Metaphors for Information Privacy," databases of personal information do not simply collect neutral facts; they create asymmetrical power structures in which those controlling the data can exert influence over individuals without accountability.[49] Solove argued that the prevalent "Big Brother" metaphor inadequately captures the privacy issues associated with computerized dossiers. Instead, he suggests that Franz Kafka's *The Trial* offers a more fitting analogy. In *The Trial*, Josef K. finds himself ensnared in a faceless bureaucratic system where he is judged and controlled by forces he cannot see or challenge—much like individuals today, whose data is used to make consequential decisions about them without their knowledge, consent, or ability to correct inaccuracies. Solove writes: "Understood with the Kafka metaphor, the problem is the powerlessness, vulnerability, and dehumanization created by the assembly of dossiers of personal information where individuals lack any meaningful form of participation in the collection and use of their information."[50] The harms resulting from this dynamic extend beyond pure privacy invasions, permeating economic, social, and political domains.

The most immediate harm caused by this conduct is the erosion of personal autonomy. *Autonomy*, broadly defined in this context,[51] refers to an individual's ability to self-govern, make independent choices, and act in accordance with their own values and reasoning.[52] Legal and political philosopher Joseph Raz describes autonomy as requiring three fundamental conditions: (1) an adequate range of options, (2) independence from coercion and manipulation, and (3) mental capacities necessary for rational decision-making.[53] When individuals lack meaningful alternatives or are subjected to covert influence that distorts their decision-making process, their autonomy is fundamentally compromised. Raz argues that autonomy is not simply the ability to choose but the ability to choose in a way that reflects

49 Daniel J. Solove, *Privacy and Power: Computer Databases and Metaphors for Information Privacy*, 53. Stan. L. Rev. 1393 (2001).

50 Id.

51 "Autonomy" is itself—like "privacy"—a concept that has no canonical definition and subject to contentious debate. *See,* for example, Julie E. Cohen, *Configuring the Networked Self: Law, Code, and the Play of Everyday Practice* (Yale Univ. Press, 2012).

52 Joseph Raz, *The Morality of Freedom* 369 (1986).

53 Id.

one's authentic values and considered judgment.[54] As Raz puts it, "[t]he autonomous person is a (part) author of [their] own life."[55]

The unchecked expansion of the data broker industry constitutes a direct assault on such self-authorship, transforming individuals into commodified data points within a vast surveillance economy, ready for covert manipulation. Data brokers amass highly sensitive personal data—including health conditions, financial stability, and religious or political affiliations—without individuals' knowledge or consent, stripping them of the ability to control their own identity. Susser, Roessler, and Nissenbaum argue that online manipulation fundamentally threatens Razian autonomy by covertly shaping individuals' choices without their awareness. Unlike overt coercion, manipulation operates through hidden influence, subtly steering decisions in ways that individuals neither recognize nor actively endorse.[56] Data brokers, by aggregating and selling extensive behavioral profiles, enable precisely this kind of manipulation—exploiting decision-making vulnerabilities and reconfiguring digital environments to nudge individuals toward behaviors that benefit corporations at the expense of their autonomy.[57] Susser et al. emphasize that manipulation violates autonomy not simply by influencing behavior but by undermining individuals' ability to reflect on and endorse their own decisions.[58] In a democratic society, autonomy is foundational to both personal freedom and collective self-governance. Data brokers, through their role as central hubs in pervasive surveillance and predictive analytics systems, erode these fundamental rights, creating an environment in which individuals are steered by forces beyond their understanding or control.[59]

Beyond individual harms, data brokers harm our collective autonomy by fueling population-level manipulation and exploitation, leveraging behavioral profiling to allow advertisers, political campaigns, and advocacy groups to tailor messages based on individuals' emotional states, beliefs, and vulnerabilities to effectuate mass behavioral outcomes and impinge on the democratic process itself. The Cambridge Analytica scandal epitomized this risk, revealing how vast troves of consumer data could be used to exploit personal vulnerabilities and manipulate political engagement as scale.[60] Julie Cohen has cautioned that such techniques are not merely about commercial advantage but about the manipulation of thought itself, posing risks to informed decision-making and democratic integrity.[61] Susser

54 Id. at 372.
55 Id. at 369.
56 Daniel Susser, Beate Roessler & Helen Nissenbaum, *Technology, Autonomy, and Manipulation*, 8 Internet Pol'y Rev. (2019).
57 Id.
58 Id.
59 Id.
60 See Chapter 3.
61 Julie E. Cohen, *Configuring the Networked Self: Law, Code, and the Play of Everyday Practice* (Yale Univ. Press, 2012).

et al. reinforce this concern, demonstrating how algorithmic targeting distorts personal autonomy by creating hidden "choice architectures" that steer individuals toward decisions they might not otherwise make.[62] Ultimately, the data broker conduct at issue in this chapter fundamentally shifts power away from individuals and into the hands of corporate entities. As Solove has observed, in a world where knowledge is power, unchecked data compilation creates an ecosystem where personal information becomes a tool for economic and political control, reinforcing structural inequalities and eroding personal agency.[63]

Another critical harm is discriminatory decision-making, enabled by algorithmic profiling. Data brokers compile dossiers on consumers that businesses, insurers, landlords, and even law enforcement agencies use to make decisions.[64] The lack of transparency in these processes means individuals often have no way to challenge incorrect or biased data about them. Reports by Justin Sherman highlight how predatory targeting in financial services disproportionately affects vulnerable populations, as data brokers sell information about low-income individuals to payday lenders and debt collectors.[65] Similarly, insurers and employers use commercial data to assess "risk," leading to discriminatory outcomes in hiring, loan approvals, and insurance pricing.[66] Recent investigations have revealed that data brokers are also collecting and selling data from vehicles—including GPS history, driving behavior, and telematic information—to insurance companies, allowing insurers to adjust premiums based on opaque and potentially biased risk assessments.[67]

The risks associated with security and identity fraud also increase as a result of data broker activity. Because these companies store and sell sensitive information—including Social Security numbers, financial histories, and home addresses—data breaches pose serious threats. Unlike credit bureaus, which at least offer some consumer protections, data brokers operate with little oversight, making them prime targets for cybercriminals.[68] Schneier warns that the mass aggregation of personal

62 Susser et al., *supra*, at 8.

63 Daniel J. Solove, *Privacy and Power: Computer Databases and Metaphors for Information Privacy*, 53 Stan. L. Rev. 1393, 1422 (2001).

64 Fed. Trade Comm'n, Data Brokers: A Call for Transparency and Accountability 39–40 (2014).

65 Justin Sherman, *Data Brokers and Sensitive Data on U.S. Individuals: Threats to American Civil Rights, National Security, and Democracy, Duke Univ. Sanford Cyber Pol'y Program 17–21* (2021). https://sites.sanford.duke.edu/techpolicy/report-data-brokers-and-sensitive-data-on-u-s-individuals/.

66 Pam Dixon & Robert Gellman, *The Scoring of America: How Secret Consumer Scores Threaten Your Privacy and Your Future*, World Priv. F. 42–48 (2014). www.worldprivacyforum.org/wp-content/uploads/2014/04/WPF_Scoring_of_America_April2014_fs.pdf.

67 Electronic Frontier Foundation, *Car Makers Shouldn't Be Selling Our Driving History to Data Brokers and Insurance Companies* (Jun. 2024). www.eff.org/deeplinks/2024/06/car-makers-shouldnt-be-selling-our-driving-history-data-brokers-and-insurance.

68 See, for example, Jesse Damiani, *Oracle's BlueKai Spilled 'Billions of Records' of Web-Tracking Data*, Forbes.com (Jun. 19, 2020). www.forbes.com/sites/jessedamiani/2020/06/19/oracles-bluekai-spilled-billions-of-records-of-web-tracking-data/.

data makes it more difficult to protect against fraud, as leaked datasets can be combined to create highly accurate profiles for identity theft.[69]

Dispelling the Myth of Legality: How Data Brokers Violate Existing Laws

Despite widespread pronouncements that data broker practices occupy a legal "gray area" even in the face of this panoply of serious privacy harms, their core business models, in fact, violate numerous existing rights and laws. The press, legislators, and even legal scholars have historically perpetuated the view that data brokers generally operate with legal impunity, and that new legislation is needed to regulate data brokers in the absence of any existing, enforceable rights. The Electronic Privacy Information Center (EPIC) has emphasized that no federal law directly regulates the data broker industry, allowing them to engage in unfettered mass surveillance.[70] Reports from Kaspersky and other cybersecurity experts opine that as long as data brokers source their information from public records or legally obtained datasets, their activities fall within legal boundaries, even though they exploit significant gaps in privacy protections: "Generally speaking, if data brokers use public records to obtain information, then their activities are legal, though there are gray areas."[71] Government agencies, such as the Consumer Financial Protection Bureau (CFPB), have also suggested that data brokers operate in a largely unregulated space, which then necessitates new proposals to limit the sale of the most sensitive personal data.[72] This legal landscape has led critics to argue that data broker conduct represents a systematic failure of privacy law, as a result of which companies can lawfully aggregate, analyze, and sell personal information without meaningful restrictions, oversight, or consumer control. Professors Meg Leta Jones and Margot Kaminski have argued:

> [D]ata privacy protections in the United States largely extend only so far as direct consumer relationships and not to the growing variety of both surveillance systems and data processing conducted by third-parties that have no direct relationships to consumers. . . . This leaves an increasingly vast ecosystem of third-party data brokers largely unregulated.[73]

69 Bruce Schneier, *Click Here to Kill Everybody: Security and Survival in a Hyper-Connected World* (2018).

70 Electronic Privacy Information Center (EPIC), *Data Brokers*. https://epic.org/issues/consumer-privacy/data-brokers/.

71 Kaspersky Security Report, *How to Stop Data Brokers from Selling Your Personal Information*. https://usa.kaspersky.com/resource-center/preemptive-safety/how-to-stop-data-brokers-from-selling-your-personal-information.

72 Consumer Financial Protection Bureau (CFPB), *CFPB Proposes Rule to Stop Data Brokers from Selling Sensitive Personal Data to Scammers, Stalkers, and Spies*. www.consumerfinance.gov/about-us/newsroom/cfpb-proposes-rule-to-stop-data-brokers-from-selling-sensitive-personal-data-to-scammers-stalkers-and-spies/.

73 M.L. Jones & M.E. Kaminski, *An American's Guide to the GDPR*. 98(1) Denver Law Review (2020).

However, contrary to this view, *current* privacy laws already provide viable mechanisms for challenging mass commercial surveillance. This section examines the multiple layers of existing laws that render data broker practices illegal, outlining how data brokers violate wiretap statutes, state consumer protection laws, constitutional privacy guarantees, and traditional privacy torts.

Statutory Violations

Data broker practices violate numerous federal and state statutes, beginning with the Federal Wiretap Act and its state analogs. As described in the previous chapter, these laws prohibit the interception of electronic communications without consent. Data brokers' systematic collection of real-time browsing data and communications through tracking pixels, cookies, and similar technologies constitutes precisely the type of interception these statutes prohibit. Data brokers—like the blackmailers that pre-digital wiretap laws sought to protect from—use surreptitious tracking "bugs" like pixels or JavaScript code to "listen" to our electronic communications and compile massive dossiers of *kompromat* on us based on that intercepted content.[74] That the ultimate use of this data is for *covert* manipulation rather than *overt* coercion (though still for profit, as with blackmail) makes the activity no less insidious. While modern digital wiretappers often claim consent through obscure privacy policies, courts have increasingly rejected such arguments when placed in context of the reality of modern surveillance infrastructures.[75]

State consumer protection and unfair competition laws provide additional grounds for liability. California's Unfair Competition Law, for example, prohibits unfair and deceptive business practices. Data brokers' systematic collection and monetization of personal information, often through obscured technical means and without meaningful notice, are arguably the type of unfair practices these laws target.[76] The lack of transparency regarding the scope of data collection and the impossibility of meaningful opt-out further support liability under these statutes. While some states have implemented statutory data broker registration requirements, such registration does not immunize companies from liability for underlying privacy violations.[77]

74 See Complaint, *Katz-Lacabe et al v. Oracle America, Inc.*, Case No. 3:22-cv-04792-RS (Aug. 19, 2022).

75 See Chapter 6.

76 *Brooks v. Thomson Reuters Corp.*, 21-cv-01418-EMC (N.D. Cal. Aug. 16, 2021).

77 *Cf.* Id. at 9 (rejected as "meritless" data broker's argument that "its conduct cannot be unfair because the CCPA expressly allows it to sell Plaintiffs' personal information if it provides Plaintiffs a mechanism to opt out of such sale").

Constitutional Privacy Rights

State constitutional privacy provisions provide strong grounds for challenging data broker practices, particularly in California, where the state constitution explicitly enshrines a right to privacy. Article I, Section 1 of the California Constitution states that "all people are by nature free and independent and have inalienable rights," including the right to privacy, which was added through the 1972 Privacy Initiative. This amendment was a direct response to growing concerns over the unchecked accumulation of personal data by both government and corporate actors. Its drafters recognized that technological advancements in data collection and surveillance posed an unprecedented threat to personal autonomy and civil liberties. The legislative history of the 1972 amendment underscores its intent to curb businesses' control over the unauthorized collection and use of personal data. The ballot argument in favor of Proposition 11 stated:

> The right of privacy is the right to be left alone. . . . It prevents government and business interests from collecting and stockpiling unnecessary information about us and from misusing information gathered for one purpose in order to serve other purposes or to embarrass us. Fundamental to our privacy is the ability to control circulation of personal information. This is essential to social relationships and personal freedom.[78]

The initiative's proponents warned against the creation of "cradle-to-grave" digital dossiers, in which corporations and government entities could compile comprehensive profiles tracking every aspect of an individual's life:

> Computerization of records makes it possible to create "cradle-to-grave" profiles of every American. At present there are no effective restraints on the information activities of government and business. *This amendment creates a legal and enforceable right of privacy for every Californian.*[79]

Data brokers systematically amass, aggregate, and monetize vast quantities of personal information, embodying the very dangers the California privacy amendment sought to prevent.

Nicole A. Ozer, in *Golden State Sword: The History and Future of California's Constitutional Right to Privacy*, provides further insight into the historical backdrop of the amendment and its implications for corporate surveillance.[80] Ozer explains that the privacy amendment was designed not only to restrict government

78 Ballot Pamp, Proposed Stats. & Amends. To Cal. Const. With Arguments to Voters. Gen. Election *26 (Nov. 7, 1972).

79 Id. (emphasis added).

80 Nicole A. Ozer, *Golden State Sword: The History and Future of California's Constitutional Right to Privacy to Defend and Promote Rights, Justice, and Democracy in the Modern Digital Age*, 39 Berkeley Tech. L.J. 961 (2024).

overreach but also to impose constitutional limits on corporate data practices. As assembly member Kenneth Cory, a key legislative advocate, made clear, the amendment was meant to put "private firms on notice that the people have this fundamental right [to privacy] and it can only be abridged when the public concern is an overriding concern."[81] This principle remains critical in modern legal challenges to data brokers; the creation of mass consumer profiles, data marketplaces, and behavioral tracking systems—as alleged in *Katz-Lacabe v. Oracle America Inc.*—demonstrates that data brokers operate in direct contravention of the California Constitution's privacy protections that have been in place for over half a century.

Common-Law Privacy Torts

Traditional privacy torts provide substantial grounds for liability that directly address data broker practices. The tort of intrusion upon seclusion protects against intrusion into private affairs in a manner highly offensive to a reasonable person.[82] Data brokers' systematic monitoring of online activities, collection of sensitive personal information, and creation of detailed dossiers readily satisfy both elements of this tort.[83] While data brokers often claim their practices are too commonplace to be considered highly offensive, this argument fundamentally misunderstands the tort's normative nature; murder is wrong, even if it is commonplace, and even if (or *especially* if) a culture is immersed in it.[84] The fact that privacy invasions have become widespread does not render them inoffensive—it heightens the need for immediate legal intervention. While data brokers typically argue that individual pieces of information come from public sources and thus do not warrant privacy protections, courts have recognized that the compilation and disclosure of comprehensive personal profiles can violate privacy rights even when built from public data points.[85]

The Inconsentability of Data Broker Conduct

Data brokers frequently defend their conduct by contending their data is "consented," that is, collected from sources that obtained consent for use of the data by data brokers.[86] However, the idea that individuals can ever, *in principle*, consent to data broker conduct is a fundamentally flawed premise resting on a misleading framework of choice that does not reflect the realities of data collection,

81 Id. at 982.
82 *Hill v. Nat'l Collegiate Athletic Assn.*, 865 P.2d 633 (Cal. 1994).
83 See Complaint, *Katz-Lacabe et al v. Oracle America, Inc.*, Case No. 3:22-cv-04792-RS (Aug. 19, 2022).
84 See Daniel J. Solove & Neil M. Richards, *Prosser's Privacy Law: A Mixed Legacy*, 98 Cal. L. Rev. 1887 (2010).
85 See, for example, *Katz-Lacabe et al v. Oracle America, Inc.*, Case No. 3:22-cv-04792-RS.
86 Id.

aggregation, and sale. The same concerns that animate Selinger and Hartzog's argument that facial recognition is "inconsentable,"[87] discussed in Chapter 5, apply to the conduct described in this chapter.

The first major obstacle to legal consent is the lack of transparency. By definition, individuals do not interact directly with data brokers;[88] rather, their information is collected indirectly from mobile apps, websites, retailers, social media, financial transactions, and even public records. Many companies that gather data do not disclose that they are selling or sharing it with third-party data brokers. A person using a weather app might assume their location data is necessary to provide accurate forecasts, but they would have no reason to expect that this information is also being sold to data brokers, which, in turn, package it and resell it to advertisers, insurers, financial institutions, and even government agencies. Similarly, a person signing up for a loyalty program at a grocery store may believe they are merely receiving discounts, without realizing that their shopping habits are being tracked, analyzed, and sold by third parties. As Helen Nissenbaum articulates in the theory of *contextual integrity*, privacy violations occur when information flows in ways that violate the norms and expectations governing a particular context. Data brokers fundamentally undermine contextual integrity by repurposing personal data collected in one setting for entirely different and often undisclosed uses, creating a pervasive and unpredictable loss of control over personal information.[89]

Even when companies do provide some form of disclosure, it is buried in legalistic privacy policies that are intentionally designed to be difficult to read. Studies have consistently found that the average consumer does not read privacy policies, and even when they do, they do not understand them. A 2019 Pew Research Center survey found that only 9% of Americans say they always read privacy policies, while another study estimated that it would take the average person 244 hours per year to read all the privacy policies they encounter.[90] As the prior chapter has shown, even experts in digital privacy and law struggle to parse the vague and ambiguous language used in these documents, making it unrealistic to expect everyday users to make informed decisions about their data.

Furthermore, many privacy policies claim that users "consent" to data collection simply by using a website, app, or service. This practice, described as "implied" consent, is an abuse of legal norms. True consent requires clear, affirmative, and

87 See Evan Selinger & Woodrow Hartzog, *The Inconsentability of Facial Surveillance*, 66 Loyola Law Rev. 101 (2019); see also Chapter 5.

88 See Cal. Civ. Code § 1798.99.80.

89 Helen Nissenbaum, *Privacy in Context: Technology, Policy, and the Integrity of Social Life* 3–7 (2010).

90 Brooke Auxier et al., *Americans and Privacy: Concerned, Confused and Feeling Lack of Control Over Their Personal Information*, Pew Rsch. Ctr. 3–5 (Nov. 15, 2019). www.pewresearch.org/internet/2019/11/15/americans-and-privacy-concerned-confused-and-feeling-lack-of-control-over-their-personal-information/.

voluntary agreement—not merely the act of opening an app or signing up for an account.[91] The notion that someone "agrees" to have their data sold to third parties simply by downloading a free flashlight app or by browsing an online store is a legal fiction that erodes the very concept of consent.[92] Beyond deception and opacity, there is also coercion. Many companies design their platforms in ways that make opting out excessively difficult or appear undesirable, a practice known as "dark patterns"—deliberate user interface tricks that nudge consumers into accepting data collection by making alternative options confusing, time-consuming, or altogether inaccessible.[93] The argument that users can provide meaningful consent is also invalidated by the fact that data brokers engage in inference-based data profiling.[94] Even if an individual were able to avoid directly providing personal information, data brokers use machine learning algorithms to infer sensitive details, such as income, sexual orientation, political beliefs, or health conditions based on seemingly innocuous behaviors.[95] Finally, the very notion of opting out is largely meaningless in the context of data brokers that never interact directly with internet users. The very structure of this industry—built on covert data collection, deceptive disclosures, inference-based profiling, and coercive design—renders true consent impossible.

Just as society does not allow people to consent to slavery because it fatally undermines autonomy, individuals cannot legally consent to the destruction of their autonomy through pervasive digital surveillance and manipulation by third parties, with which they have no direct contact. Legal scholars and international conventions have long established that consent does not legitimize fundamental violations of human dignity, as seen in the universal prohibition against contracts of enslavement.[96] Consent cannot transform slavery into lawful labor, as the prohibition against enslavement is absolute under public policy principles.[97] The same legal and policy reasoning applies to the data broker ecosystem: Agreements that claim to authorize the undermining of personal autonomy through comprehensive

91 Daniel J. Solove, *Privacy Self-Management and the Consent Dilemma*, 126 Harv. L. Rev. 1880, 1883–1885 (2013).

92 Joel R. Reidenberg et al., *Disagreeable Privacy Policies: Mismatches between Meaning and Users' Understanding*, 30 Berkeley Tech. L.J. 39, 45–48 (2015).

93 Jamie Luguri & Lior Jacob Strahilevitz, *Shining a Light on Dark Patterns*, 13 J. Legal Analysis 43 (2021).

94 Fed. Trade Comm'n, Data Brokers: A Call for Transparency and Accountability 39–40 (2014).

95 Michal Kosinski et al., *Private Traits and Attributes Are Predictable from Digital Records of Human Behavior*, 110 Proc. Nat'l Acad. Sci. 5802, 5802–5805 (2013).

96 Universal Declaration of Human Rights, G.A. Res. 217A (III), U.N. Doc. A/810 at 71 (1948), Articles 1 and 4.

97 International Labour Organization (ILO), Forced Labour Convention, 1930 (No. 29); see J. Allain, *The Legal Understanding of Slavery: From the Historical to the Contemporary* (Oxford University Press, 2012).

and indefinite surveillance by third parties fail to constitute true consent under any sound legal framework.

Litigation Roadmaps for Challenging Data Brokers

The cases discussed in the following exemplify the litigation roadmap articulated earlier, demonstrating how existing statutory, constitutional, and tort law can be effectively deployed to challenge data broker practices. They serve as exemplars of plaintiffs bringing well-crafted claims that highlight the legal vulnerabilities of data brokers and the substantial privacy harms inflicted by their surveillance-driven business models.

Brooks v. Thomson Reuters

The *Brooks v. Thomson Reuters* lawsuit represented a significant legal challenge to Thomson Reuters's CLEAR platform, a powerful database that aggregates, analyzes, and sells detailed personal profiles of individuals without their knowledge or consent.[98] Filed in the Northern District of California, this case was the first to directly challenge certain data broker practices under claims for unjust enrichment and violations of California's Unfair Competition Law.

The plaintiffs, Cat Brooks and Rasheed Shabazz, brought a class action on behalf of California residents whose personal data was sold through the CLEAR platform.[99] The plaintiffs alleged that Thomson Reuters collects and compiles a vast array of personal information—ranging from names, addresses, phone numbers, employment history, and criminal records to financial details and real-time location data—and sells it without the consent of the individuals affected. The platform allows paying customers, including law enforcement agencies, corporations, and private entities, to conduct in-depth searches on individuals, uncovering information that can be used for surveillance, tracking, and decision-making.[100] Government agencies, including US Immigration and Customs Enforcement (ICE), have been able to use this data to monitor and track individuals without judicial oversight. The plaintiffs, both Black civil rights activists, argued that the unauthorized sale of their personal data violated their rights and placed them at heightened risk, particularly given their activism and the potential for government scrutiny.[101]

The court's ruling on Thomson Reuters's motion to dismiss was an important development in defining the legal contours of data broker accountability. In August 2021, Judge Chen of the Northern District of California partially granted and

98 *Brooks v. Thomson Reuters Corp.*, 21-cv-01418-EMC, (N.D. Cal. Aug. 16, 2021).
99 Id.
100 Id.
101 Id.

partially denied the defendant's motion to dismiss. The lawsuit initially included a right of publicity claim, alleging that Thomson Reuters had unlawfully profited from individuals' identities without their permission. The court dismissed the claim, reasoning that while Thomson Reuters was monetizing individuals' personal data, its use of that information did not fit within the conventional framework of a right of publicity violation, which typically involves the unauthorized commercial use of someone's name or likeness in advertising or endorsements.[102] However, the court allowed the plaintiffs to proceed with their claims of unjust enrichment and violations of California's UCL, finding that Thomson Reuters's practice of aggregating and selling personal data without consent could plausibly constitute an unfair business practice under state law.

In its ruling, the court relied heavily on Supreme Court precedent, citing *United States Department of Justice v. Reporters Committee for Freedom of the Press*, which recognized that aggregating discrete, publicly available pieces of information into a computerized dossier could significantly impinge on privacy rights.[103] As the court explained, "[t]he Supreme Court has held that compiling disparate pieces of information about a person into a single dossier, even if the individual pieces of information are publicly available, constitutes a significant invasion of privacy."[104] This principle was particularly applicable given the scope and depth of Thomson Reuters's CLEAR database, which not only collected public records but also integrated real-time updates and proprietary datasets, creating what plaintiffs described as a "360-degree view" of an individual's life.[105] The court rejected Thomson Reuters's argument that merely compiling public records immunized it from liability. It emphasized that "[t]here is a vast difference between the public records that might be found after a diligent search of courthouse files, county archives, and local police stations throughout the country and a computerized summary located in a single clearinghouse of information."[106] Citing *Reporters Committee*, the court noted that the Supreme Court had drawn a distinction between the availability of discrete facts in the public record and the much greater privacy harm that results when those facts are systematically aggregated, indexed, and made instantly accessible. This principle, the court held, was especially applicable in this case, where the vast amount of data available in CLEAR allowed customers—including law enforcement and private entities—to instantly generate detailed and revealing reports on any given individual.[107] The court found that the plaintiffs had plausibly alleged a violation of the UCL's prohibition on unfair business practices,

102 Id. at 8.
103 Id. at 15.
104 Id.
105 Id. at 1.
106 Id. at 15.
107 Id.

stating that Thomson Reuters's sale of plaintiffs' "most private and personal information [supports] a claim under the unfair prong of the UCL."[108]

After extensive litigation, the court granted class certification in August 2023, allowing the case to proceed on behalf of all California residents whose personal information had been made available for sale through CLEAR without their consent.[109] The court determined that Thomson Reuters's business practices were uniform across the class and that class-wide relief was necessary given the broad scope of harm caused by the company's data sales.

Shortly after the class certification order, the parties entered into settlement discussions, and the case is now in the process of settling, with the settlement agreement providing both financial compensation and structural reforms to Thomson Reuters's data practices. As part of the settlement, Thomson Reuters has agreed to establish a $27.5 million non-reversionary settlement fund, which will provide proportional payments to class members who submit claims. However, the case's broader impact is best illustrated by the injunctive relief provisions, which require Thomson Reuters to make fundamental changes to its data collection and sales practices.[110] Among these measures, the company must enhance opt-out mechanisms, making it easier for California residents to remove their personal information from CLEAR. Additionally, Thomson Reuters is required to increase transparency in data collection, ensuring that individuals are informed when their information is included in the database, and the company has also agreed to restrict the sale of certain sensitive data categories, particularly those used in law enforcement and immigration tracking.[111]

The case marked a significant milestone in the quest to subject invasive data broker practices to meaningful legal oversight. The case survived challenges at both the motion to dismiss and class certification stages and was headed toward trial. The lawsuit's settlement and outcome send a clear message that the commodification of aggregated—even if otherwise public—personal data can lead to substantial legal peril. While the settlement did not wholesale eliminate the CLEAR platform, it represented a meaningful step toward curbing particularly acute abuses by data brokers.

Katz-Lacabe v. Oracle

The theoretical framework outlined earlier has found its most fulsome practical application to date in *Katz-Lacabe v. Oracle*, a first-of-its-kind privacy case challenging tech behemoth Oracle's massive digital surveillance-fuel data broker

108 Id. at 7.

109 Order on Class Certification, *Brooks v. Thomson Reuters Corp.*, 21-cv-01418-EMC, (N.D. Cal. Aug. 10, 2023).

110 Class Action Settlement Agreement, Case 3:21-cv-01418-EMC, Document 241-1 (Aug. 29, 2024).

111 Complaint, *Katz-Lacabe et al v. Oracle America, Inc.*, Case No. 3:22-cv-04792-RS (Aug. 19, 2022).

operations. The litigation demonstrated both the viability of using current law to challenge data brokers and the practical challenges of such cases.

Background and Claims

The *Katz-Lacabe* litigation challenged Oracle's massive digital surveillance infrastructure and its role in the global AdTech ecosystem. Filed by prominent privacy advocates Michael Katz-Lacabe, Dr. Jennifer Golbeck, and Dr. Johnny Ryan in the Northern District of California, the complaint challenged Oracle's systematic collection and monetization of personal information of hundreds of millions of people worldwide in its capacity as a data broker. The plaintiffs—privacy scholars and activists—alleged that the company had constructed one of the largest commercial surveillance operations in history.[112] At the heart of the complaint lay Oracle's practice of creating detailed digital dossiers about individuals without their knowledge or consent. Through its BlueKai and DataLogix functionalities, Oracle deployed sophisticated tracking technologies across millions of websites and mobile applications. These tools enabled Oracle to monitor individuals' online activities in real time, collecting intimate details about their interests, behaviors, and relationships. The company then enhanced these profiles with "offline" data purchased from other data brokers, credit card companies, and retail partners.[113]

The complaint detailed how Oracle's identity resolution capabilities allowed it to link disparate data points to specific individuals, creating comprehensive "cradle-to-grave" dossiers that included sensitive information about health conditions, financial status, political views, and personal relationships. These profiles, according to the plaintiffs and based on information ultimately obtained through discovery, contained up to 50,000 data points per individual.[114] Oracle then monetized this information by selling access to its datasets and targeting capabilities to third parties through its data marketplace. The complaint described how Oracle's tracking infrastructure employing cookies, pixels, and JavaScript was embedded in countless websites and apps, making it virtually impossible for individuals to escape the company's surveillance dragnet.[115] Through detailed technical analysis, the complaint demonstrated how Oracle's practices went far beyond traditional data collection for advertising purposes. The company's surveillance infrastructure, the plaintiffs argued, represented a fundamental threat to privacy, autonomy, and democratic values.[116]

112 Id.
113 Id.
114 Id.
115 Id.
116 Id.

Legal Theory

The legal arguments advanced in *Katz-Lacabe v. Oracle* represented a comprehensive application of existing privacy rights to pervasive corporate surveillance practices. The plaintiffs presented a combination of constitutional, tort-based, statutory, and consumer protection claims seeking to establish that Oracle's surveillance and data monetization practices were unlawful under existing legal frameworks.

The core legal claim was the assertion that Oracle's systematic collection and aggregation of personal data violated constitutional and common-law privacy rights. Drawing upon California's robust privacy protections enshrined in Article I, Section 1 of the state constitution, the plaintiffs argued that Oracle's surveillance operations constituted an unjustifiable abrogation of their fundamental right to privacy. This claim was rooted in the argument that the state's constitutional protections were deliberately and presciently drafted specifically to extend to the corporate surveillance practices such as Oracle's.[117] The plaintiffs invoked this right to challenge Oracle's alleged creation of "cradle-to-grave" digital dossiers, which aggregated extensive personal and sensitive information. As noted earlier, the California constitutional right to privacy was born from a recognition of the dangers posed by technological advancements in data collection and surveillance. The plaintiffs in *Katz-Lacabe v. Oracle* leveraged this historical context, arguing that Oracle's data practices, which include the creation of detailed digital dossiers through technologies like its ID Graph, embodied the precise harms the 1972 amendment sought to prevent.[118] Nicole Ozer's analysis details how the California right to privacy was intended to combat precisely such conduct, noting that "data brokers and how they collect, use, sell, and trade, information for profit and power [] is exactly the type of privacy harm of 'cradle-to-grave' dossiers that the California constitutional right to privacy was passed to protect against," mirroring the plaintiffs' arguments in the case.[119] The ballot materials and early court interpretations, such as *White v. Davis*, clearly envisioned robust protections against pervasive data collection and profiling activities.[120]

The complaint also invoked both state and federal wiretap laws, alleging that Oracle's tracking technologies violated CIPA and the ECPA. These claims were based on the argument that Oracle's JavaScript-based tracking code functioned

117 See Ozer, supra n. 80.

118 Id.

119 *Compare* par. 111 of the 2022 *Katz-Lacabe v. Oracle* complaint: "Oracle creates dossiers based on [extensive] online and offline data, which constitute precisely the sort of 'cradle-to-grave profiles' the right to privacy under the California Constitution was created to constrain" *with* Ozer, 2024: "The data brokers and how they collect, use, sell, and trade, information for profit and power surveillance is exactly the type of privacy harm of 'cradle-to-grave' dossiers that the California constitutional right to privacy was passed to protect against."

120 Id.

as a form of wiretapping.[121] The code allegedly intercepted the contents of communications between users and the websites they visited, capturing details such as search queries, form entries, and other user-generated content. The plaintiffs contended that because these interceptions occurred in real time and were routed to Oracle's servers without the knowledge or consent of users, they constituted unlawful wiretapping under CIPA and ECPA. They argued that Oracle's ability to extract user attributes from web traffic—including purchase intent, browsing patterns, and inferred interests—constituted the unlawful interception of the contents of their communications with websites.[122]

The plaintiffs also advanced an unjust enrichment claim under California law, asserting that Oracle wrongfully and unlawfully profited from the collection, aggregation, and sale of their personal data without their consent. The plaintiffs contended that Oracle should be required to disgorge the financial benefits it had accrued from this wrongful data exploitation.[123] Under the Restatement (Third) of Restitution and Unjust Enrichment, a person who is unjustly enriched at another's expense may be liable even if the plaintiff did not suffer a direct monetary loss.[124] The plaintiffs argued that regardless of any direct financial harm, Oracle's use of web tracking, geolocation data collection, and real-world purchase tracking amounted to an ongoing privacy invasion for profit, entitling them to disgorgement of Oracle's illicit gains.

Oracle's Motions to Dismiss

Oracle moved to dismiss the plaintiffs' claims, challenging both their standing under Article III and the sufficiency of their allegations under California and federal privacy laws. The court issued a decision granting the motion in part and denying it in part. While some claims were dismissed with leave to amend, the court allowed the plaintiffs' core claims—those related to California's constitutional right to privacy and the common-law claim of intrusion upon seclusion—to proceed. The ruling recognized the potential harm posed by large-scale commercial surveillance and affirmed that data collection and aggregation practices that exceeded reasonable consumer expectations could constitute an actionable invasion of privacy.

Oracle argued that the plaintiffs had failed to establish standing, contending that they had not demonstrated a concrete and particularized injury. The company further asserted that any alleged harm was speculative and not directly traceable to Oracle, given that third-party websites played a role in collecting and transmitting the data. The court rejected these arguments, holding that the plaintiffs had

121 Complaint, *Katz-Lacabe et al v. Oracle America, Inc.*, Case No. 3:22-cv-04792-RS.
122 Id.
123 Id.
124 See *Restatement (Third) of Restitution & Unjust Enrichment* § 1 (2011).

sufficiently alleged an invasion of privacy as a concrete injury under Article III standing jurisprudence.[125] It pointed to the fact that Oracle itself had generated and maintained detailed digital profiles on the plaintiffs, tracking their web activity and aggregating data from multiple sources.[126] The court found these allegations aligned with precedent recognizing that unauthorized data collection can constitute an injury in fact.

The court also found that the plaintiffs had sufficiently alleged invasion of privacy under the California Constitution. During the motion to dismiss hearing, the plaintiffs highlighted the ballot measure history from 1972 that introduced "privacy" into the California Constitution, noting that proponents at that time emphasized that the computerization of records and their unrestricted use could result in profiles tracking every aspect of an individual's life. The plaintiffs contended that these concerns had now materialized 50 years later in the form of Oracle's corporate surveillance practices, including the Data Marketplace and ID graph, which enabled the collection, synthesis, and sale of detailed personal profiles.[127] I argued to the court:

> [W]hat Oracle is doing is really a form of surveillance that the voters of California made a decision 50 years ago to make illegal by amending the Constitution. . . . In this context, [the word "privacy" as added to the Constitution] means you have a reasonable expectation of privacy to be free from the sort of pervasive electronic surveillance that now, 50 years later . . . a company such as Oracle is actually engaging in.[128]

While Oracle countered that much of the data collected lacked sensitivity and that the plaintiffs had no privacy interest in web browsing histories, the plaintiffs argued that *the mere aggregation of such information itself* violates constitutional protections against pervasive surveillance. Building upon the Ninth Circuit's jurisprudence in *In re Facebook Internet Tracking*, they emphasized that the sheer scale and depth of Oracle's data collection crossed the threshold of egregiousness required under California's privacy jurisprudence.[129] Oracle also maintained that its practices constituted "routine commercial behavior," arguing that its data collection and processing activities were standard in the digital advertising and analytics industry. Relatedly, Oracle argued that its conduct was not "highly offensive" under California privacy law, contending that courts regularly dismiss privacy claims

125 *Katz-Lacabe v. Oracle Am.*, 668 F. Supp. 3d 928, 940 (N.D. Cal. 2023).
126 Id.
127 Plaintiffs' opposition to motion to dismiss, *Katz-Lacabe et al v. Oracle America, Inc.*, Case No. 3:22-cv-04792-RS.
128 Transcript of motion to dismiss hearing, *Katz-Lacabe et al v. Oracle America, Inc.*, Case No. 3:22-cv-04792-RS.
129 Plaintiffs' opposition to motion to dismiss, supra n. 136.

based on data collection when the conduct in question aligns with industry standards and lacks elements of deception or misuse.[130]

The court was not persuaded. It found that Oracle's aggregation and monetization of highly detailed consumer profiles, as alleged by the plaintiffs, exceeded what a reasonable person would expect. The ruling drew on *In re Facebook Internet Tracking Litigation*, which recognized that persistent tracking and profiling can amount to a concrete privacy violation. The court emphasized that the plaintiffs' allegations regarding Oracle's data collection practices were sufficient to support a reasonable expectation of privacy, noting that "allegations that Facebook allegedly compiled highly personalized profiles from sensitive browsing histories and habits" were found sufficient in *In re Facebook Internet Tracking Litigation*, and that similar concerns were implicated in Oracle's alleged aggregation of personal data.[131] The court further observed that determinations of whether an intrusion is "highly offensive" are generally inappropriate for resolution at the motion to dismiss stage, noting that "courts must be reluctant to reach a conclusion at the pleading stage about how offensive or serious the privacy intrusion is."[132] Thus, the plaintiffs' allegations were deemed sufficient to withstand dismissal. The court additionally allowed the CIPA wiretap claim to proceed, finding that the plaintiffs had plausibly alleged that Oracle's bk-coretag.js script intercepted the "contents" of electronic communications without user consent.[133]

However, the federal ECPA was dismissed with leave to amend. The court explained that while the plaintiffs had alleged Oracle's tracking technologies intercepted user communications, they had not sufficiently demonstrated that Oracle's intent met the statutory requirement for tortious conduct under the "crime-tort exception." Quoting language from *In re DoubleClick,* the court held that the crime-tort exception "does not apply to a case such as this, where Defendant's purpose has plainly not been to perpetuate torts on millions of Internet users, but to make money.'"[134] The court also dismissed the California Unfair Competition Law claim, concluding that the plaintiffs had not adequately demonstrated an economic injury sufficient to confer standing under the statute.[135] Finally, the court dismissed the unjust enrichment claim, holding that the plaintiffs had not sufficiently alleged that they directly conferred a benefit on Oracle. The plaintiffs contended that Oracle was unjustly enriched by profiting from the collection, aggregation, and sale of their personal data without consent. However, the court reasoned that "[p]laintiffs do not demonstrate that Defendant has unjustly retained a benefit at Plaintiffs'

130 Id.
131 *Katz-Lacabe v. Oracle Am.*, 668 F. Supp. 3d 928, 942 (N.D. Cal. 2023).
132 Id. at 943.
133 Id. at 945.
134 Id.
135 Id. at 944.

expense" but dismissed the claim with leave to amend, allowing the plaintiffs to clarify how Oracle had received and unjustly retained a benefit at their expense.[136]

Despite the dismissal of several claims, taken as a whole, the court's initial motion to dismiss ruling was a significant victory for the plaintiffs, allowing key privacy claims to proceed while providing an opportunity to strengthen other claims through amendment. The decision affirmed that commercial surveillance practices by data brokers could plausibly constitute actionable invasions of privacy, and by allowing the claims under the California Constitution, intrusion upon seclusion, and CIPA to move forward, the ruling set important precedent for corporate surveillance privacy litigation.

Following this initial ruling, Oracle moved to dismiss the plaintiffs' first amended complaint. The plaintiffs had extensively amended their complaint, adding Florida privacy and wiretapping claims and adding substantial detail to the unjust enrichment claim that specifically responded to the court's articulated concerns. The court issued another decision, again granting in part and denying in part Oracle's motion.[137] The court reviewed the plaintiffs' claims under CIPA, the Florida Security of Communications Act (FSCA), unjust enrichment, and the Federal Wiretap Act. The CIPA claim was allowed to proceed, as the plaintiffs had sufficiently alleged that Oracle's tracking tools, particularly its bk-coretag.js script, intercepted the contents of online communications without consent.[138] The FSCA claim also survived, as the court found that Oracle's data collection, including information entered into online forms, constituted electronic communications protected under that statute. The court also ruled on the amended unjust enrichment claim, this time allowing it to proceed under California law for the California subclass. However, the court again dismissed the Wiretap Act claim, reasoning that the plaintiffs had not sufficiently alleged Oracle's intent to commit a tortious act under *In re DoubleClick*.[139]

Following the court's decision, the plaintiffs filed a motion to certify an interlocutory appeal under 28 USC § 1292(b).[140] This motion sought appellate review of the court's interpretation of the ECPA's "crime-tort exception." Specifically, the plaintiffs challenged the requirement of additional tortious intent, arguing that their allegations of Oracle's tortious aggregation and monetization of illegally intercepted personal data satisfied the statutory exception. The plaintiffs highlighted the conflicting interpretations of the crime-tort exception among federal district courts, citing cases such as *Brown v. Google*, arguing that the court's reliance on

136 Id. at 946.

137 Order Granting In Part And Denying In Part Motion To Dismiss, *Katz-Lacabe v. Oracle Am.*, 22-cv-04792-RS, (N.D. Cal. Oct. 3, 2023).

138 Id.

139 Id.

140 The parties has litigated a third motion to dismiss, and the Court had found (again) that the "exception to the exception" to Wiretap Act claim had not been sufficiently alleged by the plaintiffs.

DoubleClick improperly added a requirement of "insidious intent," going beyond the plain language of the statute.

Settlement and Shutdown of Oracle's Data Broker Business

Shortly after the plaintiffs filed their motion to revive their nationwide wiretapping claim, the parties entered into settlement negotiations. The resulting settlement represented an important moment in privacy litigation, not only for the substantial financial terms but also for its profound impact on the operations of one of the world's most powerful and prolific data brokers. Oracle agreed to pay $115 million to the class and was required to halt the collection of specific categories of user-generated data, including the URLs of websites visited and text entered into online forms—two of the most invasive elements of its tracking infrastructure. This restriction was imposed on data collected outside of Oracle's direct platform ecosystem, curtailing its ability to passively gather personal information from millions of users without consent.

Most striking was Oracle's announcement, shortly after the settlement, that it would exit the advertising technology industry and shut down its AdTech business—including its data broker operations—*entirely*. While the company publicly framed this move as a response to declining revenues, the timing and scope of the decision strongly suggested that the litigation and settlement had played a decisive role in forcing Oracle to reconsider the sustainability of its data broker business model. News reports confirmed as much, noting that "separate sources with contacts inside the organization claimed [privacy] concerns, ultimately, sealed the decision to close down the unit" given "it faced [the *Katz-Lacabe*] class action lawsuit for allegedly using third-party trackers without consent to build profiles."[141] This was a singular achievement in privacy litigation: compelling a global tech giant to abandon one of its core privacy-invasive business lines as a direct result of legal action.

The significance of Oracle's retreat from the AdTech sector was seismic. The company had long been a dominant force in the industry, operating one of the world's largest commercial data brokering exchanges through its BlueKai data management platform and data marketplace.[142] Its extensive data practices had been deeply integrated into the broader advertising ecosystem. By catalyzing the effective dismantlement of these surveillance operations, the lawsuit effectuated a shift in the balance of power between citizens and corporate surveillance actors.

141 Ronan Shields and Seb Joseph, *As Oracle's ad Business Collapses, Layoffs and Uncertainty Ripple Through the Industry*, Digiday (Jun. 25, 2024). https://digiday.com/marketing/as-oracles-ad-business-collapses-layoffs-and-uncertainty-ripple-through-the-industry/.
142 Id.

Katz-Lacabe v. Oracle validates the praxis of strategic privacy litigation articulated throughout this book. It demonstrates that privacy advocates, armed with robust legal theories and a willingness to challenge entrenched corporate interests, can achieve structural change. By forcing a major tech behemoth to shutter its surveillance practices, the case underscored that litigation remains a powerful tool for dismantling exploitative data ecosystems. The case also underscores the legal vulnerabilities data brokers face under *existing* legal frameworks: by leveraging historically bound constitutional privacy protections, common-law torts, and wiretap statutes, the case established that long-standing legal doctrines can be effectively applied to pervasive AdTech practices.

Conclusion

The proliferation of data brokers and their pervasive surveillance practices has reshaped our digital existence, eroding privacy, autonomy, and individual control over personal information. While legislative reform is frequently proposed as the primary solution, the litigation examined in this chapter exemplifies how strategic legal action can force meaningful structural change. As regulatory interest in data brokers grows, these cases provide a blueprint for future legal challenges and a roadmap for how courts can be leveraged to rein in mass commercial surveillance. While it is unlikely that litigation alone will be able to wholly resolve the systemic privacy issues posed by data brokers, it remains a critical lever for power realignment.

8

HARM AND DAMAGES THEORIES

Introduction

The challenge of quantifying privacy harms has long been a central tension in privacy law. While courts have increasingly recognized privacy violations as legally cognizable injuries, the question of how to assign a measurable value to privacy continues to vex both litigants and courts. This chapter, as the final chapter in Part II, examines the emerging frameworks for privacy damages through the lens of recent landmark cases and evolving legal theories. Privacy class actions present unique damages issues: Unlike traditional tort cases, where physical or economic injuries can be readily quantified, privacy harms often involve intangible injuries to dignity, autonomy, and peace of mind. This chapter examines both traditional and emerging approaches to valuing privacy violations in the context of aggregate litigation. Courts have grappled with fundamental questions about how to conceptualize and measure privacy harms, particularly in cases where any immediate economic impact may be minimal but the dignity and autonomy interests at stake are substantial.

Taxonomy of Corporate Surveillance Privacy Harms

Before examining specific damages theories, it is essential to understand the fundamental nature of the privacy harms arising from corporate surveillance practices in order to situate questions about appropriate redress. While the harms attendant to the specific commercial surveillance practices detailed in prior chapters were discussed both implicitly and explicitly, drawing from Solove and Citron's comprehensive taxonomy summarized in Chapter 1,[1] the privacy harms flowing from the

1 Danielle Keats Citron & Daniel J. Solove, *Privacy Harms*, 102 B.U.L. Rev. 793 (2022).

DOI: 10.4324/9781003413349-11

corporate surveillance practices detailed in previous chapters can be categorized into several distinct categories that illuminate why quantification of such harms in economic terms poses special questions.

Individual Autonomy and Dignitary Harms

As discussed in the previous chapter, corporate surveillance fundamentally disrupts individual autonomy by subjecting personal behaviors, choices, and interactions to constant monitoring and analysis.[2] Surveillance exerts a chilling effect on individual freedom, altering behavior even in the absence of explicit coercion or adverse consequences.[3] The mere awareness of being observed imposes autonomy harms, where individuals self-censor, hesitate to explore controversial topics, or conform to expected norms rather than act according to their true preferences. This restriction on personal liberty and self-determination constitutes a real and measurable harm, even if it does not result in a direct economic loss. Individuals lose the ability to engage in unguarded decision-making, fearing that their digital footprints may be scrutinized, monetized, or used against them in unforeseen ways. Dignitary harms also arise when individuals are stripped of control over their personal data, reducing them to passive subjects of corporate data exploitation.[4] This form of injury is closely linked to the erosion of human agency, where individuals lose the ability to dictate how, when, and by whom their information is used.[5]

Informational Power Asymmetries

The systematic collection and analysis of personal data by corporations create significant power imbalances between individuals and the entities that control their information. Scholars have identified this imbalance as an "architectural harm," in which the control over personal data is disproportionately concentrated in corporate hands, leaving individuals vulnerable to manipulation, discrimination, and coercion. As Daniel Solove explains, privacy harms often are not caused by a single organization at one time but rather arise from an architecture of data collection and use.[6] This structural imbalance makes privacy violations systemic rather than isolated, exacerbating the risks individuals face in the digital economy.

Corporations leverage the vast amounts of data they collect to develop detailed consumer profiles, predict behaviors, and influence decision-making, while individuals remain largely unaware of how their data is being used.[7] This opacity makes

2 Id.

3 Jonathon W. Penney, *Understanding Chilling Effects*, 106 Minn. L. Rev. 1451, 1453 (2022).

4 Ryan Calo, *Digital Market Manipulation*, 82 Geo. Wash. L. Rev. 995, 1029 (2014).

5 See Chapter 7.

6 Daniel J. Solove, *Privacy and Power: Computer Databases and Metaphors for Information Privacy*, 53 Stan. L. Rev. 1393 (2001).

7 See Chapter 7.

it impossible for consumers to meaningfully consent to data practices, as they lack the knowledge and bargaining power necessary to negotiate fair terms. Solove and Citron further emphasize that these power asymmetries enable privacy's hidden architectural vulnerabilities, where individual control is rendered ineffective by complex data ecosystems.[8] This imbalance also enables corporations to engage in exploitative practices, such as microtargeted advertising and price discrimination, further exacerbating economic inequalities.[9]

Aggregation and Profiling Harms

Corporate surveillance enables the aggregation of seemingly innocuous data points into highly detailed personal profiles that can reveal intimate and sensitive information about individuals. While each individual data disclosure may appear trivial in isolation, the combination of multiple data points allows corporations to construct extensive profiles that can be used to predict behavior, influence decision-making, and categorize individuals in ways that impact their economic and social opportunities.[10] As Daniel Solove recognized 20 years ago in *The Digital Person*, aggregation transforms the nature of data, allowing information that once seemed harmless to become deeply revealing.[11] This aggregation process exposes details about health conditions, political affiliations, sexual orientation, and religious beliefs, even when individuals have not explicitly disclosed these attributes. Such profiling can have far-reaching consequences, including discrimination, reputational harm, and the reinforcement of social inequalities.[12]

The risks associated with profiling are particularly concerning because they are often invisible to the individuals affected. Corporations use algorithmic decision-making processes to categorize individuals and make predictive assessments about their behavior, which can lead to biased outcomes in hiring, lending, insurance, and law enforcement. Individuals may not be aware of how their aggregated data influences automated decisions about them, making it difficult to contest unfair outcomes.[13]

Inferential Harms

Inferences drawn from aggregated data pose unique and often invisible threats to both individual and collective privacy. While each data point collected might seem benign, the synthesis of multiple data streams allows corporations to generate

8 Citron & Solove, *Privacy Harms*, supra n. 1.

9 See Chapter 7.

10 Daniel J. Solove, The Digital Person: Technology and Privacy in the Information Age (NYU Press, 2004).

11 Id.

12 Danielle Keats Citron, *The Fight for Privacy: Protecting Dignity, Identity, and Love in the Digital Age* 1–6 (2022); Alvaro M. Bedoya, *Privacy as a Civil Right*, 50 N.M.L. Rev. 301 (2020).

13 Barry Friedman & Danielle Keats Citron, *Indiscriminate Data Surveillance*, 110 Va. L. Rev. 1351, 1376–1377 (2024).

deeply revealing insights about individuals and their behaviors. For example, something as routine as music preferences on Spotify can be used to infer a person's ethnicity, while coffee purchase habits can reveal political affiliations.[14] These inferences themselves can lead to significant harms, including discrimination, economic disadvantages, and social stigmatization. As the California attorney general has recognized, "seemingly innocuous data points, when combined with other data points across masses of data, may be exploited to deduce startlingly personal characteristics."[15] Unlike explicit data disclosures, which individuals might knowingly provide, inferential privacy violations occur without awareness, making them difficult to contest. This opaque data landscape exacerbates privacy risks and demands stronger enforcement of laws that recognize the harm caused by predictive profiling and algorithmic decision-making.[16]

Economic and Opportunity Costs

Corporate surveillance generates direct economic harms that manifest through various mechanisms. One significant economic consequence arises from algorithmic scoring and profiling, where individuals are evaluated based on predictive analytics that can limit access to essential services, such as employment, housing, or credit.[17] Employers, lenders, and insurers increasingly rely on data-driven decision-making processes, which may result in individuals being unfairly penalized due to automated risk assessments that they have no ability to contest.[18] Another financial harm involves price discrimination, where companies use consumer data to charge different prices based on an individual's perceived willingness to pay. This practice disadvantages consumers who are identified as having higher spending potential, effectively exploiting personal information for corporate gain.

Privacy violations also impose costs on individuals in the form of time and resources spent managing their digital privacy. Consumers often feel compelled to take protective measures, such as using privacy-enhancing technologies or navigating complex data settings, in an attempt to regain some control over their information. These actions require effort and technical knowledge that not all individuals possess, leading to an unequal distribution of privacy protections. Additionally, corporate control over consumer data reduces individuals' bargaining power in

14 Ignacio Cofone, *The Privacy Fallacy: Harm and Power in the Information Economy* 47–50 (Cambridge University Press, 2024).

15 105 Ops. Cal. Att'y Gen. 26 (2022), 2022 WL 815641 at * 5.

16 Ignacio Cofone, The Privacy Fallacy: Harm and Protection in the Information Economy (Cambridge University Press, 2024) at 50.

17 Danielle Citron & Frank Pasquale, *Essay, The Scored Society: Due Process for Automated Predictions*, 89 Wash. L. Rev. 1 (2014).

18 M. Hurley & J. Adebayo, *Credit Scoring in the Era of Big Data*, 18 Yale J. Law Tech. 1, Article 5 (2016).

economic transactions. The monopolization of data allows companies to dictate market conditions, reinforcing consumer dependence on platforms that engage in intrusive data practices.[19] As Solove and Citron argue, the economic harms associated with corporate surveillance often emerge gradually, making them difficult to detect and quantify in the immediate aftermath of a privacy violation.[20]

Social and Democratic Harms

Privacy violations by corporate actors extend beyond individual harms to deeply affect society and democratic institutions. The widespread collection and analysis of personal data by corporations and political entities enable the manipulation of public opinion, disrupt civic participation, and distort democratic processes.[21] One of the primary social harms of unchecked data collection is the ability of corporations and governments to use microtargeted advertising and algorithmic content curation to manipulate political and social narratives at scale. As Ignacio Cofone explains, "big data threatens democracies by influencing voting outcomes around the world" through "the ease of targeted online manipulation" and the commodification of personal data for political advertising.[22] The ability of digital platforms to amplify misinformation and selectively expose individuals to tailored political messaging further erodes trust in democratic institutions.

Another significant democratic harm arises from the chilling effect of surveillance, as previously discussed, where individuals self-censor their online activity due to concerns about monitoring. Mary Anne Franks highlights that "[t]he fear of surveillance inhibits individual freedoms of expression and association, which in turn undermines the possibility of an open and democratic society."[23] Studies have shown that individuals are less likely to engage in political discussions or explore controversial topics online when they feel their activities are being tracked.[24] This fear of surveillance suppresses dissent and reduces civic engagement, which are essential components of a healthy democracy.

A further democratic harm of unchecked surveillance lies in its fundamental misalignment with democratic governance. As Salomé Viljoen argues, the current paradigm of data governance fails to account for the population-level effects of datafication, instead reducing concerns to individualist notions of privacy and

19 Lina M. Khan, *Amazon's Antitrust Paradox*, 126 Yale L.J. 710, 716 (2017).

20 Citron & Solove, *Privacy Harms*, supra n. 1.

21 S. Zuboff, *Surveillance Capitalism or Democracy? The Death Match of Institutional Orders and the Politics of Knowledge in Our Information Civilization*, 3(3) Org. Theor. 1–79 (2022).

22 Cofone, *The Privacy Fallacy*, supra at 137.

23 M.A. Franks, *Democratic Surveillance: Privacy, Security, and Public Trust*, 30 Harv. J.L. Tech. 425–489 (2016).

24 Penney.

control.[25] However, data is inherently relational, meaning that individual choices about data sharing inevitably impact others and shape the collective social and political landscape.[26] The absence of democratic oversight in data governance allows private corporations to dictate the terms of social and economic interactions, often reinforcing existing hierarchies and marginalizing vulnerable populations.[27] Without mechanisms to incorporate collective decision-making into data governance, individuals are left without meaningful participation in decisions that shape their digital and political lives, further entrenching disparities in power and representation.

The exploitation of personal data for political manipulation illustrates how privacy harms extend beyond individuals to threaten democracy itself. As Cofone observes, the Cambridge Analytica scandal discussed in Chapter 3 is emblematic of how the commodification of personal data can distort democratic processes by leveraging voters' psychological vulnerabilities.[28] The use of sophisticated data analytics allows campaigns and interest groups to craft hyper-personalized messaging, shaping voter perceptions in ways that are neither transparent nor subject to meaningful oversight.[29] Such manipulative tactics undermine the principle of an informed electorate, a cornerstone of democratic societies. These collective harms, though difficult to assign a monetary value to any single individual, represent profound threats to democratic institutions and social cohesion.

Future Risk and Anxiety Harms

Beyond immediate harms, corporate data collection imposes a persistent psychological burden on individuals. This ongoing distress stems from the knowledge that personal data, once collected, remains vulnerable to future breaches, misuse, or unauthorized access. Even when no concrete harm has yet materialized, individuals must constantly consider the potential consequences of their data being exploited in ways beyond their control. Legal scholars have emphasized that the mere existence of widespread corporate surveillance generates a state of anticipatory anxiety, where individuals experience stress over the unknown risks associated with their personal information. Daniel Solove has argued that privacy violations create harms even before any specific misuse occurs, as individuals are left in a perpetual state of vulnerability regarding how their data might be used against them in the future.[30]

25 Salomé Viljoen, *A Relational Theory of Data Governance*, 131 Yale L.J. 573 (2021).
26 Id.
27 Id.
28 Cofone, *The Privacy Fallacy*, supra at 154.
29 Id.
30 D.J. Solove, *The Digital Person: Technology and Privacy in the Information Age* (NYU Press, 2022).

The risk of data breaches further exacerbates this anxiety. Research has shown that individuals perceive privacy risks as cumulative and unpredictable—meaning that even a minor data collection event can contribute to significant long-term concerns about security and identity theft.[31] This aligns with empirical findings in behavioral economics, which demonstrate that individuals overestimate low-probability risks when the potential consequences—such as identity fraud or reputational damage—are severe.[32]

Monetary Privacy Remedies

The challenge of addressing privacy harms through monetary compensation lies in the difficulty of assigning a financial value to privacy itself. Privacy plays a critical role in individual autonomy, social relationships, and democratic participation—functions that cannot be easily reduced to economic terms.

This tension manifests in several ways. First, privacy violations often cause harm to personal dignity, autonomy, and social bonds in ways that money cannot truly repair; while financial compensation may offer some level of redress or deterrence, it does not restore lost privacy or undo the breach of personal boundaries. In some cases, accepting payment for privacy violations may even feel like an additional loss of dignity rather than a meaningful remedy.[33] Second, the effects of privacy breaches often unfold over time, making them difficult to quantify through traditional legal frameworks. Many violations do not result in immediate, concrete harm but instead create risks that may only materialize years later. Third, privacy violations often trigger a chain reaction of negative consequences: The exposure of personal information can lead to discrimination, manipulation, or loss of opportunities, with effects that extend far beyond the initial breach. Because these harms can be difficult to trace and measure precisely, monetary compensation may fail to capture the full extent of the damage.

Given these complexities, some argue that monetary damages alone are, in principle, insufficient and that privacy protections should be reinforced through structural remedies or regulatory measures.[34] However, financial penalties still play an unquestionably central role in deterring violations and holding offenders accountable.

31 C.R. Sunstein, *Probability Neglect: Emotions, Worst Cases, and Law*, 112 Yale L.J. 1 (2003), 61–107.

32 Id.

33 Alessandro Acquisti, Leslie K. John & George Loewenstein, *What Is Privacy Worth?*, 42 J. Legal. Stud. 249 (2013).

34 J.E. Cohen, *Between Truth and Power: The Legal Constructions of Informational Capitalism* (Oxford University Press, 2019).

The Role of Economic Damages in Privacy Class Actions

Economic damages serve a critical function in privacy class actions, even in cases where plaintiffs do not experience direct financial harm. Litigants have long debated the challenges of fitting privacy violations into conventional damages models. Courts sometimes dismiss privacy claims for lack of concrete injury under restrictive standing doctrines due to lack of economic harm.[35] Danielle Citron and Daniel Solove argue that the law's failure to recognize these harms has created a "misalignment of enforcement goals and remedies," allowing privacy violations to go unaddressed simply because they do not result in immediate financial loss.[36]

Despite these challenges, economic damages are widely recognized as essential for deterring privacy violations and compensating victims. Bernard Chao argues that focusing on the defendant's gains rather than the plaintiff's losses ensures that companies do not profit from privacy violations while avoiding liability.[37] Economic damages remain crucial for holding companies accountable, particularly when privacy violations result in systemic, widespread harm that is difficult to trace to individual financial losses.[38] The role of economic damages in non-privacy civil rights class actions further supports their importance in privacy litigation. Courts have long awarded damages for emotional distress and reputational harm in employment discrimination, voting rights, and housing discrimination cases, even in the absence of direct financial loss.[39] These damages serve both a compensatory and deterrent function, ensuring that systemic rights violations are not left unpunished simply because they do not fit within traditional damage models.[40]

Traditional Approaches to Privacy Damages

Monetary damages have long served as a primary legal remedy for rights violations, and legal frameworks have been developed to recognize tangible, demonstrable economic losses as the basis for compensation. These traditional approaches focus on measurable financial harms that arise from privacy violations, including direct financial losses, mitigation costs, and lost economic opportunities.

35 Citron & Solove, *Privacy Harms*, supra n. 1.

36 Id.

37 Bernard Chao, *Privacy Losses as Wrongful Gains*, 106 Iowa L. Rev. 555, 557 (2021).

38 Id.

39 See, for example, *Carey v. Piphus*, 435 U.S. 247, 264 (1978); *Memphis Community School District v. Stachura*, 477 U.S. 299, 307 (1986); Armen H. Merjian, *Nothing "Garden Variety" About It: Manifest Error and Gross Devaluation in the Assessment of Emotional Distress Damages*, 70 Syracuse L. Rev. 689 (2020); *Note, Voting Wrongs and Remedial Gaps*, 137 Harv. L. Rev. 1182, 1188–1190 (2024).

40 Lauren Henry Scholz, *Privacy Remedies*, 94 Ind. L.J. 653, 658 (2019).

Actual Damages and Economic Loss

The most straightforward approach to privacy damages involves demonstrating concrete economic losses stemming from privacy violations. Courts have consistently recognized direct financial losses from fraudulent charges or accounts as compensable damages in privacy cases. In *In re Anthem Inc. Data Breach Litigation*, the court approved a settlement that specifically compensated class members for out-of-pocket losses from identity theft, including unauthorized charges, fraudulent tax returns, and costs of resolving identity theft with creditors.[41] Similarly, in *In re Capital One Consumer Data Security Breach Litigation*, the court found that concrete financial losses from identity theft presented a clear basis for Article III standing and damages calculations.[42]

The cost of credit monitoring services has emerged as a widely recognized category of privacy damages, particularly in data breach cases. In *Hutton v. National Board of Examiners in Optometry*, the Fourth Circuit specifically recognized credit monitoring costs as a concrete injury flowing from privacy violations.[43] Courts have generally held that credit monitoring expenses are compensable when the privacy violation creates a sufficiently substantial risk of identity theft, though there is some variation in how courts assess that risk. The Seventh Circuit's decision in *Remijas v. Neiman Marcus Group* established that credit monitoring costs are compensable when there is a "substantial risk" of identity theft, while noting that the definition of "substantial" may vary based on the nature of the compromised data.[44]

Courts increasingly recognize the compensable value of time spent responding to privacy violations. In *Dieffenbach v. Barnes & Noble*, the court approved compensation for time spent reviewing account settings, implementing security measures, and monitoring for unauthorized activity.[45] Additionally, privacy violations can lead to compensable losses of income or business opportunities. In *Lewert v. P. F. Chang's China Bistro Inc.*, the Seventh Circuit recognized that time taken off work to address privacy breaches constituted concrete economic injury.[46]

Courts generally allow recovery for reasonable costs incurred to prevent or mitigate potential harm from privacy violations. However, courts typically require that such expenses be reasonably necessary given the nature of the privacy violation. In *Attias v. CareFirst, Inc.*,[47] the DC Circuit clarified that plaintiffs must demonstrate a substantial risk of harm to justify mitigation expenses; generalized concerns

41 In re Anthem, Inc. Data Breach Litigation, No. 15-MD-02617-LHK, 2018 WL 3960068 (N.D. Cal. Aug. 17, 2018).

42 *In re Capital One Consumer Data Security Breach Litig.*, 488 F. Supp. 3d 374 (E.D. Va. 2020).

43 *Hutton v. National Board of Examiners in Optometry, Inc.*, 892 F.3d 613 (4th Cir. 2018).

44 *Remijas v. Neiman Marcus Group, LLC*, 794 F.3d 688 (7th Cir. 2015).

45 *Dieffenbach v. Barnes & Noble, Inc.*, 887 F.3d 826 (7th Cir. 2018).

46 *Lewert v. P.F. Chang's China Bistro, Inc.*, 819 F.3d 963 (7th Cir. 2016).

47 865 F.3d 620 (D.C. Cir. 2017).

about data exposure alone were insufficient to support recovery. The framework established in *In re Equifax Inc. Customer Data Security Breach Litigation* further refined this approach, holding that courts must assess the type of personal information compromised and the likelihood of misuse to determine the reasonableness of mitigation measures.[48]

Courts have generally been receptive to privacy claims anchored in these demonstrable economic harms.[49] However, limiting recovery to economic losses fails to capture many of the core interests that privacy law seeks to protect.

Statutory Damages

Many privacy statutes provide for statutory damages, which allow plaintiffs to recover prescribed amounts without proving actual damages. These provisions reflect legislative recognition that privacy violations warrant remedy even absent economic loss and serve both compensatory and deterrent functions.

The California Invasion of Privacy Act (CIPA) has emerged as a particularly significant source of statutory damages in privacy class actions. Section 637.2 of CIPA provides for statutory damages of $5,000 per violation or three times actual damages, whichever is greater.[50] Courts have generally interpreted CIPA's damages provision liberally, holding that each unauthorized recording or interception can constitute a separate violation. This interpretation has led to substantial potential exposure in cases involving automated systems that routinely capture communications.[51] Similarly, the Electronic Communications Privacy Act (ECPA) provides another important statutory damages framework. The ECPA allows recovery of actual damages or statutory damages of $100 per day of violation or $10,000, whichever is greater.[52] Courts have grappled with how to apply these provisions in modern contexts involving continuous electronic surveillance or bulk data collection, particularly in class action settings where aggregate statutory damages can reach astronomical amounts.[53]

Other notable statutory damages schemes provide predefined monetary remedies for privacy violations. For instance, the Video Privacy Protection Act (VPPA) imposes a penalty of $2,500 per violation, suggesting that unauthorized disclosure of video viewing history carries significant financial consequences.[54] Similarly, the Telephone Consumer Protection Act (TCPA) establishes a tiered system of damages, ranging from $500 to $1,500 per violation, depending on the nature and

48 999 F.3d 1247 (11th Cir. 2021).
49 Citron & Solove, *Privacy Harms*, supra n. 1.
50 Cal. Penal Code § 637.2.
51 Brown v. Google LLC, No. 20-CV-03664, 2023 WL 5029899 (N.D. Cal. Aug. 7, 2023).
52 Id.
53 See, for example, *Campbell v. Facebook Inc.*, 315 F.R.D. 250, 269 (N.D. Cal. 2016).
54 Video Privacy Protection Act, 18 U.S.C. § 2710(c)(2)(A) (2018).

willfulness of the infraction, particularly in cases involving robocalls and unsolicited communications.[55] In addition, state laws addressing biometric privacy, such as Illinois's Biometric Information Privacy Act (BIPA), impose statutory damages between $1,000 and $5,000 per violation, reflecting the heightened sensitivity of biometric data and the need for strong enforcement mechanisms.[56]

These statutory frameworks present both opportunities and challenges for privacy class actions. While they obviate the need to prove actual damages, courts have sometimes expressed concern about the potential for catastrophic liability when statutory damages are aggregated across large classes.[57] Some courts have acknowledged concerns about the potential for large aggregated statutory damages in class actions but have rejected the argument that due process automatically limits such awards.[58]

Contemporary Theories of Privacy Damages

Loss of Privacy as Inherent Injury

An emerging theory posits that the loss of privacy itself constitutes a cognizable injury approrpiate for economic redress, independent of consequential harms. This approach treats privacy as an inherent good with intrinsic value, similar to property rights or bodily autonomy. Under this theory, the unauthorized collection, use, or disclosure of personal information represents an injury in fact even absent economic loss or emotional distress. Several courts have embraced versions of this theory, particularly in cases involving statutory privacy rights.[59] The approach aligns with philosophical accounts of privacy as a fundamental human right and recognizes that privacy violations alone can meaningfully harm individuals, even in the absences of additional "downstream" consequences.[60]

Market Value Approaches

Another approach involves measuring privacy damages by reference to the market value of personal information. This theory treats personal data as a form of property and measures damages through several distinct methodologies. Courts have begun to recognize evidence of market transactions involving similar personal information as a potential measure of privacy damages. In *In re Facebook Internet*

55 Telephone Consumer Protection Act, 47 U.S.C. § 227(b)(3) (2018).
56 Biometric Information Privacy Act, 740 Ill. Comp. Stat. 14/20 (2008).
57 *Parker v. Time Warner Entertainment Co.*, 331 F.3d 13 (2d Cir. 2003).
58 *Bateman v. American Multi-Cinema, Inc.*, 623 F.3d 708 (9th Cir. 2010).
59 See, for example, *In re Facebook, Inc. Internet Tracking Litigation*, 956 F.3d 589 (9th Cir. 2020); *Patel v. Facebook, Inc.*, 932 F.3d 1264 (9th Cir. 2019).
60 Neil Richards, *Why Privacy Matters* (2021); Cofone, *The Privacy Fallacy*, supra.

Tracking Litigation, the Ninth Circuit accepted plaintiffs' theory that the value of personal browsing data could be calculated based on existing data marketplace prices.[61] Similarly, in *Fraley v. Facebook Inc.*, the court approved a settlement valuation based partly on the market price advertisers paid for social media data.[62] However, courts typically require detailed expert testimony establishing the existence of genuine market comparables.[63]

Unjust Enrichment

The doctrine of unjust enrichment has been recognized as a viable remedy for privacy violations under the *Restatement (Third) of Restitution and Unjust Enrichment.* Section 1 of the Restatement establishes that "[a] person who is unjustly enriched at the expense of another is subject to liability in restitution."[64] Courts have applied this principle to privacy cases by considering whether a defendant has wrongfully obtained a benefit through the unauthorized collection or misuse of personal data. The Restatement further clarifies that a defendant's enrichment does not need to result from economic harm to plaintiffs but, rather, must involve circumstances that make it unjust for the defendant to keep the benefit. This framework has guided courts in evaluating claims where companies derive financial gain from personal information without the knowledge or consent of individuals.

Unjust enrichment has become an increasingly important theory of damages in privacy litigation. Courts have recognized that regardless of whether a plaintiff can demonstrate direct financial harm, a defendant's unjust financial gain from privacy violations may be subject to disgorgement.[65] This theory has played a critical role in corporate surveillance cases, where companies extract value from user data without consent. In *In re Facebook Internet Tracking Litigation*, the Ninth Circuit upheld the plaintiffs' unjust enrichment claims against Facebook for allegedly tracking users' browsing activity even after they had logged out of their accounts.[66] The court found that plaintiffs plausibly alleged Facebook had improperly obtained and monetized users' private data without their knowledge or consent, unjustly enriching itself in the process. The court rejected Facebook's argument that the plaintiffs had suffered no direct economic harm, emphasizing that Facebook's financial benefit from unauthorized data collection could be subject to disgorgement under an unjust enrichment theory.[67]

61 956 F.3d 589 (9th Cir. 2020).
62 *Fraley v. Facebook, Inc.*, 966 F. Supp. 2d 939 (N.D. Cal. 2013).
63 *Kumandan v. Google LLC*, 19-cv-04286-BLF, 27 (N.D. Cal. Dec. 16, 2022).
64 Restatement (Third) of Restitution and Unjust Enrichment § 1 (2011).
65 See, for example, *In re Facebook, Inc. Internet Tracking Litigation*, 956 F.3d 589 (9th Cir. 2020).
66 Id.
67 *Katz-Lacabe v. Oracle Am.*, 22-cv-04792-RS (N.D. Cal. Oct. 3, 2023).

The court in *Katz-Lacabe v. Oracle America Inc.* allowed an unjust enrichment claim to proceed, rejecting Oracle's motion to dismiss on this issue.[68] Plaintiffs successfully argued that Oracle's unauthorized collection, aggregation, and monetization of personal data unjustly enriched the company at their expense. The court found that plaintiffs sufficiently alleged that Oracle had collected and profited from user data without consent, deriving a financial benefit that would be inequitable to retain. Plaintiffs argued that Oracle's data tracking and profiling activities enabled it to sell user information to third parties, giving it a financial advantage that should be subject to disgorgement.[69] The plaintiffs further alleged that they would not have visited websites where Oracle tracked their activity had they known about the data collection, and that Oracle's conduct deprived them of control over their own personal information.

Oracle sought dismissal by contending that plaintiffs had not directly conferred a benefit upon Oracle. The company claimed that any benefit Oracle obtained was derived from third-party websites, not from plaintiffs themselves, and therefore could not support a direct unjust enrichment claim.[70] The court rejected Oracle's arguments at the motion to dismiss stage, finding that plaintiffs had sufficiently alleged that their data was involuntarily taken and monetized without their knowledge or consent.[71] The ruling also emphasized that a direct transactional relationship between the plaintiff and the defendant is not necessarily required for unjust enrichment, particularly in digital privacy cases, where companies profit from indirect, non-consensual data collection.

Nominal Damages

Nominal damages serve as an important tool for recognizing and vindicating privacy rights. Courts have awarded nominal damages in cases where privacy violations occurred but did not result in measurable economic or emotional harm.[72] The rationale behind nominal damages is to affirm that a legal right has been violated, ensuring that privacy protections remain enforceable even in cases where harm is difficult to quantify. A recent example of nominal damages in privacy cases is *Rodriguez v. Google*, where the court denied summary judgment while noting that nominal damages could still be available even if economic harm was uncertain, as discussed later in this chapter.[73] The decision reflects a broader judicial trend toward recognizing privacy violations as legally significant on their own, irrespective of the financial consequences to plaintiffs.

68 Id.
69 Id.
70 Id.
71 Id.
72 Citron & Solove, *Privacy Harms*, supra n. 1.
73 *Rodriguez v. Google LLC*, 20-cv-04688-RS, 13 (N.D. Cal. Jan. 7, 2025).

Punitive Damages

Punitive damages play a distinct and powerful role in privacy litigation, particularly in cases involving intentional, reckless, or egregious violations of privacy rights. Unlike compensatory damages, which aim to restore plaintiffs to their prior state, punitive damages are designed to punish defendants and deter future misconduct. The availability of punitive damages in privacy cases often hinges on the level of intent demonstrated by the defendant. If plaintiffs can show that a company knowingly and deliberately violated privacy rights, courts are more likely to consider substantial punitive awards.[74] Courts have awarded punitive damages in cases where defendants knowingly violated privacy rights.[75]

Cy Près as an Alternative to Damages

In privacy class actions, cy près settlements provide a practical alternative to direct monetary damages when distributing compensation to individual class members is impractical or economically unfeasible. Privacy violations often involve millions of affected individuals, each with relatively small individual claims that are difficult to quantify. Unlike financial fraud cases, where damages correspond to monetary loss, privacy harms frequently involve lost control over personal data, emotional distress, or dignitary harm, which do not always have a clear market value. Additionally, identifying and compensating individual victims in large-scale privacy cases can be prohibitively costly, making direct distribution inefficient.

The cy près doctrine, derived from the French phrase *cy près comme possible*—meaning "as close as possible"—allows courts to allocate settlement funds to organizations that serve the interests of the class, rather than issuing *de minimis* payments. This approach has been particularly useful in privacy class actions, where harm is widespread but difficult to individually quantify. In *Frank v. Gaos*, where Google allegedly shared users' search queries without consent, the court approved an $8.5 million cy près settlement directing funds to privacy advocacy groups instead of distributing a few cents per claimant.[76] While this practice has faced judicial scrutiny, courts have repeatedly recognized that cy près can ensure corporate accountability, fund privacy-enhancing initiatives, and deter future privacy violations.[77]

Despite its advantages, cy près has generated controversy. Critics argue that redirecting funds to third-party organizations deprives harmed individuals of direct

74 See, for example, *Bruce Kirby, Inc. v. Laserperformance (Eur.) Ltd.*, No. 3:13-CV-00297 (JAM), 2021 WL 328632 (D. Conn. Feb. 1, 2021); Dan D. Dobbs, Paul T. Hayden & Ellen M. Bublick, *Hornbook on Torts* § 34.4 (2nd ed., West Academic Publishing, 2015).

75 *Gutierrez v. Walker*, 2021 WL 5937586 (D.N.M. Dec. 16, 2021); *Lawlor v. N. Am. Corp. of Illinois*, 983 N.E.2d 414 (Ill. 2012).

76 *Frank v. Gaos*, 586 U.S. ___, 139 S. Ct. 1041 (2019).

77 *In re Google Location History Litig.*, 5:18-cv-05062-EJD, 3 (N.D. Cal. May. 3, 2024).

relief, raises concerns about conflicts of interest, and gives courts broad discretion in allocating funds.[78] To address these concerns, courts have established safeguards, ensuring cy près settlements align with class members' interests, favor hybrid settlements that combine direct payouts with cy près, and closely scrutinize recipient organizations.[79] As privacy class actions continue to grow, cy près is likely to remain a vital tool for addressing systemic privacy harms, particularly when direct restitution is impractical.

Privacy Damages Theories in Action: State-of-the-Art

As privacy litigation continues to evolve, courts are increasingly tasked with evaluating how to quantify and remedy digital privacy harms. The cases of *Brown v. Google LLC* and *Rodriguez v. Google LLC* represent two of the most advanced applications of privacy damages theories in modern privacy litigation. These cases showcase judicial approaches to assessing unjust enrichment, actual damages, and statutory damages while highlighting the procedural challenges plaintiffs face in seeking class certification and monetary relief.

Case Study: Brown v. Google

The Northern District of California's 2023 decision in *Brown v. Google* provides a state-of-the-art, if controversial, example of judicial treatment of class-wide privacy damages theories.[80] The plaintiffs alleged that Google's Chrome browser continued to collect user data even when users enabled "Incognito" mode, violating privacy laws and misleading users into believing their browsing activity was not being tracked. Google opposed class certification, arguing that users had different levels of knowledge, consent, and exposure to Google's privacy disclosures, making a class-wide resolution impractical. The central issue in the case was whether plaintiffs could establish a common methodology for assessing damages on a class-wide basis. Plaintiffs advanced three primary damages theories: unjust enrichment, restitution (actual damages), and statutory damages, each of which was hotly contested by Google.

Plaintiffs contended that Google was unjustly enriched by collecting and monetizing private browsing data without consent. Their expert, Michael Lasinski, proposed calculating damages based on Google's internal revenue analyses, which assessed the financial impact of disabling third-party cookies. Using this data, Lasinski estimated that Google derived between $567.4 million and $3.87 billion from improperly collected Incognito browsing data. Google contested this

78 Id.
79 Id.
80 *Brown v. Google*, LLC, No. 20-cv-3664-YGR, (N.D. Cal. Dec. 12, 2022).

model, with Google's expert, Bruce Strombom, arguing that Lasinski's approach was speculative and overstated Google's actual gains.[81] Google contended that Lasinski failed to deduct costs, calculating unjust enrichment based on gross revenue rather than net profits, which contradicts established legal precedent. Google also asserted that Lasinski overestimated private browsing traffic, assuming that a significant portion of Google's ad revenue came from Incognito users without accounting for legitimate traffic and consented data.[82] Additionally, Google argued that Lasinski did not adjust for user control settings, ignoring the fact that many users voluntarily enabled third-party tracking even in Incognito mode.

The court ultimately denied Google's motion to exclude Lasinski's damages models, finding that his methodologies for calculating unjust enrichment, restitution, and statutory damages were sufficiently reliable and admissible under the *Daubert* standard for expert evidence.[83] The court rejected Google's arguments that Lasinski's analysis was speculative, failed to deduct costs, or did not properly account for user consent and control settings. Instead, the court determined that Lasinski's models provided a reasonable framework for estimating Google's financial gains from private browsing data and could serve as common proof of damages.[84]

On unjust enrichment, the court found that Lasinski's calculations, which relied on Google's internal analyses of the financial impact of third-party cookie blocking, were grounded in a reliable methodology.[85] The court noted that Google had not provided sufficient evidence of incremental costs associated with private browsing data, making Lasinski's focus on revenue a permissible approach. For restitution damages, the court upheld Lasinski's use of Google's Screenwise Panel as a benchmark for valuing users' browsing data, rejecting Google's argument that the panel participants' consent made it an improper comparator. The court determined that Lasinski's choice of a $3-per-month baseline payment was conservative and based on Google's actual practices, making it an appropriate basis for estimating the value of improperly collected data.[86] Regarding statutory damages, the court found Lasinski's methodology for quantifying Incognito traffic and calculating potential per-violation penalties under CIPA and the Federal Wiretap Act to be sound. The court dismissed Google's claim that Lasinski's model failed to exclude instances where Google did not collect data, concluding that Google had not provided sufficient evidence to undermine the validity of the calculations.[87]

81 Id. at 5–6.
82 Id. at 11.
83 Id. at 10.
84 Id. at 10.
85 Id. at 8–9.
86 Id. at 9.
87 Id. at 12.

Although the court ruled that Lasinski's opinions were admissible, it ultimately declined to certify a damages class on separate grounds, finding that individual issues related to user consent predominated over common questions. Specifically, the court held that determining whether each user was aware of Google's data collection practices would require a fact-intensive, individualized inquiry.[88] As a result, the court granted class certification solely for injunctive relief under Rule 23(b)(2) but denied certification for monetary damages under Rule 23(b)(3).

Despite rejecting class certification, the *Brown v. Google* decision highlights several important developments in aggregate privacy litigation. Courts appear increasingly receptive to innovative theories of privacy harm, and the court's willingness to engage with theories such as unjust enrichment, restitution, and per-violation statutory damages suggests that privacy plaintiffs may have multiple viable pathways to argue for compensation in future cases. However, this ruling also imposed an unreasonably high and impractical standard for class certification of a damages class in digital privacy cases. The decision overemphasized individualized differences in user consent, exposure to privacy policies, and browsing behaviors, despite clear evidence that Google's data collection practices operated in a uniform and systemic manner. Rather than recognizing the overarching common issues of deceptive conduct and unauthorized data collection, the court erroneously focused on minor variations in user knowledge that should not have precluded class-wide adjudication. Nonetheless, the court's simultaneous acknowledgment of the validity of the plaintiffs' damages theories paved a way to a potentially substantial damages verdict.

Case Study: Rodriguez v. Google

The *Rodriguez v. Google* case centers on Google's alleged unauthorized collection of user data despite users disabling their *web and app activity* ("WAA") and *supplemental web and app activity* ("sWAA") settings. Beyond questions of liability, a crucial aspect of the litigation has been the court's resolution of competing damages theories at different procedural stages. The rulings on damages at both the class certification and summary judgment stages illustrate the evolving judicial approach to quantifying privacy harms.[89]

During class certification, plaintiffs presented multiple damages theories, arguing that Google's alleged misconduct resulted in economic harm to users and unjust enrichment for Google. The plaintiffs (again) relied on the expert testimony of Michael Lasinski, who proposed two primary methods for quantifying damages: one based on unjust enrichment, measuring the value Google derived from the unauthorized collection of WAA/sWAA-off data, and another assessing the value

88 Id. at 32.
89 *Rodriguez v. Google LLC*, No. 20-cv-04688-RS (N.D. Cal. Jan. 3, 2024).

of users' lost privacy rights by referencing Google's Ipsos Screenwise Panel, which pays users for data access.[90] Google challenged both models, arguing that plaintiffs failed to demonstrate a viable method for calculating class-wide damages. It contended that Lasinski's unjust enrichment analysis overstated Google's financial gains by failing to deduct costs and that his reliance on the Ipsos Screenwise Panel was speculative because it did not account for variations in user behavior and privacy preferences.[91] Google also asserted that individual issues related to consent, exposure to privacy disclosures, and the extent of data collection would make any class-wide damages model unreliable.

Despite these challenges, the court found that the plaintiffs had provided a sufficiently rigorous damages framework to justify certification of a damages class. The court accepted that unjust enrichment could be a viable class-wide measure and that Lasinski's methodology, while contested, was rooted in economic principles that could withstand scrutiny at later stages.[92] However, while allowing the damages models to proceed, the court acknowledged that individualized inquiries regarding user consent and data collection practices could still arise, which might affect the ultimate assessment of damages at trial.

At the summary judgment stage, the court took a closer look at whether the plaintiffs had provided sufficient evidence to support their damages claims under the applicable legal standards. Google renewed its attacks on the damages models, arguing that plaintiffs had failed to establish a concrete harm sufficient to justify monetary relief. Plaintiffs presented multiple damages theories to satisfy the elements of their claims. For their CDAFA claim, plaintiffs needed to demonstrate "damage or loss" as required by the statute, while their invasion of privacy claims required showing legally cognizable harm.[93] Google argued that plaintiffs' invasion of privacy claims failed because they could not establish that a "bare privacy harm" was actionable, contending that Article III injury alone cannot constitute harm to sustain these claims. Google further asserted that even if plaintiffs suffered Article III injury, they could not demonstrate class-wide harm since emotional harms associated with privacy claims would be available only on an individual basis.

The court addressed five distinct damages theories presented by plaintiffs. First, regarding "deprivation of privacy," the court acknowledged that while invasions of privacy themselves can be actionable without additional consequences, plaintiffs were able to show entitlement to nominal damages for emotional harms.[94] Second, the court found plaintiffs' "disgorgement of profits" theory viable, rejecting Google's argument that this was untenable after *TransUnion v. Ramirez* and finding

90 Id. at 20.
91 Id. at 22–23.
92 Id. at 21.
93 *Rodriguez v. Google LLC*, No. 20-cv-04688-RS, at 12–13 (N.D. Cal. Jan. 7, 2025).
94 Id. at 17.

that plaintiffs had "a stake in the value of their misappropriated data."[95] Third, the court determined that plaintiffs' "failure to pay for collected data" theory presented a genuine dispute of material fact, finding that "under California law, [a] stake in unjustly earned profits exists regardless of whether an individual planned to sell his or her data or whether the individual's data is made less valuable," and that it remained disputed whether plaintiffs suffered damage or loss because Google failed to pay for their data despite the existence of a market for such data.[96] Fourth, the court recognized "depletion of battery and bandwidth" as an acceptable form of damage or loss for CDAFA claims.[97] Finally, the court rejected plaintiffs' "denial of benefit of the bargain" theory due to lack of supporting authority absent a contract claim.[98]

The court concluded that while only nominal damages might be available for some theories, this did not defeat plaintiffs' claims, and several viable damages theories remained to satisfy the elements of their causes of action. Ultimately, the court's denial of summary judgment on damages reinforced the growing recognition of data privacy harms as injuries appropriate for pecuniary remedies on a class-wide basis. As the case moves toward trial, these damages theories will be central to determining whether Google will be held financially accountable for its data collection practices, and whether jurors will accept or reject the methodologies used to quantify privacy harms in class actions.

Conclusion

The evolving landscape of privacy damages theory reflects the legal system's ongoing efforts to address the unique challenges of quantifying privacy harms in the digital age. Traditional economic approaches remain foundational but exist alongside emerging frameworks that acknowledge privacy's intrinsic value to individual autonomy, democracy, and social cohesion. As demonstrated through cases like *Brown v. Google* and *Rodriguez v. Google*, courts are becoming more receptive to innovative damage theories such as unjust enrichment and market value approaches that recognize privacy violations as independently actionable harms. These developments signal a growing judicial understanding that privacy violations warrant meaningful remedy even when directly measurable economic losses are difficult to establish.

The tension between individual harm and collective impact continues to shape privacy litigation. While privacy violations affect individuals personally, their consequences ripple through society, reinforcing power asymmetries between

95 Id. at 18.
96 Id. at 19.
97 Id.
98 Id. at 19–20.

corporations and consumers, chilling democratic participation, and undermining public trust in digital spaces. This dual nature challenges traditional notions of compensable harm and demands legal frameworks that can simultaneously address individual redress and broader deterrence. The growing recognition of privacy's value—economic, dignitary, and social—suggests that damages theories will continue evolving toward more nuanced approaches that properly account for both tangible and intangible dimensions of privacy harm. This evolution is essential not only for justice in individual cases, but also for establishing meaningful constraints on corporate surveillance practices.

PART III

Critiques, Alternative Fronts, and Future

With the history and current landscape of privacy litigation covered in Parts I and II, Part III develops further theory and praxis for successfully addressing ever-encroaching corporate surveillance, with an emphasis on "outsider" approaches to current privacy law issues.

DOI: 10.4324/9781003413349-12

9

PRIVACY, PERFORMANCE, AND POWER

Over the past decade, new critiques of privacy law have cast its practice as "performative," suggesting that formulaic compliance rituals and complicit enforcement regimes legitimize, rather than limit, corporate surveillance. Ari Waldman has led this critique, demonstrating how privacy law's reliance on notice-and-consent regimes and choreographed compliance activities often cements, rather than constrains, data-extractive business models. While recognizing the validity of much of Waldman's critique, this chapter argues that class actions remain a significant countervailing force: By aggregating dispersed harms and leveraging the adversarial power of litigation, privacy class actions can challenge exploitative data practices at scale. Contrary to suggestions that privacy litigation simply reifies the status quo, successful class litigation shows promise in holding corporate actors to account, shaping public understanding of privacy harms, and driving substantive legal reforms that transcend the boundaries of a purely performative compliance culture.

The Performative Critique of Privacy Law

In a series of influential works, Ari Waldman has developed a sweeping critique of contemporary privacy law practice, arguing that it has become a largely ceremonial exercise that serves to legitimize, rather than constrain, corporate surveillance practices.[1] Informed by ethnographic observation of privacy professionals and analysis of corporate privacy programs, Waldman contends that privacy law

1 Ari Ezra Waldman, *Privacy, Practice, and Performance*, 110 Calif. L. Rev. 1221 (2022); Ari Ezra Waldman, Industry Unbound: The Inside Story of Privacy, Data, and Corporate Power (2021); Ari Ezra Waldman, *Privacy Law's False Promise*, 97(3) Wash. Univ. L. Rev. 773–848 (2020).

DOI: 10.4324/9781003413349-13

has been reduced to a series of box-checking exercises disconnected from substantive privacy protection.[2] This performative framework manifests in several ways. First, privacy professionals engage in ritualistic practices—drafting policies, conducting assessments, implementing training programs—that create the appearance of privacy protection while having little practical effect on corporate data practices.[3] Second, the focus on individual notice and choice serves to normalize privacy-invasive practices by placing the onus on consumers to protect themselves through largely illusory mechanisms of control.[4] Finally, the emphasis on procedural compliance displaces more substantive engagement with what Waldman terms "data-extractive capitalism."[5]

Waldman's analysis draws heavily from Judith Butler's theory of performativity, which posits that identities and social categories are constituted through repeated behaviors rather than being inherent or fixed. Butler originally developed this framework in *Gender Trouble*, arguing that gender is not a stable identity but is performed through continuous, routinized acts—gestures, speech, and social norms that create the appearance of natural categories.[6] Applying this framework to privacy law, Waldman contends that privacy performances—whether in regulatory settlements, corporate compliance programs, or consumer consent mechanisms—do not merely reflect privacy norms; they actively construct and reinforce them: "Performances have the capacity to create social meaning and social categories—that is, our performances are performat*ive*."[7] The result is a legal system in which the procedural performances of privacy law displace substantive privacy protections.

To show how these performances develop legal force, Waldman invokes Lauren Edelman's work on "endogenous law," which studies how internal organizational practices reshape formal regulations from within.[8] Building on that research, Waldman illustrates that once privacy professionals and regulators adopt certain routines, such as check-the-box compliance forms or predetermined audit protocols, those routines become the de facto substance of privacy law. In other words, privacy law ceases to be externally imposed and instead emerges from the very corporate structures meant to be regulated.[9] When regulators and courts bless those structures through consent decrees or settlements, they further reinforce the idea that these practices are constitutive of privacy law.[10]

2 Id.
3 Waldman, *Privacy, Practice, and Performance*, supra n. 1. at 1241.
4 Id. at 1246.
5 Id. at 1225.
6 Judith Butler, Gender Trouble: Feminism and the Subversion of Identity 33 (1990).
7 Waldman, *Privacy, Practice, and Performance*, supra n. 1. at 1241.
8 Id. at 1229.
9 Id. at 1232; Lauren B. Edelman, Working Law 12, 22 (John M. Conley & Lynn Mather eds., 2016).
10 Id.

Waldman argues that regulators in the United States, particularly the Federal Trade Commission and state attorneys general,[11] frequently resolve privacy disputes by meeting with businesses, agreeing on self-regulatory measures, and then finalizing consent decrees.[12] These negotiated settlements repeatedly signal to businesses that internal compliance programs and standardized checklists suffice for compliance. Rather than litigating to clarify more substantive limits on data use, regulators often frame their role as *partners* in ensuring businesses maintain acceptable procedures. As these agreements accumulate, they gain expressive power, shaping the field's shared understanding of what privacy law actually is.[13]

Corporations then elaborate privacy compliance protocols, such as comprehensive privacy programs, privacy trainings, risk assessments, and data audits, that Waldman labels "managerialized compliance."[14] Although such measures can encourage some attention to privacy within organizations, they often unfold in ways that prioritize formal documentation and self-certification.[15] The repeated performance of drafting policy documents, designating privacy officers, and conducting perfunctory audits can overshadow deeper inquiry into whether the company's business model is inherently data-extractive.[16]

Waldman devotes extensive analysis to individual rights of control.[17] Contemporary privacy law, he notes, relies heavily on notice-and-consent frameworks. These frameworks assign primary responsibility to individuals to manage their own privacy through read-or-click consent forms, opt-out links, and other self-service dashboards. Waldman contends that the repeated performances of clicking "Accept" or "Agree" normalizes the presumption that privacy is exclusively an issue of self-governance.[18] Waldman shows how these three forms of performance—regulatory negotiation, corporate compliance, and user self-management—collectively push privacy law toward a "rights/compliance" model.[19] Recent legislative proposals in the United States (both at the federal and state level) instantiate the same cluster of governance tools: individual rights to access or delete data, coupled with mandated organizational compliance steps. Because these proposals mirror long-standing industry and regulatory practices, Waldman sees them not as breakthroughs but as extensions of existing routines, reifying a framework that cannot confront the threats posed by data-extractive capitalism.

11 *See* discussion of Lina Kahn and her impact on the FTC's approach to both privacy and antitrust law in Chapters 4 and 12, which largely post-dates Waldman's analysis as discussed in this chapter.
12 Waldman, *Privacy, Practice, and Performance*, supra n. 1. at 1233–1240.
13 Id.
14 Id.
15 Id. at 1242.
16 Id.
17 Id. at 1246–1251.
18 Id. at 1249.
19 Id. at 1254.

Waldman notes that while new privacy bills appear to enhance individuals' control over their data, they do little to disrupt the structures that fuel indiscriminate data exploitation. Moreover, he cautions that data-extractive firms often *weaponize* consent, pointing to user "agreements" as a shield against deeper accountability.[20] Under such a regime, the repeated performance of consent normalizes corporate surveillance practices rather than meaningfully constraining them. Waldman also faults the compliance side of the legislative equation, which he sees as performative in two main ways. First, it effectively privileges technical or procedural fixes, like privacy audits, staff trainings, and privacy impact assessments, over confronting whether certain data practices should be disallowed altogether.[21] Second, compliance can foster a professional culture inside organizations where privacy officers see themselves primarily as facilitators of data flows, so long as those flows appear lawful on paper.[22] Because enforcement agencies frequently accept these procedural measures as sufficient, companies have little incentive to recalibrate the fundamentals of their data-driven business models.

A Framework for Resistance

Waldman examines ways to reorient privacy law toward more substantial privacy protection, emphasizing that performances can be harnessed to create radically different outcomes. Building on work by philosopher André Gorz, Waldman proposes a series of "non-reformist reforms," or "non-reformist performances: practices on the ground that aim not at mere tinkering with the rights/compliance model, but rather aim at fundamentally transforming the relationship between individuals and technology companies."[23] *Non-reformist reforms* are policy changes that do not merely tweak or reinforce existing systems but instead serve as stepping stones toward deeper structural transformation. Unlike incremental "reforms" that ultimately accommodate and sustain the status quo, non-reformist reforms challenge fundamental power structures, creating conditions for more radical shifts over time.[24] Waldman applies this approach to privacy law, arguing that existing compliance mechanisms and procedural routines can be repurposed to disrupt, rather than entrench, data-extractive business models. He proposes four overlapping "non-reformist reform" strategies:

First, Waldman proposes an alternative vision of privacy law that *harnesses performativity itself* in a non-reformist reform mode—meaning, that incremental

20 Id. at 1246.
21 Id.
22 Id.
23 Id. at 1270.
24 Id.

changes can nevertheless cultivate deeper structural shifts in power.[25] Rather than discarding ritualistic practices like "privacy impact assessments" ("PIAs") or negotiated settlements, he suggests *repurposing* them so they expose and challenge the commodification of personal data.[26] For example, while current PIAs often reduce privacy to mere box-checking, a revised assessment regime might demand that companies analyze whether data collection strategies deepen systemic inequalities. Organizations could be required to evaluate, document, and publicly disclose adverse impacts on marginalized populations—thereby transforming a ritualistic performance into a tool of real accountability.

Second, since language shapes how both the public and policymakers conceive of privacy, Waldman emphasizes *changing the conversation* that frames privacy as primarily about individual choice.[27] Under the existing script, each user is expected to manage a flood of consents and disclaimers, obscuring the reality that structural forces—such as platforms' profit-driven surveillance—limit meaningful autonomy. A reformist discourse would define privacy as a collective good, one integral to social participation, equality, and democratic governance.[28] Civil society groups, scholars, and the media could highlight how low-income neighborhoods, racial minorities, and other marginalized groups disproportionately bear the brunt of surveillance. Waldman contends that these rhetorical shifts may effectuate an understanding of privacy as fundamentally bound up with questions of social justice and could be ultimately emancipatory.[29]

Third, Waldman further advocates *refocusing privacy law* on deeper power imbalances, rather than relying on industry's self-regulatory performances.[30] Currently, enforcement agencies tend to settle cases in ways that preserve data-driven business models; consent decrees require formalized checklists and cosmetic reforms but rarely restrict companies' capacity to profit from user data. Instead, Waldman calls for enforcement that foregrounds substantive constraints—banning or tightly regulating manipulative advertising and continuous behavioral tracking—rather than simply mandating more compliance paperwork.[31] To accomplish this, regulators must have real resources and legal tools. They could conduct rigorous investigations, impose meaningful fines, or bring structural injunctions that limit how data is collected and used. Moreover, policymakers should invite a broader constituency—civil rights organizations, digital labor advocates, and local communities—to shape privacy rules. By making space for

25 Id.
26 Id.
27 Id. at 1272.
28 Id.
29 Id. at 1278.
30 Id. at 1274.
31 Id.

voices that have been sidelined in industry-driven "collaboration," privacy law can shift from enabling large-scale data extraction to checking it.[32]

Lastly, Waldman contends that *democratic engagement and grassroots activism* are necessary to reshape privacy law's performative script. Historically, bottom-up pressure has been crucial in galvanizing legal and cultural change, even in domains where corporate power loomed large. Privacy activism, unionization efforts in the tech sector, and public protests against data-extractive technologies all exemplify how citizen mobilization can disrupt the normalization of surveillance.[33] Over time, such protests and grassroots campaigns may denormalize the idea that collecting and aggregating vast personal datasets is inevitable. By forcing public debate on issues such as biometric surveillance, predictive policing, and targeted disinformation, protest movements spur broader questioning of corporate data practices—exactly the kind of scrutiny that performative compliance rituals function to dampen.[34] In Waldman's account, democratic interventions have the power to rewrite privacy law's core narratives, moving it beyond the illusion of user-by-user control and toward a collective project of addressing information-age inequities.

Industry Unbound: *An Ethnographic Investigation*

In *Industry Unbound*, Waldman builds out his theory presented in *Privacy, Practice, and Performance* and presents findings from nearly four years of mixed-method research, including field observations, interviews, surveys, and analyses of internal corporate documents across a range of technology companies and start-ups.[35] He describes these efforts as an ethnographic study aimed at understanding how the "social practice" of privacy law unfolds "on the ground" within the organizational hierarchies of the information industry.[36]

Waldman's research involved extensive, on-site embedding within multiple technology companies over the course of a year, supplemented by follow-up interviews and remote observations for an additional three years. He attended product design meetings, compliance trainings, and daily "standups" to capture how privacy professionals, engineers, and legal counsel interpret and implement privacy obligations in real time. In total, he interviewed dozens of privacy professionals, lawyers, and engineers, also collecting survey data from a broader set of industry workers to corroborate his in-person findings.[37] However, as Waldman explains,

32 Id. at 1277.
33 Id. at 1278–1279.
34 Id.
35 Ari Ezra Waldman, *Industry Unbound: The Inside Story of Privacy*, Data, and Corporate Power 210–231 (2021).
36 Id. at xiv.
37 Id. at 4.

large platforms like Google and Facebook refused to permit genuine independent observation, imposing what he characterizes as "extraordinarily unethical demands," including prepublication approval of his findings and editorial control over how their statements would be quoted or paraphrased.[38] Although Waldman was thus unable to embed within these particular giants, their insistence on information control is itself revealing: The biggest data-driven companies commonly restrict outside scrutiny to protect both proprietary practices and organizational structures that enable their data-extractive practices. Through his embedded fieldwork, Waldman observed how day-to-day privacy practices often legitimize rather than constrain corporate data extraction. One particularly memorable example is that of engineers relying on laminated "yes/no" cheat sheets, where the "correct" answer was predetermined, reducing privacy considerations to a mechanical exercise, leaving no room for deeper ethical or design inquiries.[39]

Organizational Structures That Undermine Privacy

Waldman argues that the erosion of privacy within technology companies is not merely a by-product of weak enforcement or corporate negligence but rather the result of deliberate organizational design choices that normalize and entrench data-extractive practices. He describes this phenomenon as the "routinization of antiprivacy norms," in which structural arrangements, internal hierarchies, and professional incentives systematically marginalize privacy concerns.[40] Compounding this problem is the fear of professional repercussions among privacy professionals. Many individuals responsible for enforcing privacy policies internally are reluctant to challenge aggressive data collection strategies, fearing that pushing back too strongly could harm their careers, what Waldman describes as the "career trap."[41] Waldman highlights how this anxiety fosters a culture of acquiescence, where privacy professionals temper their advocacy to align with the broader business priorities of their organizations rather than acting as true internal watchdogs.[42]

Another structural issue is the late-stage involvement of privacy teams in product development. Privacy concerns are often treated as an afterthought, with privacy officers brought in only after major design decisions have been finalized. This practice severely limits their ability to implement meaningful safeguards, as many critical data-collection mechanisms are already deeply embedded into the product by the time privacy teams review them.[43]

38 *See CITP Seminar: Ari Waldman—Industry Unbound: The Inside Story of Privacy, Data, and Corporate Power*, YouTube (Mar. 15, 2024), at 9:20. www.youtube.com/watch?v=-07kW31oULk.
39 Id. at 19:30.
40 Waldman, Industry Unbound, supra n. 1 at xv.
41 Id. at 152.
42 Id.
43 Id. at 161.

Finally, deliberate fragmentation of responsibilities within organizations weakens privacy oversight. Waldman describes a pattern where legal, compliance, and engineering teams are kept deliberately siloed, preventing any one group from fully understanding or controlling how user data is handled.[44] Privacy counsel may be left unaware of the specifics of data collection, engineers may not receive guidance on compliance obligations, and privacy officers may lack the authority to make meaningful interventions while ensuring that their data-intensive business models remain largely unchallenged.

Fighting Back: Waldman's Proposed Solutions

In Chapter 6 of *Industry Unbound*, Waldman insists that data extraction stems from deliberately designed organizational structures and discursive strategies that systematically subordinate privacy. To counter such entrenched power, building on the "Framework for Resistance" discussed previously, he proposes a justice-oriented approach that treats privacy not merely as a matter of individual choice but as a vital collective resource requiring substantive legal constraints and deep social change.

A core element of Waldman's vision is to adopt a law and political economy framework, positioning privacy law as an explicit counterweight to the power of the information industry.[45] Rather than deferring to industry-friendly interpretations of "innovation," he urges policymakers to confront the structural inequalities inherent in profit-driven surveillance models. Such a shift requires replacing toothless notice-and-consent rules with strong public regulation capable of imposing meaningful guardrails on the ways in which personal data are collected and exploited. In doing so, Waldman argues that law must address the broader societal contexts—he emphasizes that pervasive surveillance disproportionately harms marginalized communities, and that privacy must be understood as an issue of civil rights and social justice rather than a narrow consumer concern.

Central to Waldman's argument is the need to transform privacy discourse.[46] Too often, the dominant rhetoric frames privacy through "consent" and "choice," focusing on individuals to the exclusion of collective welfare. By contrast, Waldman highlights the perspectives of those disproportionately affected by surveillance—such as the poor, communities of color, and LGBTQ+ groups—illustrating how data extraction can exacerbate discrimination and perpetuate structural harm. Attending to these experiences shifts the privacy conversation away from purely transactional or market-based concerns and instead situates it within questions of democracy, equality, and social liberation.

44 Id. at 147.
45 Id.
46 Id. at 234.

Waldman also calls for robust public governance that stands firmly against the forces of corporate capture.[47] Part of this entails giving regulatory agencies like the FTC not only clearer legal mandates but also an unambiguous commitment to substantive oversight. Rather than issuing consent decrees or "rules of the road" that preserve data-intensive business models, agencies should consider outright bans on surveillance technologies proven to be irredeemably invasive or discriminatory. Waldman acknowledges that conventional litigation and private rights of action can play a role—he notes their historical significance in other domains—but warns that they alone cannot deliver transformative change unless courts, legislatures, and the culture at large recognize the structural injustices behind data extraction.[48]

Implementing meaningful privacy protections further requires a reorganization of corporate structures so that privacy teams wield real influence. For Waldman, simply mandating "comprehensive privacy programs" does little if privacy professionals lack independence, resources, or authority to challenge profit-driven designs. He thus proposes granting privacy departments secure budgets, direct reporting lines to the board, and freedom from hierarchical subordination that incentivizes self-censorship.[49] Equally important is ensuring that marginalized voices have a seat at the table. Waldman envisions a regulatory process where advocacy groups representing communities most harmed by surveillance actively shape both policymaking and the design stages of technology development.

Finally, Waldman stresses the power of collective action. Waldman encourages workers—especially privacy professionals, AI researchers, and software engineers—to form alliances or unions that can support whistleblowing and resist morally suspect projects.[50] On a broader scale, civil society must see privacy as part of a wider "cyber civil rights" agenda, underscoring how discriminatory data practices erode the foundations of democratic society. Educational institutions, meanwhile, must embed ethics, social context, and critical thinking throughout technical curricula so that future engineers are prepared to recognize and oppose harmful designs rather than uncritically implementing them.

Industry Unbound links these strategies to issues such as environmental impact, warning that the surging demand for data infrastructure often goes hand in hand with ecological harm and deepening digital inequities. True accountability, Waldman suggests, will require not only a reinvigorated public sector and an empowered workforce but also a willingness to see privacy as something more than an isolated civil liberty. Instead, he casts it as a collective good, essential to the pursuit of democracy, equality, and human flourishing.[51] By emphasizing these values, Waldman hopes to move privacy debates beyond stale compliance talk and to spur

47 Id. at 239.
48 Id. at 238.
49 Id. at 242.
50 Id. at 253.
51 Id. at 236.

the kinds of bold legal and cultural reforms he believes are necessary to rein in—and eventually transform—the data-extractive status quo.

Limitations of the Performative Critique

Waldman's performativity critique provides a powerful lens through which to understand privacy law as it actually functions on the ground, and he has done an invaluable service to privacy scholarship and advocacy through his years of rolling up his sleeves and immersing himself in corporate privacy practices. Waldman shows that everyday practices, whether corporate compliance exercises, user "consent," or regulator–industry settlements, actively shape the very meaning and boundaries of privacy. This performative lens explains how well-intended procedures become empty and symbolic, illuminating why corporate data extraction often remains pervasive despite multiple layers of "compliance." Waldman also explains how narrowly focusing on individual rights and consent often perpetuates rather than constrains surveillance. This contribution, bridging theory and ethnographic practice, makes Waldman's account indispensable for anyone seeking to understand and reshape the realities of privacy law. Finally, Waldman does a particularly good job of capturing and diagnosing the false consciousness endemic among privacy professionals, including defense litigators—a trait that has been a prominent feature in privacy litigation, as Waldman highlights.[52]

However, there are limitations in Waldman's proposed solutions. His emphasis on discursive transformation and consciousness-raising, while potentially valuable, does not provide sufficient practical guidance or praxis for achieving concrete reforms. Moreover, Waldman's relative dismissal of traditional legal mechanisms, including private litigation, is questionable given the historical importance of such tools in civil rights reform. While he acknowledges the potential role of regulatory enforcement, Waldman's treatment of class actions and other private rights of action is notably limited. In Chapter 6 of *Industry Unbound*, Waldman draws parallels to product safety and environmental cases where mass tort or class litigation has pushed corporations to adopt safer designs. Yet he cautions that "[i]f we flipped the switch and allowed private rights of action today, they would not be able to bring about real change for privacy on the ground as long as existing legal doctrines favor entrenched corporate interests."[53] He points to supposedly restrictive standing requirements, judicial skepticism about intangible privacy harms, and the ease with which defendants can "fall back on industry best practices" or symbolic compliance measures to avoid structural accountability.[54] Consequently, in

52 Id. at 57.

53 Id. at 238; It is not clear what Waldman means by this turn of phrase—as demonstrated by the many cases discussed in this book, the private right of action "switch" has been flipped "on" for several decades, if not for over a century.

54 Id. at 239.

Waldman's view, private rights of action—absent a wider reorientation of privacy law to explicitly counter corporate power—risk functioning as a mere theater, as does much else in privacy law: "Opening the door to impact civil litigation would mean very little without concomitant liberality from judges in recognizing privacy harms."[55]

Perhaps most significantly, Waldman's proposals face substantial implementation challenges. The tension between Waldman's radical critique and his relatively modest and incremental proposed solutions reflects a broader challenge in privacy reform. In addition to practical challenges of implementation, the application of Butler's performativity theory to privacy law is of questionable utility in addressing substantive privacy reforms. Martha Nussbaum's scathing critique of Butler's work applies to this fundamental pillar of Waldman's framework: Nussbaum contends that Butler's emphasis on performativity risks devolving into what she terms "hip quietism"—the idea that merely subverting entrenched norms through symbolic gestures or parodic acts is itself a form of political change, even when it does not address the material and institutional dimensions of injustice.[56] According to Nussbaum, the allure of focusing on flamboyant or provocative but ultimately ineffectual "counter-performances" can distract from the real conditions under which people suffer and the need for concrete and non-symbolic resistance; as Nussbaum notes, "In Butler, resistance . . . involv[es] no unironic, organized public action for legal or institutional change."[57]

This critique is relevant to Waldman's Butlerian framework. Waldman highlights how corporate actors, regulators, and even privacy professionals enact and normalize privacy invasions. Yet if the response to these hollow rituals is to meet performance with yet more performance—such as "subverting" discursive routines with pro-privacy discourse while ignoring the trenchant and frequently effective legalized warfare litigation represents—the result can be a quietistic refusal to engage in risky but substantive attempts at structural reform. Waldman's embrace of Butler's performativity, while powerful in diagnosing privacy law's structural issues, faces this Nussbaumian challenge: How do we ensure that the acknowledgment of these performances translates into tangible outcomes for those most harmed by invasive data practices?

Beyond Nussbaum's critique, philosophers have raised more general concerns about the soundness of Butler's performativity theory that undermine its utility for privacy law reform. Sally Haslanger notes that Butler's emphasis on discursive construction and repetitive performance obscures the material reality of power structures and social hierarchies that shape lived experience—a particularly

55 Id.
56 Martha C. Nussbaum, *The Professor of Parody*, New Republic (Feb. 22, 1999). https://newrepublic.com/article/150687/professor-parody.
57 Id.

significant limitation when addressing specific concrete harms in privacy contexts.[58] Haslanger's critique suggests that Waldman's focus on Butler's performativity theory may inadvertently divert attention from immediate attempts to address the tangible institutional arrangements and economic incentives that drive privacy-invasive practices through practical, non-performative means such as taking privacy invaders to court. Similarly, scholars have long criticized postmodern approaches like Butler's for their obscurantism and lack of argumentative rigor, noting they frequently rely more on rhetorical gestures than clear arguments or evidence—baggage that is not necessary for Waldman's otherwise insightful analysis.[59] These concerns are especially relevant in the context of privacy law, where effective reform requires not just recognizing the performative nature of legal rituals but aggressively engaging with the substantive economic and doctrinal forces that incentivize surveillance capitalism through challenges in the courts.

The quietism inherent in the performativity thesis is especially apparent in Waldman's dismissal of class actions. Waldman does not categorically reject privacy class actions but is deeply skeptical that they can meaningfully unsettle entrenched corporate power under current conditions.[60] However, this critique risks ignoring the real and material impacts that class actions have had in shaping corporate behavior and legal precedent, even if they fall short of completely reforming privacy-invasive conduct. Privacy class actions, like their civil rights and products liability counterparts, have historically been a crucial vehicle for forcing disclosure, securing financial accountability, and influencing regulatory and legislative agendas.[61] Waldman himself acknowledges that private litigation has historically played a crucial role in compelling corporate accountability, citing how civil litigation in other domains has led to safer consumer products, automobile safety regulations, and environmental protections. Yet dismissing privacy class actions as hopelessly ineffectual not only disregards their impact but, ironically, also mirrors the same anti-class-action rhetoric used by corporations and industry lobbyists to weaken collective legal remedies.[62] While Waldman's ethnographic work provides valuable insight into how privacy law operates "on the ground," a framework that emphasizes discursive resistance over specific and immediate material contestation

58 Sally Haslanger, *Gender and Race: (What) Are They? (What) Do We Want Them to Be?*, 34(1) Noûs 31–55 (2000); Sally Haslanger, *Resisting Reality: Social Construction and Social Critique* (Oxford: Oxford University Press, 2012); Sally Haslnger, *Feminism in Metaphysics: Negotiating the Natural.* The Cambridge Companion to Feminism in Philosophy. Eds. M. Fricker & J. Hornsby (Cambridge: Cambridge University Press, 2000), 107–126.

59 Brian Leiter, *Why Quine Is Not a Postmodernist*, 50 SMU Law Rev. 1739 (1997); Brian Leiter, *Intellectual Voyeurism in Legal Scholarship*, 4 Yale J.L.&H. 79–104 (1992).

60 Waldman, Industry Unbound, supra n1., Chapter 6.

61 See Chapters 4–7.

62 See, for example, U.S. Chamber Inst. for Legal Reform, The New Lawsuit Ecosystem: Trends, Targets and Players 88–100 (Oct. 2013). www.instituteforlegalreform.com/research/the-new-lawsuit-ecosystem-trends-targets-and-players (discussing purportedly "abusive" privacy class actions).

may ultimately fail to support the concrete legal mechanisms required to challenge entrenched corporate power. The performativity framework's greatest value may lie not in providing a fully "emancipatory" theory of privacy law but in highlighting the mechanics through which data-extractive capitalism has been normalized. This insight can inform reform efforts while recognizing the need for additional theoretical and practical tools.

Class Actions as a Vehicle for Privacy Reform

Modern class actions took shape primarily through the 1966 amendments to Rule 23 of the Federal Rules of Civil Procedure. Although the Advisory Committee was initially concerned with clarifying the old rule's confusing categories rather than devising a broad vehicle for institutional reform,[63] courts and practitioners quickly recognized that aggregated lawsuits could expose and redress systemic, large-scale harm.[64] Class suits thus became instrumental in areas such as school desegregation and employment discrimination, providing a legal mechanism to address patterns or practices affecting entire communities.[65]

By the 1980s, a backlash emerged. The Reagan administration and some courts came to view structural injunctions in class suits as instances of judicial "overreach," asserting that such relief risked transferring essentially political decisions into the judiciary.[66] This resistance dovetailed with practical constraints on plaintiffs and mounting skepticism about the judiciary's capacity to manage broad regulatory remedies.[67] Despite these pressures, class actions persisted and even expanded into mass torts, securities fraud, and consumer claims, generating ongoing debates about whether they stretched courts' powers too far or remained vital for bottom-up law reform.[68]

Ultimately, class actions demonstrated their value in forcing transparency and accountability where legislative or administrative efforts proved insufficient. They empowered affected groups to share litigation costs, develop robust factual records through discovery, and sometimes ultimately win institutional reforms through court orders or significant settlements.[69] These same qualities underlie their potential in privacy litigation today, where diffuse but large-scale data practices call for collective remedies that single plaintiffs often cannot pursue effectively.

63 David Marcus, *The History of the Modern Class Action, Part I: Sturm und Drang, 1953–1980*, 90 Wash. U.L. Rev. 587 (2013).

64 Id. at 607.

65 Id.

66 David Marcus, *The History of the Modern Class Action, Part II: Litigation and Legitimacy, 1981–1994*, 86 Fordham L. Rev. 1785 (2018).

67 Id.

68 Id.

69 Id.

Scholarly Skepticism of Privacy Litigation

Waldman's skepticism regarding the ability of privacy class actions to bring about meaningful reform is widely echoed in the academic literature, which has long argued that private litigation is ill-equipped to address the structural realities of large-scale, data-driven business models. Scholars such as Julie Cohen and Peter Ormerod emphasize a supposed mismatch between individual, lawsuit-driven enforcement mechanisms and the networked nature of modern surveillance capitalism. Their critiques argue that privacy class actions struggle to impose meaningful constraints on corporate data practices, and that, instead, legal barriers—ranging from procedural hurdles to substantive doctrinal limitations—render privacy litigation an ineffective tool for reining in entrenched data-extractive systems.

The paradigmatic articulation of this critique is found in Julie Cohen's *Information Privacy Litigation as Bellwether for Institutional Change*, where she argues that existing legal frameworks for litigation are ill-suited to problems of mass data extraction and diffuse, collective privacy harms.[70] Most privacy class actions, she argues, never reach substantive questions about whether corporate surveillance itself is legally problematic. Instead, they collapse at threshold stages, entangled in standing disputes, causation challenges, and doctrinal uncertainty.[71] The enforcement model thus functions less as a meaningful check on surveillance-based business models and more as a periodic inconvenience—one that allows companies to treat litigation costs as mere operating expenses.

Cohen argues that even when privacy class actions survive dismissal, they often fail to alter upstream design choices that facilitate pervasive data gathering.[72] The structure of privacy litigation is largely reactive, seeking compensation for past harms rather than imposing constraints on future data extraction. Furthermore, Cohen argues, private litigants—facing high costs, unsettled doctrines, and procedural barriers—are poorly positioned to mount systemic challenges to the dominant data economy; she states that "the track record of litigation achievements on the information privacy front is stunningly poor."[73] Rather than producing transformative legal change, privacy litigation is frequently absorbed into corporate compliance structures, producing settlements that legitimize rather than disrupt surveillance-based business models. As Cohen starkly puts it, "[i]nformation privacy settlements are widely regarded as having produced almost no meaningful change in business practices relating to the collection, processing, and exchange of consumer personal information."[74]

70 Julie E. Cohen, *Information Privacy Litigation as Bellwether for Institutional Change*, 66 DePaul L. Rev. 535, 536–537 (2017).

71 Id.

72 Id. at 569–570.

73 Id. at 536.

74 Id. at 569–570.

Cohen extends this critique in *How (Not) to Write a Privacy Law*, where she argues that "discussions about both the relative and absolute efficacy of litigation-centered enforcement mechanisms reflect magical thinking about litigation's upsides."[75] She critiques contemporary privacy proposals that rely on either private rights of action or public enforcement through regulatory lawsuits, arguing that both models have "not proved especially effective at constraining Big Tech's excesses."[8] Instead, Cohen and other privacy scholars advocate for alternative governance tools, including expanded agency mandates, structural remedies such as disgorgement of profits, and direct personal liability for corporate executives.[9] These proposals reflect a consensus among many scholars that traditional litigation mechanisms—while perhaps valuable for deterrence and expressive purposes—are unlikely to serve as the primary vehicle for privacy law enforcement. Because privacy litigation "is predominantly atomistic in its identification and valuation of harms," Cohen contends, it fails to discipline networked phenomena that generate privacy harms at scale.[76]

Peter Ormerod's work echoes these concerns, arguing that privacy class actions face near-insurmountable procedural and substantive barriers. Ormerod argues that despite the proliferation of privacy laws, the tech industry remains largely unaffected by these legal regimes. Surveillance-based business models, particularly those reliant on digital advertising, have continued to thrive, generating record profits even as new privacy regulations take effect.[77] As he argues, "debates about privacy law enforcement tend to outright ignore the uncomfortable reality that neither public nor private enforcement is effective at changing much of anything"[78]

Ormerod's analysis details the structural obstacles that purportedly make privacy class actions nearly impossible to sustain. He identifies major legal chokepoints that plaintiffs must overcome before a privacy lawsuit even gets off the ground. The first major hurdle is the prevalence of adhesion contracts and forced arbitration clauses, which effectively prevent consumers from banding together in collective litigation. Even if a plaintiff avoids arbitration, broad consent provisions in terms of service often undercut privacy claims on the merits by establishing prospective consent to data collection. As Ormerod notes, "terms of service don't just compel individualized arbitration; they also attempt to require users to give broad prospective consent to information collection and use, thereby effectively disclaiming any argument that mass data harvesting constitutes injury in the first place."[79] Even if a plaintiff survives these contractual hurdles, they must then navigate Article

75 Julie E. Cohen, *How (Not) to Write a Privacy Law*, Essays on Data and Democracy. Knight First Amendment Institute at Columbia University (Mar. 23, 2021). https://knightcolumbia.org/content/how-not-to-write-a-privacy-law.

76 Id.

77 Peter Ormerod, *Privacy Qui Tam*, 98. Notre Dame L. Rev. 267 (2022).

78 Id. at 273.

79 Id. at 297.

III standing requirements. Ormerod argues that the Court's decisions in *Spokeo v. Robins* and *TransUnion v. Ramirez* have narrowed the range of cognizable privacy harms, requiring plaintiffs to demonstrate concrete and particularized injury rather than abstract or probabilistic harms. Ormerod argues that privacy claims are uniquely vulnerable to dismissal under this standard because digital privacy harms do not fit neatly within the traditional categories of tort-based injuries.[80]

Once a plaintiff overcomes standing hurdles, class certification presents yet another obstacle. Courts have applied increasingly stringent interpretations of commonality and predominance under Rule 23, making it difficult for privacy class actions to proceed. Many lower courts refuse to certify privacy classes on the basis that identifying class members is too difficult or that privacy violations are too fact-specific. Ormerod describes "an atextual consideration about whether the defendant's illegal practices are so complicated that it's too difficult to identify class members."[81] Additionally, courts have introduced heightened predominance requirements, making it difficult to litigate claims that involve individualized questions of consent, data-sharing practices, or downstream harm.

The cumulative effect of these barriers, according to Ormerod, is severe. Ormerod concludes—quoting Cohen—that "in information privacy litigation, no class claims may be maintained for monetary relief of any sort, even when the wrongdoing consists of market-wide conduct for which Congress has provided a uniform remedy."[82]

Reassessing the Viability of Privacy Class Actions

As the foregoing chapters have illustrated, the claim that privacy class actions are structurally doomed does not reflect the actual trajectory of privacy litigation over the past half-decade. The notion that private enforcement mechanisms are categorically incapable of challenging corporate surveillance has been overtaken by developments in the courts, where privacy plaintiffs have successfully navigated the very procedural hurdles that critics, including Waldman, Cohen, and Ormerod, suggest make class litigation infeasible. Far from being moribund, privacy class actions have demonstrated their viability in shaping corporate accountability, challenging exploitative data practices, and securing monetary and injunctive relief. This has been borne out in case after case where privacy plaintiffs have survived standing challenges, class certification battles, and substantive legal scrutiny. These developments demand a reassessment of the structural critiques that suggest privacy litigation is an ineffective tool for systemic reform.

80 Id. at 298–303.
81 Id. at 273.
82 Id. at 306.

Cohen's and Ormerod's critiques of privacy litigation were initially formulated at a time when privacy class actions faced substantial uncertainty, particularly in light of Supreme Court rulings that heightened standing requirements[83] and made certification of consumer claims more difficult.[84] However, these critiques fail to account for the evolution of standing jurisprudence and procedural adaptability in recent privacy cases. In the last five years, privacy class actions have repeatedly withstood these purportedly insurmountable challenges, demonstrating that they are not merely symbolic or expressive but an essential mechanism for substantive corporate accountability. While it is true that some privacy class actions have struggled to establish standing or class-wide commonality, many have not only survived but also resulted in major settlements and legal precedents. The success of privacy litigation against Meta,[85] Google,[86] and Oracle[87] described in earlier chapters—companies that epitomize the data-extractive economy—illustrates how courts are increasingly willing to recognize privacy harms as legally cognizable injuries and how procedural barriers, rather than being absolute roadblocks, can be navigated by well-crafted strategies. Collectively, these cases illustrate that privacy litigation is not merely symbolic or performative but is, in fact, a rapidly evolving and increasingly viable mechanism for holding corporations accountable.

The Promise of Privacy Class Actions

While some of the limitations identified by these scholars do present some obstacles, some of the time, private rights of action through class litigation represent an essential mechanism for addressing structural privacy harms and effecting lasting institutional change. Several considerations support this conclusion.

First, the historical experience with class actions in civil rights and other contexts demonstrates their capacity to drive fundamental social transformation. As Lauren Henry Scholz has observed, just as class litigation helped dismantle institutional segregation and challenge systematic employment discrimination, it can serve as a powerful tool for confronting entrenched practices of corporate surveillance and data exploitation.[88] Additionally, as Ignacio Cofone argues, the aggregate nature of modern privacy harms makes them particularly well-suited to class treatment; when companies implement standardized technological systems that affect large populations in similar ways, class actions provide an efficient mechanism

83 *Spokeo v. Robins*, 578 U.S. 330 (2016)
84 *Wal-Mart v. Dukes*, 564 U.S. 338 (2011).
85 See Chapter 5.
86 See Chapter 6.
87 See Chapter 7.
88 Lauren Henry Scholz, *Private Rights of Action in Privacy Law*, 63 Wm. & Mary L. Rev. 1639, 1644 (2022).

for addressing these collective injuries.[89] The aggregation of claims through the class device helps overcome the economic barriers that would make individual privacy litigation infeasible while creating meaningful pressure for institutional reform. Moreover, private litigation offers distinct advantages over purely legislative approaches to privacy protection. While legislation plays an important role, the flexibility and adaptability of common law adjudication through class actions allow courts to address novel privacy threats as they emerge. This dynamic capability is particularly crucial given the rapid pace of technological change and the tendency of legislative solutions to lag behind evolving business practices. Class actions also serve vital democratic functions in privacy protection.[90] By enabling affected individuals to directly challenge corporate practices through litigation, they provide a participatory mechanism for privacy reform that complements traditional regulatory approaches.[91] This grassroots aspect of class litigation helps ensure that privacy protections reflect the actual experiences and concerns of affected communities rather than just abstract policy crafted through backroom compromises.[92]

The argument for privacy class actions extends beyond pragmatic considerations to encompass fundamental questions about power relations. As corporate and government surveillance systems increasingly shape social and economic life, class litigation provides an essential counterweight and means for collective resistance to privacy-invasive practices that might otherwise go unchallenged. In *In Praise of Litigation*, Alexandra Lahav argues that litigation is a crucial pillar of democracy, serving as a vital tool for enforcing laws, promoting transparency, enabling public participation, and fostering social equality. Her insights are particularly relevant to privacy class actions, which function as a key mechanism for holding corporations accountable for data breaches, unauthorized data use, and systemic privacy violations.[93]

Lahav argues that litigation plays an essential role in law enforcement, particularly when regulatory agencies lack resources or political independence.[94] In the privacy context, this function is critical, as agencies like the FTC often rely on settlements rather than full adjudication, leaving many privacy violations insufficiently addressed. Class actions fill this gap by allowing affected individuals to directly enforce privacy laws, compelling companies to comply with legal standards even when regulators fail to intervene.

Transparency is another major benefit of litigation that Lahav highlights, particularly through the discovery process.[95] Many corporate data practices remain

89 Ignacio Cofone, The Privacy Fallacy: Harm and Protection in the Information Economy (2024) at 159.
90 See Alexandra Lahav, In Praise of Litigation (2017).
91 Id.
92 Id.
93 Id.
94 Id. at 8.
95 Id.

opaque, shielded from public scrutiny by complex terms of service and trade secret protections. Class actions have the power to uncover these hidden practices, shedding light on how companies collect, process, and monetize personal information. This transparency not only informs consumers but also helps shape regulatory reforms and industry standards by exposing previously undisclosed privacy risks.

Lahav also emphasizes litigation's role in public participation, arguing that it provides individuals with a direct avenue for asserting their rights and influencing legal and corporate norms.[96] In privacy class actions, consumers who might otherwise have no individual leverage against major tech companies can collectively seek redress, ensuring that their voices are heard. This participatory function is particularly important in data privacy cases, where individual users often feel powerless against vast corporate data ecosystems.

Finally, social equality is a core value that litigation helps uphold.[97] Large-scale data privacy violations disproportionately harm marginalized communities, yet legislative and regulatory responses often prioritize industry preferences over progressive social protections. Class actions allow individuals, regardless of their economic status, to challenge powerful corporations and demand accountability. In doing so, they help balance the scales of justice, ensuring that privacy protections are not reserved for those with the means to navigate complex legal systems. Lahav's defense of litigation underscores its essential role in protecting privacy rights and democratic accountability. Rather than viewing privacy class actions as a burden on the legal system, her framework suggests that they are a necessary and powerful tool for enforcing privacy laws, promoting corporate responsibility, and empowering individuals in the digital age.

In *The Privacy Fallacy,* Ignacio Cofone addresses class litigation in the privacy context. He contends that privacy laws will remain ineffective unless they recognize the structural and relational nature of digital data harms.[98] In his view, corporations often profit from aggregated information in ways that create dispersed, intangible, or hard-to-measure injuries to consumers. Such injuries seldom lend themselves to straightforward individual lawsuits. Cofone therefore advocates for a "harm-based liability" framework that emphasizes class actions and collective redress.[99]

Cofone points out that collective procedures help remedy the persistent underenforcement problem plaguing privacy law. Many privacy injuries—such as data misuse, inferred profiling, or unauthorized downstream sharing—are neither obvious nor easily traceable to specific defendants by single plaintiffs. Class actions provide procedural economies of scale, reducing litigation costs and enabling counsel to

96 Id. at 6.
97 Id. at 7.
98 Ignacio Cofone, The Privacy Fallacy: Harm and Protection in the Information Economy (2024).
99 Id. at 160.

aggregate claims that would otherwise be too small or complex to litigate individually.[100] Cofone further argues that class-wide litigation is crucial to address the systemic power asymmetry between big data Goliaths and slingshot-wielding citizens. Class actions, combined with statutory damages or other remedies, can impose the kind of financial and reputational costs that create meaningful corporate accountability. Cofone thus frames collective redress not merely as a procedural convenience but as a structural counterweight to industry power, capable of setting substantive standards for acceptable data practices.[101] Finally, Cofone underscores that privacy harms, especially those arising from large-scale analytics or AI-driven profiling, frequently manifest as relational harms that affect entire groups (e.g., residents of a certain region, racial minorities, or vulnerable communities). He proposes that broad-based representative actions are well-suited to tackle these relational harms, which often transcend individual claims and require a more holistic form of legal redress.[102]

Taken together, these arguments make a powerful case for the efficacy of class litigation in privacy law enforcement. Collective legal actions can both deter pernicious data practices and supply redress mechanisms that reflect the true scope and seriousness of privacy harms. As Cofone notes, this approach shifts the focus from illusory "choice" and privatized remedies to a framework that directly confronts aggregated injuries and leverages collective power to reshape digital surveillance norms.[103]

The skepticism of privacy class actions expressed by scholars ironically (but no doubt inadvertently) echoes long-standing attempts to undermine civil rights and products liability class actions. Over the decades, critics of these collective legal mechanisms have repeatedly framed class litigation as impractical, legally untenable, or structurally unsound. However, just as civil rights and consumer protection class actions ultimately overcame these critiques to become essential tools of enforcement, privacy class actions are poised to follow a similar trajectory. A notable historical parallel is products liability class action litigation, which was initially met with fierce resistance from corporate defendants and industry groups. The US Chamber of Commerce and other corporate lobbying groups worked aggressively to limit products liability class actions, warning that they would lead to economic ruin and stifle innovation.[104] Yet over time, courts recognized that large-scale corporate misconduct—whether through defective pharmaceuticals, asbestos exposure, or unsafe consumer goods—necessitated an equally large-scale legal response.[105]

100 Id.
101 Id. at 162.
102 Id. at 51.
103 Id. at 164.
104 Brian Fitzpatrick, The Conservative Case for Class Actions (2019) at 78–81.
105 Id.

Products liability class actions ultimately forced corporations to improve safety standards and provided financial compensation to victims of widespread harm.

Dismissing privacy class actions as structurally unworkable plays directly into the hands of the Chamber. The Chamber has been a vocal opponent of private rights of action in privacy law, arguing that such lawsuits will lead to excessive litigation and economic harm.[106] However, as Brian T. Fitzpatrick details in *The Conservative Case for Class Actions*, the Chamber's opposition is rooted not in legal principle but in corporate self-interest: Class actions are one of the few mechanisms that effectively deter corporate misconduct.[107] Companies' obsessive fear of and focus on private rights of action in any newly proposed privacy legislation exemplifies this.[108] The Chamber's efforts in the privacy litigation sphere mirror its past campaigns against consumer protection class actions, where it sought to limit individuals' ability to hold corporations accountable.

The history of civil rights and products liability class actions demonstrates that courts can, and often do, adapt to new forms of harm—whether that harm arises from segregationist policies, unsafe consumer products, or exploitative data practices. Legal frameworks evolve to meet contemporary challenges, and procedural obstacles that once seemed insurmountable can be addressed through shifts in legal interpretation, statutory adjustments, and judicial willingness to engage with complex harms. Just as systemic racial discrimination and mass consumer endangerment eventually found paths to collective redress, so too do systemic privacy violations. The argument that privacy class actions are structurally unworkable echoes outdated and unbalanced critiques that history has repeatedly discredited.

Advantages Over Legislative Solutions

Scholars, pundits, and even privacy advocates frequently reflexively revert to demands for new legislation to address emerging encroachments on privacy rights. But class litigation offers several distinct advantages over purely legislative approaches that make them preferable to legislative adaptations.

Adaptability to Technological Change

Class actions demonstrate particular strength in their ability to respond dynamically to evolving technologies and business practices. Unlike legislation, which can quickly become outdated as technology advances, common-law adjudication

106 See, for example, U.S. Chamber Institute for Legal Reform, *Ill-Suited: Private Rights of Action and Privacy Claims* (Jul. 2019). https://instituteforlegalreform.com/wp-content/uploads/2020/10/Ill-Suited_-_Private_RIghts_of_Action_and_Privacy_Claims_Report.pdf.

107 Id.

108 See, for example, U.S. Chamber Institute for Legal Reform, "Ill-Suited: Private Rights of Action and Privacy Claims," *supra*.

through class actions allows courts to apply established privacy principles to novel situations as they arise.[109] This adaptability is especially crucial in the privacy context, where technological change often outpaces legislative responses. The history of privacy legislation illustrates this challenge. As Waldman notes, even relatively recent privacy laws like the GDPR and CCPA struggle to keep pace with rapidly evolving data practices.[110] By contrast, class actions can address new privacy threats as they emerge. Courts can interpret existing legal frameworks to address novel privacy violations, developing doctrine through case-by-case adjudication.

Addressing Regulatory Resource Constraints

Private enforcement through class actions helps overcome the severe resource constraints that limit regulatory oversight of privacy practices. As discussed in prior chapters, the Federal Trade Commission's limited resources and settlement-focused approach have resulted in what Waldman has identified as largely "expressive" outcomes.[111] Class actions provide a crucial supplementary enforcement mechanism that does not depend on agency resources or political will. This advantage becomes particularly apparent when examining the FTC's privacy enforcement record. As Waldman noted (as of 2021), "only three of the FTC's reported 271 privacy and security enforcement actions since 1998 ended in a judicial opinion from a federal court."[112] The rest concluded in settlements that often lack meaningful teeth. Class actions can fill this enforcement gap by enabling more rigorous testing of privacy practices through adversarial litigation. While Lina Khan's recent track record of aggressive privacy enforcement is admirable, it seems likely that under the next administration, there will be little to no meaningful federal enforcement of privacy rights against the tech industry.

Empowering Affected Individuals

Class actions provide a unique mechanism for directly affected individuals to shape privacy protections. While legislative and regulatory processes often privilege industry voices, class actions enable individuals whose privacy has been violated to participate directly in determining appropriate remedies. This participatory aspect has special importance in the privacy context, where marginalized communities often bear disproportionate privacy harms. For example, in *Brooks v. Thomson Reuters*, Cat Brooks (a Black activist and co-founder of the Anti Police-Terror Project) and Rasheed Shabazz (a Black journalist and activist)

109 Daniel J. Solove & Woodrow Hartzog, *The FTC and the New Common Law of Privacy*, 114 Colum. L. Rev. 583 (2014).
110 Waldman, *Privacy, Practice, and Performance*, supra n. 1.
111 Id.
112 Id. at 1236.

challenged the company's collection and sale of their personal information to law enforcement through its CLEAR database, illustrating how class actions empower marginalized groups to address surveillance practices that disproportionately affect their communities.[113] Class actions can amplify these voices in ways that legislative processes, vulnerable to capture by powerful interests, may not. The class action mechanism allows affected communities to challenge privacy-invasive practices directly, rather than depending on legislative or regulatory intervention.

Development of Privacy Law Through Judicial Interpretation

Class action litigation plays a crucial role in developing privacy law through judicial interpretation of both statutory and common-law rights. This process helps give concrete meaning to abstract privacy principles and establishes precedent that can guide future conduct. The adversarial process of litigation often produces more nuanced and practically grounded interpretations than legislative pronouncements alone.[114] Moreover, the development of privacy law through class litigation can inform subsequent legislative efforts. As courts grapple with specific privacy challenges through class actions, their decisions help identify areas where legislative intervention may be needed while providing practical experience with different approaches to privacy protection.

Creating Meaningful Deterrence

Class actions create more effective deterrence than many legislative solutions because they directly impact corporate bottom lines. While statutory penalties may be viewed simply as a cost of doing business, the potential for large-scale class liability creates stronger incentives for companies to take privacy seriously. This economic reality helps explain why many companies strongly oppose private rights of action in privacy legislation.[115] The class action mechanism also allows for more precise calibration of penalties to violations than typical legislative schemes, as courts can consider factors like willfulness, scope of harm, and potential deterrent effect in crafting remedies.[116]

113 See Chapter 7.

114 Daniel J. Solove & Woodrow Hartzog, *The FTC and the New Common Law of Privacy*, 114 Colum. L. Rev. 583 (2014).

115 See, for example, U.S. Chamber of Commerce, *U.S. Chamber Warns It Will Oppose Any Privacy Legislation That Creates a Blanket Private Right of Action*, U.S. Chamber of Com. (May 31, 2022). www.uschamber.com/technology/data-privacy/u-s-chamber-warns-it-will-oppose-any-privacy-legislation-that-creates-a-blanket-private-right-of-action.

116 See Chapter 8.

Conclusion

Recognizing class actions' distinct advantages over purely legislative solutions highlights their essential role in privacy reform. Rather than viewing them as mere supplements to legislation, class actions should be understood as vital mechanisms for developing and enforcing privacy rights.[117] While the performative critique provides deep insight into the nature of privacy law on the ground, it does not support abandoning powerful legal mechanisms like class litigation that can help achieve meaningful privacy reform. Rather than resigning themselves to a critique of privacy law as pure performance through and through—a hermeneutic circle that can never be escaped—privacy advocates would do well to fight the good but unpleasant fight using the democracy-fortifying mechanisms of litigation.

117 Lauren Henry Scholz, *Private Rights of Action in Privacy Law*, 63 Wm. & Mary L. Rev. 1639, 1644 (2022).

10

INTERNATIONAL PRIVACY

The Fight for Digital Sovereignty

Chapter 9 interrogated scholarly skepticism regarding private litigation's efficacy in reshaping corporate data practices and challenging entrenched power structures. The *Schrems* litigation provides a singularly compelling counterargument to such skepticism, demonstrating that strategic legal action brought by private individuals can dismantle major data transfer frameworks and compel both corporations and governments to reconsider their surveillance and data-handling policies. The *Schrems* cases illustrate how persistent legal challenges can drive meaningful regulatory and judicial interventions, reinforcing privacy rights on a global scale. This chapter builds out this perspective by shifting the focus from domestic privacy disputes to the broader struggle for digital sovereignty in the European Union. The success of the *Schrems* litigation in European courts not only disrupted transatlantic data flow practices but also forced a re-evaluation of international agreements and legal standards. This chapter examines how these legal challenges have reshaped the global privacy landscape, challenging the notion that private litigation is an ineffective tool for systemic reform.

The fundamental tension between surveillance and human rights has defined the modern privacy law landscape in the European Union. As technology has evolved from punch cards to cloud computing, the methods of collecting and processing personal data have become increasingly sophisticated yet the underlying power dynamics remain markedly similar. This chapter examines how European privacy law, particularly through the General Data Protection Regulation (GDPR) and subsequent court decisions, has emerged as a vital counterweight to both government surveillance and corporate data practices that threaten individual privacy rights. The struggle for privacy rights in the digital age cannot be understood without examining its historical antecedents. The systematic aggregation and abuse of personal data during World War II, followed by decades of authoritarian surveillance

DOI: 10.4324/9781003413349-14

in East Germany, created a uniquely European perspective on privacy as a fundamental human right. This foundation continues to influence modern privacy law and shape current debates about digital sovereignty.

Historical Background of European Privacy Law

The origins of European privacy law are inextricably linked to the darkest chapter of 20th-century history. During the 1930s, the Nazi regime implemented a comprehensive system of population surveillance and control that relied heavily on automated data processing technology. At the heart of this system was IBM's German subsidiary, Deutsche Hollerith-Maschinen Gesellschaft (Dehomag), which provided the punch card technology and technical expertise necessary for processing vast amounts of personal data.[1] The collaboration between the Nazi regime and IBM exemplifies how seemingly neutral data aggregation technologies can become powerful tools for atrocities when proper safeguards are absent. A particularly vivid illustration of this relationship can be found in a 1934 Dehomag advertisement that proudly proclaimed, "See everything with Hollerith punchcards," explicitly marketing the company's ability to enable mass surveillance and population control.[2] The Nazi regime's use of punch card technology for identifying and targeting Jews and other persecuted groups was highly sophisticated for its time. Census workers collected detailed information about individuals' religious affiliations, ethnic backgrounds, and family histories. This data was then processed using Hollerith machines, creating a comprehensive system of population surveillance that facilitated the implementation of genocidal policies.[3]

The partition of Germany after World War II starkly illustrated how such state surveillance could persist and evolve in new political contexts. In East Germany, the Ministry for State Security (Stasi) developed one of the most pervasive surveillance systems in history. The Stasi maintained detailed files on millions of citizens, monitoring their personal relationships, conversations, and daily activities. This systematic invasion of privacy is a prototypical exemplar of how mass data aggregation and analysis facilitate authoritarian control.[4] West Germany's response to this legacy of surveillance and oppression was to become a pioneer in privacy protection. In 1970, the state of Hesse enacted what is widely considered the world's first modern data protection law. This groundbreaking legislation established basic principles for the protection of personal information that would later

1 E. Black, IBM and the Holocaust: The Strategic Alliance Between Nazi German and America's Most Powerful Corporations (New York: Crown Publishers, 2012).

2 Id.

3 Id.

4 Elizabeth M. Renieris, *Beyond Data: Reclaiming Human Rights at the Dawn of the Metaverse* (The MIT Press, 2023).

influence privacy laws throughout Europe and beyond.[5] A central moment in the development of German privacy law was the 1983 Census Case, in which the German Federal Constitutional Court recognized a fundamental right to "informational self-determination."[6] This right was derived from the constitutional protection of human dignity and the right to free development of personality. The court's decision established that individuals should have control over their personal information and that any limitations on this right must be justified by compelling public interests.[7]

The GDPR Framework

The General Data Protection Regulation (GDPR) emerges from a distinctly European understanding of data protection as a fundamental human right—one that is related to, but separate from, the right to privacy. This foundation distinguishes the European approach from other global privacy frameworks and provides the normative basis for the GDPR's comprehensive protections. Understanding this foundation requires examining both how data protection differs from privacy and how fundamental rights operate in the EU legal context. While both US and EU laws protect privacy and personal data, they do so in markedly different ways. US privacy law has historically focused on protecting individuals from the dissemination of harmful information or particularly intrusive data collection.[8] This framework emphasizes restrictions on information flows; the Fourth Amendment and privacy torts exemplify this approach by focusing on "reasonable expectations of privacy" and intrusions into private spheres.[9]

Data protection, by contrast, follows personal data wherever it goes, establishing processes and transparency requirements that channel and constrain power rather than focusing on blocking information flows. As Jones and Kaminski explain, data protection operates through "rules of the game" for processing data rather than categorical prohibitions.[10] The EU explicitly protects both privacy (Article 7: "Everyone has the right to respect for his or her private and family life, home and communications") and data protection (Article 8: "Everyone has the right to the protection of personal data concerning him or her") as distinct fundamental rights in its Charter of Fundamental Rights.[11] While privacy creates zones of opacity

5 M.L. Jones & M.E. Kaminski, *An American's Guide to the GDPR*, 98(1) Denver L. Rev. (2020).
6 BVerfGE, 65 (1983), 1.
7 Id.
8 M.L. Jones & M.E. Kaminski, *An American's Guide to the GDPR*. 98(1) Denver Law Review (2020).
9 D.J. Solove, Understanding Privacy (Harvard University Press, 2008), 12–13.
10 Jones & Kaminski.
11 Charter of Fundamental Rights of the European Union [2012] OJ C326/391.

that can alter power relations,[12] data protection creates zones of transparency that foster accountability.

The fundamental rights foundation of EU data protection has several important implications. First, these rights create positive obligations to ensure protection, not just negative restrictions on state action, as in US constitutional law.[13] The GDPR operationalizes these positive obligations through detailed requirements on both public and private entities that process personal data. Second, data protection rights in the EU are not absolute but rather subject to a structured form of balancing that weighs rights against other legitimate interests. The GDPR reflects this through provisions allowing data processing when necessary for various legitimate purposes, while still requiring appropriate safeguards.[14] Third, the fundamental rights foundation means that courts, particularly the Court of Justice of the European Union (CJEU), play a crucial role in interpreting and enforcing data protection requirements. As described in what follows, the CJEU has repeatedly invalidated data transfer mechanisms that fail to adequately protect EU data subjects' fundamental rights.

The GDPR implements these fundamental rights through a hybrid system of individual rights and systemic safeguards. Individual rights, like access, correction, and erasure, give data subjects direct control over their personal information.[15] However, the GDPR does not rely solely on individual action; it also requires organizations to implement privacy by design, conduct impact assessments, and establish data protection officers.[16] This combination of individual and systemic protections reflects the fundamental rights foundation by both empowering individuals and creating institutional accountability. The GDPR is not primarily about individual consent or control but rather about ensuring comprehensive protection of fundamental rights through multiple complementary mechanisms.[17] The fundamental rights foundation also explains key differences between the GDPR and US privacy laws. Where US laws take a sectoral approach focused on specific industries or types of data, the GDPR provides comprehensive protection following personal data across contexts. Where US laws emphasize notice and consent, the GDPR creates substantive obligations that exist regardless of individual awareness or action.[18]

12 See Chapter 1.

13 J.F. Akandji-Kombe, *Positive Obligations under the European Convention on Human Rights*. Council of Europe Human Rights Handbooks (2007).

14 GDPR, Article 6(1)(f) and Recital 47.

15 GDPR, Articles 15–20.

16 GDPR, Articles 25, 35, 37–39.

17 Gabriela Zahfir-Fortuna, *10 Reasons Why the GDPR Is the Opposite of a "Notice and Consent" Type of Law*, Future of Privacy Forum (Sept. 13, 2019). https://fpf.org/2019/09/13/10-reasons-why-the-gdpr-is-the-opposite-of-a-notice-and-consent-type-of-law/.

18 Jones & Kaminski at 106–108.

Key Concepts and Structure of the GDPR Framework

The GDPR establishes a complex ecosystem of rights, obligations, and oversight mechanisms through the interaction of four primary actors. Understanding these roles and their interrelationships is necessary for comprehending how the regulation functions in practice. As the European Data Protection Board has noted, the GDPR creates an interlocking system of responsibilities designed to ensure effective protection of personal data in an increasingly complex digital environment.[19]

The GDPR's foundational category comprises *data subjects*—natural persons whose personal data falls within the regulation's scope. The definition of *personal data* is intentionally broad, encompassing "any information relating to an identified or identifiable natural person."[20] This expansive interpretation reflects the regulation's protective purpose and stands in contrast to more limited definitions found in other privacy frameworks. *Controllers* occupy a central position in the GDPR's structure, bearing primary responsibility for ensuring compliant data processing. Article 4(7) defines *controllers* as entities that "determin[e] the purposes and means of processing personal data." This role carries significant obligations, including implementing appropriate technical and organizational measures to ensure compliance. The European Data Protection Board emphasizes that the concept of controller is functional, focusing on who exercises factual influence over the processing purposes and means, rather than on formal designations.[21] *Processors* act on behalf of controllers, processing personal data according to their instructions. This relationship must be governed by a contract that sets out specific obligations under Article 28. The distinction between controllers and processors has become increasingly significant—and often controversial—in modern data processing arrangements, particularly as digital services create complex processing chains that challenge traditional concepts of controllership.[22] *Data protection authorities* serve as the regulatory cornerstone of the GDPR framework. These independent supervisory authorities possess broad investigative and corrective powers, including the ability to impose substantial fines. Their independence is constitutionally guaranteed by Article 8(3) of the Charter of Fundamental Rights and further reinforced by GDPR Article 52.

The GDPR grants data subjects an extensive set of rights. The right of access enables individuals to obtain confirmation of whether their data is being processed and allows individuals to exercise their other data protection rights effectively.[23]

19 European Data Protection Board, Guidelines 07/2020 on the concepts of controller and processor in the GDPR.

20 GDPR, Art. 4.

21 European Data Protection Board, Guidelines 07/2020 on the concepts of controller and processor in the GDPR.

22 Opinion of Advocate General Bobek in Case C-40/17 Fashion ID GmbH & Co. KG v Verbraucherzentrale NRW eV [2019] ECLI:EU:C:2019:629.

23 European Data Protection Board, Guidelines 01/2022 on data subject rights—Right of access.

Data portability, introduced as a novel right in Article 20, requires controllers to provide personal data in a structured, commonly used, and machine-readable format. This requirement facilitates data transfer between service providers, serving both data protection and competition policy objectives. The regulation also establishes rights to rectification, erasure ("right to be forgotten"), and restrictions on processing. The GDPR's accountability principle underpins this entire system. Article 5(2) requires controllers to demonstrate compliance with the regulation's principles, moving beyond mere formal compliance. While the GDPR's conceptual framework is sophisticated and ambitious, its practical application often requires difficult judgments about the scope of obligations and the balancing of rights. Nevertheless, this framework has proven influential globally, with many jurisdictions adopting similar structural elements in their own privacy legislation.

The *Schrems II* Decision

Background and Context

The *Schrems II* case represents the ongoing tension between EU privacy rights and US surveillance practices. The case began with a complaint by Max Schrems, an Austrian privacy advocate and lawyer who challenged Facebook's transfer of European users' personal data to servers in the United States. Schrems' initial complaint, filed with the Irish Data Protection Commissioner in 2013, was sparked by Edward Snowden's revelations about the scope of US surveillance programs.[24] The case's significance extends far beyond the specific challenge to Facebook's practices, and fundamentally questioned the compatibility of US surveillance law with European fundamental rights.

The central issue in the litigation concerned whether US legal frameworks, particularly Section 702 of the Foreign Intelligence Surveillance Act (FISA) and Executive Order 12333, could provide adequate protection for EU citizens' data rights. The Snowden disclosures had revealed the existence of programs like PRISM and upstream collection, which enabled bulk surveillance of non-US persons with minimal judicial oversight.[25] Schrems argued that US surveillance practices did not provide adequate protection for EU citizens' data and that the Irish DPC should suspend Facebook's data transfers to the United States under the "Safe Harbor" framework. The "Safe Harbor" was a data privacy framework established in 2000 that governed transatlantic data flows between the European Union and the United States.[26] It provided American companies with a streamlined method to purport to comply with the EU's Data Protection Directive while transferring and processing

24 See Case C-362/14, Maximillian Schrems v Data Protection Commissioner, ECLI:EU:C:2015:650 (2015).

25 See Chapter 2.

26 Commission Decision 2000/520/EC, 2000 O.J. (L 215) 7 (EC).

European citizens' personal data. Under this agreement, US companies could self-certify their compliance with seven core privacy principles: notice, choice, onward transfer limitations, security, data integrity, access, and enforcement.[27] These principles were designed to allow EU citizens to retain rights regarding how their personal information was handled, including transparency about data collection, the ability to opt out of certain processing activities, and access to their stored information. The framework purported to create a legal basis for data transfers that would otherwise have been prohibited under EU law.[28]

The case was eventually referred to the Court of Justice of the European Union (CJEU), which in a 2015 ruling (*Schrems I*) invalidated the Safe Harbor agreement, finding that US law failed to ensure "a level of protection of fundamental rights essentially equivalent to that guaranteed in the EU legal order" under the Charter of Fundamental Rights of the European Union:

> In particular, [US] legislation permitting the public authorities to have access on a generalised basis to the content of electronic communications must be regarded as compromising the essence of the fundamental right to respect for private life, as guaranteed by Article 7 of the Charter.[29]

Adoption of the GDPR and the Privacy Shield Framework

In response to the *Schrems I* decision, the European Commission and the US government sought to address the deficiencies of the Safe Harbor framework by negotiating a new transatlantic data transfer mechanism, the EU–US Privacy Shield, which came into effect in 2016.[30] The Privacy Shield introduced additional obligations on US companies receiving European data, as well as new oversight mechanisms, including an ombudsperson designed to handle EU citizens' complaints about potential US government surveillance.[31] However, even as this framework was implemented, concerns arose regarding its ability to fully comply with European privacy standards.

At the same time, the European Union significantly strengthened its data protection regime with the passage of the GDPR in 2016, which became enforceable in May 2018. The GDPR not only established comprehensive protections for

27 U.S. Dep't of Com., Safe Harbor Privacy Principles (July 21, 2000). https://web.archive.org/web/20150910081543/http://export.gov/safeharbor/eu/eg_main_018475.asp.

28 Id.

29 Case C-362/14, Maximillian Schrems v. Data Prot. Comm'r, ECLI:EU:C:2015:650 (Oct. 6, 2015).

30 European Commission. (2016, July 12). Commission Implementing Decision (EU) 2016/1250 of 12 July 2016 pursuant to Directive 95/46/EC of the European Parliament and of the Council on the adequacy of the protection provided by the EU-U.S. Privacy Shield.

31 U.S. Department of Commerce & European Commission. (2016). EU-U.S. Privacy Shield Framework Principles. Retrieved from U.S. Department of Commerce. Section II.1.d "Independent Recourse Mechanisms" and Annex A "EU-U.S. Privacy Shield Ombudsperson Mechanism."

personal data but also introduced strict requirements for international data transfers to ensure that EU citizens' information remained secure, regardless of where it was processed. Central to this framework was Article 45, which sets out the conditions under which personal data may be transferred to third countries.[32] Under Article 45, personal data may be transferred from the EU to a third country, a territory, or an international organization only if the European Commission formally determines that the recipient ensures an adequate level of data protection. This means that data transfers can occur freely—without the need for additional safeguards, such as "Standard Contractual Clauses"—so long as the Commission has issued an adequacy decision in favor of the destination country.[33]

To assess whether a country provides an "essentially equivalent" level of protection to that guaranteed in the EU, the Commission considers a range of factors. These include the rule of law, respect for fundamental rights and freedoms, the existence of independent data protection authorities, and the effectiveness of legal remedies available to individuals.[34] A particularly significant aspect of this evaluation is whether the receiving country's government has access to personal data and, if so, whether such access is limited by principles of necessity and proportionality.[35] Adequacy decisions are not permanent; Article 45 requires the Commission to periodically review its findings, at least every four years, to ensure that the country continues to uphold the necessary data protection standards. If at any point a country's legal framework is found to no longer meet EU standards, the Commission can revoke the adequacy decision, effectively prohibiting further data transfers, unless alternative legal mechanisms are put in place.[36] The decision-making process is not unilateral—before issuing an adequacy determination, the Commission must consult with the European Data Protection Board (EDPB) and obtain agreement from EU member states. For businesses and organizations, an adequacy decision simplifies the legal requirements for data transfers; companies in the EU can transfer personal data to an entity in an adequate country without the need for additional contractual safeguards or risk assessments. However, if a country loses its adequacy status, companies must find alternative legal bases for continuing such transfers.

Issues Addressed in Schrems II

The *Schrems II* decision was driven by the requirements laid out in Article 45. When the European Commission granted the United States an adequacy decision

32 Art. 45 GDPR.

33 Id.

34 Court of Justice of the European Union. (2015, October 6). Case C-362/14, Maximillian Schrems v. Data Protection Commissioner (Schrems I), ECLI:EU:C:2015:650, paragraphs 73–74.

35 Id. para. 168–185.

36 *Data Prot. Comm'r v. Facebook Ireland Ltd. & Maximillian Schrems* (Schrems II), Case C-311/18, ECLI:EU:C:2020:559, ¶¶ 1–202 (July 16, 2020).

under the Privacy Shield framework, it did so based on the premise that the United States provided sufficient legal protections for EU citizens' personal data. However, the CJEU ultimately found that US surveillance laws—particularly Section 702 of FISA and Executive Order 12333—did not provide safeguards equivalent to those required under EU law.[37] One of the most critical shortcomings identified by the Court was the lack of an independent and effective judicial redress mechanism for EU citizens whose data was collected by US intelligence agencies.[38] The Privacy Shield's ombudsperson mechanism, designed to handle complaints about US government surveillance, was deemed insufficient, as it lacked both independence and the ability to issue binding decisions. Since this fell short of the "effective judicial protection" required under Article 45 and the EU Charter of Fundamental Rights, the Court concluded that the Privacy Shield failed to meet the adequacy standard—leading to its invalidation in 2020.[39]

The *Schrems II* case revisited many of the fundamental concerns that had led to the downfall of the Safe Harbor framework just a few years earlier. At its core, the case asked whether the Privacy Shield framework and "Standard Contractual Clauses" (SCCs) offered sufficient protection for the personal data of EU citizens when transferred to the United States under GDPR Article 46(1). SCCs are pre-approved contractual agreements between data exporters and importers that impose binding obligations on the recipient to ensure that transferred data is handled in accordance with EU privacy standards, even when sent to countries without an adequacy decision. However, SCCs have been criticized as a weak and burdensome solution, arguing that they merely shift the responsibility for ensuring data protection onto companies rather than providing systemic safeguards, leaving businesses in a legally uncertain position when transferring data to the United States.[40] This inquiry required the CJEU to examine not only the legal structure of these mechanisms but also their practical effectiveness in safeguarding privacy rights.

A major point of contention was the adequacy of US surveillance protections in light of FISA Section 702 and Executive Order 12333, which authorize broad intelligence-gathering on non-US persons. The lack of judicial oversight and the expansive nature of these surveillance programs raised serious concerns about whether EU citizens' data could be protected from indiscriminate collection by US intelligence agencies.[41] The Court also scrutinized the Privacy Shield's ombudsperson mechanism, which was intended to provide EU citizens with a means of challenging

37 Id.
38 Id.
39 Id.
40 L. Bradford, M. Aboy & K. Liddell, *International Transfers of Health Data between the EU and USA: A Sector-Specific Approach for the USA to Ensure an 'Adequate' Level of Protection*. 7(1) J. Law Biosci. lsaa055, 1–19 (2020).
41 Data Protection Commissioner v. Facebook Ireland and Maximillian Schrems (Case C-311/18), ECLI:EU:C:2020:559 (2020).

US government access to their data. Unlike the independent and enforceable judicial remedies required under EU law, however, the Ombudsperson lacked the authority to issue binding decisions, making it an inadequate safeguard against disproportionate government surveillance.[42]

Beyond Privacy Shield, the CJEU also examined the role of SCCs in ensuring compliance with EU data protection standards. While SCCs had long been used as a fallback mechanism for international transfers, the Court questioned whether companies relying on them had a legal duty to assess whether the recipient country's legal framework provided sufficient protection before transferring data. This raised broader concerns about whether private contractual agreements could ever fully mitigate the risks posed by foreign government surveillance.[43]

The Court's Analysis

Ultimately, in its 2020 decision, the CJEU invalidated the Privacy Shield framework, concluding that it failed to provide adequate safeguards for EU citizens' rights.[44] However, the Court upheld the validity of SCCs, albeit with significantly stricter requirements—companies using SCCs now bore the burden of ensuring that transferred data remained adequately protected, taking into account the specific legal environment of the receiving country. This ruling reshaped the landscape of transatlantic data flows, forcing organizations to rethink their approach to international data transfers in a world where reliance on US legal frameworks was no longer sufficient, and in essence making data transfers to the United States illegal in the absence of any adequacy decision.

The Court's decision rested on two fundamental pillars: the scope of US surveillance powers and the adequacy of redress mechanisms available to EU citizens. Regarding surveillance powers, the Court found that US programs authorized by Section 702 FISA failed to meet the European standard of proportionality.[45] The Court was particularly troubled by the broad scope of collection permitted under PRISM and upstream surveillance programs, which allowed intelligence agencies to access personal data without demonstrating individualized suspicion. This wholesale approach to surveillance directly contradicted the European principle that interference with fundamental rights must be limited to what is strictly necessary in a democratic society.[46] The Court's analysis of redress mechanisms was equally damning. The Privacy Shield framework had attempted to address earlier criticisms by creating an ombudsperson mechanism within the US State Department. However, the Court found this solution fundamentally inadequate, noting

42 Id.
43 Id.
44 Id.
45 Id.
46 Id.

that the ombudsperson lacked the independence and authority necessary to provide effective remedies to EU citizens. The position's location within the executive branch and inability to issue binding decisions on US intelligence agencies rendered it incompatible with the EU Charter's requirement for effective judicial protection.[47]

Implications for International Data Flows

The invalidation of the Privacy Shield framework in *Schrems II* sent immediate shock waves through the global business and technology sectors, creating a quagmire for companies that had relied on the framework for transatlantic data transfers. The CJEU determined that US surveillance laws, particularly FISA Section 702 and Executive Order 12333, do not provide protections equivalent to those required under EU law. Given this finding, businesses using SCCs for US data transfers faced an insurmountable challenge in demonstrating that their contractual arrangements offer adequate safeguards.[48] In response to this ruling, European regulators, including the EDPB, issued guidelines requiring companies to implement additional safeguards. However, for many companies, particularly multinational corporations and cloud service providers, ceasing data flows to the United States was the only practical solution—and failing to comply with GDPR requirements could result in severe regulatory penalties and civil liability.

The *Schrems II* decision reshaped the global data transfer landscape, forcing businesses to substantially revise their data governance strategies and accelerating efforts to develop alternative legal frameworks. Some companies implemented European-hosted cloud solutions, while others have sought to negotiate bespoke data transfer agreements with regulators.[49] Meanwhile, EU and US policymakers engaged in ongoing diplomatic discussions to craft a successor to the Privacy Shield.

Post–*Schrems II* Developments

The aftermath of *Schrems II* saw increasingly assertive enforcement by European data protection authorities. The Austrian DPA's 2022 decision regarding Google Analytics marked a particularly significant development.[50] The authority found that the use of Google Analytics violated the GDPR because it necessarily involved the transfer of personal data to Google's US servers, where it could be subject

47 Id.

48 See noyb, CJEU invalidates "Privacy Shield" in US Surveillance case. SCCs cannot be used by Facebook and similar companies. (2020, Jul. 16). https://noyb.eu/en/cjeu.

49 See B. Smith, *Answering Europe's Call: Storing and Processing EU Data in the EU* (May 6, 2021). https://blogs.microsoft.com/eupolicy/2021/05/06/eu-data-boundary/.

50 Austrian Data Protection Authority, Decision on Google Analytics (2022).

to surveillance under Section 702 FISA. This decision demonstrated that even seemingly routine data transfers for website analytics could fall afoul of *Schrems II*'s requirements. The French data protection authority, CNIL, reached similar conclusions, ordering websites to cease using Google Analytics or face enforcement action.[51] The regulatory focus on Google Analytics is especially significant because it affects not just major technology companies but potentially any European website using these common analytical tools.

Perhaps the most dramatic enforcement action came from the Irish Data Protection Commission in 2023, which imposed a record €1.2 billion fine on Meta for continued data transfers in violation of *Schrems II*.[52] This unprecedented penalty reflects both the scale of the violations and regulators' determination to enforce compliance even against the largest technology companies. The decision also ordered Meta to cease transfers within five months, potentially forcing fundamental changes to its business model.

The corporate response to *Schrems II* varied significantly, reflecting different assessments of legal risk and business necessity. Meta took an aggressively histrionic stance, suggesting that a complete shutdown of its European services might be necessary if data transfers cannot continue. This position, articulated in regulatory filings and public statements, appeared designed to pressure both regulators and legislators to find a workable solution.[53] In contrast, other companies, including Microsoft—understanding that continuing to transfer data to the United States was now illegal—explored various data localization strategies, from establishing European subsidiaries with independent data processing capabilities to restructuring their services to minimize transatlantic data flows.[54]

Privacy Shield 2.0 and Future Developments

The EU–US Data Privacy Framework (DPF), implemented in 2023, represents the latest attempt to address the issues identified by the CJEU in *Schrems II*.[55] This framework introduces new safeguards for United States signals intelligence activities, including limitations on data collection for national security purposes and requirements to consider the privacy interests of non-US persons. Additionally, it establishes the "Data Protection Review Court," intended to provide independent

51 CNIL, Deliberation SAN-2022-001 (2022).

52 Irish Data Protection Commission, Final Decision in Facebook Data Transfers Case (2023).

53 Meta, Annual Report (Form 10-K) (2022).

54 *Answering Europe's Call: Storing and Processing EU Data in the EU* (May 6, 2021). https://blogs.microsoft.com/eupolicy/2021/05/06/eu-data-boundary/.

55 European Commission. (2023, July 10). Commission Implementing Decision (EU) 2023/1465 of 10 July 2023 pursuant to Regulation (EU) 2016/679 of the European Parliament and of the Council on the adequate protection of personal data by the United States under the EU-U.S. Data Privacy Framework. Official Journal of the European Union, L 194/3.

oversight and binding remedies for EU citizens subject to US surveillance.[56] While these reforms signal at least superficial efforts to bridge the gap between EU and US privacy standards, they have been met with skepticism from privacy advocates, particularly Max Schrems and noyb—European Center for Digital Rights ("none of your business"), who continue to argue that the framework remains legally inadequate and may fail to withstand judicial scrutiny.

A major concern is the framework's reliance on executive orders rather than statutory reform. The key reforms under the DPF stem from Executive Order 14086, issued by President Biden in 2022, rather than from legislative amendments to US surveillance laws. This reliance on executive authority raises doubts about the permanence and legal enforceability of the framework. Executive orders can be revoked or modified by future administrations, which makes the framework an unstable foundation for transatlantic data transfers. The CJEU in *Schrems II* explicitly emphasized the need for legally binding and enforceable protections, which, critics argue, cannot be guaranteed through executive action alone.[57] Without legislative reform addressing Section 702 of FISA and Executive Order 12333, the new framework may ultimately meet the same fate as its predecessors.

Beyond concerns about its legal foundation, critics argue that the framework fails to meaningfully limit US mass surveillance practices. One of the fundamental problems identified in *Schrems II* was that US surveillance programs lacked proportionality and necessity, as required under EU data protection principles.[58] While the DPF includes procedural safeguards, it does not establish clear limitations on bulk data collection, nor does it require prior judicial authorization for surveillance activities. This leaves fundamental concerns unaddressed, particularly regarding the lack of independent oversight of intelligence agencies. Unlike EU countries, where data access by intelligence services is subject to judicial or parliamentary review, US intelligence agencies continue to operate under a broad national security exemption, which, critics argue, fails to meet the "essential equivalence" standard required by the GDPR.

The Data Protection Review Court (DPRC), a key element of the new framework, is another source of controversy. While the DPF presents the DPRC as an independent body capable of providing legal redress to EU citizens, privacy advocates argue that it lacks genuine judicial independence.[59] The court is housed within the executive branch—meaning that its judges are appointed and overseen

56 www.justice.gov/opcl/redress-data-protection-review-court.

57 Court of Justice of the European Union. (2020, July 16). Case C-311/18, Data Protection Commissioner v. Facebook Ireland Ltd and Maximillian Schrems (Schrems II), ECLI:EU:C:2020:559, paragraphs 175–178.

58 Noyb, *Statement on EU Comission Adequacy Decision on US* (Dec. 13, 2022). https://noyb.eu/en/statement-eu-comission-adequacy-decision-us.

59 Noyb, *European Commission gives EU-US Data Transfers Third Round at CJEU* (Jul. 10, 2023). https://noyb.eu/en/european-commission-gives-eu-us-data-transfers-third-round-cjeu.

by the US Attorney General, rather than operating as an independent judicial entity. The classified nature of its decisions further undermines transparency and accountability, raising concerns about whether it provides an effective remedy as required under Article 47 of the EU Charter of Fundamental Rights. The CJEU previously rejected a similar ombudsperson mechanism under Privacy Shield, finding that it lacked sufficient independence and remedial powers. Some critics predict that the DPRC will face the same criticisms and could ultimately be deemed inadequate by the CJEU.[60]

With these shortcomings, noyb and other privacy groups have already signaled their intent to challenge the DPF before the CJEU. Schrems has stated that he expects the CJEU to strike down the framework within a few years, as it fails to alter the core structural issues identified in *Schrems II*.[61] Some scholars agree, arguing that as long as US mass surveillance laws remain unchanged, the fundamental incompatibilities with EU data protection law will persist.[62] If the DPF is invalidated, it will once again disrupt EU–US data transfers, similar to what occurred after Safe Harbor (2015) and Privacy Shield (2020) were invalidated. The continued legal uncertainty suggests that unless the United States enacts significant legislative changes to restrict mass surveillance, future transatlantic frameworks will continue to be struck down by the CJEU. Given the legal trajectory of previous frameworks and the CJEU's clear stance on surveillance safeguards, many expect "*Schrems III*" to be inevitable.[63]

The Rise of European Privacy Litigation

Dutch Class Actions

On the night of March 27, 1943, a small group of Dutch resistance fighters infiltrated the Amsterdam civil registry office with a singular goal: to destroy the records that made Nazi surveillance and persecution possible. Disguised as police officers, the group, led by artist Willem Arondéus, convinced the guards to allow them entry before setting fire to thousands of documents that identified Jews living in the Netherlands.[64] Though the act of resistance came at a grave cost—many members of the group were later executed—it was a powerful countermeasure to

60 Id.

61 Id.

62 See Sara Gerke & Delaram Rezaeikhonakdar, *Privacy Shield 2.0—A New Trans-Atlantic Data Privacy Framework between the European Union and the United States*, 45 Cardozo L. Rev. 351, 394 (2023).

63 *See* id.; see also Allison Schiff, *If There's Anything Certain in Life, It's That Schrems III Is Coming*, AdExchanger (Jul. 17, 2023). www.adexchanger.com/data-privacy-roundup/if-theres-anything-certain-in-life-its-that-schrems-iii-is-coming/.

64 Wikipedia, *1943 Amsterdam Civil Registry Office Bombing*. https://en.wikipedia.org/wiki/1943_Amsterdam_civil_registry_office_bombing.

the dangers of centralized data collection in the hands of unchecked authority. This Dutch historical moment underscores a fundamental truth that continues to shape privacy law today: Information is power, and those who control it wield massive influence over individuals' lives.

The Netherlands has recently emerged as a significant venue for collective redress in privacy and consumer protection cases, driven by a combination of progressive legal reforms and an active civil society. The 2019 Dutch Collective Damages Act (WAMCA) expanded the ability of representative organizations to file class action lawsuits on behalf of affected individuals, allowing for both injunctive relief and monetary damages.[65] Unlike many jurisdictions that require individual claimants to actively opt in, the Dutch system permits opt-out mechanisms, making it particularly well-suited for large-scale data protection claims. This approach has positioned the Netherlands as an attractive forum for challenging multinational corporations engaged in questionable data practices. The rise of privacy litigation in the Netherlands reflects broader European trends, where collective actions are increasingly being used to enforce GDPR rights in cases where regulators have been slow to act. Dutch courts have already played a pioneering role in data privacy enforcement, providing influential rulings on issues such as targeted advertising, consent mechanisms, and the misuse of personal data for commercial purposes, setting precedent that is being watched closely across the European Union.[66]

The litigation brought by the Data Privacy Stichting against Facebook exemplifies this shift. Initiated in 2019, the case challenged Facebook's business practices related to data collection and targeted advertising, alleging that the company violated Dutch and European data protection laws between April 2010 and January 2020.[67] The Foundation, acting as a representative organization, argued that Facebook unlawfully harvested and monetized users' personal data without obtaining valid consent and without providing adequate transparency about how data was processed and shared with third parties. This case followed growing global scrutiny over Facebook's role in data privacy scandals, most notably the Cambridge Analytica affair, which exposed how personal data was misused for political profiling and manipulation. The Dutch lawsuit sought to hold Facebook accountable not just for privacy violations but also for misleading consumers about the true scope of its data practices.

The legal proceedings resulted in a landmark 2023 ruling by the Amsterdam District Court, which found that Facebook had engaged in unfair commercial practices and violated Dutch privacy laws, marking the first direct judicial rebuke of

65 Xandra Kramer, *The Quest for Funding under the Dutch WAMCA: Third Party Funding and the Viability of a Procedural Fund*, 38 Emory Int'l L. Rev. 767 (2024).

66 Amsterdam District Court, *Data Privacy Stichting v. Facebook Ireland Ltd* (2023).

67 Id.

Meta's data-driven advertising model.[68] The Amsterdam District Court determined that Facebook Ireland "has acted unlawfully in the way in which it has handled the personal data of Dutch Facebook users" between April 2010 and January 2020. The Court's ruling addressed three key aspects of Facebook's data practices. First, it concluded that Facebook Ireland lacked "a legally valid basis" for processing personal data for advertising purposes, rejecting the argument that such processing was necessary to perform the user contract. Second, it held that Facebook Ireland failed to obtain "the required explicit consent" for processing special (sensitive) personal data, including certain information derived by tracking users' web browsing activity. Third, the Court found Facebook Ireland "did not sufficiently inform the Facebook users" about certain sharing of their personal data with third parties.[69]

The Court decisively rejected Meta's contention that extensive data collection and processing for advertising purposes were necessary for the performance of its contract with users. This argument, frequently advanced by social media companies, posited that personalized advertising was an inherent and essential aspect of the service provided to users. The Court found this reasoning incompatible with GDPR principles, concluding that targeted advertising serves Meta's commercial interests rather than being necessary for providing a social networking service. This distinction between core service functionality and additional commercial processing activities has significant implications for platform business models that have treated extensive data collection as a fundamental condition of service.[70]

The decision found that Meta's practice of bundling consent for targeted advertising with acceptance of general terms of service failed to meet the GDPR's requirements for freely given, specific, informed, and unambiguous consent.[71] The Court also found that Meta's tracking and profiling practices inevitably involved processing sensitive data about users' religious beliefs, sexual orientation, and health information, requiring explicit consent under Article 9(2)(a). By determining that such sensitive data processing cannot be justified by contract necessity or legitimate interests, the decision creates a significant operational impediment for platforms that rely on comprehensive behavioral profiling.[72] This aspect of the ruling thus has particular significance for the broader AdTech ecosystem: Many companies have attempted to rely on legitimate interests or contractual necessity to justify their data processing activities, avoiding the more stringent requirements of explicit consent.[73] The litigation has moved to the appellate and damages phrases,

68 District Court Amsterdam, 15 March 2023, ECLI:NL:RBAMS:2023:1407. https://dataprivacystichting.com/wp-content/uploads/Amsterdam-District-Court-Judgment-March-15-2023.pdf.
69 Id.
70 Id.
71 Id.
72 Id.
73 Id.

with the Dutch court now set to determine Meta's financial liability to Dutch Facebook users for its conduct.

Recent Developments in Collective Redress Across EU Jurisdictions

The emergence of the Netherlands as a hub for privacy class actions represents just one aspect of a broader transformation in collective redress mechanisms across the European Union. Recent legal actions in European jurisdictions demonstrate the increasing use of collective redress mechanisms to address privacy violations and consumer harm. The implementation of the EU Directive on Representative Actions (RAD) has significantly affected the EU collective action legal landscape, facilitating the rise of privacy class actions across multiple member states. Numerous recent legal developments illustrate the growing role of collective litigation in holding Big Tech accountable for data protection infringements.

Germany has seen a landmark class action targeting Meta for its mishandling of personal data. On December 9, 2024, the Federation of German Consumer Organisations (vzbv) filed a collective lawsuit against Meta Platforms Ltd. before the Higher Regional Court of Hamburg. The case concerns the 2021 Facebook data breach, which exposed personal data from 533 million users worldwide, including approximately 6 million German users. The lawsuit seeks at least €100 in damages per affected user for loss of data control, and case represents a significant shift toward data privacy enforcement through consumer collective redress.[74]

In a notable competition-related case, OCU (Organización de Consumidores y Usuarios), Spain's leading consumer protection group, filed a lawsuit against Apple on February 6, 2025. The claim focuses on Apple's anti-competitive restrictions in the music streaming market, arguing that the company unfairly overcharged iPhone and iPad users by restricting access to cheaper subscription options outside of the Apple App Store. This lawsuit follows the European Commission's €1.8 billion fine against Apple in March 2024 for similar anti-competitive behavior. OCU estimates that Spanish consumers were overcharged by a total of €25.1 million, with individual losses ranging from €39 to €200, depending on the platform used. The lawsuit seeks consumer refunds and represents a broader effort to challenge platform operators that use market dominance to extract excessive fees.[75]

Finally, in addition to the *Data Privacy Stichting* case, the Netherlands continues to play a leading role in privacy litigation, particularly through the Amsterdam District Court's ruling on January 15, 2025, allowing a privacy class action filed by the Privacy Protection Stichting against Google to proceed. The lawsuit alleges that Google engaged in large-scale unlawful data collection and sharing practices, violating the General Data Protection Regulation (GDPR). The court's ruling rejected

74 1. BEUC, From Collective Harm to Redress: What's New? (Feb. 2025), at 4.
75 Id. 6.

all of Google's objections, affirming SBP's standing to represent users and confirming the case's broad public interest scope. With over 160,000 affected users joining the claim, the foundation is seeking €750 per user in compensation.[76]

These cases underscore the rapid expansion of privacy class actions and collective consumer redress mechanisms across Europe. While regulatory authorities such as data protection agencies and competition watchdogs remain central to GDPR enforcement, private litigation is increasingly complementing public enforcement efforts. With the continued implementation of the Representative Actions Directive, consumer organizations and advocacy groups are accruing further grounds to challenge tech companies over mass privacy violations. The ongoing collective actions against Meta, Google, and Apple highlight the growing role of European courts in shaping digital rights enforcement and ensuring that individuals receive meaningful compensation for data misuse. As collective litigation frameworks become more harmonized across member states, it is likely that privacy class actions will become a key enforcement tool, reinforcing consumer rights and strengthening Europe's digital sovereignty.

Implications for Corporate Accountability

The escalation of GDPR enforcement actions in recent years reflects growing confidence among regulators and a shift toward more aggressive penalties targeting core business models rather than isolated violations. Fines against major technology firms have increased dramatically, underscoring regulators' intent to create meaningful deterrents against privacy violations. The Irish Data Protection Commission's May 2023 decision against Meta was pivotal, imposing a record-breaking €1.2 billion fine for unlawful data transfers to the United States. Beyond the scale of the penalty, the ruling directly challenged Meta's core business model, demonstrating that regulators are willing to take on the structural foundations of commercial surveillance. Similarly, Luxembourg's National Commission for Data Protection issued a €746 million fine against Amazon in July 2021, citing the company's failure to obtain valid consent for targeted advertising, reinforcing the expectation that large-scale data-driven businesses must adopt stronger privacy safeguards.[77]

France's Commission nationale de l'informatique et des libertés (CNIL) has been particularly active in pursuing violations related to deceptive consent mechanisms. In January 2022, it fined Google €150 million for the use of dark patterns

76 Id. at 5.

77 Wired, *Amazon's Massive GDPR Fine Shows the Law's Power—and Limits*, Wired (Aug. 5, 2021). www.wired.com/story/amazon-gdpr-fine-shows-power-limits/. It should be noted the CNPD's procedural rules kept the basis for this decision confidential, and the fine was ultimately rescinded by CNPD, also for unknown reasons. Nonetheless, the size of the initially-imposed fine made it one of the largest GDPR fines in history.

that made it significantly easier for users to accept cookies than to refuse them. The CNIL's ruling provided a detailed analysis of how interface design can manipulate user choices, concluding that the disparity in effort required to reject tracking cookies invalidated consent.[78] This ruling scrutinized the role of UX design in privacy compliance, an area of increasing regulatory focus.

Regulators have also moved beyond targeting isolated compliance failures to addressing systemic issues in data processing. In 2023, Italy's Garante per la protezione dei dati personali (Italian DPA) imposed a €79 million fine on TikTok for failing to implement effective age verification measures and for targeting minors with personalized content. The decision emphasized that technical challenges do not justify non-compliance, especially when dealing with vulnerable data subjects like children.[79] Regulators have also demonstrated growing sophistication in tackling industry-wide technical standards. The Belgian Data Protection Authority's (APD) enforcement action against IAB Europe's real-time bidding (RTB) system highlighted the inherent privacy risks in the online advertising ecosystem, shaping broader regulatory approaches to behavioral advertising across the EU.[80]

Increasingly, GDPR enforcement has become more coordinated across jurisdictions, with the EDPB playing a crucial role in ensuring consistency. The EDPB's binding decisions have often pushed for higher penalties and stricter enforcement. In the Meta case, for instance, the EDPB mandated that the Irish DPC significantly increase its initially proposed fine; Andrea Jelinek, EDPB chair, stated:

> Meta IE's infringement is very serious since it concerns transfers that are systematic, repetitive and continuous. Facebook has millions of users in Europe, so the volume of personal data transferred is massive. The unprecedented fine is a strong signal to organisations that serious infringements have far-reaching consequences.[81]

This coordinated regulatory effort underscores a broader trend in targeting commercial surveillance practices. Recent enforcement trends suggest a shift toward even more stringent regulatory approaches. The Norwegian Data Protection Authority's

78 Commission Nationale de l'Informatique et des Libertés (CNIL), Closure of Injunction Issued Against Google, CNIL (Feb. 2023). www.cnil.fr/en/closure-injunction-issued-against-google.

79 Garante per la Protezione dei Dati Personali, Decision No. 9574709, GDPR Hub (2021). https://gdprhub.eu/index.php?title=Garante_per_la_protezione_dei_dati_personali_(Italy)_-_9574709.

80 Belgian Data Protection Authority, *The BE DPA to Restore Order to the Online Advertising Industry: IAB Europe Held Responsible for a Mechanism That Infringes the GDPR*, Data Protection Authority Belgium (Feb. 2022). www.dataprotectionauthority.be/citizen/iab-europe-held-responsible-for-a-mechanism-that-infringes-the-gdpr.

81 European Data Protection Board, *Binding Decision 1/2023 on the Dispute Submitted by the Irish SA on Data Transfers by Meta Platforms Ireland Limited for Its Facebook service (Art. 65 GDPR)*, EDPB (May 2023). www.edpb.europa.eu/system/files/2023-05/edpb_bindingdecision_202301_ie_sa_facebooktransfers_redacted.pdf.

2023 ban on behavioral advertising without explicit consent, accompanied by daily fines of €100,000, reflects regulators' willingness to go beyond fines and impose structural remedies requiring fundamental changes to surveillance-based business models.[82]

Private Litigation as a Catalyst for Privacy Reform

The *Schrems* litigation has profoundly reshaped the global privacy landscape, demonstrating that private legal action brought by a single highly motivated individual can serve as a catalyst for systemic privacy reform in ways that traditional regulatory enforcement often cannot. As noted in the previous chapter, academic skepticism has questioned the efficacy of private privacy litigation, with critics arguing that private lawsuits lacked the institutional force to challenge corporate surveillance models at scale. However, the strategic efforts of Max Schrems and his organization noyb have directly countered this assumption. Through carefully crafted legal actions, Schrems has not only forced the invalidation of two major transatlantic data transfer frameworks—Safe Harbor and Privacy Shield—but has also exposed fundamental weaknesses in US surveillance practices and their compatibility with EU privacy laws.

The significance of these cases extends beyond Meta and transatlantic data flows. The legal challenges have reaffirmed the principle that global technology firms are subject to the rule of law, despite their efforts to position themselves as sovereign actors beyond international regulatory control. This issue is particularly pronounced in the context of the *Schrems* rulings, where Meta, Google, and other tech giants have engaged in systematic resistance to regulatory enforcement. Nowhere has this been clearer than in the EU–US data transfer debate, where companies have continued transferring data under legally dubious mechanisms even after multiple court rulings against them.

Meta and Google, two of the most dominant technology firms in history, increasingly seek to operate as quasi-sovereign entities. Indeed, Mark Zuckerberg has made no effort to hide these sovereign aspirations, stating that, in his view, "[i]n a lot of ways Facebook is more like a government than a traditional company."[83] Meta's response to *Schrems II*, for example, was not to immediately cease the unlawful transfer of personal data but to attempt to reinterpret the ruling in a way that justified continued data flows, and to simply continue business as usual. This strategy, which Schrems has described as "Facebook fully ignor[ing] the Court of Justice, despite two explicit rulings," is illustrative of a larger trend in which

82 European Data Protection Board (EDPB), *EDPB Publishes Urgent Binding Decision Regarding Meta* (Dec. 7, 2023). www.edpb.europa.eu/news/news/2023/edpb-publishes-urgent-binding-decision-regarding-meta_en.

83 David Kirkpatrick, *The Facebook Defect*. Time (online) (Apr. 12, 2018). http://time.com/5237458/the-facebook-defect.

tech giants treat adverse rulings not as binding legal constraints but as temporary roadblocks to be worked around through strategic noncompliance.[84] The *Schrems* litigation is thus a direct challenge to Meta's ongoing attempts to openly flout the rule of law.

The *Schrems* litigation serves as a model for future privacy advocacy, demonstrating that private litigants, equipped with legal expertise and strategic persistence, can disrupt even the most entrenched commercial surveillance systems. The success of noyb's legal challenges has already influenced privacy class actions in various European jurisdictions, including the Dutch Data Privacy Stichting's ongoing lawsuit against Meta, which has incorporate claims based on the *Schrems II* litigation into its lawsuit seeking redress for Dutch citizens.[85] These developments suggest that the future of privacy rights enforcement will increasingly rely on private litigation as a complement to regulatory action, pushing back against corporate overreach in ways that governments alone have struggled to achieve.

Conclusion

The ongoing struggle over international data flows reflects a fundamental contest over digital sovereignty in the 21st century. The GDPR represents Europe's assertion of its citizens' fundamental rights in the face of both government surveillance and corporate data practices. The historical arc from the Nazi regime's abuse of then cutting-edge surveillance technology to today's debates over digital surveillance illustrates the enduring relationship between data, power, and human rights.

While the *Schrems* and *Data Privacy Stichting* cases were litigated under a distinctly European legal framework that recognizes privacy as a fundamental right—differing significantly from the less-protective US environment—they nonetheless exemplify the profound impact a single motivated individual or organization can have on global privacy norms. By challenging assumptions that pervasive US government surveillance was simply an unavoidable aspect of modern life for European citizens, the *Schrems* litigation catalyzed a re-evaluation of corporate practices and governmental policies worldwide. In doing so, it underscored that robust legal protections, strategic advocacy, and persistent pursuit of judicial recourse can, even in the face of formidable corporate and political resources and will, reshape the balance of power between commercial interests and individual rights on a global scale.

84 4th Advent Reading: Facebook fully ignores "Schrems" rulings by Court of Justice. https://noyb.eu/en/4th-advent-reading-facebook-fully-ignores-schrems-rulings-court-justice.

85 Extract for the Central Register of Collective Actions within the Meaning of Article 1018C DCCP. https://dataprivacystichting.com/wp-content/uploads/DPS-v.-Meta.pdf.

11

THE RISE OF HIPSTER ANTITRUST

A New Front in the Fight for Privacy

Introduction

As digital platforms have grown to unprecedented scale and power, traditional regulatory frameworks have struggled to address novel forms of market power built on the exploitation of personal data. This chapter examines how antitrust law, historically focused on economic harm and consumer prices, has evolved to recognize privacy as a crucial dimension of market competition and consumer welfare. The emergence of what critics have dubbed "Hipster Antitrust"—a movement calling for broader consideration of non-economic harms in antitrust analysis—has created new opportunities for addressing privacy concerns through competition law. This development marks a return to antitrust's historical roots as a tool for checking concentrated private power while adapting those principles to the unique challenges posed by digital platforms and data-extractive surveillance capitalism.

Foundations of American Antitrust Law

American antitrust law emerged during the Gilded Age as a response to unprecedented concentrations of economic and political power in the hands of industrial "trusts," large business combinations that dominated entire industries in the late 19th century, often through anti-competitive practice.[1] This period, characterized by rapid industrialization and corporate consolidation, saw the rise of powerful monopolies in industries ranging from oil and steel to railroads and telecommunications. The public and political reaction to these developments reflected concerns

1 National Archives, Sherman Anti-Trust Act (1890). www.archives.gov/milestone-documents/sherman-anti-trust-act.

DOI: 10.4324/9781003413349-15

not just about economic efficiency but about the fundamental compatibility of such private power with democratic governance.[2] The Sherman Act of 1890 represented Congress's first comprehensive attempt to address these concerns through federal legislation. While modern antitrust analysis often focuses on economic efficiency, the Act's original purposes were considerably broader. As Senator Sherman himself argued, the accumulation of private power through monopolies and trusts threatened to create "a kingly prerogative, inconsistent with our form of government."[3] Early Supreme Court jurisprudence recognized this, noting that "among the purposes of Congress in 1890 was a desire to put an end to great aggregations of capital because of the helplessness of the individual before them."[4] The law thus aimed not merely to promote competition but to prevent concentrations of private power that could rival or capture legitimate governmental authority.

The core provisions of American antitrust law are found in two key statutes: the Sherman Act and the Federal Trade Commission Act. Section 2 of the Sherman Act establishes the basic prohibition on monopolization, making it unlawful to "monopolize, or attempt to monopolize, or combine or conspire . . . to monopolize" trade or commerce.[5] Courts have interpreted this provision to require three essential elements for a monopolization claim: possession of monopoly power in the relevant market, willful acquisition or maintenance of that power through exclusionary conduct, and causal antitrust injury. Section 1 of the Sherman Act addresses anticompetitive agreements, prohibiting "every contract, combination . . . or conspiracy, in restraint of trade."[6] This provision reaches beyond single-firm conduct to address collusive behavior among multiple market participants. Courts have interpreted this section to require proof of both an agreement and that the agreement unreasonably restrained trade, developing sophisticated frameworks for distinguishing between legitimate business arrangements and anticompetitive collusion. The Federal Trade Commission Act, passed in 1914, created the Federal Trade Commission and empowered it to prevent "unfair methods of competition."[7] This broader language gave the agency flexibility to address anticompetitive practices beyond those specifically enumerated in the Sherman Act. The FTC's dual authority over both competition and consumer protection matters makes it particularly relevant to contemporary issues at the intersection of antitrust and privacy law.

Despite the early origins of antitrust laws as counterweights to concentrations of corporate power, beginning in the 1970s, antitrust law underwent a profound

2 Tim Wu, The Curse of Bigness: Antitrust in the New Gilded Age (2018).

3 John Sherman, Statement in support of the Sherman antitrust act. Congressional Record, March 1890. 51st Congress, 1st Session, Senate.

4 *United States v. Aluminum Co. of America*, 148 F.2d 416, 428 (2d Cir. 1945).

5 15 U.S.C. § 2.

6 15 U.S.C. § 1.

7 15 U.S.C. §§ 45.

transformation under the influence of the Chicago School of economic thought. This approach, championed by scholars like Robert Bork in his influential book *The Antitrust Paradox*, argued that antitrust law should focus exclusively on promoting consumer welfare as measured by economic efficiency and consumer prices.[8] The Chicago School's influence led courts to increasingly view antitrust cases through the lens of price theory and economic efficiency. This shift had several consequences. First, it led to greater skepticism of antitrust enforcement generally, as Chicago School scholars argued that many supposedly anticompetitive practices could actually enhance efficiency.[9] Second, it narrowed the scope of antitrust analysis to focus primarily on short-term price effects, making it harder to challenge conduct that harmed competition in other ways.[10]

As Richard Hofstadter observed, this transformation turned antitrust from a political movement into a technical exercise managed by economists and lawyers: "Once the United States had an antitrust movement without antitrust prosecutions; in our time there have been antitrust prosecutions without an antitrust movement."[11] This observation captured how antitrust law had become increasingly disconnected from its original broader purposes. The tension between antitrust law's broad original purposes and its narrower modern interpretation has particular relevance for contemporary privacy issues; the Chicago School's focus on price effects has made it difficult for antitrust law to address forms of consumer harm that do not manifest in higher prices, such as privacy degradation or reduction in service quality. This limitation has become increasingly problematic as digital platforms gained prominence, as these businesses provide services to consumers which purport to be "free," while extracting economic value through data collection and surveillance. Moreover, the Chicago School's skepticism toward structural remedies and preference for narrowly targeted interventions has presented a barrier to addressing systemic issues through antitrust enforcement. Where earlier antitrust thinking might have supported breaking up companies that accumulated too much power over consumer data, modern doctrine has required detailed proof of specific anticompetitive effects, often focusing on price impacts that may be difficult to demonstrate in digital markets.[12]

The "Neo-Brandesian" movement, discussed in the next section, represents in many ways an attempt to recover antitrust law's original broader purposes while adapting them to contemporary market conditions.[13] For half a century, the Chicago School's influence transformed antitrust enforcement into a technical exercise focused on price theory, erasing its broader concerns about corporate power.

8 Robert H. Bork, The Antitrust Paradox: A Policy at War With Itself 50 (The Free Press, 1978).
9 Richard Posner, *The Chicago School of Antitrust Analysis*, 127. U. Pa. L. Rev. 925 (1979).
10 Herbert Hovenkamp, *Antitrust Policy after Chicago*, 84 Mich. L. Rev. 213 (1985).
11 Richard Hofstadter, The Paranoid Style in American Politics and Other Essays 188 (1965).
12 Id.
13 Erika Douglas, *The New Antitrust/Data Privacy Law Interface*, 130 Yale L.J.F. 647 (2021).

The Neo-Brandesian movement represents an explicit repudiation of this narrow approach, arguing that corporate dominance poses risks that extend beyond short-term price effects—including harms to privacy, competition, and democracy itself.

The Rise of Hipster Antitrust

The term "Hipster Antitrust" emerged as a pejorative label for what scholars have more formally termed the "Neo-Brandesian" movement in antitrust law.[14] The movement takes its name from Supreme Court Justice Louis Brandeis, whom Ralph Nader quoted as warning that "we can have democracy in this country, or we can have great wealth concentrated in the hands of a few, but we can't have both."[15] This sentiment has gained renewed relevance in an era of unprecedented corporate concentration and technological power. The Neo-Brandesian movement represents a fundamental challenge to the dominant paradigm in antitrust law that has prevailed since the 1970s. Where the Chicago School focused narrowly on consumer prices and economic efficiency, Neo-Brandeisians argue for a return to antitrust's original broader purposes of preventing excessive concentrations of private power. This approach recognizes that market concentration creates risks beyond simply higher consumer prices, including threats to democratic governance, innovation, and consumer privacy. The movement gained particular momentum through the work of scholars like Lina Khan, whose influential article "Amazon's Antitrust Paradox" demonstrated how traditional antitrust analysis failed to capture the anticompetitive potential of digital platform business models.[16] Khan's subsequent appointment as FTC chair marked a significant victory for the movement, signaling its evolution from academic criticism to enforcement policy.

The Neo-Brandesian movement rests on a theoretical framework that challenges several core assumptions of contemporary antitrust law. Rather than treating consumer welfare as synonymous with low prices, the movement argues for considering a broader range of market outcomes and competitive dynamics.[17] Central to this analysis is the recognition that market structure fundamentally shapes economic and social outcomes. Neo-Brandeisians argue that high levels of market concentration tend to produce negative effects across multiple dimensions. These include suppressed wages and reduced worker bargaining power as labor markets

14 Wright et al., *Requiem for a Paradox: The Dubious Rise and Inevitable Fall of Hipster Antitrust*, 51 Ariz. St. L.J. (May. 2019).

15 This oft-repeated quote is perhaps apocryphal, even if an accurate representation of Brandeis's thought; *see* Peter Scott Campbell, Democracy v. Concentrated Wealth, In Search of a Louis D. Brandeis Quote, 16. Green BAG 2nd 251, 256 (2013) ("Whatever the circumstances and whatever the exact wording, the quote rings true. While there is no positive proof Brandeis ever said these exact words, he expressed a similar sentiment numerous times. If it is not a Brandeis quote, it is at least a Brandeisian one.")

16 Lina M. Khan, *Amazon's Antitrust Paradox*, 126 Yale L.J. (2016).

17 Id.

become more concentrated.[18] They also point to diminished innovation, as dominant firms can either acquire or copy potential competitors rather than competing through improvement.[19]

The movement also emphasizes the relationship between economic and political power. As Tim Wu argues in *The Curse of Bigness*, extreme economic concentration yields "gross inequality and material suffering, feeding an appetite for nationalistic and extremist leadership."[20] This analysis draws on historical parallels between the current era and the Gilded Age, suggesting that unchecked private power poses fundamental threats to democratic governance.[21] The theoretical framework also addresses the unique challenges posed by digital markets. Neo-Brandeisians argue that network effects, data advantages, and ecosystem control create powerful barriers to entry that make digital markets particularly prone to monopolization and the deleterious social effects that flow from those monopolies.[22] Traditional antitrust tools focused on price effects struggle to address these dynamics, especially in markets where services are nominally free to users.

The Neo-Brandesian movement has proven particularly significant for privacy law, as it provides a framework for understanding how market power enables privacy degradation. By recognizing that competition occurs along multiple dimensions of quality, not just price, the movement helps explain how lack of competition can lead to deteriorating privacy protections even in free services. As Frank Pasquale presciently argued in 2013, the leaders of dominant digital platforms "are not simply in it for the money" but rather seek "to create platforms that nearly everyone must use to navigate and participate in an increasingly digital reality. They are seeking a power akin to that held by media barons of old: to shape individuals' reality and perceptions."[23] This insight helps explain why traditional antitrust analysis, focused solely on economic metrics, fails to capture the full scope of platform power and its implications for privacy.

The movement's emphasis on structural analysis also illuminates how privacy problems stem from market structure rather than just individual firm conduct. When firms achieve dominant positions through network effects and data advantages, they can degrade privacy protections without losing users to competitors. This dynamic suggests that protecting privacy requires addressing market structure, not just regulating specific privacy practices. The Neo-Brandesian framework helps connect privacy concerns to these broader issues of corporate power and democratic governance. The movement supports the argument that surveillance

18 Id.
19 Id.
20 Tim Wu, The Curse of Bigness: Antitrust in the New Gilded Age (2018) 5.
21 Id. at 8.
22 Id.
23 Frank Pasquale, *Privacy Antitrust, and Power*, 20 Geo. Mason L. Rev. 1024 (2013).

capitalism, enabled by market concentration, poses fundamental threats to individual autonomy and democratic discourse.[24]

Privacy-Antitrust Theory

Concomitant with the rise of Hipster Antitrust is a growing recognition of privacy as a dimension of market competition. Scholars and regulators have observed that in digital platform markets, consumer data and user attention are often the dominant currency rather than any direct monetary exchange.[25] As a result, privacy has been theorized to be a parameter of product quality in ways that traditional antitrust analysis—centered primarily on price and output—has struggled to capture.[26] This reconceptualization has led some scholars to argue that antitrust law should address privacy harms directly, whether by treating privacy degradation as a form of consumer harm or by questioning whether large-scale data collection reflects or reinforces monopoly power.[27]

This approach to privacy-antitrust theory contends that dominant digital platforms acquire and maintain market power in part through the accumulation of user data and the ensuing network effects that entrench their positions.[28] A platform with access to vast personal information can more effectively microtarget advertisements and develop novel features, reducing users' incentives to switch to potential rivals, even if those rivals offer more privacy-protective services.[29] As discussed in what follows, scholars such as Dina Srinivasan have argued that the ability to degrade privacy terms without losing users is itself probative evidence of market power.[30] Frank Pasquale has similarly warned that the ever-expanding commercial surveillance capabilities of Big Tech platforms have made privacy an antitrust concern and not merely a matter of consumer protection: According to this view, as major players grow larger through acquisitions and data-driven economies of scale, their power to unilaterally dictate privacy terms only increases.[31]

24 See Matthew Sipe, *Covering Prying Eyes with an Invisible Hand: Privacy, Antitrust, and the New Brandeis Movement*, 36 Harv. J.L. & Tech. 359 (2023).

25 See Erika M. Douglas, *The New Antitrust/Data Privacy Law Interface*, 130 Yale L.J.F. 647, 649 (2021).

26 See Frank Pasquale, *Privacy, Antitrust, and Power*, 20 Geo. Mason L. Rev. 1009, 1009–1010 (2013).

27 See Dina Srinivasan, *The Antitrust Case Against Facebook: A Monopolist's Journey towards Pervasive Surveillance in Spite of Consumers' Preference for Privacy*, 16 Berkeley Bus. L.J. 39, 46–48 (2019).

28 Cf. Lina M. Khan, *Amazon's Antitrust Paradox*, 126 Yale L.J. 710, 717–719 (2017).

29 See Matthew Sipe, *Covering Prying Eyes with an Invisible Hand: Privacy, Antitrust, and the New Brandeis Movement*, 36 Harv. J.L. & Tech. 355, 366–367 (2023).

30 Srinivasan, *Antitrust Case Against Facebook*, supra, at 49–50.

31 Pasquale, supra note 2, at 1009–1010.

This focus on privacy as an element of product quality has appeared in high-profile agency actions and policy proposals. The FTC has contemplated privacy-based harms in merger reviews and monopolization cases, recognizing that, in some circumstances, diminished privacy may constitute a reduction in service quality.[32] However, important confounding factors persist. As some commentators note, privacy preferences when engaging directly with platforms are sometimes heterogeneous or inconsistent, making it challenging to quantify privacy harm under conventional antitrust tools.[33] Moreover, privacy-focused remedies—such as mandating data portability or interoperability—can inadvertently facilitate more pervasive data sharing if not carefully designed, thus underscoring the nuanced interplay between privacy and competition goals.[34] Nonetheless, the newfound willingness to integrate privacy concepts into antitrust analysis constitutes a major shift in antitrust doctrine, setting the stage for more robust enforcement against firms that leverage data-driven network dominance to the detriment of both competition and consumer privacy.

The Antitrust Case Against Facebook

This pattern of corporate overreach—where dominant firms leverage their market power to erode privacy protections once competitive pressures subside—is exemplified by Facebook's trajectory. Nowhere is this more apparent than in the stark contrast between Facebook's public commitments to privacy and its actual internal attitudes and business practices, which reveal a deliberate strategy of surveillance expansion, masked by consumer-friendly rhetoric.

The disconnect between Facebook's public privacy commitments and its founder's private attitudes was evident from the company's earliest days. While publicly positioning Facebook as a privacy-protective alternative to existing social networks, Mark Zuckerberg expressed striking contempt for user privacy in private communications. A leaked instant messenger exchange from Facebook's first weeks revealed Zuckerberg boasting about his access to Harvard students' personal information:

ZUCK: yea so if you ever need info about anyone at harvard

ZUCK: just ask

ZUCK: i have over 4000 emails, pictures, addresses, sns

FRIEND: what!? how'd you manage that one?

ZUCK: people just submitted it

32 See, for example, Federal Trade Commission, Substitute Amended Complaint, *FTC v. Facebook, Inc.*, No. 1:20-cv-03590 (D.D.C. Aug. 19, 2021).

33 See Sipe, at 367–370.

34 See Douglas, supra, at 653–654.

ZUCK: i don't know why
ZUCK: they "trust me"
ZUCK: dumb fucks

This exchange, later published by Silicon Valley Insider and documented in Julia Carrie Wong's firsthand account of Facebook's early days, provides a revealing glimpse of the cynicism underlying Facebook's privacy promises.[35] The casual derision of users who trusted the platform with their personal information stands in stark contrast to the company's careful public positioning around "respect" for privacy. This duplicitousness—public commitments to privacy coupled with private exploitation of user trust—would become a recurring pattern in Facebook's conduct.

Theoretical Framework

Dina Srinivasan's 2019 article "The Antitrust Case Against Facebook" directly contributed to reshaping the landscape of antitrust enforcement.[36] The article's central insight was that privacy degradation could constitute anticompetitive conduct. Srinivasan argued that privacy protections represent a crucial dimension of product quality in social networking markets, similar to how safety features function in automobile markets or food quality standards operate in restaurant markets.[37] The theoretical framework rests on three key pillars. First, Srinivasan established that privacy was a material factor in early competition between social networks, with Facebook explicitly positioning itself as the privacy-protective alternative to MySpace's more open approach.[38] The materiality of this to competition was evidenced by Facebook's numerous public statements, privacy-focused product decisions, and market research showing user privacy concerns influenced platform choice. Second, the framework showed how Facebook's privacy commitments functioned as quality guarantees in a market characterized by information asymmetry and network effects.[39] Users could not easily evaluate the technical details of data collection and use, making Facebook's promises particularly significant in shaping market behavior. These commitments helped Facebook overcome early user skepticism and achieve critical mass in the network effects–driven social media market. Third, Srinivasan developed a novel theory of anticompetitive conduct based on quality

35 Julia Carrie Wong, *I Was One of Facebook's First Users. I Shouldn't Have Trusted Mark Zuckerberg*, The Guardian (Feb. 2, 2019). www.theguardian.com/technology/2018/apr/17/facebook-people-first-ever-mark-zuckerberg-harvard.
36 Dina Srinivasan, *The Antitrust Case Against Facebook*, 16 Berkeley Bus. L.J. 39 (2019).
37 Id.
38 Id.
39 Id.

degradation rather than price increases.[40] She argued that Facebook's systematic reversal of privacy protections after achieving market dominance represented an extraction of monopoly rents through reduced quality rather than increased prices. This framing helped bridge the gap between traditional antitrust analysis and the zero-price markets characteristic of social media.

This process is a particularly clear manifestation of what Cory Doctorow has termed "enshittification": the gradual degradation of online platforms as they shift from prioritizing user experience to maximizing profit extraction.[41] Initially, platforms offer high-quality services to attract users, but then eventually degrade the experience by imposing constraints, monetizing engagement, and leveraging market dominance to exploit users and businesses alike. Enshittification exemplifies a broader pattern of anticompetitive behavior, as platforms leverage their control over digital ecosystems to extract rents from both consumers and third-party businesses. The phenomenon has been observed across multiple industries, from social media to e-commerce and search engines, where dominant platforms incrementally worsen service quality while increasing monetization strategies.[42]

Facebook's Pattern of Deceptive Conduct

During its ascent to market dominance, Facebook engaged in a systematic pattern of privacy-related misrepresentations while simultaneously laying the groundwork for future invasive surveillance practices. The company repeatedly assured users it would not leverage "backdoor access" for commercial surveillance purposes, as it had attempted with the failed "Beacon" program. The Beacon program was an advertising process launched in 2007 that surreptitiously tracked users' online purchases and then shared them with their Facebook friends without consent.[43] The program, introduced with select third-party partners such as Blockbuster and *The New York Times*, initially sought user permission through pop-ups but secretly transmitted browsing data to Facebook even when users declined. Following backlash, independent security researchers exposed that Facebook was collecting data from users who explicitly opted out, users who were logged out, and even individuals without Facebook accounts. Public outrage led to class action lawsuits and petitions, forcing Facebook to dismantle Beacon entirely by 2009, with Mark Zuckerberg later calling it a "mistake."[44]

40 Id.

41 Cory Doctorow, *The 'Enshittification' of TikTok*, Wired (Jan. 23, 2023). www.wired.com/story/tiktok-platforms-cory-doctorow/

42 Matthew Gault, *'Enshittification' Is Officially the Biggest Word of the Year*, Gizmodo (Nov. 26, 2024). https://gizmodo.com/enshittification-is-officially-the-biggest-word-of-the-year-2000530173.

43 Srinivasan, supra.

44 Id. at 61.

These assurances were particularly prominent in Facebook's response to subsequent concerns about its social plug-ins, especially the ubiquitous "Like" button that began appearing across the internet. When confronted with evidence that these plug-ins could enable tracking, Facebook's chief technology officer Bret Taylor made categorical denials, stating, "We don't use them for tracking and they're not intended for tracking."[45] The company continued consistently characterized any data collection through these tools as being solely for security purposes and user protection. Such representations proved crucial in maintaining user trust during Facebook's critical growth phase.[46] However, even as Facebook made these public commitments, it was systematically dismantling mechanisms for user control and oversight. The most notable example was the company's retreat from its promised "democratic" approach to privacy governance.[47] After the Beacon controversy, Facebook had implemented a system allowing users to vote on privacy policy changes. This voting right was incorporated into Facebook's governing documents as a binding commitment. Yet as Facebook's market position strengthened, it eliminated this accountability mechanism, foreshadowing more dramatic privacy reversals to come.[48]

Once Facebook achieved market dominance, it began systematically implementing the very surveillance practices it had previously disavowed. In June 2014, Facebook announced it would leverage its code presence on third-party applications to track users' online behavior for advertising purposes.[49] This represented a complete reversal of the company's long-standing promises about social plug-ins and tracking. The implementation of commercial surveillance extended beyond Facebook's own practices: The company began requiring its business partners to modify their privacy policies to obtain user consent for Facebook tracking.[50] Facebook even provided standardized legal language for websites to adopt: "Third parties, including Facebook, may use cookies, web beacons, and other storage technologies to collect or receive information from your websites, apps and elsewhere on the internet and use that information to provide measurement services [and] target ads."[51] This coordinated approach catalyzed the normalization of invasive commercial surveillance practices across the internet.

At each stage, Facebook followed its by now well-worn playbook: Deploy a new invasive practice, face public outrage, issue denials, apologize, make token concessions, and then quietly reinstate or expand the surveillance in another form. This cycle of *lie, apologize, backtrack, and repeat* incrementally set a lower and

45 Id. at 66.
46 Id.
47 Id.
48 Id.
49 Id.
50 Id.
51 Id. at 73.

lower bar for invasive data practices, paving the way for the normalization of mass surveillance as an unavoidable feature of modern digital life—a process privacy scholars have termed "surveillance creep."[52] The world populace, virulently resistant to pervasive tracking, found itself increasingly subjected to commercial surveillance not because consumers consented to it but because Facebook systematically pushed the boundaries, each time retreating just enough to quell backlash before pushing forward again. In this way, Facebook is uniquely responsible for establishing data-extractive surveillance capitalism as the de facto business model of the digital economy, as documented throughout this book. Through this process, Facebook forced on an unwilling public levels of digital surveillance that would have been unthinkable in the era before social networking.

Facebook's surveillance capabilities were significantly enhanced by its ability to connect user activity across devices and contexts through persistent identification mechanisms. The company developed sophisticated methods to compile detailed dossiers on users by connecting their activities across multiple websites and devices.[53] This enabled highly targeted advertising based on sensitive personal information. Srinivasan provides an example of how this surveillance could affect users: If someone used a shared family computer to read articles about marital problems on a local news site, Facebook could record this activity and associate it with that person's profile. This could lead to that individual—or their spouse using the same computer—being shown advertisements for divorce lawyers in their Facebook feed, potentially revealing private concerns in highly sensitive domestic situations.[54] That this example may perhaps now seem trite or sadly unsurprising only exemplifies the extent to which Facebook's conduct has systematically eroded resistance to its all-pervasive and highly invasive surveillance practices.

As users became increasingly aware of and concerned about Facebook's surveillance practices, many attempted to resist through various technical means. Facebook's response to these attempts at privacy self-help demonstrated its ability to leverage market power to override user preferences. The company adopted a three-pronged approach to defeating user privacy efforts. First, Facebook simply refused to offer any meaningful opt-out mechanism for its off-site tracking.[55] Second, the company explicitly chose to ignore "Do Not Track" signals from web browsers, despite these representing clear user privacy preferences.[56] Finally, when users attempted to employ ad-blocking technology, Facebook developed technical countermeasures to circumvent these tools.[57] This pattern of conduct was particularly

52 See Evan Selinger & Judy Hyojoo Rhee, *Normalizing Surveillance*, 22 N. Eur. J. of Phil. 49, 56–61 (2021).
53 Id.
54 Id. at 75.
55 Id. at 76.
56 Id. at 78.
57 Id. at 79.

significant from an antitrust perspective because it demonstrated how Facebook's market power enabled it to ignore user preferences regarding privacy; in a competitive market, such systematic disregard for user privacy preferences would likely have resulted in user exodus to alternative platforms. Facebook's ability to override user privacy choices without business consequences provides strong evidence of its monopoly power.

Klein v. Facebook: Testing Privacy-Based Antitrust Claims

The theories developed by Srinivasan and other privacy-focused antitrust scholars received their first major judicial test in *Klein v. Facebook*, a consumer class action filed in federal court in the Northern District of California.[58] The case represents the integration of privacy and antitrust law, as it required the court to directly confront whether and how privacy harms can constitute actionable anticompetitive conduct.

The litigation's significance extended beyond its immediate context, as it coincided with parallel enforcement actions by the FTC and state attorneys general.[59] While those government actions focused primarily on Facebook's acquisition strategy and platform access policies, *Klein* squarely presented the privacy-based theories of anticompetitive conduct. The case thus became a crucial test of whether private plaintiffs could successfully advance antitrust claims based on privacy degradation. The forum was felicitous (if unavoidable, given the location of Facebook headquarters in Menlo Park), as the Northern District of California has developed substantial expertise in both privacy and antitrust litigation through previous cases against major technology platforms. The case was assigned to Judge Lucy Koh, who had presided over several landmark technology cases and had recently authored important decisions addressing similar issues in privacy litigation against Google (*Brown v. Google*, *Calhoun v. Google*), discussed in Chapter 6.

The *Klein* complaint advanced a theory of how Facebook's privacy practices violated Section 2 of the Sherman Act predicated largely on Srivinasian's article. At its core, the complaint alleged that Facebook engaged in a two-pronged strategy to acquire and maintain monopoly power in the social network and social media markets through privacy-related conduct. The first prong focused on Facebook's representations about privacy practices.[60] The complaint meticulously documented how Facebook had made numerous statements about protecting user privacy and not engaging in commercial surveillance. These representations, plaintiffs argued, were both material to Facebook's early market success and demonstrably false.

58 Maximilian Klein, et al., v. Facebook, Inc., Case No. 20-CV-08570-LHK (N.D. Cal).

59 See *FTC v. Facebook, Inc.*, No. 20-cv-03590 (D.D.C.); *New York v. Facebook, Inc.*, No. 20-cv-03589 (D.D.C.).

60 Class Action Complaint (Dec. 3, 2020) Klein et al., v. Facebook, Inc. Case No. 20-CV-08570-LHK (N.D. Cal.).

The complaint drew particular attention to Facebook's promises regarding the use of cookies, third-party information sharing, and the surveillance capabilities of social plug-ins. The second prong addressed Facebook's "Copy, Acquire, Kill" strategy for dealing with competitive threats.[61] The complaint alleged that Facebook used its surveillance capabilities to identify emerging competitors, then either acquired them (as with Instagram and WhatsApp), copied their distinctive features (as with Snapchat's Stories feature), or cut off their platform access to handicap their growth. This pattern of conduct, plaintiffs argued, worked to entrench Facebook's monopoly position and enable privacy degradation.[62] The complaint also included state law claims for unjust enrichment, arguing that Facebook's deceptive privacy practices had allowed it to obtain valuable user data and attention without proper compensation. This theory complemented the antitrust claims by providing an alternative framework for understanding how Facebook extracted value from users through privacy degradation.

The court's order on Facebook's motion to dismiss was a groundbreaking victory for privacy-based antitrust theories. Judge Koh's thorough analysis addressed several issues that had previously raised uncertainty about the viability of such claims. The court's treatment of antitrust injury was particularly important: Judge Koh rejected Facebook's argument that privacy harms could not constitute antitrust injury, instead recognizing that user data and attention had concrete economic value in the digital advertising market.[63] The court pointed to Facebook's own financial statements, which described earnings in terms of average revenue per user, as evidence that users' information and attention represented quantifiable economic value. This analysis built on the court's previous decisions in *Brown v. Google* and other cases recognizing the economic impact of privacy harms.[64]

The court further developed a framework for analyzing when privacy-related representations could constitute anticompetitive conduct. Drawing on securities fraud jurisprudence, the court distinguished between actionable false statements and mere puffery. The order identified several categories of "clearly false" representations that were "capable of objective verification," including statements about third-party data sharing, the Beacon program, social plug-in functionality, and cookie-based tracking.[65] The court also addressed market definition, a central element of antitrust claims that had proven challenging in digital platform cases. While expressing some skepticism about certain aspects of the plaintiffs' market definition, the court found their allegations sufficient at the pleading stage. Notably, the court rejected Facebook's argument that services like Twitter and TikTok

61 Id.
62 Id.
63 *Klein v. Facebook, Inc.*, 580 F. Supp. 3d 743, (N.D. Cal. 2022).
64 Id. at 804.
65 Id. at 795.

necessarily competed in the same market, finding that Facebook had failed to substantiate its claims about product interchangeability.[66] The court's order demonstrated how traditional antitrust principles could be adapted to address novel forms of anticompetitive conduct in digital markets. By recognizing privacy as a dimension of competition and accepting that its degradation could constitute antitrust injury, the decision provided a potential roadmap for future privacy-based antitrust litigation.

The viability of privacy-based antitrust theories faced another crucial test in the class certification proceedings before Judge James Donato (to whom the case was transferred after Judge Koh was elevated to the Ninth Circuit). While Judge Koh's motion to dismiss order established that privacy degradation could constitute antitrust injury in theory, class certification required plaintiffs to demonstrate that such injury could be proven on a class-wide basis through common evidence. The certification proceedings focused heavily on the plaintiffs' proposed damages models. Their primary theory argued that Facebook's privacy violations enabled it to generate supracompetitive profits by collecting and monetizing user data in ways that would have been impossible in a competitive market.[67] This approach sought to measure the difference between users' actual privacy-related losses and what would have occurred in a market where Facebook faced meaningful competition.

Judge Donato expressed significant skepticism about whether traditional antitrust damages methodologies could capture privacy harms. During one hearing, he questioned whether economic models designed to measure price effects could be meaningfully adapted to privacy degradation, asking the plaintiffs' lawyers: "Are you aware of a single social media company at any time to ever offer a consumer any money to obtain their personal data?"[68] The court ultimately rejected the plaintiffs' approach, finding that their proposed economic model for measuring privacy harm was speculative and unsupported by real-world evidence.[69] Judge Donato concluded that the plaintiffs' economist, Dr. Nicholas Economides, failed to establish that Facebook would have compensated users for their data in a competitive market. The court found his theory—that Facebook users suffered antitrust injury because they were not paid $5.00 per month for their data—was not grounded in factual evidence or reliable economic methodology.[70] Judge Donato also dismissed the argument that privacy harm could be measured through Facebook's own financial metrics, such as average revenue per user. He ruled that while Facebook

66 Id. at 772.

67 Id.

68 Bonnie Eslinger, *Meta Users Fight Uphill For Cert., But Advertisers Have A Shot*, Law360.com (Oct. 31, 2024). www.law360.com/articles/2254721/meta-users-fight-uphill-for-cert-but-advertisers-have-a-shot.

69 *See* Order Re Dr. Nicholas Economides and User Class Certification at 6–7, Klein v. Meta Platforms, Inc., No. 20-cv-08570-JD (N.D. Cal. Jan. 24, 2025).

70 Id. at 8.

monetized user data, there was no precedent or economic support for the claim that competition would have compelled Facebook to pay users instead of improving privacy protections.[71] The court emphasized its finding that neither Facebook nor any other firm in the personal social networking services market had ever competed by offering direct payments to users.[72]

Ultimately, the court denied class certification, holding that the plaintiffs failed to present a viable method for proving antitrust injury on a class-wide basis. Because their theory of harm was entirely dependent on the excluded expert testimony of Dr. Economides, they could not meet the requirements of Rule 23.[73] As of this writing, the Plaintiffs are appealing the Court's denial of class certification.

Despite Judge Koh's initial ruling blessing the Plaintiffs' theory of antitrust harm, Judge Donato's decision underscores the challenges of using privacy degradation as the basis for antitrust claims and highlights the evidentiary hurdles that plaintiffs must overcome to establish causation and damages in such cases, reflecting tensions scholars have regarding the role of privacy harms in competition analysis. As Matthew Sipe has argued, integrating privacy considerations into antitrust doctrine poses structural challenges because privacy and competition are not always aligned.[74] While policymakers increasingly look to antitrust enforcement as a tool for addressing the privacy harms inflicted by dominant digital platforms, the traditional consumer welfare framework seemingly continues to prioritize efficiency and price effects, making non-price harms like privacy erosion more difficult to quantify and litigate successfully. Moreover, as Sipe notes, the structural remedies typically pursued in antitrust cases—such as breaking up dominant firms or imposing interoperability requirements—may not necessarily enhance consumer privacy and could, in some cases, lead to greater privacy intrusions by fragmenting markets and increasing data-sharing across a wider number of firms.[75] The inability of plaintiffs in this case to demonstrate class-wide antitrust injury based on privacy degradation highlights these evidentiary and conceptual challenges of using competition law to address privacy harms.

Nevertheless, the fight against corporate power on this new front continues, moving the dispute to the Ninth Circuit Court of Appeals. While Meta appeared to have won this round, as in *In re Facebook Internet Tracking*, it is conceivable that an unfavorable district court ruling will transform into a substantial pro-consumer victory on appeal.

71 Id. at 9.
72 Id. at 11–12.
73 Id. at 15.
74 Matthew Sipe, *Covering Prying Eyes with an Invisible Hand: Privacy, Antitrust, and the New Brandeis Movement*, 36 Harv. J.L. & Tech. 360 (2023).
75 Id.

The Transformation of Antitrust Law

Despite this apparent setback in the practical application of Neo-Brandesian antitrust theory to privacy harms, there is no question that the theoretical landscape has shifted. The evolution of privacy-based antitrust theories demonstrates how emerging scholars working outside traditional power centers can fundamentally reshape legal doctrine. This transformation has been particularly noteworthy for being led by young scholars—in this case both women of color—who brought novel and contrarian perspectives to long-standing questions of market power and consumer protection, thereby transforming an entire legal field.

Lina Khan's meteoric rise from law student to FTC chair exemplifies this phenomenon. While still a law student at Yale, Khan published "Amazon's Antitrust Paradox" in the *Yale Law Journal*, challenging fundamental assumptions about how antitrust law should address digital platform power. The article's impact went far beyond academic circles, helping spark the Neo-Brandesian movement and eventually influencing enforcement policy. Khan's subsequent appointment as FTC chair at age 32 marked a remarkable trajectory from academic critic to enforcement leader. Khan's appointment in 2021 created intense debate as she sought to challenge entrenched competition policies, particularly in Big Tech–dominated markets, by prioritizing structural concerns over the traditional consumer welfare standard.[76] Her ambitious vision, rooted in the Neo-Brandesian school of antitrust thought, faced skepticism from legal and business communities, with critics arguing her approach was untested and risked judicial setbacks that even sympathetic critics argued could weaken the FTC's regulatory authority.[77] Early legal defeats, internal dissent, and concerns about expanding antitrust law beyond its economic focus cast doubt on the feasibility of her enforcement strategy.[78] Nevertheless, Khan's leadership has driven a significant shift in US antitrust enforcement, reinvigorating efforts to curb corporate consolidation and influencing global regulatory trends. Under her tenure, the FTC has aggressively challenged mergers and acquisitions, shaping policy discussions that extend beyond litigation and placing antitrust reform at the forefront of economic regulation.[79] Even as critics questioned the viability of her approach, Khan succeeded in shifting the Overton window of competition law, ensuring that structural antitrust arguments—once considered fringe—are now central to policy debates. Whether these lawsuits ultimately prevail, her tenure has laid the groundwork for a more interventionist

76 Sheelah Kolhatkar, *Lina Khan's Battle to Rein in Big Tech*, The New Yorker (Nov. 29, 2021). www.newyorker.com/magazine/2021/12/06/lina-khans-battle-to-rein-in-big-tech.

77 Jacob M. Schlesinger, *The Return of the Trustbusters*, Wall St. J. (Aug. 27, 2021). www.wsj.com/articles/the-return-of-the-trustbusters-11630076102.

78 Daniel A. Crane, *The Radical Challenge to the Antitrust Order*, 59 Wake. Forest L. Rev. 399 (2024).

79 Id.

regulatory framework, solidifying her role as one of the most consequential figures in modern antitrust enforcement.

Similarly, Dina Srinivasan's path-breaking work on Facebook emerged from an unusual background. Rather than following a traditional academic career path, Srinivasan, working outside of any position in academia, drew on her experience in digital advertising to develop novel theories about how privacy degradation could constitute anticompetitive conduct. Her 2019 article provided a detailed blueprint for subsequent private and regulatory enforcement actions, demonstrating how out-of-the-box interrogation of regnant yet pernicious business practices can uncover otherwise-overlooked rights violations.

These scholars succeeded by getting "under the hood" of both fundamental legal doctrine and technology business models, reshaping the contours of the law on the ground in court. They combined groundbreaking legal analysis with detailed understanding of how digital platforms actually operate, allowing them to identify anticompetitive patterns that traditional antitrust analysis had obscured. The success of these emerging scholars suggests similar opportunities exist in privacy law, where many foundational questions about privacy rights in the digital age remain unresolved. Just as Khan and Srinivasan revealed new ways of understanding platform power through antitrust law, emerging scholars may discover novel approaches to privacy protection by examining existing legal frameworks from unconventional perspectives.

12

THE FUTURE OF PRIVACY LAW

As the surveillance technologies discussed in previous chapters grow ever more sophisticated, invasive, and pervasive, predictions about the future of individual autonomy, democratic governance, and human agency have become increasingly dire. This chapter examines competing theoretical frameworks for understanding these challenges, evaluates current legislative approaches, and argues that the courts may offer the best hope for preserving privacy rights that are essential to democratic society.

Surveillance/Informational Capitalism

Surveillance Capitalism

Shoshana Zuboff's now well-known work on surveillance capitalism provides one accessible theoretical lens for understanding the unprecedented challenges to privacy discussed throughout this book. She defines this new economic order as one that "claims human experiences as free raw material for hidden commercial practices of extraction, production and sales."[1] In Zuboff's analysis, surveillance capitalism represents a fundamental threat to human autonomy and agency, as technology companies convert intimate details of human behavior into predictive products traded in "behavioral futures markets."[2] Zuboff argues that this represents a radical

1 Shoshana Zuboff, The Age of Surveillance Capitalism: The Fight for a Human Future at the New Frontier of Power (PublicAffairs, 2019).
2 Id.

DOI: 10.4324/9781003413349-16

departure from traditional market capitalism, constituting "a new economic order that claims human experience as a free source of raw material."[3]

The pervasiveness of this new form of capitalism, according to Zuboff, stems from its ability to operate largely undetected while gathering vast amounts of data about individuals through digital interfaces. This information asymmetry creates what she terms "instrumentarian power"—a form of behavioral control that operates through prediction and modification rather than physical coercion.[4] Unlike earlier forms of industrial capitalism that primarily extracted value from natural resources and labor, surveillance capitalism extracts value from human experience itself, creating markets where predictions about behavior become valuable commodities.

However, while Zuboff's framework has gained considerable public attention, it has significant limitations as a tool for understanding how to effectively regulate privacy. As Amy Kapczynski argues, Zuboff's account suffers from a surprisingly uncritical view of non-surveillance forms of capitalism.[5] As Kapczynski notes, "[g]iven the manifesto-like quality of the book, it is something of a shock when you realize that Zuboff's dream is a world dominated by firms like Apple, instead of firms like Google."[6] Perhaps most problematically, Zuboff's framework rests on a flawed premise that surveillance capitalism operates in a kind of lawless space, overlooking the extensive legal infrastructure that enables and shapes corporate surveillance practices. Kapczynski contends that by framing surveillance capitalism as a merely rogue form of capitalism, Zuboff's narrative inadvertently obscures how existing legal frameworks actively facilitate data extraction and behavioral prediction markets. This framework, ultimately, does not "help us think about many of the extraordinarily important modes of private power facilitated by information technologies today."[7]

Informational Capitalism

Julie Cohen offers a more nuanced analytical political economy framework, situating current privacy challenges within a broader transformation she terms "informational capitalism."[8] Rather than focusing narrowly on surveillance and behavioral control, Cohen's analysis examines how "informationalism" has become a foundational mode of development in contemporary political economy. This broader frame captures not only surveillance practices but also the rise of platform power,

3 Id.
4 Id.
5 Amy Kapczynski, *The Law of Informational Capitalism*, 129 Yale L.J. 1460 (2020).
6 Id. at 1465.
7 Id.
8 Julie E. Cohen, Between Truth and Power: The Legal Constructions of Informational Capitalism (Oxford University Press, 2019).

monopolistic tendencies, and technology's role in reshaping relationships between capital, labor, and governance.

Cohen's approach identifies how the shift toward informational capitalism represents a fundamental restructuring of economic organization that extends beyond mere surveillance. She argues that under the "regime of informational capitalism, market actors use knowledge, culture, and networked information technologies as means of extracting and appropriating surplus value, including consumer surplus."[9] Unlike Zuboff's framing, which often characterizes surveillance capitalism as a novel deviation from prior forms of capitalism, Cohen situates current developments within the broader historical evolution of capitalism, emphasizing how informational capitalism represents a continuation and intensification of existing patterns of economic power and legal transformation.

Cohen demonstrates how law mediates these developments at every stage, enabling de facto property regimes in both data and algorithms despite neither being formally recognized as property.[10] This insight illustrates how legal frameworks simultaneously construct and constrain private power in the digital age, suggesting potential points of intervention for privacy advocates.[11] Cohen identifies how various legal domains—including antitrust, intellectual property, contract, and consumer protection—work together to establish and maintain informational capitalism's foundations.[12] Her analysis reveals that far from operating in a lawless zone, technology companies navigate a complex legal landscape that often provides the very infrastructure enabling their business models.

Cohen's framework helps explain why purely market-based approaches to privacy protection have proven insufficient. As she argues, under informational capitalism, "[i]nformation platforms and other information businesses are largely unaccountable for behavioral manipulation, for practices of behavioral microtargeting and content optimization that amplify collective unreason, and for the security vulnerabilities that distributed architectures for data harvesting, storage, and processing engender."[13] This structural misalignment suggests that meaningful privacy protections demand reconceptualizing the legal frameworks that govern information flows and platform operations.

The Ghost of the Ascendant Surveillance Society's Future

Surveillance/informational capitalism's critical frameworks teach that contemporary surveillance practices are not accidental or inevitable but rather the result of deliberate economic and legal structuring. Surveillance capitalism warns that

9 Id. at 6.
10 Id. at 25–46.
11 Id. at 4–5.
12 Id. at 16–29.
13 Id. at 106.

private corporations extract, analyze, and manipulate human behavior as raw material for predictive markets, fundamentally shifting the nature of power in society. Informational capitalism explains that surveillance is not just a business strategy but a core structural feature of the digital economy, embedded within legal and regulatory institutions that legitimize and entrench data exploitation. These critiques demonstrate that the future of democratic governance, and ultimately human autonomy, is not simply at risk from the increasing incursions of technological advancements but from the economic and legal incentives that drive increasingly invasive surveillance infrastructures.

This erosion of democratic foundations is now unfolding in ways that once existed only in the realm of dystopian futurism. Science fiction authors have long explored the possible futures facilitated by totalizing surveillance, as extrapolations of existing technological and social developments.

Orwell's telescreens from *1984* seem almost quaint compared to the reality of billions of internet-connected devices constantly harvesting behavioral data. Consider a near-future scenario where the failure to achieve meaningful privacy preservation has allowed surveillance infrastructure to become completely embedded in daily life. Unlike the overt oppression of Orwell's dystopia, this future more closely resembles Aldous Huxley's *Brave New World*, where control is maintained through pleasure and manipulation rather than force.[14] As Neil Postman observed, "Orwell feared those who would deprive us of information. Huxley feared those who would give us so much that we would be reduced to passivity and egoism."[15] In this world, the "smart" environment constantly adjusts itself to optimize human behavior for commercial and political ends. Every surface becomes an interface, every interaction a data point, every moment an opportunity for manipulation. This further resembles the world imagined in works like Dave Eggers's *The Circle*, where transparency becomes a form of tyranny and privacy is viewed as selfishness or even treason.[16] Eggers's dystopian vision is particularly relevant because it anticipates how privacy erosion might occur not through government oppression but through voluntary adoption of surveillance technologies marketed as enhancing connection and social good. The novel's central corporation promotes transparency through banal doublespeak slogans like "Privacy is theft" and "Secrets are lies," echoing contemporary tech companies' vacuous rhetoric about "making the world more open and connected."[17] The protagonist's gradual acceptance of total surveillance mirrors our society's incremental surrender of privacy through acquiescence

14 Aldous Huxley, Brave New World (Chatto & Windus, 1932).

15 Neil Postman, Amusing Ourselves to Death: Public Discourse in the Age of Show Business (Penguin Books, 1985).

16 Dave Eggers, The Circle (Alfred A. Knopf, 2013).

17 Id.; see also A.L. Hoffmann, N. Proferes & M. Zimmer, *"Making the World More Open and Connected": Mark Zuckerberg and the Discursive Construction of Facebook and Its Users*, 20 New Media & Society 1 (2018).

to life-embedded digital services. Eggers depicts how privacy becomes reframed as antisocial behavior—those who resist constant sharing and surveillance are viewed as suspicious, selfish, or potentially dangerous. The novel thus illustrates how privacy rights might be lost not through sudden authoritarian imposition but through gradual social reconstruction of privacy itself as a negative value incompatible with modern society—a return to the religious quest to eliminate "zones of opacity" in thought itself, as discussed in Chapter 1.

The technical infrastructure for such a future has long since emerged. The Cambridge Analytica scandal demonstrated how surveillance infrastructure can be weaponized to manipulate democratic processes,[18] yet this may represent only a primitive version of what is possible. As Philip K. Dick explored in *The Minority Report*, predictive technologies powered by vast data collections can move beyond merely influencing behavior to actively preventing certain actions deemed undesirable by those in power.[19] This fictional warning has found troubling real-world parallels—as has so much of Dick's nearly supernaturally-prescient work—in the rise of predictive policing systems, which use historical data and machine learning algorithms to forecast potential criminal activity. As Andrew Ferguson has documented, these systems often reinforce existing patterns of discriminatory enforcement while creating "digital dragnets"—perpetual surveillance systems that treat entire communities as perpetually suspicious.[20] The biases embedded in historical policing data become self-fulfilling prophecies, as increased surveillance of targeted communities leads to more arrests, which in turn "proves" the initial targeting was justified. This has been termed the "tyranny of the algorithm"—a system where past patterns of discrimination become laundered through seemingly neutral technical systems into future enforcement decisions.[21] Moreover, predictive policing represents a form of digitized social control that extends well beyond traditional law enforcement, incorporating data from social services, education, housing, and health care to create comprehensive systems of surveillance and control over marginalized populations.[22] This reality suggests Dick's dystopian vision may have been optimistic; rather than waiting for actual "precrime" capabilities, current systems are already using predictive analytics to impose preemptive restrictions on individual liberty based on demographic categories and zip codes rather than individual conduct.

18 See Chapter 3.

19 Philip K. Dick, Minority Report and Other Classic Stories (Citadel Press, 1987).

20 Andrew Guthrie Ferguson, The Rise of Big Data Policing: Surveillance, Race, and the Future of Law Enforcement (NYU Press, 2017).

21 Daniel J. Solove, *The Tyranny of Algorithms*, TeachPrivacy (Dec. 8, 2024). https://teachprivacy.com/the-tyranny-of-algorithms/.

22 Sarah Brayne, Predict and Surveil: Data, Discretion, and the Future of Policing (Oxford University Press, 2020).

The psychological and social implications of permanent surveillance are explored in Yevgeny Zamyatin's 1921 novel *We*, in which a society of complete transparency destroys the internal space necessary for individual development and authentic human relationships.[23] When every action is observed, recorded, and analyzed, human behavior becomes increasingly performative, leading to what sociologist Erving Goffman described as "front stage" behavior becoming permanent.[24] This psychological burden manifests in what might be termed "surveillance stress"—the constant awareness of being watched, analyzed, and judged by invisible systems. Such stress would fundamentally alter human development, particularly for generations who have never known true privacy. As explored in Shteyngart's *Super Sad True Love Story*, the resulting society might be one where authentic human connection becomes nearly impossible, replaced by algorithmically mediated relationships and carefully curated digital personas.[25]

The increasing consolidation of power among a small number of technology conglomerates has accelerated the likelihood of these dystopian near-futures. Companies like Apple, Google, Meta, Microsoft, Amazon, and X have amassed unprecedented economic and political influence through their control of digital infrastructure, data repositories, and algorithmic systems. This concentration creates what Lina Khan describes as "platform power"—the ability not just to dominate markets but to establish the very terms under which others can participate in economic and social life.[26] As these corporations increasingly operate essential infrastructure for communication, commerce, health care, transportation, and even governance, they acquire quasi-governmental powers without corresponding democratic accountability. Frank Pasquale characterizes this as the rise of "digital feudalism"—entities that control critical resources while setting and enforcing their own rules.[27] Neal Stephenson anticipated this development in *Snow Crash*, which depicts a future where nation-states have largely collapsed, replaced by corporate sovereigns that control distinct territories and populations.[28]

While current reality has not yet fully reached this extreme, the trend toward corporate control of social structures is alarmingly evident. As these companies expand into all aspects of social life and infrastructure, their surveillance capabilities grow correspondingly more extensive and intrusive. The endgame of this trajectory is a society effectively controlled by corporate technocracy, where democratic institutions exist in name but have been hollowed out by private power. Elon Musk's gutting of the federal workforce in early 2025—with the intention of

23 Yevgeny Zamyatin, We (Gregg Press, 1978).
24 Erving Goffman, The Presentation of Self in Everyday Life (Anchor Books, 1959).
25 Gary Shteyngart, Super Sad True Love Story (Random House, 2010).
26 Lina M. Khan, *Sources of Tech Platform Power*, 2 Geo. L. Tech. Rev. 325 (2018).
27 Frank Pasquale, *Paradoxes of Digital Antitrust*, (2013) Harvard Journal of Law & Technology Occasional Paper. Series, July 2013.
28 Neal Stephenson, Snow Crash (Bantam Books, 1992).

replacing it with a more "efficient," privately owned infrastructure under the control of tech oligarchs—points to this trajectory.[29]

Legislative Approaches and Groundhog Day

The reflexive reaction to such dystopian prognostication is to look to legislation—usually omnibus federal legislation—to somehow forestall it. However, it has become a ritual for the US Congress and state legislatures to introduce similar-sounding privacy bills every year or so—think "American Privacy Rights Act of 2024," "Online Privacy Act of 2023," "American Data Privacy and Protection Act of 2022"—that never get passed. This pattern is now decades old; the early 2000s saw proposals like the "Consumer Internet Privacy Enhancement Act of 2001," the "Consumer Privacy Protection Act of 2005," and the "Personal Data Privacy and Security Act of 2009" generate similar fanfare before silently fading into legislative oblivion. Each cycle, these proposals spark initial excitement, garner headlines, and generate optimism that *this time*, comprehensive data protection might finally pass. Yet as soon as the media attention subsides, the legislative session concludes with no real change to the statutory landscape, and the same process repeats the following year. This repetitive cycle underscores a deeper problem: Much of the legislation is rooted in the same incremental fixes and superficial consent provisions that have already proven inadequate, making it all too easy for lobbyists and lawmakers to table or dilute the bills before any truly transformative reform emerges. As a result, the structural issues that Julie Cohen and other critics identify—from the monopolistic data practices of major tech firms to the entrenched notice-and-choice paradigm—remain unaddressed, even as each new Congress appears poised to "finally" enact comprehensive privacy protections

However, even were one of these bills to finally make it into law, it would almost certainly be inherently and systematically flawed. In *How (Not) to Write a Privacy Law*, Cohen argues that virtually all contemporary privacy bills suffer from a misguided focus on individual control rights at the expense of regulating the architecture of surveillance embedded in today's data-driven business models.[30] Cohen warns that lawmakers generally recycle older regulatory approaches—such as the notice-and-choice paradigm and weak managerial box-checking—and thus fail to address the actual design and networked scale of surveillance technologies. She contends that truly effective legislation must disrupt the underlying structural incentives of the data economy, unlike current proposals that generally merely add more disclosure or user consent requirements. As Cohen writes, "[o]rganizing a

29 The Guardian, *Elon Musk's Mass Government Cuts Could Make Private Companies Millions* (Feb. 16, 2025). www.theguardian.com/technology/2025/feb/16/elon-musk-doge-government-privatization.

30 Julie E. Cohen, *How (Not) to Write a Privacy Law* (2021). https://knightcolumbia.org/content/how-not-to-write-a-privacy-law.

regulatory regime around individual control rights imports a governance structure that is atomistic and post hoc," leads to a system of regulation that "cannot meaningfully discipline networked processes that operate at scale."[31] Such legislation "purports to map the road forward but promises only to excuse business as usual and further entrench systemic surveillance abuses."[32]

Moreover, the history of American privacy legislation reveals a pattern of reactive, sectoral responses to specific privacy threats rather than comprehensive protection. From the Video Privacy Protection Act of 1988—passed in response to a Supreme Court nominee's video rental history becoming public—to the Children's Online Privacy Protection Act of 1998, privacy legislation has typically emerged only after privacy violations become publicly salient. The American Privacy Rights Act (APRA) of 2024, like its predecessor, the American Data Privacy and Protection Act (ADPPA) of 2022, attempts to establish baseline privacy protections across sectors. But despite their ambitions, these legislative proposals suffer from fundamental limitations and remain deeply wedded to the paradigms that have proven inadequate in the face of modern data practices. As Cohen observes, this "continuing optimism about consent-based approaches to privacy governance is mystifying, because the deficiencies of such approaches are well known and relatively intractable."[33] The APRA, for instance, continues to rely heavily on consumer consent mechanisms, despite clear evidence that such mechanisms cannot meaningfully constrain data collection and processing at scale. Consent-based models fundamentally misunderstand how modern data ecosystems operate; when data collection and processing occur continuously and invisibly across networked systems, meaningful individual consent becomes impossible.[34]

Perhaps no issue better illustrates the structural challenges that face federal privacy legislation than the debate over preemption. Both APRA and ADPPA would largely preempt state privacy laws, with limited exceptions for certain categories of regulation.[35] This approach has drawn sharp criticism from state regulators and privacy advocates, who argue that preemption would undermine stronger state protections and stifle regulatory innovation. The California Privacy Protection Agency (CPPA) and California Attorney General have been particularly vocal in opposing federal preemption, arguing that it would effectively lower privacy standards for California residents.[36] Their concerns reflect a broader tension in privacy

31 Id.

32 Id.

33 Id.

34 Cohen, Between Truth and Power, supra n. 8.

35 *See* California Privacy Protection Agency, *The California Privacy Protection Agency Opposes the American Privacy Rights Act* (Jun. 26, 2024). https://cppa.ca.gov/announcements/2024/20240626.html.

36 Id.

federalism: While national standards might reduce compliance complexity for commercial actors, they almost certainly create a ceiling, rather than a floor, for privacy protection.

Finally, the effectiveness of privacy legislation ultimately depends on its enforcement mechanisms. Current proposals typically rely on a combination of FTC enforcement and state attorney general action. The FTC, despite its growing privacy expertise, remains underfunded and understaffed relative to the scale of its regulatory responsibilities. Under the Trump administration, the situation will likely deteriorate dramatically, with the systematic dismantling of regulatory bodies like the Consumer Financial Protection Bureau serving as the canary in the coal mine for privacy enforcement.[37] Indeed, under the Trump administration, it seems likely corporate surveillance behemoths will enjoy virtually unfettered freedom to operate as they please, provided they demonstrate sufficient loyalty and financial support to the president and his allies. This regulatory capitulation will transform agencies like the FTC from watchdogs into lapdogs, creating not merely a vacuum of enforcement but an actively hostile environment for privacy protection. State attorneys general, while often more nimble and sometimes less politically constrained than federal regulators, face resource constraints and jurisdictional limitations that make comprehensive oversight impossible. Finally, private rights of action, even when included in proposed legislation, are often heavily circumscribed.[38]

Of course, the limitations of current privacy legislation are ultimately a function of the political economy of its creation. As Waldman has documented, industry stakeholders exercise enormous influence over the legislative process, often shaping privacy bills to preserve existing business models while creating the appearance of reform.[39] Thus, proposed legislation always and ineluctably emphasizes procedural performativity over substantive restrictions. The influence of industry stakeholders is particularly evident in the treatment of algorithmic decision-making and artificial intelligence: While these technologies pose some of the most significant privacy challenges, legislative proposals typically address them through weak transparency requirements rather than meaningful restrictions on their development and deployment.[40]

37 *See* Arnold & Porter, *Trump Administration Seeks to Dismantle CFPB Amid Legal Challenges* (Feb. 18, 2025). www.arnoldporter.com/en/perspectives/advisories/2025/02/trump-administration-seeks-to-dismantle-cfpb.

38 See Electronic Frontier Foundation, *Americans Deserve More From Current American Privacy Rights Act, EFF* (Apr. 16, 2024). www.eff.org/deeplinks/2024/04/americans-deserve-more-current-american-privacy-rights-act.

39 See Chapter 9.

40 Id.

Situating the Courts in the Fight for Privacy and Democracy

Given the apparently insurmountable shortcomings of legislative efforts to curb corporate surveillance and the structural barriers to meaningful regulatory reform, as this book has argued, litigation presents the current best opportunity to challenge and constrain the rise of surveillance capitalism and to realign the balance of power between individuals, corporations, and democratic institutions. By leveraging existing legal doctrines—ranging from constitutional protections and consumer rights to antitrust doctrine—litigation has the capacity to serve as a counterweight to the dominance of informational capitalism. Courts, as Alexandra Lahav has argued, play an active role in shaping the legal landscape to protect public interests against systemic imbalances of power. In this context, litigation is not only a legal tool but also a structural safeguard for democracy itself.[41] As scholars such as Carissa Véliz and Ignacio Cofone have emphasized, legal interventions must extend beyond procedural corrections to challenge the very business models that depend on data exploitation.[42] Such models pose an existential threat to democratic participation by transforming citizens into passive subjects within a system that preemptively shapes behaviors, choices, and political engagement. Litigation has a unique role in addressing this challenge by defining and enforcing privacy rights as fundamental democratic protections.

One of the most profound dangers posed by unchecked corporate surveillance is its ability to facilitate what Julie Cohen calls "modulated democracy." In her seminal and generative work "What Privacy Is For," Cohen describes how pervasive surveillance reshapes democratic governance by subtly conditioning and directing individual behaviors through data-driven prediction and manipulation.[43] Unlike traditional authoritarian control, which relies on direct coercion, modulated democracy operates through invisible infrastructures that guide individual choices, influence public discourse, and shape social and political participation in ways that serve corporate and governmental interests. As Cohen explains, "[a] society that permits the unchecked ascendancy of surveillance infrastructures cannot hope to remain a liberal democracy" because governance itself becomes an instrument of those who control the data flows. Modulated democracy undermines agency, dissent, and the deliberative processes that are essential to democratic self-governance.[44] As Cohen explains, "[b]y these increasingly ordinary processes, both public and private regimes of surveillance and modulation diminish the capacity for democratic self-government."[45] When individual choices are conditioned

41 Id.

42 Carissa Véliz, *Privacy Is Power: Why and How You Should Take Back Control of Your Data* (2021); Ignacio Cofone, *The Privacy Fallacy: Harm and Power in the Information Economy* (2024).

43 Julie E. Cohen, *What Privacy Is For*, 126 Harv. L. Rev. 1904 (2013).

44 Id.

45 Id.

by algorithmic intervention, democratic participation ceases to be an exercise in self-governance and instead becomes a controlled process dictated by corporate self-interest.

The implications of this transformation are already evident in the ways digital platforms mediate political participation. The Snowden revelations exposed the deep entanglement between corporate data collection and government surveillance programs, revealing how technology firms such as Google and Facebook actively collaborated in state surveillance efforts through programs like PRISM.[46] The Cambridge Analytica scandal further demonstrated how digital platforms can be weaponized to manipulate elections, illustrating how mass surveillance has evolved from a passive tool of commercial profiling to an active mechanism for political engineering.[47]

Litigation is not only an avenue for redress but also a necessary mechanism for preserving democracy itself. Alexandra Lahav's work on litigation as a tool for systemic reform underscores the judiciary's role in addressing the power imbalances that manifest in a modulated democracy.[48] As Lahav explains:

> Litigation enables people to protect and promote core democratic values in the course of bringing a lawsuit. Lawsuits enforce the law by forcing wrongdoers to answer for their conduct; they increase transparency by eliciting information from their adversaries that often benefits the public; and in so doing, they help people participate in self-government.[49]

As Lahav contends, the judicial system is not merely a forum for resolving disputes but a battleground where power is negotiated.[50] Private litigants are uniquely positioned to challenge the privatization of governance through informational capitalism by asserting historic constitutional protections and enforcing common-law and statutory constraints on corporate data exploitation. As preceding chapters have shown, private litigation is a viable means to challenging the structural conditions that enable corporate surveillance, reinforcing doctrines that constrain private sector participation in state surveillance and curbing the monopolistic control of data markets. Indeed, even class action skeptics such as Julie Cohen recognize that private remedial litigation "can serve important expressive and normative functions."[51] Cohen notes that "[p]ublic enforcement proceedings against those who flagrantly violate public mandates reassert the importance of the values those

46 See Chapter 2.
47 See Chapter 3.
48 Alexandra D. Lahav, In Praise of Litigation (2017).
49 Id.
50 Id.
51 Julie E Choen, *How (Not) to Write a Privacy Law, Knight First Amend. Inst.* (Mar. 23, 2021). https://knightcolumbia.org/content/how-not-to-write-a-privacy-law.

mandates express," thereby "affording adequate scope for such proceedings can demonstrate a public commitment to holding powerful, for-profit entities accountable to the citizens whose interests the laws were enacted to protect."[52]

In the face of modulated democracy and the privatization and co-optation of governance through informational capitalism, private litigation thus emerges as a key tool for democratic preservation. As this book has argued, courts offer a vital institutional counterweight to the unchecked expansion of corporate surveillance regimes that threaten to fundamentally reshape democratic participation. While legislative and regulatory approaches have proven insufficient against the political and economic might of corporate surveillance purveyors, litigation provides a pathway for reasserting democratic values and reclaiming individual agency from algorithmic determination. By enforcing historic constitutional and common-law protections, consumer rights, and antitrust principles, private litigants can challenge the structural conditions that enable data exploitation and help re-establish the boundaries between corporate influence and democratic self-governance. The battle for privacy is ultimately a battle for democracy itself—one that must be waged in courtrooms as vigilantly as in legislatures. As surveillance infrastructures continue to evolve and expand ever deeper into the substrate of our lives and minds, the judiciary's role in safeguarding the democratic foundations will only grow more essential.

Conclusion

We must confront the uncomfortable truth that the ambitions of the largest surveillant technology actors have evolved far beyond mere commercial dominance. Companies like Google, Meta, and their counterparts no longer simply seek to monetize our attention and behaviors—they now aspire to direct our very cognitive processes and co-opt our autonomy. Former Google CEO Eric Schmidt articulated this vision with surprising frankness in 2010 when he told the *Wall Street Journal*: "I actually think most people don't want Google to answer their questions. They want Google to tell them what they should be doing next."[53] This statement was a pure declaration of intent to develop increasingly sophisticated predictive and prescriptive algorithms that shape our choices before we even recognize them as choices. Their new frontier is the extraction and subordination of human autonomy itself. Each recommendation, each "helpful" suggestion, each curated feed serves not merely as a vehicle for advertising but as a mechanism to gradually reshape human behavior in service of corporate objectives.

52 Id.

53 Holman W. Jenkins Jr., *Google and the Search for the Future*, Wall St. J. (Aug. 14, 2010). www.wsj.com/articles/SB10001424052748704901104575423294099527212.html.

As of early 2025, with the alliance between the executive branch and tech oligarchy working feverishly and openly to dismantle the structures of American democracy, Lord Acton's dictum that "absolute power corrupts absolutely" appears to have become an ironclad physical law. We might add its corollary: Absolute surveillance leads to the complete corrosion and eventual breakdown of a society composed of autonomous individuals. We face the prospect of a society where the capacity for independent thought and action is progressively surrendered to the AI-powered "God-mind" controlled by the current and soon-to-be tech oligarchs who position themselves as the architects of our collective future. The battle for privacy is thus, at its core, a battle for the preservation of human agency in a world increasingly ruled by digital despotism.

As surveillance infrastructures become ever more embedded in our physical and digital environments, privacy advocates seeking to protect what is left of our democratic autonomy would do well to employ the litigation strategies outlined throughout this book, leveraging the rich history of privacy jurisprudence developed over the past 150 years. Innovative applications of historical privacy doctrine provide powerful mechanisms to hold corporate surveillance actors accountable and constrain surveillance excesses before they further irreparably damage the social fabric. The success of some (but not all) of the cases discussed through this book demonstrates that existing legal frameworks, when properly leveraged, can force even the most powerful technology companies to respect boundaries that protect human autonomy.

INDEX

Acxiom 138
adequacy decisions (EU) 7, 47, 51, 65, 94–95, 142, 177, 211–225, 227–231, 242
AdTech industry 162
Akandji-Kombe, J.F. 214
algorithmic bias 11, 24, 93
algorithmic regulation 44, 46
Allen, Anita L. 24, 38, 95–96
Amazon 47, 55, 168, 228, 235, 237, 247, 254
Amsterdam District Court 225–227
Angel, María P. 11
Anthem Inc. Data Breach Litigation 172
antitrust law 7, 189, 232–235, 237, 243, 247–248, 254
anxiety harms 169
Apple 32, 39, 138, 227–228, 250, 254
Ariès, Philippe 12, 18
Article III standing 4–5, 35–36, 49, 56–59, 102–104, 106, 110–111, 122, 124, 158–159, 172; *Clapper v. Amnesty International* 35; *Patel v. Facebook* 103; post-*TransUnion* developments 106–111; *Spokeo v. Robins* 57, 104, 106; *TransUnion LLCv. Ramirez* 5, 106
artificial intelligence 17, 19–20, 22, 42, 138, 257
Attias v. CareFirst 172
autonomy harms 26, 28–30, 100, 144–145, 164–165

ballot initiative (California 1972) 149, 157, 159
Bateman v. American Multi-Cinema 174
Beacon program (Facebook) 240, 244
Bedoya, Alvaro 25, 166
behavioral modification 44, 250
Belgian Data Protection Authority 229
Bentham, Jeremy 13–14
Biometric Information Privacy Act (BIPA); overview 95–96, 100, 174
biometric privacy 95–98, 100–106, 111, 174
Black Opticon 24, 96
BlueKai (Oracle) 146, 156, 162
Bork, Robert H. 234
bounty hunters, location data access 77
Boyd v. United States 19
brain-computer interfaces 22
Brandeis, Louis D. 3, 13, 19–23, 28, 105, 235, 237, 246
Brayne, Sarah 143, 253
Bridges, Khiara M. 23
Brooks v. Thomson Reuters 148, 153, 155, 208
Brown, P. 18
Browne, Simone 24
Brown v. Google 115, 120, 126–130, 178–180

Calhoun v. Google 132–133, 243
California constitutional privacy right 82, 130, 149, 157

California Consumer Privacy Act (CCPA) 59, 81, 98, 148, 208
California Invasion of Privacy Act (CIPA) 113–114, 116–118, 121–124, 157–158, 160–161, 173, 179
Cambridge Analytica scandal 4–5, 47, 49, 51, 68, 71, 122, 125, 135–136, 253, 259
Campbell v. Facebook 104, 110–111, 121–123, 173
Capital One Consumer Data Security Breach Litigation 172
Carey v. Piphus 171
Carpenter v. United States 71–73, 83, 86, 105
castle doctrine 19
cell site location information 72, 80, 105
Chao, Bernard 108, 171
Charter of Fundamental Rights (EU) 211–225
Chicago School (antitrust) 7, 234–235
chilling effects 27, 32, 42–44, 165
China, social credit system 32, 44–46
Christl, Wolfie 78, 137–139, 142–143
Citron, Danielle Keats 26–28, 30, 43, 80, 97, 106–108, 110, 164, 166–168, 171, 173, 176
civil rights, privacy as 195
Clapper v. Amnesty International 35–38
class actions; advantages over legislation 199–209
CLEAR platform (Thomson Reuters) 153, 155
Clearview AI litigation 100–103
Cofone, Ignacio 17, 109, 167–169, 174, 203–206, 258
Cohen, Julie E. 8, 14, 17, 40, 75, 141, 144–145, 170, 200–203, 250–251, 255–256, 258–259
collective harm 17, 99–100, 109, 145, 169, 182, 200, 205, 227
commercial purpose exception (ECPA) 119–120
commonality (class actions) 202–203
Computer Fraud and Abuse Act (CFAA) 117, 119–120
concrete injury requirement 56, 106
consent fatigue 61
consent theory 49, 196
consent trap 61
constitutional privacy rights 6, 38, 149, 157
contextual integrity 151
cookies 117–119, 138, 140, 148, 156, 178, 229, 241, 244
Copy, Acquire, Kill strategy (Meta) 244
Court of Justice of the European Union (CJEU) 214, 217–224
cradle-to-grave profiles 123, 149, 157
Crawford, Kate 24, 95
credit monitoring costs 27, 172
Creemers, Rogier 46
crime-tort exception 119, 127, 160–161
cross-device tracking 140
Cuddihy, William John 19
cybersurveillance state 32, 39
cy près settlements 177–178

damages theories 164–183
dark patterns 62, 142, 152, 228
data brokers 3, 6, 27, 41–42, 68–69, 75, 77–81, 84, 87–89, 136–163
data localization 222
data portability 216, 238
data protection (EU concept) 59, 66, 81, 88, 95, 98, 103, 211–225, 227–230, 255
Data Protection Review Court 222–223
data subject rights 98, 214–215
Dean, Mitchell 12
democratic harms 168–169
deterrence 43–44, 170, 183, 201, 209
Dick, Philip K. 91, 253
Dieffenbach v. Barnes & Noble 172
digital dossiers 2, 6, 15, 26, 113, 136–137, 149, 156–157
digital feudalism 254
digital resignation 140
digital sovereignty 211–212, 228, 231
dignitary harms 165, 177
discrimination harms 27, 29–30, 165, 167, 207
Dobbs v. Jackson Women's Health Organization 4, 79–81
Doctorow, Cory 240
Do Not Track signals 242
DoubleClick litigation 112, 116, 118, 120–121
Douglas, Erika 234, 237–238
Duby, Georges 12, 18
Dutch class actions 224, 231

economic harms 26–27, 30, 109, 144, 164–165, 167–168, 173, 182, 244–245
Eggers, Dave 252–253
Electronic Communications Privacy Act (ECPA) 58, 113–116, 118, 120–123, 127, 157–158, 160–161, 173

Elliott, Heather 57
emotional distress damages 171
enshittification 240
Equifax Inc. Customer Data Security Breach Litigation 173
European Data Protection Board (EDPB) 215, 218, 221, 229–230
European privacy law; collective redress 227–228
EU-US Data Privacy Framework 222–224

Facebook cases 54, 64, 104, 115, 126, 134, 175
Facebook/Meta; antitrust case against 243–246
face clustering 94
face detection 92–94
face identification 93–94
face templates (faceprints) 92
face tracking 94
face verification 93–94
Fashion ID GmbH & Co. KG v Verbraucherzentrale NRW eV 215
Federal Trade Commission (FTC) 4, 28, 66, 84, 87, 137, 189, 208, 233, 238
Ferguson, Andrew Guthrie 253
Fitzpatrick, Brian T. 206–207
Foreign Intelligence Services Act (FISA) 35, 216
Foreign Intelligence Surveillance Act (FISA) 35, 40, 216, 219–223
Foucault, Michel 13–14, 23, 25
Fourth Amendment 19, 32–33, 39, 72–74, 76, 83, 142, 213
Fraley v. Facebook Inc. 175
Franks, Mary Anne 24–25, 168
Frank v. Gaos 177
Friedman, Barry 24, 166
friend permission feature 51, 64
FTC v. Facebook, Inc. 238, 243

Gajda, Amy 22
General Data Protection Regulation (GDPR); data subject rights 66, 211, 213, 227
geofence warrants 76
geolocation tracking 3–4, 69–89, 136, 139, 158
Goffman, Erving 254
Google 4–7, 30–32, 47–48, 65, 74–76, 81–84, 110, 115, 118, 120–122, 126–135, 137–138, 175–182, 221–222, 227–230, 243–244, 259–260
Google cases 6, 30, 82–83, 112, 115, 126, 129, 134, 161, 176, 178, 182, 244
Gorz, André 190
government-corporate surveillance nexus 40–42
Graph API (Facebook) 50–51
Greenwald, Glenn 32, 38–41
Gutierrez v. Converse 113

harms, privacy 26–29
Hartzog, Woodrow 61, 68, 88, 97–99, 109, 151, 208–209
Haslanger, Sally 197–198
Hernandez v. Hillsides, Inc. 82
Hill v. National Collegiate Athletic Association 150
Hipster Antitrust 7, 232–247
Hofstadter, Richard 234
Hovenkamp, Herbert 234
Hu, Margaret 39–40
Hutton v. National Board of Examiners in Optometry 172
Huxley, Aldous 252

identity resolution 138, 140, 156
identity theft 27, 54, 56, 58, 95, 98, 109, 147, 170, 172
Illinois Biometric Information Privacy Act (BIPA 95–96
incognito mode 126–128, 178–179
inconsentability 98, 150–151
inferential harms 166
informational capitalism 14, 17, 141, 170, 249–252, 258–260
informational self-determination 213
In re Anthem Inc. Data Breach Litigation 172
In re Capital One Consumer Data Security Breach Litigation 172
In re DoubleClick Inc. Privacy Litigation 112, 116, 118, 120
In re Equifax Inc. Customer Data Security Breach Litigation 173
In re Facebook Biometric Info. Privacy Litigation 104–105
In re Facebook Inc. Consumer Privacy User Profile Litigation 50, 53
In re Facebook Inc. Internet Tracking Litigation 5, 82, 112, 174–175
In re Google Inc. Cookie Placement Consumer Privacy Litigation 124
In re Google Location History Litigation 81
In re Meta Pixel Healthcare Litigation 117
instrumentarian power 250

internet activity tracking 5, 112–136
intrusion upon seclusion 82, 124, 130, 150, 158, 161
Irish Data Protection Commission 222, 228

JavaScript tracking 118, 148, 156–157
Javier v. Assurance IQ, LLC 117
Jones, M.L. 147, 213

Kafka, Franz 15, 144
Kaminski, Margot E. 37–38, 147, 213–214
Kapczynski, Amy 250
Katz-Lacabe v. Oracle 6, 86, 110, 118, 148, 150, 155, 157–161, 163, 175–176
Katz v. United States 32, 113
keystroke logging 117
Kim, Nancy 98
Klein v. Facebook 243–246
Kochava 84–89, 139–140
Kramer, Xandra 225
Kreimer, Seth F. 57
Kumandan v. Google LLC 175

Lahav, Alexandra 204–205, 258–259
Lawlor v. North American Corp. of Illinois 177
Leiter, Brian 198
Lewert v. P. F. Chang's China Bistro Inc. 172
Like button (Facebook) 125, 241
location data marketplace 76–77
Luhrmann, T.M. 12–13
Lujan v. Defenders of Wildlife 36, 56

machine learning 42, 45, 93, 95, 138–139, 152, 253
Madison Square Garden, facial recognition 91–92
managerialized compliance 189
market definition (antitrust) 244
market value approaches to damages 174–175
Mayson, Sandra 24
Memphis Community School District v. Stachura 171
metadata collection 33, 39
Meta *see* Facebook/Meta
microtargeting 51, 251
Miller, Arthur R. 72, 114
mobile advertising IDs 85–86
modulated democracy 258–260
monopoly power 233, 237, 243
Moy, Laura M. 24

national security surveillance 41, 44, 48
Nazi surveillance 212, 224, 231
Neo-Brandesian movement 234–236, 247
Netherlands, collective actions 225
network effects 236–237, 239
New York v. Facebook, Inc. 243
Nietzsche, Friedrich 12
Nissenbaum, Helen 145, 151
nominal damages 176, 181–182
non-reformist reforms 190
nothing to hide argument 33–34
noyb (organization) 223, 224, 230, 231
Nussbaum, Martha C. 197

obscurity, right to 96
Ohm, Paul 17, 74
Olmstead v. United States 21, 32
ombudsperson mechanism 217, 219–220, 224
opt-out mechanisms 63, 102, 155, 225, 242
Oracle case 30, 148, 150, 155, 158–159
ordinary course of business exception 121
Ormerod, Peter 109, 111, 200–203
Orwell, George 15, 39, 44–45, 252
Overton window 89, 247
Ozer, Nicole A. 149, 157

panopticon 13, 49–67
Parker v. Time Warner Entertainment Co. 174
Pasquale, Frank 47, 167, 236–237, 254
Patel v. Facebook 86, 103–105, 124, 174
Penney, Jonathon 43–44, 165, 168
People v. Superior Court (Smith) 114
performative critique of privacy law; framework for resistance 187–192
Perkins v. LinkedIn 28
physical harms 26–27, 30, 164
Pitt, William 19
platform power 65, 236, 247–248, 250, 254
Posner, Richard 234
Postman, Neil 252
predictive policing 24, 143, 192, 253
preemption, federal 256
PRISM program 32, 38–40, 216, 220, 259
privacy as civil right 25
privacy as power relation 11, 13–29
privacy by design 13, 75, 116, 142, 149, 151, 177, 192–195, 200, 214, 219, 229, 238, 245
privacy class actions 6–7, 53, 84, 109–110, 128–129, 164, 171, 173–174, 177–178, 182, 187, 198–210, 227–228, 231

privacy harms; aggregation and profiling 166
privacy policies 55, 62, 127, 132–133, 141, 148, 151–152, 188–189, 193, 238, 241, 243
Privacy Shield framework 217, 219–221, 224, 230
profiling harms 166, 206
proportionality principle 218, 223
psychographic targeting 50
punitive damages 177

Quality degradation theory 238
Quon v. Arch Wireless Operating Co. 116

Raz, Joseph 144–145
real-time bidding (RTB) 110, 140, 229
reasonable expectation of privacy 32, 62, 72–73, 81–82, 89, 124–125, 159–160, 213
redressability 36, 56
relationship harms 27, 29, 122–123
Remijas v. Neiman Marcus Group 172
Remsburg v. Docusearch Inc. 27
reproductive health surveillance 78–79
reputational harms 26–27, 30, 109
Richards, Neil 14–15, 21, 24, 61, 98, 109, 150, 174
Richardson, Rashida 24
right to be forgotten 216
right to be let alone 23
Riley v. California 76
Robertson v. Allied Solutions 29
Robins v. Spokeo, Inc. 56–58, 122–123, 204
Rodriguez v. Google 130–132, 180–181
Roessler, Beate 145
Rosenbach v. Six Flags Entertainment Corp. 102–103
Rozenshtein, Alan Z. 40, 142
Ryan, Johnny 142–143, 156

Safe Harbor framework 216–217, 219, 230
Schauer, Frederick 43
Schmidt, Eric 260
Scholz, Lauren Henry 171, 203, 210
Schrems litigation 216–224
Schultz, Jason M. 24
Schwartz, Paul M. 61, 92, 108, 138
Scott, James C. 18, 76, 235
search warrants 80, 100
self-censorship 43, 195
Selinger, Evan 20, 98–99, 142, 151, 242
Semayne's Case 19
session replay software 118
Sherman, Justin 75, 78, 80, 142–143, 146
Sherman Act 22, 232–233, 243
Shteyngart, Gary 254
Snowden revelations 38–41
social conformity theory 43
social credit system (China) 32, 44, 46–47
social plug-ins 241, 244
Solove, Daniel J. 11, 15–17, 22, 25–28, 33–34, 60–61, 88, 97, 106–108, 113–115, 144, 146, 164–166, 168–169, 171, 208–209
Spokeo Inc. v. Robins 57, 106, 111, 122
Srinivasan, Dina 237, 239–240, 242–243, 248
Standard Contractual Clauses (SCCs) 218–219
standing doctrine; *Clapper v. Amnesty International* 35
Stasi surveillance 212
statutory damages 97, 100, 103, 108, 134, 173–174, 178–180, 206
Steagald v. United States 76
Stephenson, Neal 254
Stored Communications Act (SCA) 54, 116, 192, 132
Sunstein, Cass R. 56–57, 170
surveillance capitalism 8, 13, 16–17, 20, 24, 45, 47, 67–68, 198, 200, 202, 249–252, 258
surveillance creep 142, 242
surveillance-innovation complex 40
surveillance intermediaries 40, 42, 142
Susser, Daniel 145–146

Tag Suggestions feature 103
Tau, Byron 42–43, 142
Telephone Consumer Protection Act (TCPA) 28, 173–174
terms of service 60–62, 115, 117, 121, 133, 201, 205, 226
third-party cookies 117, 138, 178, 244
TikTok 97, 229, 240, 244
Tokson, Matthew 73, 142
tracking pixels 117–118, 148, 156
TransUnion LLC v. Ramirez 5, 28, 106–108, 181, 202
Turow, Joseph 141

United States Department of Justice v. Reporters Committee for Freedom of the Press 154
United States v. Aluminum Co. of America 233

United States v. Chatrie 76
United States v. Jones 105
unjust enrichment damages theory 175–176
upstream collection 39, 216, 220

Van Buren v. United States 117
Véliz, Carissa 16, 258
Video Privacy Protection Act 54, 173, 256
Viljoen, Salomé 168–169

Waldman, Ari Ezra 6, 62–63, 66–68, 88, 141, 187–198, 200, 202, 208, 257
Wal-Mart v. Dukes 203
Warren, Samuel D. 3, 13, 19–22, 28, 80–81, 105
web and app activity (WAA) settings 130–131, 180
Werbach, Kevin 44–47
Westin, Alan 113–114
whitelisting (Facebook) 50, 54
White v. Davis 157
Wu, Tim 233, 236
Wylie, Christopher 50

X-Mode Social 88

Zamyatin, Yevgeny 254
zones of negative privacy 12–13
Zuboff, Shoshana 8, 17, 20, 47, 138, 168, 249–251
Zuckerberg, Mark 52, 59, 230, 238–240, 252

FSC
www.fsc.org
MIX
Papier | Fördert
gute Waldnutzung
FSC® C083411

Kolibri 360 GmbH
Ferdinand-Jühlke-Straße 7
99095 Erfurt, Deutschland
produktsicherheit@kolibri360.de